Fodor's

HONG KONG

TOP REASONS TO GO

★ **Amazing eats:** Dim sum reigns supreme, and celebrity chefs reinvent classic dishes.

★ **Marvelous markets:** Whether you want goldfish or jade earrings, you'll find them here.

★ **Sacred spaces:** The Tian Tan Buddha beckons, as do many other places to find enlightenment.

★ **After dark:** Everyone from hipsters to high-rollers can indulge in serious barhopping.

★ **Great outdoors:** Amazing hikes, verdant parks, and far-flung beaches provide some R&R.

Welcome to Hong Kong

With a population of over 7 million people living on a land mass smaller than London, Hong Kong is one of the most densely populated regions in the world. From its past as a British colony to now, it has evolved into a bustling metropolis with a unique sense of identity and a dynamic culture that blends the old with the new.

Nowhere is this more apparent than in Hong Kong's food scene: a million shades of neon point the hungry masses to storefront noodle shops and penthouse-level restaurants with wraparound views. Ultramodern restaurant concepts open each month, while decades-old local eateries serve up classics from Hong Kong French toast and wonton noodles to dim sum. Gleaming late-night dessert shops draw lines from young couples, while grab-and-go snack stalls offer cheap delicacies from condensed milk and peanut butter–filled waffles to *siu mai* and pig intestines.

Beyond the culinary, Hong Kong offers the pleasures of a dazzling urban center. Its gravity-defying skyline is breathtaking, especially when the sun goes down and the glittering glass towers are reflected in Victoria Harbour. Take it all in from a vintage ferry, or ride the rumbling tram up lofty Victoria Peak. At street level, spot British colonial landmarks in Central or explore the mazelike alleys of Sham Shui Po. Wander through cramped antiques shops, sprawling malls packed with designer boutiques, or street markets—in spaces high and low, big and small, Hong Kong has something for everyone.

It is possible to find a semblance of peace in Hong Kong, with 75% of the region made up of beaches, mountains, and woodland. There are more islands than McDonald's in Hong Kong—a fact that escapes most visitors. Buddhism—the region's ancestral religion—continues to influence the daily lives of many, with temples and monasteries offering places of worship, refuge, meditation, and learning.

However you choose to explore this multifaceted region, Hong Kong's lively pulse will remain with you long after you depart. As you plan your upcoming travels to Hong Kong, please reconfirm that places are still open and let us know when we need to make updates by writing to us at ✉ *corrections@fodors.com.*

Contents

MAPS

About Our Writers

Kowloon Walled City Park

Piera Chen is an anglophone writer and poet from Hong Kong. She has coauthored some 20 travel guides to Hong Kong, Taiwan, and China for Lonely Planet. Her translation of Hong Kong poet PK Leung's work was one of three Highly Commended entries in the 2024 Stephen Spender Prize. Piera's favorite corners of her native city are the riveting Hong Kong Geopark and the winding alleys of Tsim Sha Tsui, where she grew up. She updated the Travel Smart chapter.

Jonathan DeLise is a travel writer and speaker from the U.S. In addition to having lived in Orizaba, Mexico, Jakarta, Jeddah, and Japan, the majority of his five years as an expat was lived in Shenzhen, China, and Hong Kong. He has covered food and tourism topics for CNBC, Wanderlust, CNN, and Matador Network, and has spoken about culinary travel at Arabian Travel Market and the New York Travel & Adventure Show. He updated the Lantau Island and the New Territories chapter.

Doris Lam is a lifestyle and food journalist from Hong Kong, currently based in Italy to learn pasta making. She spent her young adult years exploring Kowloon, eating ramen in Mong Kok and cafe hopping in Sham Shui Po. After two years at *Tatler*, she moved to the United Kingdom to pursue a culinary apprenticeship while writing for publications such as *BBC*, *Serious Eats*, and *The Telegraph*. She still believes that there's no other place in Hong Kong that encapsulates the local essence and culture quite like Kowloon. She updated the Kowloon Peninsula chapter.

Wong Tai Sin Temple

Thomas O'Malley is a travel writer specializing in China, Hong Kong, and East Asia. Originally from the UK, he lived in mainland China for 12 years and is a regular visitor to Hong Kong, writing about the city for various guidebook publishers and travel magazines. He has also written travel and food pieces for the *BBC*, *The Guardian*, *Playboy*, and more, and is the China Travel Expert for *The Telegraph*. He updated the Western, Central, and Southside chapter.

Audrey Phoon is a travel writer and contributor to *Conde Nast Traveler, Time,* and *South China Morning Post.* While she's Singapore-based, Hong Kong is her second home: she has family there and roots in Canton, where her great-grandparents were born and where most Hong Kongers migrated from. She believes Hong Kong has one of the world's best culinary scenes and can't resist a few pilgrimages a year for dim sum and typhoon shelter crab. She updated the Experience and Wan Chai, Causeway Bay, and Eastern chapters.

Craig Sauers has spent 14 years exploring Asia. Formerly based in Bangkok and Hong Kong, where he edited travel and lifestyle magazines, he began contributing to Macao News after going freelance in 2021. A frequent visitor with a deep affinity for the city, he regularly edits articles and books on Macau's history and advocates for staying much longer than the typical one-night visit to experience it to the fullest. He updated the Side Trip to Macau chapter.

Chapter 1

EXPERIENCE HONG KONG

15 ULTIMATE EXPERIENCES

Hong Kong offers terrific experiences that should be on every traveler's list. Here are Fodor's top picks for a memorable trip.

1 Stroll through the Markets

You can find almost anything your heart desires at one of Hong Kong's street markets, whether it be flowers, birds, jade, street food, or sneakers. Visit Mong Kok in Kowloon, where such markets abound. (*p. 178*)

2 Ride the Star Ferry

The iconic Star Ferry has been shuttling passengers across Victoria Harbour for more than a century. Take one to admire the famous Hong Kong skyline. *(p. 83)*

3 Yum Cha

No trip to Hong Kong is complete without a *yum cha* ("drink tea") experience. Along with their tea, guests nibble on small plates of dim sum dishes. *(p. 156)*

4 Take the Tram

These rattling cars have become giant rolling advertisements, carrying everyone from schoolboys to grannies through all the main street action straight across Hong Kong Island. (*p. 41*)

5 Indulge in Nightlife

Head to Lan Kwai Fong or SoHo in Sheung Wan for award-winning bars and rooftop clubs. Don't miss Bar Leone, a casual spot that belies its status as Hong Kong's most-awarded watering hole. (*p. 76*)

6 Go for a Walk

In town, you can take in colonial architecture during an hour-long stroll through Western between the University of Hong Kong and Western Market. (*p. 67*)

7 Ride the Central–Mid-Levels Escalator

The longest outdoor escalator system in the world covers half a mile of moving stairs, walkways, and passageways, from the business hub of Central to the residential heights of Mid-Levels. (*p. 79*)

8 Visit the Kowloon Walled City Park

Once a lawless, labyrinthine slum occupied by triads, gambling houses, and brothels, the park was resurrected as a peaceful and expansive Qing Dynasty–style garden. *(p. 183)*

9 Go to the Races

Even if you're not a gambler, it's worth heading to Hong Kong's horse-racing tracks in Happy Valley. Grab a snack and enjoy live music as the horses thunder past. *(p. 125)*

10 Trek to Tian Tan Buddha

The true path to divine ascension is by way of 268 steps leading up to the 275-ton Tian Tan Buddha (the Big Buddha), which sits on a hill next to the Po Lin Buddhist Monastery. *(p. 194)*

11 Have afternoon tea at The Peninsula

Tuck into sandwiches and scones while sipping tea from silver-plated teapots in the imposing, high-ceilinged lobby of the posh Peninsula, the territory's oldest hotel. *(p. 162)*

12 Visit the Wong Tai Sin Temple

One of the busiest religious shrines in the territory, Wong Tai Sin Temple is packed with dedicated worshippers looking to have their prayers answered or their fortunes read. *(p. 184)*

13 Scale Victoria Peak

At over 1,800 feet, this is Hong Kong Island's highest point, and the best spot to take in a 360-degree panorama of the city center and harbor. It's also a great place to get into nature. *(p. 84)*

14 Explore Tai Kwun Centre

This 170-year-old compound is a hub for local arts and culture, housing art galleries, tea shops, fashion boutiques, and restaurants. (*p. 84*)

15 Relax at the Chi Lin Nunnery

A tranquil oasis in the middle of residential Diamond Hill, the nunnery and surrounding garden are built in the Tang Dynasty style and feature Buddhist treasures. (*p. 182*)

WHAT'S WHERE

1 Western, Central, and Southside. Western has long been known for its Chinese produce shops, old-school swimming shed, and traditional craft businesses. Nowadays it's becoming a hip area where visitors can find quirky restaurants, bars, and independent boutiques. Central is Hong Kong's world-famous finance hub that extends through Admiralty and boasts skyline high-rises. Head up the Central–Mid-Levels Escalator to enjoy drinks in trendy SoHo or take the funicular to Victoria Peak for postcard views of the city and harbor. In Southside, Stanley attracts visitors with its colonial remnants, outdoor market, waterfront restaurants, and annual Dragon Boat races. But don't let it stop you from visiting its beaches, from Repulse Bay to Shek O.

2 Wan Chai, Causeway Bay, and Eastern. Wan Chai still has its strip of harmless red-light venues, though not so far away are furniture and home-accessories shops and wine bars. Shoppers flock to Causeway Bay's Times Square, Hysan Place,

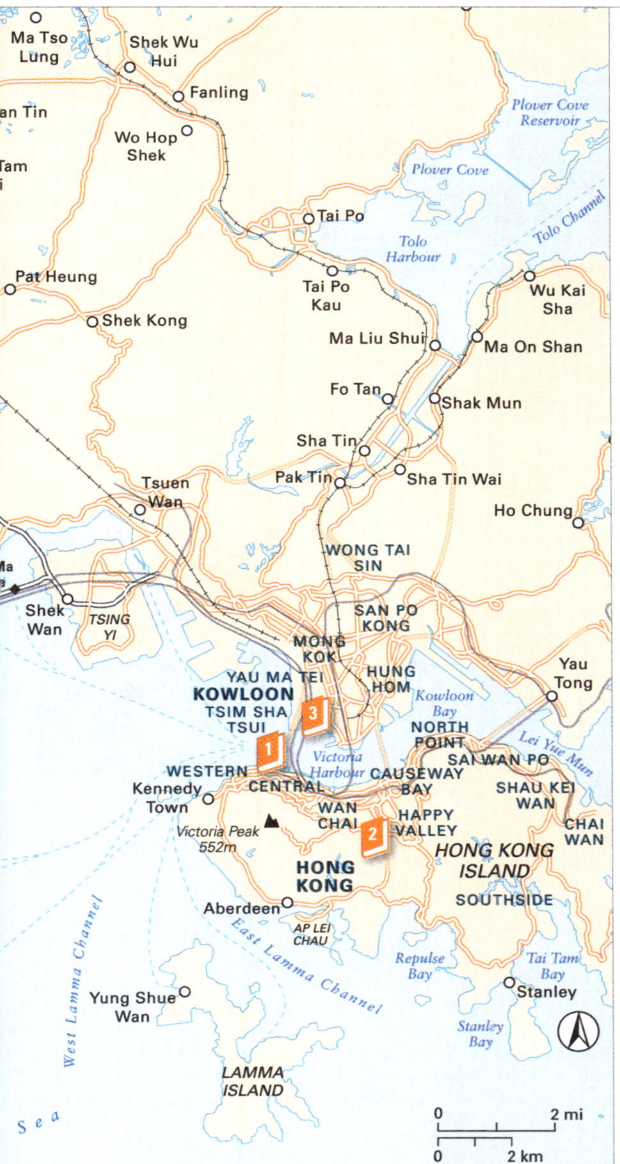

Sogo, and Lee Gardens, as well as the many boutique shops that pepper the area. The Eastern District, which used to be primarily residential and industrial, is picking up pace as a hub for the arts and hip cafés.

3 Kowloon Peninsula. Moving across the harbor to Kowloon, Tsim Sha Tsui begins at the nearly 70-year-old Star Ferry Terminal followed by the eastward promenade along the Avenue of Stars, which offers front-row views of the famous Hong Kong Island skyline. Yau Ma Tei and Mong Kok are the epicenters of night and day markets, where you can score souvenirs and knickknacks on the cheap. North of here are residential areas and attractions, including the famed and storied Kowloon Walled City Park.

4 Lantau Island and the New Territories. Of the Hong Kong archipelago of 260 islands, Lantau is by far the largest. It's home to the Big Buddha and Disneyland. The New Territories are the sites of still-inhabited historic villages and relatively unspoiled natural beauty, in addition to the Ten Thousand Buddhas Monastery and Hong Kong Heritage Museum in the town of Sha Tin.

What to Eat and Drink in Hong Kong

CHAR SIU

In Hong Kong, *char siu*—sweet, smoky barbecued pork—is many things: comfort food; a symbol of joy; a talisman against bad luck. It's also delicious. Although the dish originated in the Chinese province of Guangdong, it's Hong Kong chefs who have earned a reputation for it.

DIM SUM

Dim sum in Hong Kong is both a show of culinary artistry and a social ritual. Families and friends gather to chat, often at lunchtime on weekends, over delicate dumplings served in bamboo steamers and plates piled with baked and fried tidbits.

BEEF BRISKET NOODLES

This soul-warming Cantonese favorite pairs different cuts of beef with thin egg noodles in clear or curry-flavored broth. Often eaten at lunch or dinner, it's a fixture on the menus of *dai pai dong* (street stalls) and *cha chaan tengs* (Hong Kong–style cafés)—though in recent years, restaurants have started offering elevated versions.

EGG PUFFS

These slightly sweet waffles feature clusters of soft, puffy spheres surrounded by crispy edges. A popular street snack, they're usually eaten plain or with toppings like fruit or ice cream. Locals swear by the egg waffles sold by Master Low-Key Food Shop in the Eastern District, though the more accessible Mammy Pancake (at several locations) does a nearly comparable version.

DAI PAI DONG MEALS

Dai pai dong—street stalls licensed by the government—are lively odes to local cuisine where food is cooked *a la minute* and served fast and hot. The government stopped issuing licenses for new stalls in 1983, but they remain wildly popular. Today, many of the remaining *dai pai dong* are run by second-generation owners.

TYPHOON SHELTER CRAB

Typhoon shelter cuisine gets its name from the food fishermen used to cook in storm shelters while waiting for squalls to pass. It typically involves seafood that is deep-fried or showered in fried garlic. Of this genre, typhoon shelter crab (sweet mud crabs fried with garlic) is the most popular.

CURRY FISHBALLS

It may sound like an odd combination, but this quintessential street food is worth a try. Made of fried fish paste shaped into balls and blanketed in thick curry sauce, it's the perfect in-between-meal snack (and a great hangover cure). Eat it standing and out of paper bowls, as the locals do.

EGG TARTS

Crisp on the outside and silky smooth on the inside, egg tarts—locally known as *daan tat*—are a snack beloved by Hong Kong's young and old. They were introduced by the British in the 1920s, and are now sold everywhere from *cha chaan tengs* to hip bakeries.

ROAST GOOSE

Among Hong Kong's *siu mei*—fire-roasted meats—goose is often considered king because of its rich, succulent flesh. Both casual joints and fancy restaurants serve this Cantonese staple, usually with rice or noodles, and always with a tart plum dipping sauce.

CHA CHAAN TENG FARE

You can't visit Hong Kong without dining at one of its *cha chaan tengs*, or "tea restaurants"—casual cafés that embody the territory's East-meets-West culture with menus blending local and Western influences. Think bowls of instant noodles topped with Spam, or pork chops clapped between crusty buns.

What to Buy in Hong Kong

JADE

TikTok has made the old-school gemstone jade cool again, and Hong Kong—one of the world's top production and trade centers—is where to buy it. If you're looking for a bargain, head to the indoor Jade Market and be prepared to do some serious haggling. Higher-quality pieces can be found at the jewelry boutiques that line nearby Jade Street.

PERSONALIZED SEALS

Have your name engraved in Chinese, English, or both on traditional chops (seals). Made of wood, stone, or even jade, they're usually ornately carved, often with animals of the Chinese zodiac. Sets come with a tub of sticky red ink.

SECONDHAND LUXURY GOODS

Shops filled with secondhand designer goods flood the city center. But do your homework before buying, because not every store peddles authentic products. Japanese chain Brand Off is one reliable name that stocks a mind-boggling range of Hermes, Louis Vuitton, and Chanel items, many in pristine condition.

MAH-JONGG SETS

Hong Kong has a reputation for producing beautifully hand-carved and hand-painted mah-jongg tiles, and traditional and more unique modern versions can be found at shops around the territory. The best places to buy sets include Kung Yau Cheung (Mong Kok) and Glocal Mahjong (Central).

CALLIGRAPHY SUPPLIES

Granted, becoming a master brush painter takes years. But calligraphy equipment makes a wonderful display, even if your brushwork doesn't. Boxed sets of bamboo-handled brushes, porcelain inkwells, and smooth ink stones start at about HK$200 at Yue Hwa.

SILKWARE

Silk dressing gowns and basic *cheongsams* (silk dresses with Mandarin collars) are excellent buys in Hong Kong. They come in a variety of colors, patterns, and styles and range from bargains at Yue Hwa to luxurious splurges at Blanc de Chine.

Tea shop

TEA ACCOUTREMENT
Yixing teapots are made from uniquely porous clay, which absorbs and retains the flavor of the teas brewed over time. The best pots pour in thin, quiet streams without splashes. Those from the homegrown brand Fook Ming Tong will melt even coffee-guzzlers' hearts.

KITCHEN SOUVENIRS
Remind yourself of all those dim sum meals with souvenirs to dress up your dining room. You'll find black-lacquer chopsticks and brocade place mats in street stalls all over town. Stanley Market has beautiful appliqué table linen.

DRIED PRODUCE
Re-create your Hong Kong culinary experience by taking home the preserved foods—such as liver sausages, century eggs, and dried scallops—that form the foundation of Cantonese cooking. They're easy to transport (though you should check your country's customs restrictions), and shops often help to pack purchases for air travel.

Best Fests and Fêtes in Hong Kong

LUNAR NEW YEAR
The Lunar New Year brings Hong Kong to a standstill each year in late January or early February with markets, parades, and fireworks. Shops shut down, and everywhere you look there are red and gold signs, kumquat trees, and pots of yellow chrysanthemums, all considered auspicious.

LANTERN FESTIVAL
The Lunar New Year festivities end with the overwhelmingly red Lantern Festival. Hong Kong's parks—especially Victoria Park—become a sea of light as people, mostly children, gather with beautifully shaped paper or cellophane lanterns. It's held on the 15th day of the first moon, usually in February.

CHEUNG CHAU BUN FESTIVAL
Thousands make the yearly trip to Cheung Chau Island for the exuberant Cheung Chau Bun Festival, a four-day-long Taoist thanksgiving feast. Outside Pak Tai Temple, 60-foot towers covered in sweet buns welcome climbers to collect them—the higher the bun the better the bestowed fortune. It's held on the eighth day of fourth moon, usually in May.

WINE AND DINE FESTIVAL
Every year in October, the Hong Kong Tourism Board throws a monthlong culinary extravaganza packed with restaurant deals, tours, and street carnivals. The highlight event is the four-day Wine and Dine Festival, which has booths offering tasty snacks and tipples, as well as live music and entertainment.

HUNGRY GHOST FESTIVAL

Food left out on the street and smoldering piles of paper are everywhere during the Hungry Ghost Festival, held in August or September. Replicas of houses, cars, and traditional "hell money" are burned as offerings to the ancestral spirits, who are believed to be roaming the streets for two weeks.

DRAGON BOAT FESTIVAL

The Dragon Boat Festival, usually held in June, pits long dragon-head boats against one another in races to the shore. The festival commemorates Qu Yuan, a scholar who drowned himself in the 3rd century BC to protest government corruption. These days it's one big beach party.

MID-AUTUMN FESTIVAL

In September or October, friends and families gather to admire the full moon while munching on moon cakes stuffed with lotus-seed paste. Colorful paper lanterns fill Hong Kong's parks, and a 220-foot-long "fire dragon" dances through the streets of Tai Hang near Victoria Park.

CLOCKENFLAP

Hong Kong's biggest outdoor music and arts festival is one of the best ways to connect with the territory's energetic arts scene. Held every year, it draws tens of thousands of people and blends indie music, art installations, food, and interactive experiences against the stunning backdrop of Victoria Harbour. Headliners include big international names and local talent. It's usually held in December.

CHING MING

Ancestor worship is important in Hong Kong culture, and on Ching Ming families meet to sweep the graves of departed relatives and burn paper offerings. It's usually held in early April.

HONG KONG ARTS FESTIVAL

Held each year in February and March, the Hong Kong Arts Festival showcases music, drama, and dance. The festival's past visitors have included Mikhail Baryshnikov, Pina Bausch, and José Carreras.

Best Free Things to Do in Hong Kong

MUSEUM WEDNESDAYS

Visit the Hong Kong Heritage Museum in Sha Tin on a Wednesday, when admission is free. This expertly curated museum chronicles Hong Kong's changing face, from scattered agricultural communities to booming towns. Other museums like the Hong Kong Museum of Art also offer free admission on Wednesday. (*p. 200*)

GALLERY HOPPING

Visitors are free to browse antiques and artworks at private galleries in Central, SoHo, Sheung Wan, Chai Wan, and Aberdeen. Kowloon Park's winding Sculpture Walk features 19 works—including an Eduardo Paolozzi—against a leafy backdrop. And be sure to keep your eyes open at the malls, most notably Harbour City and Times Square, where you'll see pop-up art exhibitions. (*p. 151*)

VIEWFINDING

For fabulous harbor views, ride up to the Bank of China's 43rd-floor observation deck or visit the Hong Kong Monetary Authority on the 55th floor of the International Finance Centre. For a glorious panoramic bay view of Victoria Park, visit the main library in Causeway Bay. (*p. 82*)

CULTURE CLASSES

Various government departments and government-run facilities run regular classes in tai chi, table tennis, and more across the island that are free for anyone to take part in. At Kowloon Park, you can join kung fu sessions every Sunday from 2:30 pm to 4:30 pm. (*p. 151*)

TEMPLES

Inner peace is priceless, and though it's customary to make a small donation, all of Hong Kong's temples are free. Don't miss out on Man Mo Temple in Sheung Wan, dedicated to Man, the god of literature, and Mo, the god of war. Built in the 19th century, the temple is still visited regularly by locals. (*p. 71*)

AVENUE OF STARS

Join the families and lovers strolling down the Avenue of Stars, a waterfront boulevard that pays tribute to Hong Kong's cinematic history and the stars who helped make it a world-famous. Apart from taking in the magnificent harbor views, you can also snap photos with statues of actors. (*p. 150*)

Symphony of Lights

SYMPHONY OF LIGHTS

Victoria Harbour's Symphony of Lights is performed every evening at 8 pm to a crowd of mesmerized visitors and proud residents. Music and narration blast through low-fi outdoor speakers as more than 40 skyscrapers are synchronized to light up on cue. Watch from the waterfront promenade in Tsim Sha Tsui, Golden Bauhinia Square in Wan Chai, or Central Harbour-front. (*p. 150*)

HIKING

For a small territory, Hong Kong has a surprisingly large number of hiking trails that reveal how diverse its landscape is. From paths that snake through centuries-old geological formations to treks that lead to cloud-swathed peaks, what lies beyond Hong Kong's concrete façade may surprise and invigorate you. Head for the hills and hike along the Dragon's Back or up to Lion Rock. (*p. 101*)

BIRD-WATCHING

See our feathered friends up close and personal without leaving town—either at the Yuen Po Street Bird Garden in Kowloon or at the Edward Youde Aviary in the heart of Hong Kong Park. (*p. 79*)

Hong Kong Today

Hong Kong's skyline of gleaming glass towers, streets plastered with neon signs, and alleys crammed with street vendors have long served as the backdrop for local and international films, but this multifaceted territory's charms go beyond its photogenic qualities. Even though political developments have altered the landscape in recent years, it remains a cultural melting pot that's full of surprises for everyone from first-timers to those who've visited year after year.

COSMOPOLITAN HUB

Living up to the title of Asia's World City, Hong Kong is a buzzing stage that attracts millions of visitors from all over the globe. Business travelers pass through frequently and Hong Kong's soaring market development makes it one of the world's leading financial hubs. And just as many people come here for leisure travel. Navigation is easy within the city center, since road signs, maps, and directions on public transportation are spelled out in Chinese and English. Most major tourist attractions—including museums, parks, and performance venues—also have bilingual directories and information centers. While the territory has a distinct tradition of its own, you'll also find foreign influences embedded in its culture, language, food, and lifestyle.

SHOPPERS' PARADISE

You can score great bargains here on everything from electronics to clothing—on top of heavily discounted prices on many items, there's no sales tax. You'll find all the world-renowned brands at modern shopping malls and boutiques in the main shopping hubs of Central, Causeway Bay, and Tsim Sha Tsui, but it's worth visiting the loud and crowded local markets, where you can haggle for cheap trinkets. At the larger markets, like the one on Temple Street in Yau Ma Tei and Tung Choi Street in Mong Kok, most of the vendors are used to tourists and can speak basic phrases of English. Fashion and design connoisseurs might want to look into the independent boutiques hidden away in complexes such as Island Beverly mall in Causeway Bay or in trendy areas like Tai Ping Shan Street, Star Street, and Tin Hau. These shops offer unique items from local and international designers, but be warned that they don't usually open before noon.

FOOD LOVERS' DELIGHT

There is no reason not to eat well in Hong Kong, regardless of your budget. While Hong Kong's Michelin-starred Asian and European restaurants continue to add names to their wait lists, it's also not unusual to see queues outside humble-looking local eateries and *dai pai dongs*—the open-air food stalls that line Temple Street and other major arteries. Immigrants from other parts of Asia also marked out their territories on the region's culinary map, with Kowloon City known for its Thai food, Tsim Sha Tsui for Indian and Korean, and Causeway Bay for Japanese. In the hip neighborhoods of Hong Kong many trendy restaurants have opened their doors to an eager clientele. Private kitchens were once the rage, and small restaurants serving artisanal cuisine continue to flourish. Waves of food trends in Hong Kong also mean that every other year or so there's a boom in eateries serving a particular dish or cuisine, with two-dish rice shops—cheap pick-and-mix stalls serving homestyle Chinese cooking—being one of the most recent fads.

GETTING GREENER

Despite its expansive rural landscape, Hong Kong has always been identified more as a concrete jungle plagued by urban development and inner-city pollution than as an eco-destination. But the times they are a-changin', and residents have really stepped up their efforts to turn their home into an eco-friendly place. The most notable change is the increase of interest in farming and a back-to-basics lifestyle, especially from the younger community. Weekend trips to farms out in the New Territories are gaining popularity as a way to relieve stress from the hustle and bustle of city-center life. And while Hong Kong's size makes it difficult to find arable land, some enterprising farmers are looking up and building rooftop gardens right in the heart of the city. Restaurants are also doing their part, with more chefs designing menus based on sustainable seafood and locally grown produce.

FOCUSED ON HEALTH

In recent years traditional Chinese medicine has received a lot of holistic hype in the West. Around here, though, it's been going strong for a while—more than 2,000 years, to be precise. Although modern Hong Kongers may see western doctors for serious illnesses, for minor complaints and everyday pick-me-ups they still turn to traditional remedies. To get to the root of your body's disequilibrium, a traditional Chinese medicine practitioner takes your pulse in different places, examines your tongue, eyes, and ears, and talks to you. Your prescription could include herbal tonics, teas, massage, dietary recommendations, and acupuncture.

LGBTQ+ COMMUNITY

In recent years, Hong Kong has made big strides in LGBTQ+ rights. While it doesn't yet recognize same-sex partnerships, a landmark court ruling in 2023 required the government to introduce a legal framework for same-sex civil unions by the end of 2025. Recent studies show the majority of Hong Kongers support the community. It's just a pity that the Pride Parade, the territory's annual LGBTQ+ march, is a shadow of its former self—it has down-geared into an exhibition and a market, following 2019's government crackdown on mass demonstrations.

POLITICAL DEVELOPMENTS

Since 2019, major political shifts have reshaped Hong Kong's social landscape, governance, and its relationship with mainland China. That year's explosive pro-democracy mass protests—sparked by an extradition bill and driven by concerns over increasing mainland influence and an erosion of civil rights—surfaced deep-seated tensions between the territory's autonomy and Beijing's growing control. In response, the Hong Kong government, backed by Beijing, implemented a sweeping National Security Law in 2020, curtailing freedoms of expression, assembly, and press. The move marked a sharp departure from the "one country, two systems" framework that governed the territory since its 1997 handover from British rule.

These developments have led to more controlled political and civil environments, with increased censorship and restrictions on political opposition. Many of those who can—expats and wealthy Hong Kongers with homes overseas—have packed up and left because of uncertainty over what may happen next. For tourists, the effects can be felt in a slightly subdued atmosphere (the bar scene, for one, is tangibly quieter), but the region is very much still a dynamic metropolis buzzing with creativity and ambition.

WHAT'S NEW

Although its reputation as a world-class shopping and dining destination is well known, Hong Kong has also been making a real effort to showcase its many cultural attractions. Historic sites—known here as heritage buildings—are being rejuvenated into cultural hubs, the latest being Tai Kwun Centre for Heritage and Art, which opened in 2018 after a decade of restoration. Formerly the site of Hong Kong's central police operations, the space is now filled by local shops and restaurants as well as arts exhibitions and events.

Off-the-beaten-track neighborhoods are also being revitalized through the Design District Hong Kong project, which draws visitors to less touristy areas like Tsuen Wan and Sha Tau Kok through art festivals and weekend markets. But the biggest—and most controversial, because of concerns over how the area's heritage is going to be preserved—redevelopment effort on the cards is a decade-long transformation of the iconic Mong Kok Flower Market into a commercial and residential center. It involves an ambitious 31 buildings and is expected to be completed by 2035.

Hong Kong with Kids

One child's buzz is another child's bore, so plan a variety of amusements to keep everyone entertained. Hong Kong has two major amusement parks, but so many more opportunities to laugh and learn at museums, parks, and wildlife reserves.

HONG KONG DISNEYLAND

Hong Kong's petite version of the Magic Kingdom, on Lantau Island, is growing more adult-size thanks to a multiyear expansion. You can still go on every ride at least once and see all the attractions in a day, but there's now more to thrill both older and little kids, like the world's first Frozen-theme park that includes a high-speed coaster and a musical boat ride.

Don't miss snapping a photo in front of the Castle of Magical Dreams, the park's newly revamped centerpiece. While Disney castles are usually designed to reflect one particular Disney princess, this unique citadel is an ode to 12 diverse Disney heroines.

HONG KONG PARK

This large public park is an oasis of lush greenery, populated with historic buildings and several facilities. The highlight is the Edward Youde Aviary, home to about 600 birds of 90 species indigenous to the endangered rain forests around Southeast Asia. Plant lovers should pay the Forsgate Conservatory, complete with three plant houses, a visit.

HONG KONG ZOOLOGICAL AND BOTANICAL GARDENS

Hong Kong has grown around these gardens, which opened in 1864, and although they're now watched over by skyscrapers, a visit here is still a delightful escape. Burmese pythons, Chinese alligators, Bali mynahs, Bornean orangutans, ring-tailed lemurs, and lion-tailed macaques are among its 400 birds, 70 mammals, and 50 reptiles in the zoo enclosures.

OCEAN PARK

This homegrown marine theme park offers a balance of toned-down thrills and high-octane rides suitable for toddlers to teenagers, as well as a giant aquarium and the popular giant-panda enclosure. The park stretches out over 200 hilly acres, which you can gaze down upon from the mile-long cable car that connects the tamer Lowlands area to the action-packed Headland.

SCIENCE MUSEUM

Kids can spend a full day bouncing from one exhibition zone to another at this science-theme museum. Take the fitness challenge or learn about light, sound, and motion through interactive presentations and activities.

HONG KONG SPACE MUSEUM

Take the kids to infinity and beyond at this dome-shape museum with a planetarium that screens immersive 3-D and Omnimax movies. The 100 interactive exhibits spanning two exhibition halls will keep them entertained for hours, though they may not want to budge from the virtual space station that simulates what weightlessness in space feels like.

What to Read and Watch Before You Go

A MANY-SPLENDOURED THING BY HAN SUYIN

This semi-autobiographical novel set in 1940s Hong Kong tells the story of a forbidden love affair between a Eurasian doctor and a British war correspondent, exploring the question of cultural identity in the territory's postwar society.

CITY AT THE END OF TIME BY LEUNG PING-KWAN

What was life like in Hong Kong just before 1997? This meditative poetry collection by one of Hong Kong's foremost cultural critics, penned in the run-up to the region's handover to China, is a reflection on the territory's changing urban landscape and shifting identity.

MY CITY: A HONG KONG STORY BY XI XI

Written by one of Hong Kong's most beloved authors, this emotive collection of essays and vignettes presents a rare, intimate view of local life, touching on Hong Kong's urban chaos, unique culture, and the resilience of its people.

GWEILO: MEMORIES OF A HONG KONG CHILDHOOD BY MARTIN BOOTH

Britain-born Booth lived in Hong Kong for three years in the 1950s as a boy, and his critically acclaimed memoir captures a sense of what the territory was like then—a time when Hong Kong was still a British colony but growing and evolving rapidly from an influx of migrants from mainland China. It's a story about cultural tension and identity.

THE WORLD OF SUZIE WONG BY RICHARD MASON

In recent years, Hong Kong's seedy side has been scrubbed fairly clean, but this love story paints a picture of the territory's ongoing social complexities and the relationship between expat and local lives, through the lens of its vibrant 1950s nightlife scene.

HONG KONG: CULTURE AND THE POLITICS OF DISAPPEARANCE BY ACKBAR ABBAS

An invaluable resource for understanding Hong Kong's complexity, this critical analysis by the former chair of comparative literature at the University of Hong Kong investigates how the city has grappled with its colonial past, modern influences, and coming under Chinese power.

A MODERN HISTORY OF HONG KONG BY STEVE TSANG

From 19th-century fishing village to 21st-century financial hub: Tsang's extensively researched, easy-to-read overview of Hong Kong's history is a fast track to understanding the territory's incredible political, economic, and social evolution over the past two centuries.

IN THE MOOD FOR LOVE (2000)

Few things have inspired visits to Hong Kong more than this cinematic masterpiece set in the 1960s. Directed by Wong Kar-Wai, one of the territory's most famous filmmakers, it's a love story set against a romantic, nostalgic portrait of Hong Kong and an ode to the region's vintage charm.

A BETTER TOMORROW (1986)

Hong Kong director John Woo revolutionized action cinema with his stylized, operatic approach to storytelling. This violent classic tells a story of brotherhood, loyalty, and redemption that also sheds light on the territory's influential triads.

INFERNAL AFFAIRS (2002)

This thriller about an undercover cop infiltrating a triad and a triad mole within the police is a heart-thumping tale of Hong Kong's struggle with duality: good and bad; east and west. It's said to have inspired the Hollywood remake *The Departed*.

Chapter 2

TRAVEL SMART

Updated by
Piera Chen

★ CAPITAL:
Beijing

POPULATION:
7,414,909

LANGUAGE:
English, Cantonese

$ CURRENCY:
Hong Kong Dollar (HK$)

COUNTRY CODE:
852

⚠ EMERGENCIES:
999

DRIVING:
On the left

ELECTRICITY:
220V/50Hz; plugs with three round or rectangular prongs

TIME:
12 hours ahead of New York (Eastern Standard Time)

WEB RESOURCES:
www.discoverhongkong.com
www.weather.gov.hk
www.timeout.com.hk

Know Before You Go

Hong Kong is a fast-paced and crowded place where no-nonsense efficiency reigns supreme. While that means it's a convenient place to visit, winging it is probably not the best approach. Here are some tips to help you get the most out of your trip.

ENGLISH IS SPOKEN, BUT KNOWING CANTONESE HELPS

Hong Kong's official languages are Chinese and English, but its native dialect is Cantonese. Most people speak English with varying levels of proficiency, but many drivers and hawkers do not. The ability to recognize a few basic Cantonese expressions such as "*do ze*" and "*mm-goi*"—which mean "thank you" in different contexts—will help you navigate the territory. Feel free to ask anyone for directions in English, but in particular, MTR employees or police officers. Get your concierge to write down your destination in Chinese if you're headed off the main trail.

LOOKS DECEIVE

On the surface, Hong Kong is a huge jumble of bustling alleys and streets punctuated by skyscrapers and shopping malls. A closer look reveals that rural mountains, forests, and outlying islands comprise more than 70% of Hong Kong's landmass.

BE MINDFUL OF THE EATING CULTURE

Meals are a communal event, so food in a Chinese restaurant is always shared. You usually have a small bowl or plate in which to transfer food from the center platters. Although cutlery is common in Hong Kong, chopsticks are ubiquitous. Be sure not to mistake serving chopsticks with your own. Avoid leaving your chopsticks standing up in a bowl of rice, which will make them resemble the ritual of offering food to the deceased. When someone pours tea into your cup, lightly tap your index and middle fingers twice on the table as a gesture of thanks. When doing the honor, fill others' cups before your own.

SPLIT THE BILL BUT ACCEPT GENEROSITY

The Hong Kong people are a pragmatic bunch who are comfortable "going dutch" when going out. Among acquaintances, expenses are split to prevent the owing of favors, which makes socializing more of a pleasure and less of an obligation. Special occasions like birthdays or entertaining visitors are exceptions. In such cases, Hong Kongers will want to show generosity. Offer to pay your share, but if your local friends insist on treating, accept. You can express gratitude by buying them drinks or a small gift.

RENT, BUT NOT POLITICS, IS FREELY TALKED ABOUT

In recent years, Hong Kongers have shied away from talking to strangers about politics, but real estate and salaries remain topics that are freely discussed. You may also find that certain older people are comfortable commenting on weight, marital status, and appearance. Take it in stride. You are not obligated to respond, but know that it's not meant maliciously.

ABIDE BY THE RULES

By and large, Hong Kongers are a rule-abiding bunch. Avoid jaywalking, eating on public transport, and cutting lines. Smoking is not allowed in bars and restaurants, museums and shopping malls, and even public areas like beaches and parks. A whopping fine of HK$1,500 should deter even the most diehard smoker. Littering is also frowned upon, and when caught, litterbugs will be handed a HK$3,000 fine.

EFFICIENCY AND SPEED REIGN SUPREME

Hong Kongers work hard and move fast, as do their escalators. When riding on one, make sure you stand on the right, leaving the left for those in a hurry. Don't be surprised if your server gets straight to the point without asking how your day has been. Don't be offended if no one other than the doorman holds the door open for you. Though Hong Kongers may not bother with certain niceties that you're used to, they don't mean to be rude. Once you get to know them, they can be as warm, helpful, and friendly as people anywhere else.

IT'S SAFE BUT USE COMMON SENSE

Hong Kong is generally very safe and crimes against tourists are almost unheard of. But as always, exercise caution. In crowded places, beware of pickpockets. Stick to illuminated areas if walking alone after dark. When using a taxi, make sure the driver's identity plate (with a light blue background) is displayed and they start the meter. When partying, do not leave your drink, mobile phone, or purse unattended.

PEOPLE DRESS MORE CASUALLY THAN YOU THINK

While there are uber-fashionable Hong Kongers, most of the city's inhabitants are casual dressers. Jeans and windbreakers are not uncommon at banquets. Shorts and flipflops, however, are almost a rarity, thanks in part to the ubiquity of indoor air-conditioners. Showing cleavage, the mid-section, or legs is fine—if you don't mind the occasional gawker. Modest dressing is recommended for temples and churches.

HONG KONG IS BECOMING AN INCLUSIVE PLACE

Hong Kong has a vibrant and welcoming LGBTQ+ scene, with party spots aplenty. The Pride Parade takes place in November, while the territory's largest queer event Pink Dot occurs in September. It is safe to be out after dark and handholding in public, though not common, is accepted. That being said, same-sex marriage is not recognized and bureaucratic impediments to the holding of LGBTQ+ events seem to have heightened in recent years. By comparison, Hong Kong fares extremely well in gender equality. Of the economies studied by the World Economic Forum in 2024 for a global gender-gap report, Hong Kong has the highest score of all Asian economies, as well as a score higher than those of the U.S., South Africa, and Singapore.

RESERVE, RESERVE, RESERVE

Check exact dates of traditional festivals, and book tickets to concerts and other key cultural events at least two months before you go. If you're a foodie, two or even three months in advance is not too early to reserve the town's hottest tables. For intimate live shows and niche festivals, buy tickets at least a month before. You'll want to book tours at least two weeks ahead, but a month is preferred for popular ones. A week or two ahead should suffice for Hong Kong's busiest small drinking dens.

Getting Here and Around

The many public transportation options in Hong Kong are generally clean, safe, and inexpensive. If you're a smartphone user, the first step in navigating Hong Kong is to download the navigation and payment apps. Handy ones include **HKeMobility,** an all-in-one journey planner developed by the Transport Department that gives information on routes, fares, duration, and real-time traffic conditions. All major bus companies also have their own apps, as do ferry operators. Another essential app is the **Octopus App for Tourists.** The Octopus Card is a mobile payment device usable for all public transportation options and designated taxis. You can also obtain a physical Octopus Card from any Mass Transit Railway (MTR) or Airport Express station. It is more convenient than buying a ticket for each train trip or digging for change on the bus. The card comes with a deposit of HK$50, and when it's no longer needed, you can apply for a refund through the app or in person at any MTR station. You can top up the physical card at Customer Service Centres and Add Value machines at MTR stations, or at convenience stores, supermarkets, and some fast-food chains.

The quickest and perhaps safest way to travel is with the ever-reliable MTR (underground railway), which links to most of the areas you'll want to visit. There's no timetable because trains run so frequently. Signs and announcements are in both Chinese and English, and posted maps help visitors navigate outside the stations, too.

When boarding a bus or entering a subway, simply look for the rectangular yellow sensor (on top of the MTR turnstiles or next to the fare box on buses and minibuses) and place the card or QR code on it until you hear a beep. The sensors are sensitive enough to scan through wallets and bags, so you don't need to take your card out. Once your card has been read, the remaining balance appears on the sensor screen.

Although you can cross the harbor on the MTR, the Star Ferry is a cheaper ride, with the added bonus of letting you enjoy the fantastic harbor views during the 10-minute journey between Hong Kong Island and Tsim Sha Tsui, or Tsim Sha Tsui and Wan Chai. Fast and regular ferries are also available for the outlying islands.

If you prefer street-level travel, the city's air-conditioned double-decker buses can take you anywhere, provided you know which number and route to take. On the northern side of Hong Kong Island you can also take the tram (listen for the distinctive "ding-ding"), a fun and inexpensive way to get from one side of the island to the other—and it's the same route that the MTR follows, so you should be able to walk to an MTR station from any tram stop between Sheung Wan and Shau Kei Wan.

If you do get lost, you can always hail a cab. Prices are reasonable if you're not traveling too far, and tipping is not required. Not all drivers are willing to cross the harbor, though, so be sure to ask before getting in. Unless it's a designated cross-harbor vehicle, expect to be charged for the return-trip toll as well.

Uber is available in Hong Kong and you can use the app as you would anywhere else in the world. However, keep in mind that Uber operates in a legal "gray area" in Hong Kong, as the drivers generally do not have a "car hire" permit and passengers are not insured.

Perhaps best of all, Hong Kong is easy to explore on foot. In Central, a covered walkway connects major buildings in the business district, and Mid-Levels is easily accessed by an outdoor escalator, thus avoiding stoplights, exhaust fumes, and weather conditions (but not crowds). The same can apply to the pedestrian overpasses all around the city.

Before you leave Hong Kong, you can cash in your Octopus Card at MTR stations. If your balance is less than HK$500, you will receive that amount plus the HK$50 deposit. There is a refund processing fee of HK$11 for cards that are returned within three months of purchase.

 Air

Flying time to Hong Kong is around 16 hours nonstop from New York City, 16 hours nonstop from Los Angeles, or 15 hours nonstop from San Francisco.

AIRPORTS

Easy to navigate and full of amenities, **Hong Kong International Airport** (HKG)—also known as Chek Lap Kok, after its location on Lantau Island—is a traveler's dream. Terminal 1, one of the largest in the world, handles arrivals and departures for most major airlines. The smaller Terminal 2 handles all other airlines, including budget carriers.

Although the lines usually move quickly at security and immigration checkpoints, it's advisable to arrive at least two hours before departure. Remember that check-in counters are a long distance from the gates. Most major airlines let you use the In-Town Check-In service at the Hong Kong or Kowloon Airport Express stations up to 24 hours before your flight (confirm with your airline first). You can check luggage as well, saving you the bother of lugging bags out to the airport.

Travelex currency-exchange machines in each terminal make it easy to get rid of your leftover Hong Kong dollars. Another way is to take advantage of the wealth of duty-free shopping choices throughout the airport, especially in Terminal 1. If you'd rather relax before or after a flight, you can pay to use one of the 24-hour Plaza Premium Lounges (🌐 *www.plazapremiumlounge.com*) with restrooms, showers, massage services, online access, and hot meals. Packages range from HK$960 to HK$1,300. Free resting lounges (without showers and other perks) and miniature gardens with comfortable seating are at the Departure Level near Gates 21, 26, 34, 41, and 61.

When arriving in Hong Kong, you'll be asked to fill out an immigrations form. An immigrations officer will collect an arrivals slip and give you a departure slip that you must show when you leave the city. An airport tax is normally included in your ticket price. If it's not, the fee is HK$120. It's levied only on those 12 years and older and is waived for all transit and transfer passengers who arrive and leave on the same day.

GROUND TRANSPORTATION

The Airport Express (🌐 *www.mtr.com.hk*) train service is the quickest and most convenient way to and from the airport. High-speed trains whisk you to Kowloon in 21 minutes and Central in 24 minutes. Trains run daily every 10 minutes between 5:54 am and 11:28 pm and every 12 minutes between 11:28 pm and 12:58 am. The last train from the airport departs at 12:48 am. The trains have Wi-Fi access, plenty of luggage space, and comfortable seating with video screens showing tourist information and the latest news.

The Airport Express station has stops at the AsiaWorld-Expo, Tsing Yi, Kowloon, and Central stations. Excluding the AsiaWorld stop, all stations connect to the MTR. One-way or same-day return tickets are HK$100 to Kowloon and HK$110 to Central. Round-trip tickets

Getting Here and Around

valid for one month cost HK$185 to Kowloon and HK$205 to Central. Tickets are cheaper if purchased online or through a travel agent. It's the most expensive public transport option, but the speed and dependability justify the extra cost.

The Airport Express also provides free in-town check-in service, and free MTR connections if you change to an MTR line using the same Octopus card within one hour of arrival. Free shuttle buses run every 12 or 20 minutes between major hotels and the Hong Kong and Kowloon stations—there are several routes, and a list of stops is displayed prominently at the boarding area. Service begins at 6:12 am and ends at 11:12 pm. To board, you must show your Airport Express ticket and airline ticket or boarding pass.

Citybus (🌐 *www.citybus.com.hk*) runs five buses ("A" precedes the bus number) from the airport to popular destinations. They make fewer stops than regular buses (which have an "E" before their numbers). Two useful routes are the A11, serving Central, Admiralty, Wan Chai, and Causeway Bay and ending in North Point; and the A21, going to Tsim Sha Tsui, Jordan, and Mong Kok. The A11's operating hours are from 6:10 am to 12:30 am, while the A21 runs from 6 am to 12 am. Should you arrive in Hong Kong outside of these hours, you can take the N11 or the N21, which are night buses serving the same routes. The buses are comfortable, have adequate luggage space, and include free Wi-Fi access. The onboard announcements are in Cantonese, Putonghua, and English, so you won't miss your stop.

Several small shuttle buses with an "S" before their numbers run to the nearby Tung Chung MTR station, where you can get the MTR to Central and Kowloon. MTR trains run parallel to the Airport Express route, but they cost much less (HK$27.50 from the airport to Central). However, you won't have the same amenities, and travel time is longer as the trains make more stops.

Taxis from the airport are reliable and plentiful. Trips to Hong Kong Island destinations cost around HK$360 to HK$450, while those to Kowloon are around HK$260 to HK$345. There is also an HK$6 charge per piece of luggage stored in the trunk. **Blacklane** (🌐 *www.blacklane.com*) offers limousine service to the city for HK$800 to HK$2,000 one-way.

Ground Transportation to Kowloon

Transport Mode	Time	Cost
Airport Express	19 mins	HK$100
Citybus Line A (Cityflyer)	45 mins	HK$41.90
Citybus Line E (Regular)	60 mins	HK$21.70
Limo	35 mins	HK$900
Taxi	35 mins	HK$375
Tung Chung (S1 bus) + MTR (train)	10 mins + 38 mins	HK$3.70 + HK$23.50

FLIGHTS

Cathay Pacific is Hong Kong's flagship carrier. It maintains high standards, with friendly service, good food, an extensive in-flight entertainment system, and an excellent track record for safety. Cathay has nonstop flights from both Los Angeles and San Francisco on the West Coast and from New York–JFK on the East Coast, with connecting services to many other U.S. cities. **Singapore Airlines** is also another highly rated airline with flights to Hong Kong from multiple American cities, including daily flights from San Francisco.

If you are on a tight budget, **Air China** and **China Airlines** offer lower-cost flights between New York and Los Angeles and Hong Kong, although the savings are reflected in the service and amenities. Several other airlines also offer service from the United States to Hong Kong, usually with connections in Asia.

If you're planning to travel to three or four Asian destinations, you might want to consider **One World's Visit Asia Pass,** which provides travel throughout Southeast Asia via an array of airlines. Cities are grouped into zones, and there's a flat rate for each zone. The pass doesn't cover flights from the United States, Europe, or Australia and New Zealand, however. Inquire through American Airlines, Cathay Pacific, or any other One World member.

Boat and Ferry

With fabulous views of both sides of Victoria Harbour, the **Star Ferry** (🌐 *www.starferry.com.hk*) is so much more than just a boat. This icon has been circling the harbor since 1888. Double-bowed, green-and-white vessels connect Central and Wan Chai with Kowloon in under 10 minutes, daily from 6:30 am to 11:30 pm. A ride on the upper deck costs HK$5 on weekdays and HK$6.50 on weekends and public holidays, making it the cheapest scenic harbor tour in town. You can use cash or your Octopus Card to pay the fare.

There's also regular ferry service to outlying islands, such as Lantau. Ordinary ferries are cheap but slow, while fast ferries travel at twice the speed for twice the price. As a general rule, fares are more expensive at night. Check ferry schedules on the HKeMobility app or pick up printed copies at the Hong Kong Tourist Board information center at the Tsim Sha Tsui Star Ferry Concourse.

Ferry Travel

Line/ Route	Fre-quency	Travel Time	Fare
Central–Mui Wo (Lantau)	30–45 mins	35–55 mins	HK$17.20–HK$48.90
Star Ferry Central–Tsim Sha Tsui	6–12 mins	7 mins	HK$2.50–HK$3.40
Star Ferry Wan Chai–Tsim Sha Tsui	10–14 mins	8 mins	HK$5–HK$6.50

Bus

An efficient network of double-decker buses covers most of Hong Kong, often with stops at locations not accessible via MTR. The best way to figure out the routes is by using a combination of the **HKeMobility** journey planner app and those of the individual bus companies. Citybus and New World First Bus (NWFB) share a common app, as do Kowloon Motor Bus (KMB) and Long Win Bus Company (LWB).

More intrepid visitors can take a chance on a minibus, officially called Public Light Buses. These cream-color vehicles with a red or green stripe seat 16 people and rattle through the city at breakneck speeds. Routes and prices are prominently displayed in front. Red-stripe minibuses are free to operate anywhere without fixed routes or fares, while green-stripe ones are the opposite. While faster than buses, minibuses are risky if you aren't sure of your destination. There are designated stops, but minibus drivers will also pick up and drop off passengers at other points along the way. To get off, you'll have to shout out "*yau lok!*" ("getting off") to the driver and hold on tight as he screeches to a halt.

FARES

Double-decker bus fares range from HK$3.50 to HK$60.70; minibus fares from HK$5.70 to HK$30.50. The best way to pay is by Octopus Card. Otherwise, you'll need to have exact change. Some minibuses, particularly the overnight ones, accept only cash, but they do give you change.

 Car

Frankly, you'd be mad to rent a car on Hong Kong Island or in Kowloon. Traffic jams, hard-to-navigate streets, and next to no parking make driving here severely stress inducing. What's more, gasoline prices are among the most expensive in the world. So why bother, when public transportation is excellent and taxis are inexpensive?

If you must have your own wheels, consider hiring a driver. Most top-end hotels can arrange this; the Peninsula in Kowloon and the Island Shangri-La even have their own fleets of chauffeur-driven Rolls-Royces and Mercedes available for hourly hire. Avis can also provide chauffeur services along with car rentals.

If you're determined to drive yourself, your driver's license must be valid in Hong Kong for up to a year if you're 18 to 70 years old (those over 70 must pass a physical examination before driving). You'll need an International Driver's Permit (HK$80) for stays up to 12 months. Check the AAA and Hong Kong Transport Department websites for more info.

The cheapest option for car rentals may be **Hawk Rent-a-Car** (🌐 *www.hawkrentacar.com.hk*), which has lots of models and prices; there are special rates for weekends and longer-term rentals. Rental rates begin at around HK$480 per day and HK$2,550 per week for an economy car with air-conditioning, automatic transmission, and unlimited mileage. **Parklane Limousine** has a fleet of more than 100 Mercedes-Benzes with hourly rates for chauffeur services.

PARKING

There's next to no on-street parking in Hong Kong, and the extremely vigilant traffic police hand out copious parking tickets. If you luck out and find a metered space, you'll have to use an Octopus Card to pay.

Most drivers take advantage of parking garages, which cost up to HK$40 per hour in prime locations. However, some mall garages will subsidize parking if you make purchases at their shops or eat in one of their restaurants. Be sure to have the receipt validated by the staff before leaving.

RULES OF THE ROAD

Driving is on the left-hand side of the road in Hong Kong. Wearing a seat belt is mandatory in the front and back of private cars. The standard speed limit is 50 kph (30 mph) and 70 or 80 kph for expressways, unless signs state otherwise. The police spend a lot of time setting up speed traps and giving out juicy fines. Using handheld cell phones while driving is forbidden. You can't make a right turn on a red light, and you should scrupulously obey lane markings regarding turns.

Drunk driving is taken very seriously: the legal limit is 50 mg of alcohol per 100 ml of blood (or 22 micrograms of alcohol per 100 ml of breath), and there are penalties of up to HK$25,000 and three years in prison for those who disobey. You can get highly detailed information on

Hong Kong's road rules on the Transport Department's website.

 Cruise

Cunard (*www.cunard.com*), the crème de la crème of cruisers, docks in Hong Kong on its round-the-world trips. **Princess Cruises** (*www.princess.com*) has a wide variety of packages that call at Hong Kong and many other Asian destinations. **Holland America** (*www.hollandamerica.com*) has two-week Asian cruises as well as round-the-world options. Be sure to check out last-minute special offers from all these lines.

Subway

By far the best way to get around Hong Kong is on the MTR (*www.mtr.com.hk*). The network now provides all subway and train services in Hong Kong. The trains are among the cleanest in the world, with hardly any litter to be found. Eating or drinking on the trains or in the paid areas is prohibited, with fines of HK$2,000.

There are nine main lines, all color-coded for convenience. The MTR is extremely safe, even late at night. Glass screens have been installed between the edges of platforms and tracks, preventing falls and other mishaps. Emergency stop buttons and help lines are easy to access and ensure instant response from the staff. Trains run every two to eight minutes during peak times between 6 am and 1 am daily. Entrances, platforms, and exits are clearly marked and signposted, and all MTR areas are air-conditioned. Most stations have wheelchair access, and all have convenience stores and other shops or services. All MTR stations have free Wi-Fi.

FARES AND SCHEDULES

You can buy tickets from ticket machines (using coins or notes) or from English-speaking staff behind glass-windowed Customer Service Centres. Fares range from HK$5 to HK$63, depending how far you travel. Instead of paying cash, consider a rechargeable (and refundable) **Octopus Card.** It saves time lining up for tickets and fussing for change, gives you a discounted fare on each trip, and can also be used for buses and other forms of transportation.

Another alternative is the **Tourist Day Pass.** For HK$75 (HK$35 for children age 3 to 11), this pass allows you unlimited travel on the MTR—excluding the Airport Express or to Lo Wu or Lok Ma Chau Stations—for one day. However, you cannot use the pass on other public transport or to purchase items.

 Taxi

Taxis are easy to find in Hong Kong, although heavy rush hour traffic in Central, Causeway Bay, and Tsim Sha Tsui means they aren't always the best option for getting around the city quickly. They're most useful other times of the day, especially after the MTR closes. Drivers usually know the terrain well, but many don't speak English; having your destination written in Chinese is a good idea.

You can hail cabs on the street, provided you're in a stopping area (i.e., not marked by double yellow lines). The white "taxi" sign is lit when the cab is available. Not all taxis will drive from Hong Kong Island to Kowloon (or vice versa). You can usually identify cross-harbor taxis by the red plastic "No Service" sign on their dashboards; you'll find cross-harbor taxi ranks at the Star Ferry terminal and elsewhere

Getting Here and Around

around town. It's sometimes hard to find a taxi between 3 pm and 4 pm, when the drivers switch shifts.

There are three types of taxi: red, green, and blue, with each color representing a geographical area. Red taxis are found throughout most of Hong Kong, and fares start at HK$29 for the first 2 km (1½ miles), then HK$2.10 for each 0.2 km (0.1 mile) or minute of waiting time. (Fares add up fast in bumper-to-bumper traffic.) After the fare reaches HK$102.50, you're charged HK$1.40 for each 0.2 km or minute of waiting time. The Hong Kong Kowloon Taxi and Lorry Owners Association and the Kowloon Taxi Owners Association operate red taxis.

There's a surcharge of HK$6 for each piece of luggage you put in the trunk. The Cross-Harbour Tunnel, Eastern Harbour Crossing, and Western Harbour Crossing all incur surcharges of the toll plus HK$25 return toll. Passengers must pay the toll amount for other tunnels and roads, except the toll for the Tai Lam Tunnel, which is paid by the driver.

In the New Territories, taxis are green; on Lantau Island they're blue. Fares are lower than in urban areas, but while red urban taxis may travel into rural zones, rural green and blue taxis can't cross into urban zones. Call the **Lantau Taxi Call Station** (☎ *2984–1368* ☎ *2776–7888*) for blue taxis, and the **NT Taxi-call Service Centre** (☎ *2657–2267* ☎ *2476–4247*) for green taxis.

Passengers are required by law to wear a seat belt when available. Most locals don't tip; however, if you round up the fare by a few Hong Kong dollars you're sure to earn yourself a winning smile from your underpaid and overworked driver. Taxis are usually reliable, but if you have a problem, note the taxi's registration number and the driver's name, which are usually prominently displayed on the dashboard, and call the Transport Complaints Unit (☎ *2889–9999*). If you've left an item behind in your taxi, you can call the Road Co-op Lost and Found hotline (☎ *1872–920*).

In urban areas it's as easy and safe to hail a cab on the street as it is to call one. There are hundreds of taxi companies, so it's usually best to get your hotel or restaurant to call a company it works with. Note that there's a HK$5 surcharge for phone bookings.

 Train

The ultra-efficient MTR train network connects Kowloon to the eastern and western New Territories. Trains run every five to eight minutes, and connections to the subway are relatively quick. This is a commuter service and, like the subway, has sparkling-clean trains and stations—smoking, eating, and drinking are strictly forbidden.

The train network has three main lines. The East Rail line begins at Hung Hom, with notable stops at Mong Kok, Kowloon Tong, Sha Tin, Racecourse, Chinese University, and Tai Po on its way to Lo Wu at the mainland Chinese border. East Rail is the fastest way to get to Shenzhen—it's a 40-minute trip from Hung Hom to Lo Wu. The Hung Hom train station terminus connects via a series of walkways with East Tsim Sha Tsui; you can also transfer to the MTR at Kowloon Tong.

The short Ma On Shan Rail service starts at Tai Wai and has eight stops in the northeastern New Territories.

West Rail starts at East Tsim Sha Tsui, moves on to Tsim Sha Tsui for a possible connection to the subway, then extends westward through 10 more stops to Tuen Mun, in the New Territories. Here West Rail connects with the local Light Rail Transit, an aboveground train serving mainly residential and industrial areas in the western New Territories.

The regular fare from Central to Lo Wu is HK$55.50, but using an Octopus Card will save you HK$3.30.

Trains have television screens that constantly barrage you with news and advertisements. To avoid this, avail yourself of the cars marked "Quiet."

Tram

PEAK TRAM

It's Hong Kong's greatest misnomer—the **Peak Tram** (🌐 *www.thepeak.com.hk*) is actually a funicular railway. Since 1888 it's been rattling the 1,365 feet up the hill from Mid-Levels to the Victoria Peak tram terminus. As well as a sizable adrenaline rush due to the steepness of the ascent, on a clear day the trip offers fabulous panoramas. Most passengers board at the Lower Terminus between Garden Road and Cotton Tree Drive. (The tram has six stations.) The fare is HK$76 one-way, HK$108 round-trip, and the tram runs every 15 to 20 minutes between 7:30 am and 11 pm daily. You can walk up to the Lower Terminus or take Bus 15C, which shuttles passengers from the Star Ferry.

STREET TRAMS

Old-fashioned double-decker trams (🌐 *www.hktramways.com*) have been running along the northern shore of Hong Kong Island since 1904. Most of the six routes start in Kennedy Town or Western Market, and go eastward all the way through Central, Wan Chai, Causeway Bay, North Point, and Quarry Bay to Shau Kei Wan. A branch line turns off in Wan Chai toward Happy Valley, where horse races are held in season.

Destinations are marked on the front of each tram and route maps are displayed at the stops; you board at the back and get off at the front, paying a flat rate of HK$3 (by Octopus or with exact change) as you leave. Avoid trams at rush hours, which are generally weekdays from 7:30 to 9:30 am and 5 to 7:30 pm. Although trams move slowly, for short hops between Central and Western or Admiralty they can be quicker than going underground to take the MTR. A leisurely top-deck ride from Western to Causeway Bay is a great city tour. There is no air-conditioning on trams.

Essentials

Business and Trade Services

BUSINESS CENTERS

Hong Kong has many business centers located outside the major hotels, and some are considerably cheaper. You can arrange for everything from a fully equipped workspace to a serviced office. Amenities include secretarial support, access to printers and photocopiers, and maintenance services. Many centers are affiliated with accountants and lawyers who can expedite company registration. Some will even process visas for you.

Jumpstart Business Centre (*www.jumpstartoffices.com*), **Regus** (*www.regus.hk*), and the **Executive Centre** (*www.executivecentre.com*) are international business services companies with several locations in Hong Kong. They provide secretarial support and office rentals, along with meeting and conference facilities. Coworking spaces like **The Hive** (*www.thehivecausewaybay.com*) are also gaining popularity.

Most business centers offer delivery service, and you can sometimes arrange a delivery through your hotel concierge. Courier services such as **City-Link International** (*www.citylinkexpress.com*) will pick up from your hotel, as will FedEx and DHL, which also have drop-off points all over Hong Kong. Price is based on weight and distance. Hong Kong Post also has a dependable and speedy courier service. You can drop off your package at a post office or at any one of the local courier post boxes in the city.

Communications

INTERNET

Going online is extremely easy in Hong Kong. Free public Wi-Fi is available at multiple locations, including public libraries, major museums, public parks, indoor markets, MTR stations, ferry terminals, and popular tourist spots. Some buses, including all Kowloon Motor Bus vehicles, and buses to and from the airport, also provide free onboard Wi-Fi—look for the Webus sticker by the door. Many fast-food outlets, cafés, and shopping malls also offer free Wi-Fi service.

CSL, a Hong Kong–based communications company, has more than 15,000 Wi-Fi hotspots scattered around the city, including areas near universities, convenience stores, and shopping malls. You can access these hotspots via a prepaid Discover Hong Kong Tourist SIM Card. A seven-day 5G card costs HK$88 and can be used in both Hong Kong and Macau. The cards can be purchased at convenience stores, CSL locations, and the Hong Kong Tourism Board's Kowloon Visitor Centre.

Public libraries and the Hong Kong International Airport provide free access to computer terminals.

PHONES

Hong Kong was the first city in the world with a fully digitized local phone network, and the service is efficient and cheap. Even international calls are inexpensive relative to those in the United States. You can expect clear connections and helpful directory assistance. Don't hang up if you hear Cantonese when calling automated and prerecorded hotlines; English is usually the second or third language option. The country code for Hong Kong is 852; there are no local area codes.

CALLING WITHIN HONG KONG

Hong Kong phone numbers have eight digits: landline numbers usually start with a 2 or 3; cell phones with a 9, 6, or 5.

If you're old enough to talk in Hong Kong, you're old enough for a cell phone. This means public phones can be difficult to find, although you'll find a few tucked away in MTR stations. Local calls to both land and cell lines cost HK$1 per five minutes. If you're planning to call abroad from a pay phone, remember that convenience stores like 7-Eleven sell international phone cards. You may need to specify the country you're calling to get the right type of card. Some pay phones also accept credit cards.

Some hotels may charge as much as HK$5 for a local call, while a few others include them for free in your room rate. In a pinch, restaurants and shops will often let you use their phones for free.

Dial 1081 for directory assistance from English-speaking operators; 10013 for international inquiries and for assistance with direct dialing; 10010 for collect and operator-assisted calls to most countries, including the United States; and 10011 for credit-card, collect, and international conference calls.

CALLING OUTSIDE HONG KONG

International rates from Hong Kong are reasonable, even more so between 9 pm and 8 am. The international dial code is 001, followed by the country code.

The country code for the United States is 1, so you must dial 0011 before the area code and number. You can dial direct from many hotel and business centers, but always with a hefty surcharge.

MOBILE PHONES

Most GSM-compatible mobile phones work in Hong Kong. Roaming fees can be steep, however—99¢ a minute is considered reasonable—and overseas you normally pay the toll charges for incoming calls. It's almost always cheaper to send a text message than to make a call, since text messages have a very low set fee (often less than 5¢).

If you can unlock your phone, buying a SIM card locally is the cheapest and easiest way to make calls. PCCW's prepaid Discover Hong Kong Tourist Card can be found at convenience stores, PCCW outlets, and the Hong Kong Tourism Board's Kowloon Visitor Centre. A standard five-day pass costs HK$69.

Cellular Abroad (🌐 *www.cellularabroad.com*) rents and sells GSM phones and sells SIM cards that work in many countries. **Mobal** (🌐 *www.mobal.com*) and **PlanetFone** (🌐 *www.planetfone.com*) rent and lease GSM phones that will operate in countries around the world, though per-call rates can be expensive.

Customs and Duties

You're allowed to bring goods of a certain value back home without having to pay duty or import tax. But there's a limit on the amount of tobacco and liquor you can bring back duty-free, and some countries have separate limits for perfumes; for exact figures, check with your customs department. When you shop abroad, save all your receipts, as customs inspectors may ask to see them along with the items you purchased. If the total value of your goods is more than the duty-free limit, you'll have to pay a tax (most often a flat percentage) on the value of everything beyond that limit.

Essentials

Except for the usual prohibitions against endangered species, narcotics, explosives, firearms, and ammunition, and limits on alcohol, tobacco products, and perfume, you can bring almost anything you want into Hong Kong. Visitors bringing over HK$120,000 into the territory need to declare to the authorities. Cannabis is prohibited in Hong Kong. See 🌐 *www.customs.gov.hk* for more details.

Dining

No other city in the world boasts quite as eclectic a dining scene as Hong Kong. Michelin-star restaurants, both opulent and humble, such as The Chairman, Yat Lok, and Chaat, as well as Asian outposts of international celebrity chefs like Joël Robuchon, are just a custard bun's throw from humble eateries doling out excellent egg noodles and shrimp wonton, or juicy slices of barbecued meat piled atop bowls of fragrant jasmine rice.

One of the key lessons here is to never judge a book by its cover—the most unassuming eateries are often the ones that provide the most memorable meals. At noodle-centric restaurants, fish-ball soup with rice noodles is a great choice, and the goose, suckling pig, honeyed pork, and soy-sauce chicken are good bets at the roast-meat shops. A combination plate, with a sampling of meats and some greens on a bed of white rice, is generally a foolproof way to go if you're not sure what to order. Street foods are another must-try; for under HK$20, you can sample curry fish balls, egg waffles, stinky tofu, and all sorts of other delicious tidbits. If you have the chance, visit a *dai pai dong* (outdoor food stall) or a *cha chaan tang* (local café), and try the local specialties.

Finally, remember that Hong Kong is the world's epicenter of dim sum. While you're here you must have at least one dim sum breakfast or lunch in a teahouse. Those steaming bamboo baskets you see conceal tasty dumplings, buns, and pastries—best washed down with cups of Chinese tea.

HOURS

A typical breakfast at a *cha chaan tang* consists of scrambled eggs with buttered toast and/or macaroni or noodles in soup, and a cup of aromatic and insomnia-inducing Hong Kong–style milk tea, coffee, or *yin yeung* (tea-coffee). Congee with a side of crullers is also a popular option. Most hotels serve western-style breakfasts, and coffee, pastries, and sandwiches are readily available at *cha chaan tangs* and cafés. Lunchtime is between noon and 2 pm; normal dinner hours are from 7 until 11 pm, but Hong Kong is a 24-hour city, and you'll be able to find a meal here at any hour. Dim sum can begin as early as 7:30 am, and though it's traditionally a daytime food, you'll find plenty of specialist restaurants that serve dim sum late into the evening.

PRICES, TIPPING, AND TAX

Many restaurants in Hong Kong serve main dishes that are meant to be shared, so take this into account with respect to prices. It's also worth noting that some specialty dishes—like abalone, bird's-nest soup, and dried seafood—are outrageously expensive. And when you get your check, don't be shocked that you've been charged for everything, including tea, rice, and those side dishes placed automatically on your table. At upmarket and western-style restaurants tips are appreciated (10% is generous); the service charge on your bill doesn't go to the waitstaff.

⇨ *Restaurant reviews throughout this guide have been shortened. For full information, visit Fodors.com. Restaurant prices are the average cost of a main course at dinner or, if dinner is not served, at lunch.*

What It Costs in HK$

$	$$	$$$	$$$$
AT DINNER			
under HK$100	HK$100–HK$200	HK$201–HK$500	over HK$500

RESERVATIONS

Book ahead at all restaurants, except cafés, noodle joints, roast meat stalls, shopping mall eateries, *cha chaan tangs*, and *dai pai dongs*, especially if you're going on the weekend or during major holidays and the eves of public holidays. For the hottest tables, it is advisable to book months in advance. It's usually easier to land a table for lunch than dinner. Certain dishes that are tedious or costly to prepare require reserving not just a table but the dish itself. Ask the restaurant when booking if any of their dishes require reservation.

SHARE AND SHARE ALIKE

In Hong Kong, food is meant to be shared. Instead of ordering individual main dishes, it's usual for those around a table—whether a couple or a dozen people—to share several. Four people eating together, for example, might order a whole or half chicken, another type of meat, a fish dish, a vegetable, and fried noodles—all of which would be placed on the table's revolving tray. Restaurants may adjust portions and prices according to the number of diners.

Western-style cutlery is common in all upmarket Chinese restaurants in Hong Kong, but what better place to practice your chopstick skills? Serving chopsticks are usually provided for each dish. You should use these to serve yourself and others. If no serving chopsticks are provided, serve yourself using your own chopsticks; just be sure to use the ends that you haven't put into your mouth.

WHAT TO WEAR

Casual dress—sports shirts, T-shirts, clean jeans, and the like—is acceptable almost everywhere in Hong Kong, although shorts and sneakers or flip-flops will feel out of place at trendy venues and five-star restaurants where people dress to impress. Generally, the dress code in Hong Kong is smart casual.

WINE OR BEER?

French reds have long had a cachet in Hong Kong, but since the repeal of the city's wine tax in 2008, the city's wine selection has blossomed. Wine is very popular in Hong Kong and it's not uncommon to see Chinese restaurants—especially the higher-end ones—create tasting menus designed specifically to go with various wines. Many midrange restaurants and some *dai pai dongs* allow you to bring your own wine for a corkage fee.

For Cantonese food, tea is traditional, but Hong Kong likes its beer—before, during, or after dinner. It's generally light stuff, like Heineken, the locally brewed San Miguel, or a Chinese lager such as the immensely popular Tsing Tao. Craft beers have also taken off. Many pubs import interesting microbrews, and you may also want to try one of dozens of locally brewed artisanal ales with funky names like Gweilo, HK Lovecraft, and Nine Dragons. When it's time to hit the karaoke bars or clubs, though, people switch to stronger spirits. If you like cocktails, check out some of the trendy upscale bars, which take their mixed drinks and decor very seriously.

Essentials

Electricity

The current in Hong Kong is 220 volts, 50 cycles alternating current (AC), so most American appliances can't be used without a transformer. Exceptions are most laptops and mobile phone chargers, which are dual voltage (i.e., they operate equally well on 110 and 220 volts), and thus require only an adapter. The same may be true of some hair dryers and other small appliances. Always check labels and manufacturer instructions to be sure. Don't use 110-volt outlets marked "for shavers only" for high-wattage appliances such as hair dryers.

Most plugs have three square prongs, like British plugs, but you can buy adapters in just about every supermarket and at electronics stalls in street markets. If you travel frequently, consider making a small investment in a universal adapter, which has several types of plugs in one lightweight, compact unit.

Emergencies

Locals and police are usually very helpful in emergencies. Most police officers speak some English or will contact someone who does. For police, fire, and ambulance emergency services, dial 999.

There are 24-hour accident and emergency services at the **Pamela Youde Nethersole Eastern Hospital** (🌐 *www.ha.org.hk/pyneh* ☎ *2595–6111*), **Prince of Wales Hospital** (🌐 *www.ha.org.hk/pwh* ☎ *3505–2211*), **Queen Elizabeth Hospital** (🌐 *www.ha.org.hk/qeh* ☎ *3506–8888*), **Queen Mary Hospital** (🌐 *www8.ha.org.hk/qmh* ☎ *2255–3838*), **Ruttonjee** (🌐 *www.ha.org.hk* ☎ *2291–2000*), and **Tseung Kwan O Hospital** (🌐 *www.ha.org.hk* ☎ *2208–0111*). Nonresidents are charged a set fee of HK$1,190 for each use of the public health-care system. Private hospitals (🌐 *www.privatehospitals.org.hk*) charge more but the waiting time is shorter.

The following hospitals also have 24-hour pharmacies: Pamela Youde Nethersole Eastern Hospital, Prince of Wales Hospital, Queen Elizabeth Hospital, and Queen Mary Hospital. Local drugstore chains **Watsons** (🌐 *www.watsons.com.hk*) and **Mannings** (🌐 *www.mannings.com.hk/eng*) have shops throughout the city; closing times generally vary between 7:30 pm and 10:30 pm.

Health

When visiting Hong Kong, it's a good idea to be immunized against typhoid and hepatitis A and B, and in winter, a flu vaccination is also advisable, especially if you're infection-prone or are a senior citizen. Speak with your physician and check the Centers for Disease Control and Prevention (CDC) or World Health Organization (WHO) websites for health alerts, particularly if you're pregnant, traveling with children, or have a chronic illness.

Most locals don't drink water straight from the tap. Expect to pay HK$10 to HK$20 for a 1½-liter bottle of distilled or mineral water, or drink boiled tap water. Better still, bring your own bottle and use the Water for Free app to find the nearest water dispenser (🌐 *waterforfree.org*).

Avian influenza, commonly known as bird flu, is a form of influenza that affects birds (including poultry) but can be passed to humans. It causes initial flu symptoms, followed by respiratory and organ failure. Although rare, it's often lethal. The Hong Kong government now exercises strict control over poultry farms and markets, and there are signs warning against contact with birds. Pay heed to warnings, and make sure that any poultry or eggs you consume are well cooked.

You can easily find most familiar over-the-counter medications (like aspirin and ibuprofen) in pharmacy chains like Watsons or Mannings, and usually in supermarkets and convenience stores. Acetaminophen—or Tylenol—is known as paracetamol and is sold under the brand name Panadol. Oral contraceptives are available without a prescription at pharmacies.

Hours of Operation

Banks are open weekdays from 9 to 4:30 or 5; some branches are also open on Saturday from 9 to 1. Office hours are generally from 9 to 5 or 6, although working longer hours is common. Some offices are open from 9 to noon on Saturday. Lunch hour is usually 1 pm to 2 pm; don't be surprised if offices close during lunchtime. Museums and tourists attractions are usually open weekdays 9 to 6, a bit longer on weekends and public holidays. Most are closed one day a week, usually Monday or Tuesday. Pharmacies are generally open from 10 am until about 9 or 10 pm. Many 24-hour pharmacies are located in local hospitals.

Business hours for most shopping malls and boutiques are from 11 am until 8 or 9 pm, though hours may be extended during weekends and festive seasons. Small family-owned businesses might close for big public holidays—especially Lunar New Year—but major operations, supermarkets, and chain stores usually stay open year-round.

Hong Kong will keep you well fed through the day and deep into the night. Breakfast can start as early as 6 am with options such as congee, dim sum, or scrambled eggs on toast with a cup of milk tea. In between lunch and dinner, most cha chaan tangs (Hong Kong–style cafés) offer an afternoon tea menu, which is basically the regular menu at a discounted price. Typical closing time for restaurants is 10:30 or 11 pm, but you'll find plenty of late-night dining establishments, including street snack stalls that sell local delicacies, including fish balls on a stick, until well past midnight.

HOLIDAYS

Public holidays in Hong Kong are: New Year's (January 1), Lunar New Year (three days in late January or early February), Ching Ming (April 4 or 5), Good Friday and Easter Monday (April), Labor Day (May 1), Buddha's Birthday (May), Dragon Boat Festival (late May or early June), Hong Kong SAR Establishment Day (July 1), Mid-Autumn Festival (late September or early October), National Day (October 1), Chung Yeung (October), and Christmas and Boxing Day (December 25 and 26).

Lodging

FACILITIES

Unless stated otherwise in the review, hotels are equipped with elevators and all guest rooms have air-conditioning, TV, telephone, Wi-Fi, and private bathrooms. Note that bathrooms with showers but no bathtubs are the norm in smaller hotels, so be sure to check if you want a tub. Hong Kong's smoking ban on all indoor public places and workplaces does not extend to hotel rooms. If the smell of cigarette smoke bothers you, select a no-smoking hotel; also know that all hotels have designated no-smoking rooms or floors. All upmarket and some midrange hotels are wheelchair-accessible with "special access" rooms for guests in wheelchairs.

Essentials

All hotels, even budget ones, offer Wi-Fi in the rooms and public areas. Most moderately priced hotels will offer up-to-date technologies such as plasma screens, entertainment on demand, iPod docks, and sometimes even cell phones. Most hotels are conveniently situated near the MTR subway system, and those that are not will often provide free shuttle services to the nearest station, as well as to popular downtown destinations.

PRICES

Prices vary depending on season and occupancy. Most hotels offer their best rates and special offers on their websites—look for long-stay or advanced-purchase discounts, or for that matter, last-minute booking deals. Hong Kong's high seasons are generally May through June and October through November, though rates also go up during certain holiday periods and events such as the Hong Kong Sevens rugby tournament in March. While many hotels put on lavish breakfast buffets, breakfast is usually extra and not included in basic room rates.

⇨ *Hotel reviews throughout this guide have been shortened. For full information, visit Fodors.com. Hotel prices are for a standard double room in high season, excluding 10% service charge and a 3% government tax.*

WHAT IT COSTS in HK$

	$	$$	$$$	$$$$
FOR TWO PEOPLE	under HK$1,000	HK$1,000–HK$2,000	HK$2,000–HK$3,000	over HK$3,000

RESERVATIONS

Most hotels have reliable online booking systems, but phone reservations are also accepted, and receptionists speak English. Specify arrival and departure dates, number of guests, room type (standard, deluxe, suite), and any specific preferences. Make sure to find out what is, and what is not, included in the room rate, such as breakfast, in-room Wi-Fi, and local calls. A credit-card deposit is generally required to secure reservations.

Flights from the United States often arrive in the evening, so it's a good idea to inform the hotel when you plan to arrive. Some hotels will not otherwise hold a booking after 6 pm.

Whether you're a business traveler or a casual tourist, you'll inevitably be caught up with the manic pace of life in Hong Kong. Luckily, hotels are constantly increasing their efforts to provide guests with a restful haven, often bundling spectacular views of the famous skyline and harbor with chic luxury, snazzy amenities, and soothing ambience.

From budget guesthouses to gleaming towers, you're sure to find a style and site to fit your needs. Prices tend to reflect quality of service and amenities as well as location, so it's worth the effort to examine neighborhoods closely when making your choice—you may end up paying the same to stay exactly where you want to be as you would to be off the beaten path.

The rock stars of Hong Kong's hotel industry are perfectly situated around Victoria Harbour, offering unobstructed harbor views, sumptuous spas, and reputable service to compete for the patronage of business-suited jet-setters, and any visitor willing to splurge for uncompromised luxury. Farther up the hills on both Kowloon and Hong Kong Island, cozy hotels seduce travelers who simply want a safe and practical place to crash in a trendy locale.

Travelers familiar with European cities might be surprised by the lack of provenance among Hong Kong hotels—the Peninsula passes as the venerable old-timer in this relatively young city where most hotels are perched in modern towers. And the scene keeps changing: Hong Kong's continued growth as a top tourist destination and business capital means that when it comes to choice of lodging, the next big thing is always around the corner.

CHECKING IN

Typical check-in and checkout times are 3 pm and noon, respectively, although most hotels will be flexible if they are not fully booked and if you make a request in advance. Many major hotel chains have privilege clubs that allow their members to extend their checkout times until the evening, and some hotels now offer completely flexible checkout times, with checkout based on when you check in, rather than a set time. Some hotels also offer you the opportunity to check out online, so you can simply pack up and leave.

EXECUTIVE PRIVILEGE

Most high-end hotels have a VIP executive floor or lounge, and these tend to come with sweeping panoramic views. Complimentary breakfast (not a regular feature in most Hong Kong hotels) and cocktails are usually served in these clubs, while business facilities tend to include Wi-Fi, laser printing, special dedicated concierges, and sometimes a miniconference room. Entry to these clubs and lounges is based on the type of room you book, although some hotels allow guests staying in less expensive rooms to pay an additional fee for executive privileges.

ROOMS WITH A VIEW

It's no secret that the prime waterfront properties have the best views in Hong Kong. On the Kowloon side, hotels in Tsim Sha Tsui and West Kowloon generally have the most compelling skyline views across Victoria Harbour. Because of the curvature of the bay, hotels in Causeway Bay and North Point can also have an equally exhilarating view down the coast of Hong Kong Island as well as of Kowloon. Remember that silence speaks loudly; if the hotel doesn't advertise views, no matter how hip it is, it probably has none. And while more low-profile small hotels are cleverly designing their rooms to optimize limited square footage, nothing opens up a room like a far-reaching view, be it harbor (preferably) or city (high-rise horizons).

WHERE TO STAY?

Mail

Hong Kong's postal system is efficient and inexpensive. Airmail letters to anywhere in the world should take three to eight days. The Kowloon Central Post Office in Yau Ma Tei (✉ *405 Nathan Rd.*) is open weekdays 9:30 to 6 and Saturday 9:30 to 1. The General Post Office in Central (✉ *2 Connaught Rd.*) is open Monday to Saturday 8 to 6. All other post offices are open weekdays 9:30 to 4:30 and Saturday 9:30 to 1.

Airmail sent from Hong Kong is classified by destination into one of two zones. Zone 1 covers all of Asia except Japan. Zone 2 is everywhere else. International airmail costs HK$2.90 (Zone 1) or HK$3.70 (Zone 2) for a letter or postcard weighing 20 grams or less. To send a letter within Hong Kong, the cost is HK$1.70. The post office also has a dependable overnight international courier service called Speedpost.

Where Should I Stay?

	NEIGHBORHOOD VIBE	PROS	CONS
Western	A sprawling neighborhood with hidden alleyways, antiques shops, Chinese medicine markets, temples, and hip eateries.	Western is akin to the residential extension of Central, with less traffic and similarly spectacular views. Accessible on foot.	May require steep footwork if your destination is away from the main roads, where the trams and MTR run.
Central	A dense international finance center full of banks, shopping malls, restaurants, and footbridges. High up the escalators, Mid-Levels is an exclusive residential getaway.	Home to major luxury brands' flagship stores, as well as grand hotels, fine dining, and the famous nightlife area, Lan Kwai Fong. Mid-Levels offers quiet views.	Congested streets by day, crowded bars by night. Central–Mid-Levels Escalator runs uphill only after morning rush hour. Relatively expensive.
Wan Chai, Causeway Bay, and Beyond	Wan Chai hosts a strip of street-level bars in addition to the boutique Star Street area. Causeway Bay is the haven of hip young locals who come to eat, shop, and hang out in upstairs cafés.	Wan Chai has a good mix of sights and restaurants, the convention center, and performing-arts venues. Causeway Bay is absurdly busy but conveniently situated with hotels in all price ranges.	The Wan Chai bar strip can get seedy, while Causeway Bay is extremely crowded on weekends. Eastern is mostly for business or residents.
Southside	Lower building density means more green space and fewer people, with a relaxing fishing-village atmosphere around Aberdeen.	Proximity to great beaches and treks on Hong Kong Island, as well as to Stanley Market.	Be prepared for a lot of car and bus rides along winding roads, often in slow traffic.
Lantau Island	Hong Kong's largest island hosts disparate attractions: an international airport, an outlet shopping mall, natural scenery, Hong Kong Disneyland, and AsiaWorld-Expo.	Tung Chung, at the end of the MTR line, is the point of access to the Ngong Ping cable car. Those with kids may prefer the resort-like setting inside Disneyland.	Inconvenient for exploring the rest of Hong Kong, as even Tung Chung is a half-hour MTR ride from Central.
Kowloon	Kowloon generally feels more down-to-earth than Hong Kong Island, with less of a "financial hub" vibe. Tsim Sha Tsui is the city's seat of culture, the area where the city's most important museums are located.	Shopping paradise indeed, for both malls and markets. The TST promenade offers endless postcard views of the Hong Kong skyline. Hotel rooms are generally slightly cheaper than on Hong Kong Island.	In Yau Ma Tei and Mong Kok, the streets are generally noisy, crowded, and congested.

SHIPPING PACKAGES

Packages sent via airmail to the United States can take up to two weeks. Airmail shipments to the United Kingdom—both packages and letters—arrive within three to five days, while mail to Australia often arrives in as little as three days.

You are probably best off shipping your own parcels instead of letting shop owners do this for you, both to save money and to ensure that you are actually shipping what you purchased and not a quick substitute—though most shop owners are honest and won't try to cheat you in this way. The workers at Hong Kong Post are extremely friendly and will sell you all the packaging equipment you need at unbelievably reasonable prices. Large international couriers in Hong Kong include DHL, Federal Express, and S.F. Express, which also has an international forwarding service.

$ Money

Very few shops or restaurants accept U.S. dollars, so either exchange your cash or withdraw Hong Kong dollars direct from an ATM. Traveler's checks aren't accepted in most shops, and can be a pain to cash—avoid them, if possible. Getting change for large bills isn't usually a problem, although you will find that some shops will refuse to accept HK$1,000 bills for fear they might be counterfeit.

An increasing number of restaurants and shops prefer digital payment. Mobile wallets commonly used in Hong Kong include: Alipay, PayMe, Octopus Card, FPS, Apple Pay, and WeChat Pay.

ATMS AND BANKS

Your own bank will probably charge a fee for using ATMs abroad; the foreign bank you use may also charge a fee.

Sample Prices	
Cup of Coffee/Tea	HK$30–HK$60
Glass of Wine	HK$68–HK$120
Glass of Beer	HK$55–HK$70
Sandwich	HK$30–HK$90
Fresh Juice from a Stall	HK$20–HK$30
Bowl of Noodle Soup	HK$35

Nevertheless, you'll usually get a better rate of exchange at an ATM than you will at a currency-exchange office or when changing money in a bank. And withdrawing funds as you need them is a safer option than carrying around a large amount of cash.

Reliable, safe ATMs are widely available throughout Hong Kong. In a pinch, MTR stations usually have at least one Hang Seng Bank ATM. If your card was issued from a bank in an English-speaking country, the instructions on the ATM machine will appear in English.

TIP→ PINs with more than four digits are not recognized at ATMs in many countries. If yours has five or more, remember to change it before you leave.

CREDIT CARDS

Major credit cards are widely accepted in Hong Kong, but be sure to ask first at small shops and restaurants. You may also get better rates paying in cash. When adding tips to restaurant bills, be sure to write "HK$" and not just "$."

It's a good idea to inform your credit-card company before you travel, especially if you're going abroad. Otherwise, the company might put a hold on your card owing to unusual activity—not a good thing at the beginning of your trip. Record all your credit-card numbers—as well as the phone numbers to call if your cards are lost or stolen—in a safe place, so you're prepared should something go wrong. Both MasterCard and Visa have general numbers you can call (collect if you're abroad) if your card is lost, but you're better off calling the number of your issuing bank, as MasterCard and Visa usually just transfer you to your bank; your bank's number is usually printed on your card.

Although it's often cheaper (and safer) to use a credit card rather than cash for large purchases you make abroad (so you can cancel payments or be reimbursed if there's a problem), note that some credit-card companies *and* the banks that issue them add substantial percentages to all foreign transactions, whether they're in a foreign currency or not. Check on these fees before leaving home, so there won't be any surprises when you get the bill. If you plan to use your credit card for cash advances, you'll need to apply for a PIN at least two weeks before your trip—but remember, most banks charge heavily for issuing cash advances.

■ TIP→ **Before you charge something, ask the merchant whether they plan to do a dynamic currency conversion (DCC). In such a transaction the credit-card processor (shop, restaurant, or hotel, not Visa or MasterCard) converts the currency and charges you in U.S. dollars. In most cases you'll pay the merchant a 3% fee for this service in addition to any credit-card company and issuing-bank foreign-transaction surcharges. Plus, the exchange rate is often less favorable than that offered by the credit-card company.**

Dynamic currency conversion programs are becoming increasingly widespread. Merchants who participate in them are supposed to ask whether you want to be charged in dollars or the local currency, but they don't always do so. And even if they do offer you a choice, they may well avoid mentioning the additional surcharges.

CURRENCY AND EXCHANGE

The only currency used is the Hong Kong dollar, divided into 100 cents. There are bronze-color coins for 10, 20, and 50 cents; silver-color ones for 1, 2, and 5 dollars; and chunky bimetallic 10-dollar pieces. Bills can be confusing, as there are a range of designs and issuing banks. There are new purple and a few remaining older green $HK10 bills in circulation, as well as bills for HK$20 (blue-green), HK$50 (purple), HK$100 (red), HK$500 (brown), and HK$1,000 (yellow). Don't be surprised if two bills of the same value look different: three local banks (HSBC, Standard Chartered, and Bank of China) all issue bills, and each has its own design. Although the image of Queen Elizabeth II doesn't appear on new coins, old ones bearing her image are still valid.

The Hong Kong dollar has been pegged to the U.S. dollar at an exchange rate of HK$7.8 to US$1 since 1983. You can exchange currency at the airport, in hotels, in banks, and through private money changers scattered through the tourist areas. Banks usually have the best rates, but as they charge a fee of up to HK$100 for nonaccount holders, it's best to change large sums. Money changers do not charge fees, and they are open at conveniently late hours, but the rate of exchange is usually less favorable than it is at banks.

Nightlife

A riot of neon announces Hong Kong's nightlife districts. Clubs and bars fill to capacity, evening markets pack in shoppers looking for bargains, restaurants welcome diners, cinemas pop corn as fast as they can, and theaters and concert halls prepare for full houses.

The neighborhoods of Wan Chai, Lan Kwai Fong, Sheung Wan, and SoHo are packed with bars, pubs, and nightclubs that cater to everyone from the hippest trendsetters to bankers ready to spend their bonuses and more laid-back crowds out for a pint. Partying in Hong Kong is a way of life; it starts at the beginning of the week with a drink or two after work, progressing to serious barhopping and clubbing on the weekends. Wednesday is a big night out here, too. Work hard, play harder is the motto in Hong Kong, and people follow it seriously.

Because each district has so much to offer, and since they're all quite close to each other, it's perfectly normal to pop into two or three bars before heading to a club. You simply cannot go home without a Hong Kong nightlife story to tell.

Hong Kong's arts and culture scene is also lively, with innovative music, dance, and theater among the regular offerings. Small independent productions as well as large-scale concerts take to the stage across the territory every weekend.

Good online sources of nightlight and cultural information include **Hong Kong Clubbing** (🌐 *www.hkclubbing.com*) ***Time Out Hong Kong*** (🌐 *www.timeout.com/hong-kong*), the **HK Hub** (🌐 *thehkhub.com*), and the website of the **West Kowloon Cultural District** (🌐 *www.westk.hk*).

WHERE TO GO

From champagne decadence to sports bars lined with peanut shells, each of Hong Kong's districts has its own distinct nighttime personality. Even on a single street, dress codes and drink prices can vacillate wildly. The bar- and pub-lined streets of Wan Chai and Kowloon are fairly casual, though shorts and flip-flops will limit your options. A beer or a mixed drink will cost from HK$80 to HK$180. The Central, SoHo, and Wyndham Street areas are home to classy bars and glamorous nightclubs where a cosmopolitan mix of high rollers and partiers comes out to play. Drinks are expensive, and a martini might set you back more than HK$200.

Nightclubs range from down-to-earth dives with boisterous cover bands to uberstylish caverns pulsing techno, R&B, disco, house, or reggae. Cover charges, if levied, can be steep, from HK$250 to HK$500, but often include a drink or two. If you're prepared to pay a steep minimum for bottle service (HK$2,000 to HK$10,000 depending on the venue), you can reserve a table for your party at some of these swanky establishments. Door trolls abound, so dress up to get in and blend in—shorts, flip-flops, and sneakers are definite no-nos.

WHEN TO GET THERE

Around-the-clock liquor licenses are common, so strict closing times are not. Bars start closing around 2 am, clubs around 4 am, with some still hopping around sunrise. Happy hours are from late afternoon to 8 or 9 pm on weekdays. Closing times listed refer to Friday, Saturday, and the eves of public holidays; you can expect things to wind down an hour or two earlier midweek. Bars are typically open nightly, but nightclubs are closed or quiet on Sunday and Monday.

MEMBERS ONLY

Many bars and clubs have a "members-only" policy, but don't let this deter you. It's mostly a way of prioritizing the guest list on busy nights or get around no-smoking regulations. It can also mean that you're required to pay a cover charge, usually in the region of HK$200 to HK$300, including a drink on the house.

Essentials

STAYING SAFE

All premises licensed to serve alcohol are supposedly subject to stringent fire, safety, and sanitary controls, although at times this is hard to believe, given the overcrowding at the hippest places. Think twice before succumbing to the city's raunchier hideaways. If you stumble into one, check out cover and table charges *before* you get too comfortable. If you don't have a table, pay for each round of drinks as it's served (in cash rather than by credit card).

Hong Kong is an extremely safe place, but, as in many destinations, the art of the out-of-towner rip-off has been perfected. If you're unsure, visit places signposted as approved by the Hong Kong Tourism Board.

LATE-NIGHT TRANSPORTATION

The clean and reliable subway (MTR) shuts down at around 1 am, depending on your location. Taxis are your most convenient way home after that, unless you Uber or the HKeMobility app says there's an overnight bus going that way. Taxis are relatively cheap and can easily be flagged down on the street; when the light on the car roof is on, it's available for hire. If the cab has an "out of service" sign over its round "for hire" neon sign on the dashboard, it means it's a cross-harbor taxi. Fares start at HK$29.

Packing

Pack your nicer pairs of jeans, slacks, or skirts, especially if you're planning on going to a nice restaurant or out on the town. Flip-flops and more casual wears are fine for the beach and pool.

From May through September, conditions are seriously hot and sticky, but air-conditioning in hotels, restaurants, museums, and movie theaters can be arctic, so keep a crushproof sweater or shawl in your bag. Don't forget your swimsuit and sunscreen; many large hotels have pools, and you may want to spend some time on one of Hong Kong's many beaches. In October, November, March, and April, a jacket or sweater should suffice, but from December through February bring a light overcoat, preferably waterproof. Compact folding umbrellas can come in handy to protect against either rain or sun, but hotels will also lend you larger ones for the day.

Passports and Visas

Citizens of the United States need only a valid passport to enter Hong Kong for stays of up to 90 days. Your passport must be valid for at least six more months. All minors regardless of age, including newborns and infants, must also have their own passports. Upon arrival, you'll have to fill in an immigrations form. Keep the departure portion of the form safe—you'll be asked to present it again for your return trip home. If you're planning to pop over the border into mainland China, you must first get a visa, although it's not necessary for Macau.

Travel agents in Hong Kong can issue visas to visit mainland China. If you have time, it's less hassle to let a company like **China Travel Service** (🌐 *www.ctshk.com*) handle this for you. It has branches all over Hong Kong and can generally get you a visa in between three to five business days starting at HK$1,770 (single entry; not more than three months' stay). If you prefer to apply for a China visa before leaving home, the wait time is usually four to five days and the fee is US$140.

Restrooms

Big shopping malls, especially high-end ones, are your best bet for clean, well-stocked restrooms. If there isn't one nearby, you will likely find public toilets near indoor markets, public parks, and MTR stations. (There's a handy guide on the MTR website.) It's best to carry bathroom tissue with you, and don't expect to find tampon or sanitary napkin dispensers in Hong Kong toilets.

Safety

Hong Kong is an incredibly safe place—day and night. The police do a good job maintaining law and order, but there are still a few pickpockets about, especially in Tsim Sha Tsui and Mong Kok. Exercise the same caution you would in any large city: be aware of your surroundings, avoid crowded areas, and don't carry large amounts of cash or valuables with you.

Nearly all consumer dissatisfaction in Hong Kong stems from the electronics retailers in Tsim Sha Tsui. Get some reference prices online before buying, and always check the contents of boxed items before you leave the shop. Have a good idea of what you're looking for before you shop, and keep all receipts.

■TIP→ Distribute your cash, credit cards, IDs, and other valuables between a deep front pocket, an inside jacket or vest pocket, and a hidden money pouch. Don't reach for the money pouch once you're in public.

Shopping

It's true the days when everything in Hong Kong was mind-bogglingly cheap are over. It *is* still a tax-free port, so you can get some good deals—but it isn't just about the savings. Sharp contrasts and the sheer variety of experiences available make shopping here very different from back home, and exhilaratingly so. You might find a bargain or two elbowing your way through a chaotic open-air market filled with haggling vendors selling designer knockoffs. But then you could find a designer number going for half the usual price in a hushed marble-floor mall. What's more, in Hong Kong the two extremes are often within spitting distance of each other. With space at a premium, shops and small businesses are tucked into all sorts of places—up the back staircase of a scruffy building, down an alleyway, or on an office tower's 13th floor.

As a rule of thumb, stores are generally open until 7 or 8 pm; many don't close their doors until 10 pm. They close on just three days a year—Christmas Day and the first two days of Lunar New Year. From late December through February and July through September, prices plummet.

SHOPPING PLANNER

Prices vary hugely. For big items, do research before the trip and then comparison shop in different districts. Ask clerks to record prices on store business cards: it helps you to keep track and ensures that you get the quoted rate if you return to buy. Keep expectations realistic. A US$10 (about HK$80) pure silk shirt probably isn't pure silk. That said, it may still be a good shirt at a great price.

Essentials

Prices are always negotiable at markets, and you can expect discounts in small shops, too, especially for electronics or if you buy several things at once. We usually suggest starting to bargain at half the advertised price: you might end up with anything from 10% to 50% off. Be firm and decisive: walking away from a stall can often produce a radical price drop.

Be wary of absurd discounts, designed purely to get you in the door. Product switches are also common—after you've paid, they pack a cheaper model. Check purchases carefully, ensuring that clothes are the size you wanted, jewelry is what you picked, and electronics come with the accessories you paid for. *Always* get an itemized receipt. Without one, forget about getting refunds.

Shops displaying the Hong Kong Tourism Board's "quality tourism service" sticker (an easily recognizable red junk) are good bets. You can complain about prices or service at one of several HKTB offices strewn throughout the city or submit an inquiry online (*www.discoverhongkong.com*). Find centers at the Peak, at the Star Ferry concourse in Kowloon, and even at the airport. For complaints about all shops not approved by the Hong Kong Tourism Board, call the Hong Kong Consumer Council (*www.consumer.org.hk*).

The Hong Kong government has seriously cracked down on designer fakes. Depending on how strict the police are being, you may not find the choice of knockoffs you were hoping for. Bear in mind that designer fakes are illegal, and you could get into trouble if you get caught with them going through customs.

Tipping Guidelines for Hong Kong

Bartender	HK$10–HK$20 per round of drinks, depending on the number of drinks
Bellhop	HK$10–HK$20 per bag, depending on the level of the hotel
Hotel Concierge	HK$20–HK$50, more if they perform a service for you
Hotel Doorman	HK$10 if they help you get a cab
Hotel Maid	HK$10 a day
Restroom Attendants	HK$5
Porter at Airport or Train Station	HK$10–HK$20 per bag
Waiter	5%–10% if service was good

 Taxes

Hong Kong levies a 10% service charge and a 3% government tax on hotel rooms. There's no other sales tax or V.A.T. Many restaurants also include a 10% service charge.

 Tipping

Tipping isn't a big part of Hong Kong culture. Hotels and restaurants usually add a 10% service charge; however, in almost all cases this money does not go to the waiters and waitresses. In restaurants, add up to 10% more for good service, or simply round up the tab. In hotels, tip bellhops and other helpful staff members. Tipping restroom attendants is common, but it is generally not the custom to tip taxi drivers.

Visitor Information

Swing by the **Hong Kong Tourism Board** (🌐 *www.discoverhongkong.com*) visitor center before even leaving the airport. It publishes stacks of helpful (and free) booklets and maps and operates a multilingual helpline. Its detailed, comprehensive website is a fabulous resource.

The ***Standard*** (🌐 *www.thestandard.com.hk*) is a free English-language tabloid that you can pick up at MTR stations, and the ***South China Morning Post*** (🌐 *www.scmp.com*) is Hong Kong's local English-language daily. **Hong Kong Free Press** (🌐 *hongkongfp.com*) is a nonprofit news website, while ***Time Out Hong Kong*** (🌐 *www.timeout.com.hk*) is the local edition of the well-known city guide magazine. ***Hong Kong Outdoors*** (🌐 *www.hkoutdoors.com*) is the authority on hiking, camping, and all things wild in Hong Kong. ***Love HK Film*** (🌐 *www.lovehkfilm.com*) reviews the latest Hong Kong and Asian releases.

The government portal of the **Hong Kong Leisure and Cultural Services Department** (🌐 *www.lcsd.gov.hk/en/home.php*) is a useful resource that provides access to the websites of all parks and some museums, as well as information on government-sponsored events. You can also book tickets on the website. **The West Kowloon Cultural District** (🌐 *www.westk.hk/en/home*) has information on the excellent M+ Museum, the Palace Museum, the Xiqu Center, and all performing arts events under the West Kowloon umbrella.

For up-to-date weather information, check out the website maintained by **Hong Kong Observatory** (🌐 *www.weather.gov.hk*). **Centamap** (🌐 *www.centamap.com*) provides online Hong Kong street maps so detailed they give street numbers and building names.

When to Go

High season, from September through late December, sees sunny, dry days and cool, comfortable nights. January and February are mostly cool and damp, with periods of overcast skies. March and April are pleasant, and by May the temperature is consistently warm and comfortable.

June through August are the cheapest months for one reason: they coincide with the hot, sticky, and very rainy typhoon (hurricane) season. Hong Kong is prepared for blustery assaults; if a big storm approaches, your hotel will post the appropriate signals (a No. 10 signal indicates the worst winds; a black warning means a rainstorm is brewing). This is serious business—bamboo scaffolding and metal signs can hurtle through the streets, trees can break or fall, and large areas of the territory can flood. Museums, shops, restaurants, and transport shut down at signal No. 8, but supermarkets, convenience stores, and cinemas typically stay open.

Helpful Cantonese Phrases

BASICS

Hello	哈佬 / 你好	haa lo / nei ho
Yes/No	係/唔係(As in, are you British/sick?) 要/唔要 (As in, do you want to buy tickets?) 好/唔好 (As in, tea? Can I take your bags?)	hai / mm-hai yiu / mm-yiu ho / mm-ho
Please	唔該	mm-goi
Thank you	唔該 (for a service)/ 多謝 (for a gift)	mm-goi / daw jeh
You're welcome	唔使客氣	mm-sai haak hei
I'm Sorry (apology)	對唔住	deui mm jyu
Sorry (Excuse me)	唔好意思/唔該	mm ho yee see / mm-goi
Good morning	早晨	zo sun
Good night	早	zo tau
Goodbye	拜拜 / 再見	baai baai / zoi geen
Mr. (Sir)	先生	seen saang
Mrs.	太太	taai taai
Miss	小姐	siu zeh
Ms.	女士	neui si
Pleased to meet you	好高興認識你	ho go hing ying sik nei
How are you?	你好嗎？	nei ho ma?

NUMBERS

one-half	一半	yat boon
one	一	yat
two	二 (as in No.2/ second) 兩 (as in two oranges/o'clock)	yi leung
three	三	saam
four	四	sei
five	五	ng
six	六	luk
seven	七	chat
eight	八	baat
nine	九	gau
ten	十	sap
eleven	十一	sap yat
twelve	十二	sap yi
thirteen	十三	sap saam
fourteen	十四	sap sei
fifteen	十五	sap ng
sixteen	十六	sap luk
seventeen	十七	sap chat
eighteen	十八	sap baat
nineteen	十九	sap gau
twenty	二十	yi sap
twenty-one	二十一	yi sap yat
thirty	三十	saam sap
forty	四十	sei sap
fifty	五十	ng sap
sixty	六十	luk sap
seventy	七十	chat sap
eighty	八十	baat sap
ninety	九十	gau sap
one hundred	一百	yat baak
one thousand	一千	yat cheen
one million	一百萬	yat baak maan

COLORS

black	黑色	haak sik
blue	藍色	laam sik
brown	咖啡色	gaa fe sik
green	綠色	luk sik
orange	橙色	chaang sik
red	紅色	hung sik
white	白色	baak sik
yellow	黃色	wong sik

DAYS

Sunday	星期日/禮拜日	sing kei **yat**
Monday	星期一	sing kei yat
Tuesday	星期二	sing kei yi
Wednesday	星期三	sing kei saam
Thursday	星期四	sing kei sei
Friday	星期五	sing kei ng
Saturday	星期六	sing kei luk

MONTHS

January	一月	yat yewt
February	二月	yi yewt
March	三月	saam yewt
April	四月	sei yewt
May	五月	ng yewt
June	六月	luk yewt
July	七月	chat yewt
August	八月	baat yewt
September	九月	gau yewt
October	十月	sap yewt
November	十一月	sap yat yewt
December	十二月	sap yi yewt

USEFUL PHRASES

Do you speak English?	你識唔識講英文？	nei sik-mm-sik gong ying-man?
I don't speak [Language]	我唔識講 [ ]	ngaw mm sik gong [ ]
I don't understand.	我唔明	ngaw mm ming
I don't know.	我唔知	ngaw mm zi
I understand.	明白	ming baak
I'm American.	我係美國人	ngaw hai mei-gwok-yan

I'm [ ].	我係英國人 (English) 我係蘇格蘭人 (Scottish) 我係愛爾蘭人 (Irish) 我係威爾斯人 (Welsh)"	ngaw hai ying-gwok-yan (English) ngaw hai so-gaak-laan-yan (Scottish) ngaw hai ngoi-yi-laan-yan (Irish) ngaw hai wai-yi-si-yan (Welsh)
What's your name?	你叫咩名?	nei giu meh meng?
My name is ...	我叫...	ngaw giu...
What time is it?	而家幾點?	yi gaa gei dim?
How?	點樣?	dim yeung?
When?	幾時?	gei si?
Yesterday	琴日	kam yat
Today	今日	gam yat
Tomorrow	聽日	ting yat
This morning	今朝早	gam ziu zo
This afternoon	今日晏晝	gam yat ngaan zau
Tonight	今晚	gam maan
What?	咩事?(when someone calls your name or gestures at you.)	meh si?
Why?	點解?	dim gaai?
Who?	邊個?	bin gaw?
Where is ...		
... the train station?	火車站係邊度?	faw-che-zaam hai bin dou?
... the subway station?	地鐵站係邊度?	dei-teet-zaam hai bin dou?
... the bus stop?	巴士站係邊度?	baa-see-zaam hai bin dou?
... the airport?	機場係邊度?	gei-cheung hai bin dou?
... the post office?	郵局係邊度?	yau-guk hai bin dou?
... the bank?	銀行係邊度?	ngan-hong hai bin dou?
... the hotel?	酒店係邊度?	zau-deem hai bin dou?
... the museum?	博物館係邊度?	bok-mut-goon hai bin dou?
... the hospital?	醫院係邊度?	yi-yuen hai bin dou?
... the elevator?	電梯係邊度?	deen-tai hai bin dou?
Where are the restrooms?	洗手間係邊度?	sai-sau-gaan hai bin dou?
Here/there	呢度/度	ne dou / gaw dou
Left/right	左/右	zaw / yau
Is it near/far?	近唔近?/遠唔遠?	kan m kan? / yuen m yuen?
I'd like ...	我想要...	ngaw seung yiu...
... a room	...間房	... gaan fong
... the key	...鎖匙	... saw si
... a newspaper	...報紙	... bo zi
... a stamp	...郵票	... yau piu
I'd like to buy ...	我想買...	ngaw seung maai...
... a city map	...張地圖	... dei tou
... a book	...本書	... boon syu
... a magazine	...本雜誌	... boon zaap zi
... envelopes	...信封	... seon fung
... writing paper	...寫字紙	... se zi zi
... a postcard	...明信片	... ming seon peen
... a ticket	...飛	... fei
How much is it?	幾錢?	gei cheen?
It's expensive/cheap	好貴/平	ho gwai / ho peng
A little/a lot	好少/好多	ho siu / ho daw
More/less	多/少	daw di / siu di
Too little	太少	taai siu
Enough/too (much)	啦/太多	gau laa / taai daw
I am ill/sick	我病	ngaw beng zaw
Call a doctor	叫醫生嚟, 唔該	giu yi-saang lai, mm-goi
Help!	救命!	gau meng!
Stop!	停!(Trying to get out of a car.) 你好停啦!(You'd better stop! When you're being harassed.)	ting! nei ho ting laa!

DINING OUT

A bottle of ...	一支/ 一樽...	yat zi / yat zeon...
A cup of ...	一杯...	yat bui...
Beer	啤酒	be zau
Bill/check	帳單	jeung daan
Bread	麵包	meen baau
Breakfast	早餐	jo chaan
Butter	牛油	ngau yau
Cocktail/aperatif	雞尾酒	gai mei zau
Coffee	咖啡	gaa fe
Dinner	晚飯	maan faan
Fixed-price menu	套餐	tou chaan
Fork	叉	chaa
I am a vegetarian/I don't eat meat	我食齋/我唔食肉	ngaw sik zaai / ngaw mm sik yuk
I cannot eat ...	我唔可以食...	ngaw mm haw yi sik...
I'd like to order ...	我要...	ngaw yiu...
Is service included?	包唔包服務費?	baau mm baau fuk-mo-fai?
I'm hungry/thirsty	我肚餓/我口渴	ngaw tou ngaw / ngaw hau hot
It's good/bad	好味/唔好味 (taste of food)	ho mei / mm ho mei
It's hot/cold	好熱/好凍	ho yeet / ho dung
Knife	刀	dou
Lunch	午餐	ng chaan
Menu	菜單	choi daan
Napkin	餐巾	chaan gan
Pepper	胡椒	wu ziu
Plate	碟	deep
Please give me ...	唔該, 我要...	mm-goi, ngo yiu...

Best Tours in Hong Kong

The right guided tour can shed light on a complex territory like Hong Kong and help you appreciate its multiple facets through experiences curated by those in the know. Whether your interest is history, nature, food, or a particular aspect of local life, here are some excellent tours that will give you an in-depth take.

BUS AND TRAM TOURS

Big Bus Tour. These double-decker tourist buses cover three main routes—Hong Kong Island, Kowloon, and Stanley—with recorded commentary in 10 languages. Tourists can hop on or off at any stop along the way to take in the neighborhood sights. There's also a tour to the Star Ferry, and a night-time bus tour that takes visitors through the neon-lit streets of Kowloon. ☏ *2723–2108* 🌐 *www.bigbustours.com.*

TramOramic Tour. Aboard an open-top faux-vintage tram, you can savor sights and history as Hong Kong Island unfurls cinematically before your eyes. The one-hour tour starts at the Western Market Terminus in Sheung Wan and ends at the Causeway Bay Terminus. You will pass by a host of landmarks, from bazaars and tenements to monuments and skyscrapers. Alternatively, you can choose the three-day unlimited access that will allow you to hop on and off any regular tram and embark on thematic journeys covering a total of 60 sights. 🌐 *www.hktramways.com.*

FOOD TOURS

Foodie Tasting Tour. Celebrating the vibrant flavors of Hong Kong, the Foodie Tasting Tour takes visitors to six or seven culinary spots in one of four areas—Central and Sheung Wan, Sham Shui Po, Tai Po Market, or Temple Street—in the company of a certified foodie guide who will decipher menus and explain eating customs. All meals are included in the ticket price. Arrive hungry because you'll be feasting on everything from traditional pastries to freshly steamed dim sum. ☏ *9233–7466 WhatsApp* 🌐 *www.hongkongfoodietours.com* ⏲ *Closed Sun.*

Kowloon Walled City & Food Adventure. Hear dark and delicious stories about the Kowloon Walled City and eat your way through modern-day Kowloon City. You will stroll through a graceful Chinese garden that sits on the site of the former Walled City, where Qing dynasty relics of the once-lawless enclave remain. You'll also visit restaurants and grocery stores that existed before the advent of supermarkets. Expect multiple food tastings throughout the 2½-hour tour. ☏ *5511–4839* 🌐 *walkin.hk.*

HISTORY AND LOCAL LIFE TOURS

Old Town Central Tour. This 2½-hour tour takes you to historic Sheung Wan where you'll find an endearing mélange of old and new: intriguing temples and former hospitals alongside artisanal bakeries and craft beer dens. As you wander the area with a guide, you'll be treated to accounts of Sheung Wan's storied past and anecdotes by local shop owners. 🌐 *walkin.hk.*

Ex-Sham Shui Po Reservoir Tour. This highly popular 90-minute tour run by the Waterworks Department is the only way to see the underground Romanesque cistern (circa 1900s) in Shek Kip Mei. In 2020, plans to demolish the 4,300-square-meter reservoir with brick pillars, water pipes, and chambers were met with public outcry, and the site was given heritage status and a new lease of life. It's an important component of Hong Kong's waterworks heritage, and a handsome one at that. Tours run twice daily on weekend afternoons. All slots for a particular month are released for online booking at the start of the previous month. ⊕ *www.waterconservation.gov.hk.*

Aberdeen Fishermen Cultural Tour. The former fishing settlement of Aberdeen may have a few high-rise residences now, but a closer look with pointers from a local will unveil mesmerizing remnants of its former self: the typhoon shelter full of vessels, temples devoted to sea deities, a bustling market, and hangouts few outsiders know about. The guide, an Aberdeen native, will tell you about the traditions and superstitions of the fishing community and what life is like today. After a dim sum lunch, you'll take the minibus to Stanley for some retail therapy and chilling at the beach. ⊕ *www.withlocals.com.*

NATURE TOURS

Tai Po Kau Nature Walk. This half-day guided walk takes you through Tai Po Kau, a lush 460-hectare reserve that shelters one of Hong Kong's most varied old growth forests. Expect to encounter at least a few among the hundreds of species of birds, butterflies, and dragonflies flitting around. You'll also see trees like Chinese Red Pine, Camphor, and Sweet Gum. Even those not particularly into birds and bees will enjoy forest-bathing in a lush and beautiful setting. ⊕ *www.walkhongkong.com.*

R2G Tour. The most informative and ecologically responsible way to see Hong Kong's stunning UNESCO-crowned Global Park is by joining a tour led by a Recommended Geopark Guide (R2G). These park-endorsed tours are led by trained English-speaking guides, have a low guide-to-participant ratio, and respect off-limits protected areas. Dispersed over 150 square km of land and sea, the park's geological gems include honeycomb-shape volcanic rock columns formed 140 million years ago, and sedimentary rocks from 400 to 55 million years ago. Depending on the month or the tour (half- or full-day), you will see the rocks as well as islands, precipitous cliffs, sea arches, and/or walled villages. ⊕ *www.geopark.gov.hk; www.hkr2g.net.*

Great Itineraries

Hong Kong is a delightful mix of the old and the new, the East and the West, and the urban and the rural. These are our suggested itineraries to get a holistic feel for the territory.

Hong Kong in 3 Days

DAY 1: VICTORIA PEAK, SHEUNG WAN, AND YAU MA TEI

Catch Bus route 15 to Victoria Peak—try to get a window-seat on the upper deck. Power-walk the 3.5 km- (2.2 mile-) loop around the Peak or stroll part of it for vistas of the harbor and Kowloon. Descend by Peak Tram (it's more scenic coming down) and hop on a West-bound "ding ding" tram.

After getting off in Sheung Wan, head back to Central on foot, checking out the dried seafood stores, stone wall trees, and coffin shops on the way. Lunch on old-school dim sum at Lin Heung Lau Tea House. Visit the historic Man Mo Temple and the vibey neighborhood around Tai Ping Shan Street, before pausing at Tai Kwun for colonial history, handsome courtyards, and art.

Navigate to the Star Ferry Pier via the Central–Mid-Levels Escalator and the repurposed Central Market. Cruise across Victoria Harbor to Kowloon. Watch the boats against the backdrop of Hong Kong Island from Tsim Sha Tsui Promenade—the view from this side of the harbor is superior. Take the MTR to the Temple Street Night Market. Browse eclectic fashion and digital doodads or simply take in the atmosphere. Dine on sizzling claypot rice to end your day.

DAY 2: WEST KOWLOON AND WAN CHAI

Spend the morning at the West Kowloon Cultural District. Linger over post-1970 Chinese art and other contemporary gems at M+ Museum and ogle imperial treasures at the Palace Museum. Don't forget to browse M+'s museum shop for unique souvenirs of Hong Kong. Grab a bite on-site, then catch a cross-harbor bus to Wan Chai. Explore the Blue House cluster of pre–World War II Chinese tenements, moody Pak Tai Temple, and old-fashioned toy shops on Tai Yuen Street. For a well-deserved pause, sip a cocktail at Tai Lung Fung.

To pick up where you left off the day before, return to Soho in Sheung Wan for a closer look at its open-air markets, antiques shops, and hipster bars. Splurge on a Michelin-star dinner at The Chairman (if you have a reservation) or devour pizza at one of several pizzerias in the area. Finish off with a quiet Bellini or a bar crawl.

DAY 3: SAI KUNG AND ITS GEOPARK

Make your way to Sai Kung in the New Territories for your land or sea tour of the spectacular Hong Kong UNESCO Global Geopark. The sites in the 150 square km park are spread out and comprise islets, sea caves, and villages; the star may be the honeycomb-shape columns formed by volcanic eruptions 140 million years ago. An informative and environmentally responsible way to experience these geological wonders is by joining an R2G guided tour recommended by the park, but you'll need to book in advance.

Alternatively, as a couple of sites are strewn along the Maclehose Trail, you can combine sightseeing with hiking. The stunning East Dam of High Island Reservoir, a half-hour cab ride from town, is where you'll find the rocks and the trail. Spend the remainder of the day chilling in Sai Kung town center with its fishing junks and seafood restaurants.

Hong Kong in 5 Days

Spend the first three days as outlined above.

DAY 4: KOWLOON

Devote your morning to two temples: one Taoist and one Buddhist, both served by adjacent MTR stops. At the vibrant Sik Sik Yuen Wong Tai Sin Temple, explore ornate altars to Taoist deities and a garden populated by carp and zigzag bridges. At tranquil Chi Lin Nunnery, admire the subtle aesthetics of Tang dynasty–style architecture.

Ride a few stops to working-class Sham Shui Po, a former textile hub recently revitalized by artist advocates, bookstore owners, and young restaurateurs. It's great for finding out what Hong Kong's dreamers are up to.

Next up is Tsim Sha Tsui. If there's no time for Earl Grey and scones at The Peninsula, take a peek inside the legendary hotel, then for contrast, zip across the road to Chungking Mansions to see its labyrinth of budget guesthouses and South Asian grocery stores. This is where Hong Kong auteur Wong Kar-wai's *Chungking Express* was filmed. Young children will be tickled by the spacious Middle Road Children's Playground nearby. From the park's southern exit, cross the podium garden to Tsim Sha Tsui East where drinking and dining options abound.

DAY 5: TIAN TAN BUDDHA AND TAI O

You may have caught a glimpse of the 34-meter-tall Tian Tan Buddha flying into Hong Kong, but now's your chance to get intimate with the seated behemoth. Coach buses run from the town of Tung Chung on Lantau Island to the bronze statue, but the cable car affords panoramic views. After paying homage to the icon, have a quick look inside Po Lin Monastery then duck into its vegetarian restaurant for lunch.

Instead of returning to Tung Chung, hop on Bus route 21 for Tai O, an old fishing town on Lantau's western coast. Highlights here are stilt houses built over tidal flats, which offer glimpses into the old way of life. Snack on grilled cuttlefish as you meander through the narrow streets. Return to the city via Tung Chung, or Mui Wo, a settlement on the eastern coast, where you can dine at a *dai pai dong* before cruising back to Central.

Hong Kong in 7 Days

Spend the first five days as outlined above.

DAY 6–7: ISLAND SOUTH

Bus it to To Tei Wan and begin your ascent to Dragon's Back, an 8.5 km- (5.3 mile-) ridgeline trail in Shek O Country Park, whose windy peak overlooks the entire Shek O Peninsula and beyond. The final section of the trail snakes past villages, drying kayaks, and boulders popular with climbers. The route ends on Big Wave Beach where you can swim and unwind at an alfresco restaurant.

Continue on to the seaside town of Stanley, known for its mazelike garment-and-souvenir market and sprinkle of historic sights. Dragon boat races are held here in the summer. If that's too much beach, go instead to Béthanie in Pok Fu Lam for an unusual slice of Hong Kong history. Tour the 19th-century complex and its museum on your own, or with a docent (by booking the service ahead) who will detail the history of the French Mission in Hong Kong and how they came to build the former sanatorium, the neo-Gothic chapel, and the Dairy Farm cowsheds. For dinner, feast on fresh seafood cooked a la minute at the Ap Lei Chau Cooked Food Market.

Chapter 3

WESTERN, CENTRAL, AND SOUTHSIDE

Updated by
Thomas O'Malley

NEIGHBORHOOD SNAPSHOT

TOP REASONS TO GO

■ **Ride the iconic Peak Tram:** The Peak Tram seems to defy gravity as it clunks up through jade-green jungle to a plateau close to the summit of Hong Kong's highest peak. From up top the skyline and harbor views are sensational, while a web of all-abilities trails makes it prime territory for walkers.

■ **Take the Star Ferry:** The Star Ferry is a workaday commute masquerading as one of the world's great sightseeing sojourns. There's no better vantage point from which to take in Hong Kong's remarkable skyline.

■ **Drink and dine:** From Michelin meals to masterful mixology, the world-class restaurants and bars of Central and Western are pure heaven for gastronomes.

■ **Admire Tai Kwun:** Central's hulking colonial-era police compound has been reborn into the territory's hottest lifestyle destination.

MAKING THE MOST OF YOUR TIME

Central is Hong Kong's financial and business hub, packed with skyscrapers that house banks and multinationals. Beyond its corporate veneer, it also features a vibrant dining and nightlife scene, along with notable colonial-era landmarks such as St. John's Cathedral and Tai Kwun, offering a glimpse into the city's historic past.

Western retains more of a classic Hong Kong vibe, where traditional shops stand beside hip cafés and neighborhood restaurants. You can see Western's colonial buildings on an hour-long stroll from the University of Hong Kong, heading eastward. You might also spend an hour wandering through Sheung Wan's old shops on Queen's Road West, Bonham Strand West, Wing Lok, and more.

In Southside, it's best to pick one hub and explore in and around it: Aberdeen with its busy harbor on the southwest coast; Stanley and its market on the south-central coast; or Shek O with its beaches and trails far to the southeast.

GETTING HERE AND AROUND

■ Central MTR station is an underground hive with a host of far-flung exits. A series of moving walkways joins it with Hong Kong station, where Tung Chung Line and Airport Express trains arrive and depart. Outside on the harborfront, Star Ferry vessels to Kowloon leave Pier 7 every 6 to 12 minutes.

■ The Peak Tram, which climbs from Central to Victoria Peak, is actually a funicular railway with its lower terminus at Garden Rd., directly opposite the U.S. Embassy. Also climbing partway up toward Victoria Peak is the Central–Mid-Levels Escalator, which ascends from Queen's Road. Central to the residential towers of the Mid-Levels. From Central MTR, it's the best way to reach Tai Kwun and the bars and restaurants of SoHo.

■ To get to Southside, it takes anywhere between 15 to 50 minutes from Central. For Aberdeen, take the South Island Line of the MTR to Lei Tung, then hop over the harbor on a sampan ferry. Buses 6, 6A, and 260 depart from Central Exchange Square and stop at Deep Water Bay, Repulse Bay, and Stanley. For Shek O, take the MTR to Shau Kei Wan and then Bus 9 to the last stop.

Central is Hong Kong's corporate playground, home to sleek office towers and a retinue of high-end malls and urbane restaurants that cater to the bulging wallets of the city's elite. In the spaces between, you'll also discover humble noodle shops, laptop-friendly cafés, lively pubs, and pockets of heritage that showcase a more laid-back and authentic side of the territory.

Western is where you'll find an intriguing mix of old-school charm and contemporary energy. You'll encounter colorful local shops selling everything from pungent dried seafood to funerary goods and Chinese antiques, as well as hip neighborhood cafés, bars, and galleries that offer a bohemian contrast to Central's business hub.

Beach lovers usually head to the south side of Hong Kong Island, where the seaside communities of Repulse Bay, Stanley, and Shek O are perched next to popular stretches of golden sand. But you never get too far from civilization in Hong Kong—the ever-popular Ocean Park, a theme park and zoo, is also set amid dramatic Southside coastal scenery.

Western

Since the MTR was extended westward in 2014, gentrification has reshaped the once stubbornly local neighborhoods of Sai Ying Pun and Kennedy Town. While you can still experience an authentic tableaux of rattling trams, old-world medicine shops, and neighborhood temples, these now sit alongside third-wave coffee shops, art galleries, and international bistros. The hipster enclave of Tai Ping Shan perfectly captures this compelling blend of old and new, while farther east, cosmopolitan Sheung Wan, with its cocktail bars and independent boutiques, blends almost seamlessly into corporate Central.

Sights

Street life is the big appeal of Western, taking in the sights, sounds, and scents as you puff up steep "ladder streets" through enticingly jumbled neighborhoods like Tai Ping Shan—home to an eclectic mix of cool cafés and incense-shrouded temples. Man Mo Temple, dedicated to the gods of war and literature, is one of Hong Kong's oldest, and all around are stores crammed with antiques and curios. Small but diverting museums can be found in the vicinity, covering everything from Chinese art to medical science.

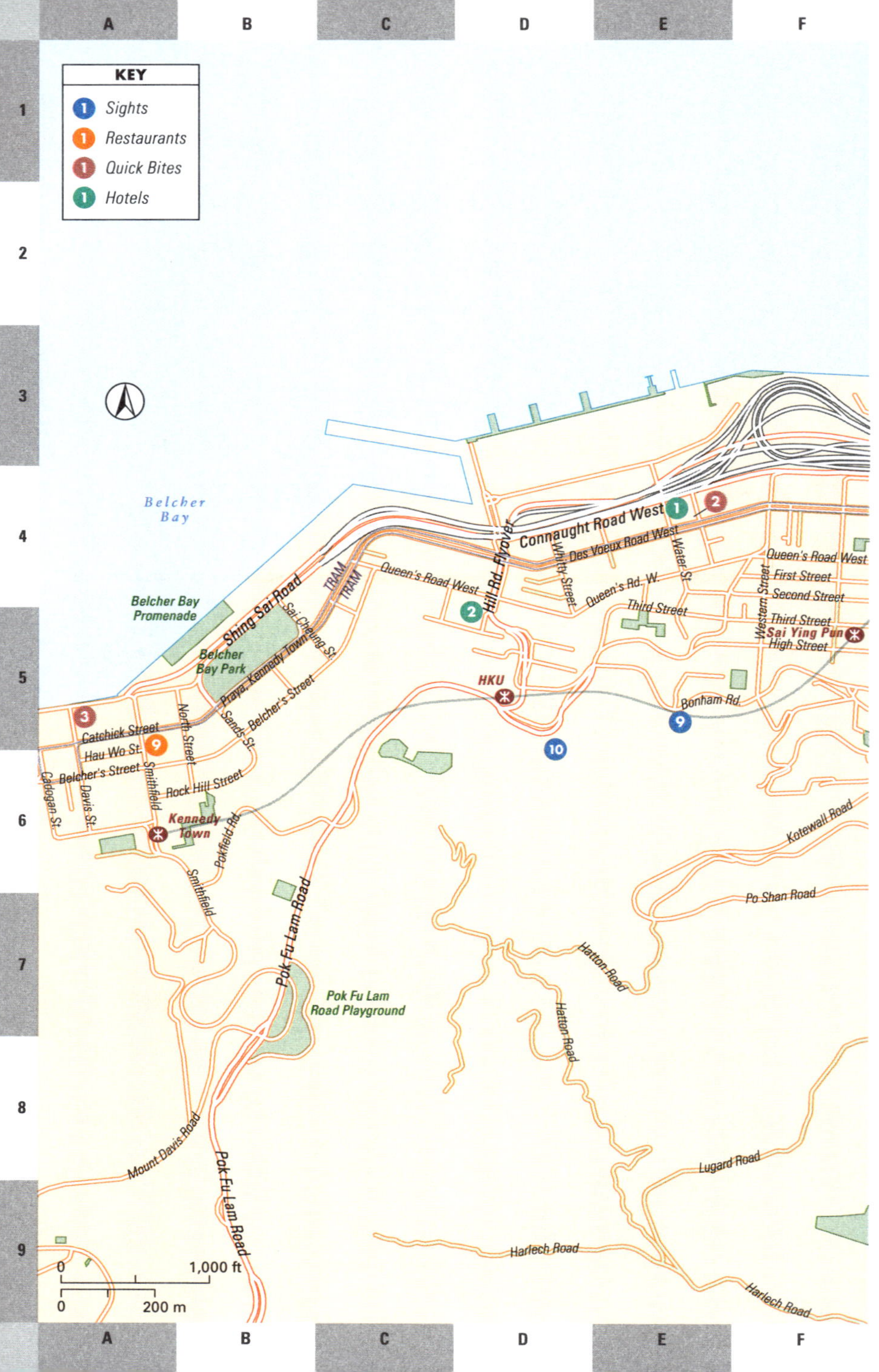

A
B
C
D
E
F
1
2
3
4
5
6
7
8
9
KEY
Sights
Restaurants
Quick Bites
Hotels
Belcher Bay
Belcher Bay Promenade
Belcher Bay Park
Shing Sai Road
Sai Cheung St.
Praya, Kennedy Town
TRAM
Queen's Road West
Hill Rd. Flyover
Connaught Road West
Des Voeux Road West
Whitty Street
Water St.
Queen's Rd. W.
Third Street
Queen's Road West
First Street
Second Street
Western Street
Third Street
Sai Ying Pun
High Street
HKU
Bonham Rd.
Catchick Street
Hau Wo St.
North Street
Sands St.
Belcher's Street
Belcher's Street
Smithfield
Rock Hill Street
Cadogan St.
Davis St.
Kennedy Town
Pokfield Rd.
Smithfield
Kotewall Road
Po Shan Road
Pok Fu Lam Road
Hatton Road
Hatton Road
Pok Fu Lam Road Playground
Mount Davis Road
Pok Fu Lam Road
Lugard Road
Harlech Road
Harlech Road
0
1,000 ft
0
200 m

Sights

1 Dr Sun Yat-Sen Museum........... I6
2 Hollywood Road I5
3 Hong Kong Museum of Medical Sciences I5
4 Liang Yi Museum I5
5 Man Mo Temple I5
6 PMQ..J5
7 Possession Street H5
8 Tai Ping Shan....................... H5
9 University Museum and Art Gallery E5
10 The University of Hong Kong.......................... D5
11 Western Market I4

Restaurants

1 ABC Kitchen.......................... H4
2 The Chairman J5
3 Kau Kee.................................J5
4 Lin Heung Lau Tea House..........J5
5 Little Bao...............................J5
6 Queen Street Cooked Food Market.............. H4
7 Ronin.....................................J5
8 Samsen, Sheung Wan J5
9 Sun Hing A5
10 Yardbird I4

Quick Bites

1 Mammy Pancake, Sheung Wan J5
2 NOC Coffee........................... E4
3 % Arabica, Kennedy Town A5

Hotels

1 Courtyard Hong Kong E4
2 JEN Hong Kong by Shangri-La.......................... D4
3 The Jervois I5
4 The Mercer.............................J5
5 99 Bonham............................ I4
6 Sohotel................................. I4

PMQ is a hub for creative endeavors, housing art and design studios, restaurants, and cultural centers.

Dr Sun Yat-sen Museum

HISTORY MUSEUM | The life of Sun Yat-Sen, the revolutionary who helped overthrow the Qing dynasty in 1911 and usher in China's first Republic, is examined in detail at this museum in the Mid-Levels. The building itself is a handsome colonial-era mansion that belonged to the brother of a prominent Eurasian businessman. Dr Sun spent significant time in Hong Kong, and you can follow in his footsteps by walking the **Dr Sun Yat-sen Historical Trail,** a self-guided tour available for free by downloading a smartphone app called iM Guide. The walk starts at Hong Kong University in Western and finishes in Central, stopping at 16 waypoints connected to Dr Sun. ✉ *Mid-Levels, 7 Castle Rd., Central* ☎ *2367–6373* 🌐 *hk.drsunyatsen.museum* 🎫 *Free* 🕒 *Closed Thurs.* Ⓜ *Central.*

Hollywood Road

STREET | The best of Hong Kong's antiques sellers can be found on Hollywood Road, named after the holly trees that once grew nearby. On nearby Upper Lascar Row, a flea market known as Cat Street sells curios, porcelain, and not-so-old trinkets masquerading as artifacts. They might not be authentic, but they do make for great souvenirs and affordable gifts. ✉ *Hollywood Rd., Western* ✥ *Between Arbuthnot Rd. and Queen's Rd.* Ⓜ *Sheung Wan, Exit A2.*

Hong Kong Museum of Medical Sciences

SCIENCE MUSEUM | Housed in an Edwardian-style redbrick building at the top of Ladder Street, this quirky museum was formerly Hong Kong's Bacteriological Institute, set up after a plague outbreak in 1894 ravaged the surrounding Tai Ping Shan neighborhood. The most interesting exhibits are to do with the outbreak and its aftermath; in the rather chilling basement are a selection of primitive surgical tables and a former autopsy room. ✉ *2 Caine La., Mid-Levels* ☎ *2549–5123* 🌐 *www.hkmms.org.hk* 🎫 *HK$20* 🕒 *Closed Mon.* Ⓜ *Central.*

Liang Yi Museum

ART MUSEUM | A few steps away from Man Mo Temple, this private museum is accessible by guided tour only, and visits must be reserved online in advance. It's well worth it, however, not only because of the superb collections—which include fine Chinese lacquerware, porcelain, and Ming and Qing dynasty furniture—but also because nothing is behind glass and you are even permitted to feel, pick-up, and interact with some of the treasures. ✉ *181–199 Hollywood Rd., Sheung Wan* ☎ *2806–8280* 🌐 *www.liangyimuseum.com* 🎫 *HK$200* ⏲ *Closed weekends* Ⓜ *Sheung Wan.*

★ **Man Mo Temple**

TEMPLE | No one knows exactly when Hong Kong Island's most atmospheric Taoist temple was built, but the consensus is sometime between 1847 and 1862. The temple is dedicated to the gods of literature and war: Man, who wears green robes and carries a writing brush, and Mo, dressed in red with a sword. The temple bell, cast in Canton in 1847, and the drum next to it are sounded to attract the gods' attention when a prayer is being offered. ✉ *124 Hollywood Rd., Sheung Wan, Western* 🌐 *www.man-mo-temple.hk* Ⓜ *Sheung Wan.*

PMQ

STORE/MALL | A one-stop showcase of independent Hong Kong design, this enclave of shops, pop-ups, and workshops is set inside the old Police Married Quarters, a modernist housing complex built in 1951. You can take the elevator up either of the main residential buildings to explore a beehive of boutiques selling clothes, handbags, leatherware, metalwork, and more. There's also a small history exhibition on Level 5 of the Staunton Block, where you can learn about the police families who once occupied the small units now serving as shops. PMQ is easily reached by taking the Central–Mid-Levels Escalator. ✉ *35 Aberdeen St., SoHo, Sheung Wan* ☎ *2870–2335* 🌐 *www.pmq.org.hk.*

Possession Street

STREET | This street is roughly at the spot where Captain Charles Elliott stepped ashore in 1841 to claim Hong Kong for the British empire. Back then, this was the waterfront, but aggressive reclamation means it is now several blocks inland. At the top of the street stands Hollywood Centre, home to the nonprofit contemporary art space Asia Art Archive. ✉ *Possession St., Western* ✣ *Between Queen's Rd. and Hollywood Rd.* Ⓜ *Sheung Wan, Exit A2.*

Tai Ping Shan

NEIGHBORHOOD | Centered on Tai Ping Shan Street, the area known as Tai Ping Shan (the Chinese name for Victoria Peak, which towers above it) is one of the city's oldest residential districts. This gentrifying neighborhood retains a local feel, with arty shops, small temples, and cozy cafés to pitch up in. ✉ *Tai Ping Shan St., Western* ✣ *Between Upper Station St. and Square St.* Ⓜ *Sheung Wan, Exit A2.*

The University of Hong Kong

COLLEGE | With time on your hands, take a trip out to the western end of the Mid-Levels to see the imposing Edwardian-era buildings of Hong Kong's oldest university. The institution opened in 1912 with its first faculty, the Faculty of Medicine, which had been known as the Hong Kong College of Medicine since 1887. Today the exteriors of University Hall, the Hung Hing Ying Building, and the Tang Chi Ngong Building are on the government's Declared Monument List. ✉ *Bonham Rd., Western* ✣ *At Pok Fu Lan Rd.* ☎ *2859–2111* 🌐 *www.hku.hk.*

University Museum and Art Gallery

ART MUSEUM | Set inside a heritage building, this museum and gallery is filled with a small but excellent collection of Chinese antiquities. On view are ceramics and bronzes, some dating from 3,000 BC, as well as paintings, lacquerware, and carvings in jade, stone, and wood. The museum also has the world's largest collection of Nestorian crosses, dating from the Mongol Period (1280–1368). There are usually two or three well-curated temporary exhibitions on view; contemporary artists who work in traditional media are often featured. The museum is a seven-minute walk from Sai Ying Pun MTR station. ✉ *University of Hong Kong, 90 Bonham Rd., Western* ☎ *2241–5500* 🌐 *www.umag.hku.hk* 🎫 *Free* ⏲ *Closed Mon.* Ⓜ *Sheung Wan.*

Western Market

NOTABLE BUILDING | Sheung Wan's iconic market, a hulking Edwardian-era brick structure, is a good place to get your bearings. Built in 1906, it functioned as a produce market for 83 years. Mostly of interest to architecture buffs, today it's a shopping center selling fabrics. Nearby you'll find herbal medicine on Ko Shing Street and Queen's Road West, dried seafood on Wing Lok Street and Des Voeux Road West, and ginseng and bird's nest on Bonham Strand West. ✉ *323 Des Voeux Rd. Central, Sheung Wan, Western* ☎ *6029–2675* 🌐 *www.westernmarket.com.hk* Ⓜ *Sheung Wan, Exit B or C.*

Restaurants

For authentic local cuisine, Western has got you covered. Choose between restaurants specializing in handmade dim sum, beef-brisket noodles, traditional congee (rice porridge), sausage-topped claypot rice, and much more. Bringing all these tastes together under one roof are Hong Kong's municipal Cooked Food Centers: the Sheung Wan Market & Cooked Food Center and Queen Street Cooked Food Market are two of the city's best. Western's trademark authenticity extends to the area's top-end eateries too: you can find what many foodies have decreed the city's most remarkable Cantonese food at The Chairman.

ABC Kitchen

$$ | **EUROPEAN** | Hong Kong is no stranger to European eateries, but ABC ranks as one of the most quirky. Serving dishes like suckling pig, soufflé, and duck confit, it's made up of a few stand-alone plastic chairs and tables in the utilitarian surrounds of Queen Street Cooked Food Market, a place more used to joints selling wonton noodles and milk tea. **Known for:** offering BYOB on wine; serving the cheapest genuine foie gras in the city; crisp-skinned suckling pig with mash and gravy. Ⓢ *Average main: HK$200* ✉ *Queen St. Cooked Food Market, Shop CF7, 38 Des Voeux Rd. W, Sheung Wan* ☎ *9278–8227* 🌐 *www.abckitchen.com.hk* 💳 *No credit cards* ⏲ *Closed Sun.*

★ **The Chairman**

$$$$ | **CHINESE** | Consistently one of the hottest tables in Hong Kong, The Chairman gets booked up months in advance by foodies yearning to taste chef-owner Danny Yip's set menus of levelled-up Cantonese classics. Using only the freshest possible fare—from locally reared organic chicken to wild-caught seafood—this unique eatery focuses on the intrinsic flavors of each ingredient, putting quality and simplicity to the fore. **Known for:** steamed crab with aged Chinese wine; one of the hardest reservations to score in Hong Kong; chef-owner Danny Yip, an icon of Hong Kong's dining scene. Ⓢ *Average main: HK$650* ✉ *The Wellington, 3rd fl., 198 Wellington St., Sheung Wan* ☎ *2555–2202* 🌐 *www.thechairmangroup.com* Ⓜ *Sheung Wan.*

Kau Kee

$ | **CANTONESE** | Tender beef with noodles in soup is the mainstay dish of this humble Hong Kong diner, which, like many similar small local restaurants, only accepts payment in cash. Choose the type of noodles you want (flat rice noodles, thin egg noodles, or vermicelli), beef cut (brisket or tendon), and consider opting for the curry soup version, which lends the dish a spicy-sweet richness. **Known for:** long lines at lunchtime; utilitarian ambience and decor; sharing tables with other diners. Ⓢ *Average* *main: HK$60* ✉ *21 Gough St., Sheung Wan* ☎ *2850–5967* ▭ *No credit cards* ⏲ *Closed Sun.* Ⓜ *Sheung Wan.*

Lin Heung Lau Tea House

$$ | **CANTONESE** | Faded decor, cranky waiters, and old men reading the newspapers: there's nothing fancy about Lin Heung Lau Tea House, but it's been doing great dim sum for years. Stop by any time after 6 am and fill up on such dishes as *har gow* (steamed shrimp dumplings) and *char siu bao* (barbecue pork buns), washed down with lots of tea. **Known for:** old Hong Kong atmosphere; dim sum served on traditional push-carts; busy, bustling atmosphere. Ⓢ *Average main: HK$100* ✉ *160 Wellington St., Central* ☎ *2116–0670* ▭ *No credit cards* Ⓜ *Central.*

★ **Little Bao**

$$ | **ECLECTIC** | Duck into this cute counter-top restaurant for delicious *baos*— fluffy steamed buns sandwiched with all types of delicious ingredients, from teriyaki fried chicken to slow-braised pork belly. The rest of the menu is more globally inspired and includes sharing plates such as drunken clams, beef brisket dumplings, and truffle fries. **Known for:** founding-chef May Chow, a reality TV star; ice-cream baos for dessert; creative cocktails made with local ingredients. Ⓢ *Average main: HK$108* ✉ *1–3 Shin Hing St., SoHo, Sheung Wan* ☎ *2818–1280* 🌐 *www.little-bao.com* ⏲ *Closed Mon.* Ⓜ *Sheung Wan.*

Queen Street Cooked Food Market

$ | **CHINESE** | Refurbished in 2024, this old-school municipal food hall is packed to the rafters with vendors hawking various affordable eats, from Chinese noodles and dumplings to cheap Thai, Indian, Vietnamese, and even Italian fare. You first order from your chosen kitchen then find a spot at the plastic chairs and tables, which you might be expected to share with other diners at busy periods. **Known for:** early breakfasts and late-night eats; bright, bustling atmopshere; wide range of dishes and cuisines. Ⓢ *Average main: HK$70* ✉ *1st fl., 38 Des Voeux Rd. W, Sheung Wan* ☎ *3542–5915* 🌐 *www.fehd.gov.hk* ▭ *No credit cards* Ⓜ *Sheung Wan.*

Ronin

$$$ | **JAPANESE** | Behind an unmarked door is this ultraslick *izakaya*-style restaurant, where diners perch along the counter ordering mouthwatering sharing dishes like grilled seafood and meat skewers, seasonal sashimi, and artfully assembled salads. With only 14 seats lining the bar, it's a hip, sociable hangout. **Known for:** skewers grilled over premium binchotan charcoal; Instagram-worthy sashimi platters; huge selection of Japanese whiskies. Ⓢ *Average main: HK$250* ✉ *8 On Wo La., Sheung Wan* ✣ *At the end of Kau U Fong* ☎ *2547–5263* 🌐 *www.roninhk.com* ⏲ *Closed Sun. and Mon. No lunch* Ⓜ *Sheung Wan.*

Samsen, Sheung Wan

$$ | **THAI** | Feast on diverse Thai street food at this warehouse-chic branch of a Wan Chai stalwart. Popular dishes include Pad Thai with tiger prawns, crabmeat fried rice, and a chef's-kiss rendition of Chiang Mai's famous khao soi noodles that are brim full of spicy-sweet, aromatic goodness. **Known for:** yummy fruit slushies (with or without alcohol); easygoing, hipster vibes; bare-concrete interior with color accents. Ⓢ *Average main: HK$180* ✉ *23 Jervois St., Sheung Wan* 🌐 *www.samsen-hk.com* Ⓜ *Sheung Wan.*

Sun Hing

$ | **CANTONESE** | Dim sum joints don't get more local than this Kennedy Town institution, which starts service at 3 am every day. From the juicy, taut *har gow* (crystal shrimp dumplings) to the sweet and sour fried spareribs, everything is prepared by hand. **Known for:** local clientele of taxi drivers and night shift workers; old timey dishes like deep-fried milk; humble decor and battered furniture. Ⓢ *Average main: HK$75* ✉ *Markfield Bldg., 8 Smithfield, Western* ☎ *2816–0616* ▭ *No credit cards* Ⓜ *Kennedy Town.*

★ Yardbird

$$ | **JAPANESE** | This hip Sheung Wan eatery has consistently been one of the hottest places to eat in Hong Kong since it opened in 2011. *Yakitori* (Japanese-style grilled chicken) is the menu mainstay, particularly nose-to-tail treats like chicken hearts, livers, and oysters (tender morsels from the back of the chicken). **Known for:** Korean fried cauliflower (dubbed KFC); bar stocked with house-brand junmai sake, Japanese beer, and whiskey; noisy and bustling. *Average main: HK$200 154–158 Wing Lok St., Sheung Wan, Western 2547–9273 www.yardbirdrestaurant.com Closed Sun. and Mon. No lunch Sheung Wan.*

Coffee and Quick Bites

Mammy Pancake, Sheung Wan

$ | **DESSERTS** | Head to Mammy's in Sheung Wan for her famously fluffy egg waffles: Hong Kong pastries with the appearance of bubble-wrap and the taste of sweet, egg-rich waffles. You can choose from a huge variety of sweet or savory fillings, from banana chocolate-chip to white sesame pork floss. **Known for:** no tables, just a counter; many popular branches throughout the territory; inspiring nostalgia in older eaters. *Average main: HK$30 32 Bonham Strand, Sheung Wan www.mammypancake.com Sheung Wan.*

NOC Coffee

$ | **CAFÉ** | Bright, white, and postindustrial, this smart Sai Ying Pun café is a buzzy place to brunch (think healthy, ingredient-packed "buddha bowls" and smashed avocado on sourdough toast), hang out with friends, or tap away on a computer while nursing a flat white and a pastry. NOC roasts its single-origin beans in-house; the rich coffee aromas whump you in the nose as soon as you enter the café. **Known for:** handful of branches in Hong Kong; wide choice of international brunch fare; excellent milk-based coffee drinks. *Average main: HK$95 321 Des Voeux Rd. W, Western 3611–5300 www.noc.coffee Sai Ying Pun.*

% Arabica, Kennedy Town

$ | **CAFÉ** | Ride the Hong Kong tram to its terminus in Kennedy Town and you can reward yourself with a meticulously crafted coffee at this waterfront favorite a few steps from the tram stop. Floor-to-ceiling windows frame the blue waters of Victoria Harbour just across the road; the views are even better from upstairs. **Known for:** "Kyoto latte" made with sweet condensed milk; excellent location on the waterfront; small selection of pastries and baked goods. *Average main: HK$50 Grand Fortune Mansion, Shop 4, 1 Davis St., Western 2326–4578 arabica.com Kennedy Town.*

Hotels

The steep, narrow streets of Western are a natural setting for smaller, boutique-styled hotels catering to those who favor local flavor over opulence. As a rough rule of thumb, the further west from Central you stay, the cheaper the price. You'll also be further from the crowds and noise, while still having a wealth of more intimate dining and drinking options on your doorstep.

Courtyard Hong Kong

$$ | **HOTEL** | Smart and comfortable (if business-like) rooms here have harbor views from higher floors, and the quiet Sai Ying Pun location means its a short walk to trendy neighborhood bars, cafés, and restaurants. **Pros:** good facilities for business travelers; great restaurants on its doorstep; nice views of Kowloon West from upper floors. **Cons:** nearest MTR station an eight-minute walk away; rooms on lower floors look out over a lot of traffic; fitness center but no pool. *Rooms from: HK$1,350 167 Connaught Rd. W, Western 3717–8888 www.marriott.com 245 rooms No Meals Western.*

JEN Hong Kong by Shangri-La
$ | **HOTEL** | This comfortable hotel has modern guest rooms with cushioned seats set into bay windows that are perfect for reading while taking in the city and harbor views. **Pros:** rooftop pool and a gym with Victoria Harbour panoramas; MTR stop and numerous restaurants within minutes; authentic local neighborhood. **Cons:** rooms are on the small side; on-site bar lacks character; some rooms looking worn. *Rooms from: HK$990 508 Queen's Rd. W, Western 2974–1234 www.shangri-la.com 283 rooms No Meals HKU.*

The Jervois
$$ | **HOTEL** | This slick apart-hotel ditches traditional hotel trappings like a grand lobby, restaurants, and bars, instead channeling its focus into spacious, minimalist rooms that boast floor-to-ceiling windows, kitchenettes, luxurious bedding, and skyline views. It's a stylish base from which to explore Sheung Wan's vibrant cultural and dining scene. **Pros:** suites have double corner windows; all suites have private lift lobbies; only two suites per floor for more privacy and quiet. **Cons:** limited traditional hotel services; no swimming pool; signs of wear and tear. *Rooms from: HK$1,613 89 Jervois St., Sheung Wan 3994–9000 www.thejervois.com 49 suites Sheung Wan.*

The Mercer
$$ | **HOTEL** | Choose from a range of serviced-apartment-inspired studios and suites (many with kitchenettes) at this tower residence, all of which are light, airy, and contemporary. **Pros:** a fun neighborhood to explore; nicely situated in between Sheung Wan and Central; five minutes to the nearest MTR station entrance. **Cons:** smallest studios are rather narrow; surrounding area can get congested with traffic; glass-walled bathrooms are not popular with some guests. *Rooms from: HK$1,575 29 Jervois St., Sheung Wan 2922–9988 www.themercer.com.hk 55 rooms No Meals Sheung Wan.*

99 Bonham
$$ | **HOTEL** | The living concept at this slender glass tower hotel in Sheung Wan combines boutique comfort with apartment convenience—each "suite" (either one or two-bed) comes with separate areas for lounging, dining, and preparing food, as well as spacious marble-clad bathrooms. **Pros:** rooms are more like serviced apartments; only three guest rooms per floor; superb location in heart of Sheung Wan. **Cons:** no swimming pool; lacks hotel services like concierge; breakfast arranged with nearby cafés. *Rooms from: HK$1,238 99 Bonham Strand, Sheung Wan 3940–1111 www.99bonham.com 84 rooms Sheung Wan.*

Sohotel
$ | **HOTEL** | Functional, clean, and no-frills rooms are good value for the spec at this hotel tucked away in a lively neighborhood of galleries, bars, and local shops. **Pros:** good standards of housekeeping; hip Tai Ping Shan neighborhood is a short walk uphill; cheap rates for the location. **Cons:** basic in-hotel facilities; some rooms are tiny; free morning pastry but no breakfast. *Rooms from: HK$886 139 Bonham Strand, Sheung Wan 2851–8818 www.sohotel.com.hk 37 rooms No Meals Sheung Wan.*

Nightlife

Less ritzy and commercial than Central, Western offers Hong Kong's hippest night out. Sheung Wan is the preserve of wildly creative cocktail bars, several of which have been voted among Asia's Top 50 bars in successive years. Bottle shops with fridges full of craft beer line the steep "ladder streets," and on warm nights the steps pack out with alfresco drinkers. Farther west, bars take on a more chill neighborhood vibe, many serving coffee during the day and wine or whiskey after dark.

BARS

★ Bar Leone

COCKTAIL BARS | Awarded first place in Asia's 50 Best Bars 2024, this Italian-run, casual-cool bar is known for its signature "filthy martini," pepped up with a smoked olive and brine for extra oomph. More genteel is the small but perfectly formed mezcal negroni, which goes beautifully with bar snacks like Leone's best-selling mortadella sandwich—stacked layers of thinly sliced Italian garlic sausage squeezed between crisp home-baked focaccia. ✉ *11–15 Bridges St., Sheung Wan* 🌐 *www.barleonehk.com* Ⓜ *Sheung Wan.*

Coa

COCKTAIL BARS | There can't be many cocktail bars in the world that have fans queuing at 5 pm to sample their libations, but such is the allure of Coa, crowned Asia's Best Bar for three consecutive years (2021–23). The meticulously crafted drinks spotlight the spirits and flavors of Mexico, showcasing the smoky depth of artisanal mezcal. Coa boasts a standout collection of over 200 agave-based spirits, while the bar's name is a reference to *coa de jima,* a traditional machete-like tool used for harvesting agave plants. ✉ *Wah Shin House, Shop A, 6–10 Shin Hing St., Sheung Wan* ☎ *2813–5787* 🌐 *coa.com.hk* Ⓜ *Sheung Wan.*

The Old Man

COCKTAIL BARS | This Hemingway-theme cocktail speakeasy takes its name from one of the author's stories, *The Old Man and the Sea*. There's nothing fishy about the superb drinks on offer, which are best savored while sitting along the central bar-table, cleverly inset with a slab of ice to keep them at optimum temperature as you imbibe. ✉ *37–39 Aberdeen St., SoHo, Sheung Wan* 🌐 *www.theoldmanhongkong.com* Ⓜ *Sheung Wan.*

★ Ping Pong 129

COCKTAIL BARS | Hidden behind an unmarked red door is one of the coolest bars in Sai Ying Pun. Converted from an old table-tennis parlor, the basement space serves gin and tonic cocktails and features works by local artists on the walls. It also offers an array of Spanish tapas. ✉ *Nam Cheong House, 129 2nd St., Western* ☎ *9835–5061* 🌐 *www.pingpong129.com* Ⓜ *Sai Ying Pun.*

LGBTQ+

FLM

DANCE CLUB | Dance anthems fill the floor until the wee hours at this friendly LGBTQ+ club. "Game nights" lure visitors and locals alike with alternating themes such as drag bingo or karaoke. ✉ *62 Jervois St., Sheung Wan, Western* ☎ *2799–2883* 🌐 *www.flmhk.net* Ⓜ *Sheung Wan.*

Shopping

Hong Kong's enduring traditions are writ large in Western's shops, selling rare ingredients for Chinese medicinal teas or dried abalone and fish maw for grand banquets. Hong Kong's biggest cluster of antique shops lines Hollywood Rd. through Central and Sheung Wan to the vicinity of Man Mo Temple, while nearby Upper Lascar Row, a.k.a. Cat Street, does a brisk trade in communist retro paraphernalia, mah-jongg tiles, and fans. More contemporary wares are on sale at PMQ, Sheung Wan's hive of independent designers and local artisans.

ANTIQUES AND COLLECTIBLES

Select 18

VINTAGE | Almost more museum than shop, this Sheung Wan vintage store is packed from floor to ceiling with nostalgic Hong Kong ephemera. Dig through old toys, books, vinyl records, faded posters, watches, jewelry, retro lighting, furniture, and more to find something irreverent to take back home. ✉ *14 Tung St., Sheung*

Wan ☎ *9121–3011* 🌐 *www.instagram.com/select18_mido* Ⓜ *Sheung Wan.*

ART

Asia Art Archive

ART GALLERY | Back in 2000, the Asian Art Archive set out to address the lack of information on the emerging field of Asian art, and to record its growth. Open to the public as a resource center, archive, and library, AAA is a magnet for art experts and the art-curious, providing comprehensive research and reading facilities. ✉ *Hollywood Centre, 11th fl., 233 Hollywood Rd., Sheung Wan, Western* ☎ *2815–1112* 🌐 *www.aaa.org.hk* Ⓜ *Sheung Wan.*

DEPARTMENT STORES

Wing On

DEPARTMENT STORE | Opened in 1907, this old-style Hong Kong department store in Sheung Wan made its name with cheap deals on household appliances, kitchenware, and crockery. Of chief interest to overseas visitors are the local cosmetics, porcelain tea sets, and snacks. ✉ *211 Des Voeux Rd., Sheung Wan, Western* ☎ *2852–1888* 🌐 *shop.wingon.hk* Ⓜ *Sheung Wan, Exit E3.*

FOOD

Wing Lok Street

FOOD | Also known as Dried Seafood Street, Wing Lok Street is a hot spot for stores selling dried delicacies. You can find almost anything your heart desires, whether it be dried goji berries or dried bird's nest. ✉ *Wing Lok St., Sheung Wan* Ⓜ *Sheung Wan.*

SPECIALTY STORES

Glocal Mahjong

LOCAL GOODS | This small shop in PMQ makes mah-jongg tiles with unique designs and themes, which are also customizable. ✉ *PMQ, 4th fl., Shop 405, Aberdeen St., Central* 🌐 *www.glocalmahjong.com* Ⓜ *Sheung Wan.*

Personalized Chinese Seals

Head to Man Wa Lane in Sheung Wan for a unique souvenir—a personalized Chinese chop (seal). Used traditionally in place of a signature on contracts, chops can be inscribed with your name in Chinese script. Carvers along the alley speak English and can transliterate your name into Chinese characters. Prices start at HK$200, with a one-day turnaround.

Thorn & Burrow

SOUVENIRS | A treasure-trove of Hong Kong–theme souvenirs, this appealingly cluttered first-floor emporium sells towels, mugs, fridge magnets, and cute, affordable homewares, greetings cards, ornaments, and the like. Notable are the impressionistic paintings of Hong Kong street scenes by British artist Louise Hill. ✉ *30 High St., Western* ☎ *9840–3886* 🌐 *www.thornandburrow.com* Ⓜ *Sai Ying Pun.*

Central

Hong Kong's historic heart has been a global hub of trade and commerce since its mid-19th-century British colonial beginnings. Streets and squares are dotted with architectural relics, though these have long been overshadowed by soaring spires of contemporary architecture—but somehow, the mishmash works. Central is still the city center, a kinetic jumble of businesspeople, shoppers, and tourists, all rubbing shoulders in restaurant queues, air-conditioned malls, and on the moving walkways of the Central–Mid-Levels Escalator. Framed by the harbor on one side and Victoria Peak on the other, Central boasts some of the city's most iconic views—if you get high enough to see them, whether from an office tower or the hillsides that rise above the district. The higher you go, the more serene Central becomes, especially in lush green sanctuaries like the Botanical Gardens and Hong Kong Park.

Sights

Central blends history and culture at revamped heritage sights like Tai Kwun, a colonial police compound turned museum, dining and arts hub, and the Bauhaus-styled Central Market, reopened in 2021 as a shopping and lifestyle venue. For colonial-era charm, explore St. John's Cathedral, the tranquil Botanical and Zoological Gardens, and Hong Kong Park, with its Victorian buildings and aviary. For iconic views, ride the historic Peak Tram to Victoria Peak, where observation decks and trails showcase the city and harbor. And no visit is complete without a jaunt on the Star Ferry, an enduring symbol of Hong Kong, offering stunning vistas as it links Central with Kowloon.

Asia Society Hong Kong Center

OTHER ATTRACTION | Nestled in a pocket of lush hillside, this heritage site was once a store for British Army explosives, and now hosts exhibitions, film screenings, and lectures pertaining to Asian countries and cultures. The complex, designed by acclaimed NYC architects Tod Williams and Billie Tsien, adds contemporary design to the 19th-century compound, incorporating sleek glass-and-metal structures with green terraces. Views from the lush roof garden are spectacular; a walk on the grounds is a must. The Center's AMMO (Asia, Modern, Museum, Original) restaurant and bar is a lovely spot for lunch or a drink. Check the website for heritage tours in English. ✉ *9 Justice Dr., Admiralty, Central* ☎ *2103–9511* 🌐 *www.asiasociety.org/hong-kong* 🎫 *Free* 🕙 *Closed Mon.* Ⓜ *Admiralty, Exit C1.*

Favorite Places

Thomas O'Malley: For an invigorating blend of leaping lemurs and balmy banyan trees, nothing beats a morning stroll in the Hong Kong Zoological & Botanical Gardens. It is a quiet and peaceful escape in the middle of a bustling city.

Bank of China Building

NOTABLE BUILDING | The Art Deco building at the southern end of Statue Square (beside the HSBC Building) is the former headquarters of the Bank of China built in the 1950s. The building now houses offices, as well as the members-only, colonial-chic China Club restaurant. Don't confuse it with the newer Bank of China Tower, one of the most iconic skyscrapers in the city, just down the street on Garden Road. Completed in 1990 and designed by I.M. Pei, this imposing structure is said to resemble bamboo—a symbol of the city's strength, growth, and enterprising nature. ✉ *2A Des Voeux Rd. Central, Central* Ⓜ *Central, Exit K.*

Bishop's House

NOTABLE BUILDING | Formerly the campus of St. Paul's College, Bishop's House dates back to 1843. This historic Victorian building, which is a pale shade of yellow, served as the official residence of the Anglican bishop. ✉ *1 Lower Albert Rd., Central* Ⓜ *Central, Exit D1.*

Central Market

MARKET | Once a bustling commercial market selling meat and produce, Central Market is today one of Hong Kong's rare heritage success stories. Rather than tearing down the 1939 building—one of the city's few surviving structures designed in the art deco–adjacent Streamline Moderne style—it has been redeveloped into a tourist-focused hub of market-style shops selling old-timey souvenirs, a food court, and areas for art exhibitions. The architecture is certainly worth admiring, and a small museum exhibit downstairs tells the story of the market of yesteryear. ✉ *93 Queen's Rd. Central, Central* ☎ *3618–8668* 🌐 *www.centralmarket.hk* 🎫 *Free* Ⓜ *Hong Kong.*

Central–Mid-Levels Escalator

TRANSPORTATION | By far the best way to navigate the steep slopes that rise up from the Western and Central districts toward Mid-Levels is the world's longest covered outdoor escalator. Free of charge and protected from the elements, this series of moving walkways makes the uphill journey a cinch. It connects to several main residential streets, the bars, and restaurants of SoHo, and also provides direct access to Tai Kwun via a ramp. From 6 to 10 am the escalators only move downward, carrying an endless stream of workers and their cups of coffee. The escalator ceases operation at midnight. ✉ *Next to 100 Queen's Rd. Central, Central* Ⓜ *Central, Exit D1.*

Former French Mission Building

NOTABLE BUILDING | A tree-lined lane called Battery Path was built by the British in the 1840s to provide access to the artillery batteries that defended the colony—hence the name. At the top of Battery Path sits the elegant Former French Mission Building, a neoclassical redbrick structure with white columns and green shutters. Completed in 1917, it is a declared monument subject to protection. St John's Cathedral and Cheung Kong Park sit nearby. ✉ *1 Battery Path, Central* Ⓜ *Central, Exit D1.*

Government House

HISTORIC HOME | This handsome white Victorian mansion was constructed in 1855 as the official residence of British governors, and is now home to Hong Kong's chief executive. During the Japanese occupation the house was significantly rebuilt, so it exhibits a strong Japanese influence, particularly in the roof eaves. The house occasionally opens to the public for guided tours on certain days of the year. ✉ *Upper Albert Rd., Mid-Levels, Central* ☎ *2878–3300* 🌐 *www.ceo.gov.hk/gh/eng* Ⓜ *Central, Exit D1.*

Hong Kong Maritime Museum

HISTORY MUSEUM | **FAMILY** | Housed in Central Ferry Pier No. 8, this family-friendly museum explores over 2,000 years of Hong Kong's maritime history. There are interactive exhibits and historic artefacts aplenty, including hoards of precious Chinese porcelain salvaged from Ming dynasty wrecks in the harbor. In the basement, an exhibition on the opium trade takes an uncompromising look at Britain's colonial takeover of Hong Kong. Don't miss the chance to have a drink and snack on the terrace of **Cafe 8** above the museum. The views are world class, and your money supports a local charity that finds vocational opportunities for adults with learning difficulties. ✉ *Central Pier No. 8, Central* ☎ *2813–1723* 🌐 *www.hkmaritimemuseum.org* 🎫 *HK$30.*

Hong Kong Observation Wheel

AMUSEMENT RIDE | Soaring high over Victoria Harbour, this scenic Ferris wheel is just the ticket to keep little ones entertained before or after a trip on the Star Ferry, which docks a couple of hundred meters away. Ice-cream kiosks and an old-school carousel are further distractions, and the family-friendly Maritime Museum is close by at Pier 8. ✉ *Central Harbourfront, 33 Man Kwong St., Central* 🌐 *hkow.hk* 🎫 *HK$20* Ⓜ *Hong Kong.*

★ Hong Kong Park

CITY PARK | **FAMILY** | One of the prettiest parks in the city proper is a sloping arrangement of rock gardens, water features, and leafy pathways. It's common to stumble on locals practicing tai chi or reading in a secluded spot. This welcome respite from the surrounding skyscrapers occupies the site of a former garrison called the Victoria Barracks, and some buildings from 1842 and 1910 are still standing.

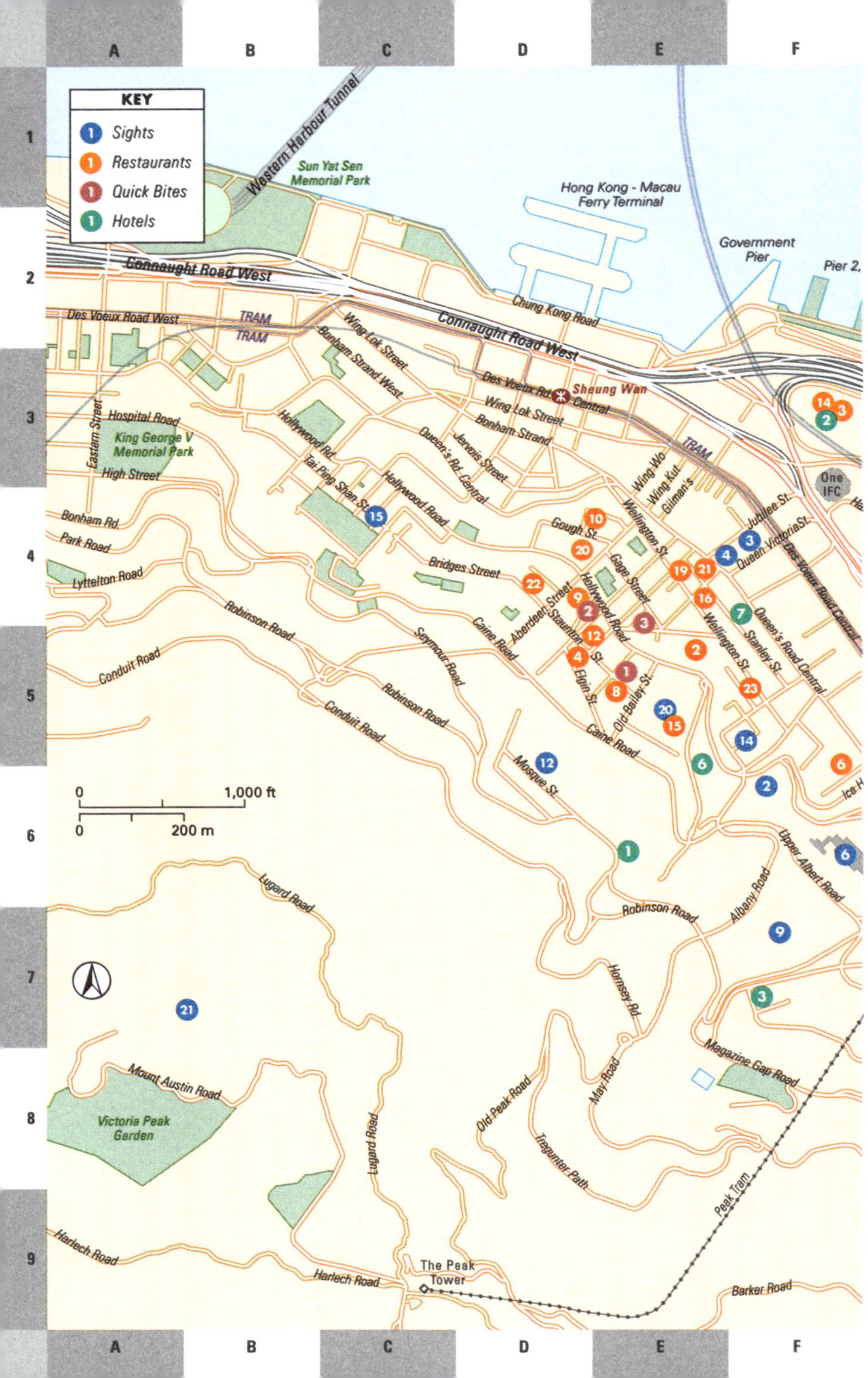
A
B
C
D
E
F
1
2
3
4
5
6
7
8
9
KEY
Sights
Restaurants
Quick Bites
Hotels
Western Harbour Tunnel
Sun Yat Sen Memorial Park
Hong Kong - Macau Ferry Terminal
Government Pier
Pier 2
Connaught Road West
Des Voeux Road West
TRAM
Chung Kong Road
Wing Lok Street
Bonham Strand West
Sheung Wan
Des Voeux Rd. Central
Bonham Strand
Hospital Road
Eastern Street
King George V Memorial Park
High Street
Hollywood Rd.
Tai Ping Shan St.
Queen's Rd. Central
Jervois Street
Hollywood Road
Wing Wo
Wing Kut
Gilman's
Jubilee St.
Queen Victoria St.
One IFC
Des Voeux Road Central
Bonham Rd.
Park Road
Lyttelton Road
Gough St.
Wellington St.
Gage Street
Bridges Street
Aberdeen Street
Staunton St.
Robinson Road
Caine Road
Seymour Road
Elgin St.
Old Bailey St.
Stanley St.
Queen's Road Central
Conduit Road
Mosque St.
Ice H
0
1,000 ft
0
200 m
Upper Albert Road
Lugard Road
Albany Road
Hornsey Rd.
Mount Austin Road
Victoria Peak Garden
Magazine Gap Road
May Road
Old Peak Road
Tregunter Path
Peak Tram
Harlech Road
The Peak Tower
Barker Road

Central

Sights

1 Bank Of China Building G6
2 Bishop's House F6
3 Central Market F4
4 Central–Mid-Levels Escalator E4
5 Former French Mission Building G6
6 Government House F6
7 Hong Kong Maritime Museum H3
8 Hong Kong Observation Wheel H3
9 Hong Kong Zoological and Botanical Gardens F7
10 HSBC Main Building G6
11 International Finance Centre G3
12 Jamia Mosque D6
13 Jardine House G4
14 Lan Kwai Fong F5
15 SoHo C4
16 St. John's Cathedral G6
17 Standard Chartered Bank Building G5
18 Star Ferry H3
19 Statue Square G5
20 Tai Kwun E5
21 Victoria Peak B7

Restaurants

1 Amber G5
2 Bo Innovation E5
3 Caprice F3
4 Chôm Chôm D5
5 Cuisine Cuisine G3
6 Duddell's F6
7 8½ Otto e Mezzo Bombana G5
8 Fiata Pizza E5
9 Ho Lee Fook D4
10 Kau Kee D4
11 La Rambla by Catalunya G3
12 La Vache! D5
13 Liberty Exchange Kitchen & Bar G4
14 Lung King Heen F3
15 Magistracy Dining Room E5
16 Mak's Noodles E4
17 Mandarin Grill + Bar G5
18 Mott 32 ..... G5
19 Shui Kee E4
20 Sing Heung Yuen D4
21 Sing Kee E4
22 22 Ships D4
23 Yung Kee F5

Quick Bites

1 Bakehouse E5
2 Leaf Dessert E4
3 Tai Cheong Bakery E5

Hotels

1 Bishop Lei International House E6
2 Four Seasons Hotel Hong Kong F3
3 Garden View Hong Kong F7
4 Mandarin Oriental Hong Kong G5
5 The Murray G6
6 Ovolo Central E6
7 The Pottinger Hong Kong F4

The park is home to the **Flagstaff House Museum of Tea Ware.** With its simple white facade, wooden monsoon shutters, and colonnaded verandas, the house is the earliest surviving example of colonial Greek revival architecture in Hong Kong. Built in 1846 as the office and residence of the Commander of the British forces, it now serves as a museum dedicated to the art of tea, exhibiting hundreds of delicate tea sets from the Tang (618–907) through the Qing (1644–1911) dynasties. Look out for the understated beauty of Yixing teapots, crafted from unadorned brownish-purple *zisha* clay, where perfection lies in their flawless form and the subtle, tactile texture of the clay. You will also be able to find the **Edward Youde Aviary,** containing hundreds of tropical birds. A raised boardwalk gets you close to the ornithological action.

The Peak Tram has its lower terminus just beyond the park's northwest exit. ✉ *19 Cotton Tree Dr., Central* ☎ *2521–5041* 🌐 *www.lcsd.gov.hk* 🎫 *Free* 🕑 *Flagstaff House closed Tues.* Ⓜ *Admiralty, Exit C1.*

Hong Kong Zoological and Botanical Gardens

GARDEN | **FAMILY** | A verdant holdover from colonial times, Hong Kong's Botanical Gardens opened back in 1864, and remain a delightful showcase of subtropical Asian flora, with bamboo groves, towering banyans, and groves of colorful rhododendrons. The fauna arrived much later and is a garden highlight: Lemurs, sloths, meerkats, and all manner of acrobatic monkeys swing about in well-tended enclosures. A menagerie of colorful birdlife includes flamingos housed in an aviary. The walk from the Central MTR stop is long and uphill, so consider taking a bus or taxi. Buses 1A, 3, and 22 go there from Central Ferry Pier. ✉ *Albany Rd., Central* ✣ *Between Robinson and Upper Albert Rds.* ☎ *2530–0154* 🌐 *www.hkzbg.gov.hk* 🎫 *Free* Ⓜ *Central.*

HSBC Main Building

NOTABLE BUILDING | Dubbed the "robot building" by locals, this iconic Norman Foster–designed skyscraper was the world's most expensive building when completed in 1985. The pair of bronze lions out front, named Stephen and Stitt, belonged to an earlier version of the bank's Hong Kong headquarters and still bear shrapnel scars from the Japanese invasion during World War II in 1941. Look up into the atrium through the curved glass panels, or step inside to admire the building's exposed structural mechanics, a hallmark of Foster's high-tech architecture. ✉ *1 Queen's Rd. Central, Central* ✣ *Across from Statue Square* 🎫 *Free* Ⓜ *Central, Exit K.*

International Finance Centre

NOTABLE BUILDING | Above the Central skyline, one skyscraper rules them all: Two IFC, the slender second tower of the International Finance Centre. Designed by Argentine architect Cesar Pelli, its 88 floors top a whopping 1,352 feet. Opposite stands its dinky little brother, the 38-floor One IFC. The massive IFC Mall stretches between the two, and Hong Kong station is underneath. If you wish to see the views from Two IFC, visit the 55th-floor Hong Kong Monetary Authority. While there, take a quick look at exhibits tracing the history of banking in Hong Kong. Upon arrival, you will need to register your passport with the concierge and get a visitor pass. ✉ *8 Finance St., Central* 🌐 *www.ifc.com.hk* 🎫 *Free* Ⓜ *Hong Kong, Exit A2.*

Jamia Mosque

MOSQUE | The Central–Mid-Levels Escalator provides easy access to this hidden gem, the first mosque in Hong Kong. Known as the Lascar Temple in the early days, the original 1840s structure was rebuilt in 1915 and reveals its Indian and Islamic heritage in the perforated arches and decorative facade work. The mosque interior isn't open to non-Muslims, but the small enclosure surrounding the building is a peaceful retreat. ✉ *30 Shelley St., Central ✣ Above Caine Rd.* ☎ *2523–7743* 🌐 *www.amo.gov.hk* Ⓜ *Central, Exit D1.*

Jardine House

NOTABLE BUILDING | Just behind the IFC stands Jardine House, a notable 1970s skyscraper recognizable by its grid of round porthole-style windows. The 52-level building serves as the Hong Kong headquarters for Jardine, Matheson & Co., once the greatest of the British "hongs" (trading companies) that dominated trade with imperial China. Historically linked to the opium trade, Jardine Matheson has since transformed into a global conglomerate in retail, property, and financial services. ✉ *1 Connaught Pl., Central* ☎ *2500–0555* Ⓜ *Hong Kong, Exit A2.*

Lan Kwai Fong *(LKF)*

STREET | A few narrow lanes filled with bars and clubs uphill from the intersection of Queen's Road Central and Pedder Street, Lan Kwai Fong has long been the epicenter of Hong Kong nightlife. Though much subdued after the protests and the COVID-19 pandemic, visit during the Hong Kong Sevens in April and you'll see it at its raucous, beer-soaked best. ✉ *Lan Kwai Fong and D'Aguilar St., Central ✣ Between Wyndham and Wellington Sts.* 🌐 *www.lankwaifong.com* Ⓜ *Central, Exit D1.*

SoHo

NEIGHBORHOOD | Known for its chic neighborhood bars and urbane eateries, this roughly defined area on the western edge of Central gets its name from being south of Hollywood Road. The bars here are a chiller alternative to the rowdier drinking spots in Lan Kwai Fong, while the narrow lanes reveal hips cafés, eclectic restaurants, and independent boutiques. This hilly neighborhood is reached by the Central–Mid-Levels Escalator, also the very reason for the rise of SoHo as a drinking and dining destination. ✉ *SoHo, Central ✣ South of Hollywood Rd. and north of Caine Rd., just off Central–Mid-Levels Escalator* Ⓜ *Central, Exit D1.*

St. John's Cathedral

CHURCH | A gap in the skyscrapers accommodates the graceful Gothic form of this Anglican church, completed in 1849 and one of Hong Kong's oldest European-style buildings. Inside, the rows of cane wicker pews and low-slung ceiling fans will transport you to the early days of the British administration. ✉ *4–8 Garden Rd., Central* ☎ *2523–4157* 🌐 *www.stjohnscathedral.org.hk* 🎟 *Free* Ⓜ *Central, Exit K.*

Standard Chartered Bank Building

NOTABLE BUILDING | This wedgelike building includes a pair of stained-glass windows by Remo Riva that represent visions of "Hong Kong Today" and "Hong Kong Tomorrow." ✉ *4 Des Voeux Rd. Central, Central* Ⓜ *Central, Exit K.*

★ **Star Ferry**

BOATING | For decades since it launched in 1898, the Star Ferry was the main mode of transport between Kowloon and Hong Kong Island. The MTR might be faster, but no visitor to Hong Kong should pass on the chance to ride the Star Ferry across Victoria Harbour. The skyline views are to die for, and journeying on these iconic mid-century vessels with their distinctive green and white livery is just plain fun. An evening ride is the most spectacular, especially if you can time your ride to coincide with the 8 pm Symphony of Lights show.

The Central Star Ferry Terminal is at Pier 7. On ferries between Central and Tsim Sha Tsui, you can choose to ride upper deck or lower. The roomier upper deck has air conditioning and better views for taking photos, while the grungier lower deck is a tad more atmospheric. **TIP→ For trips from Central to Tsim Sha Tsui, seats on the eastern side have the better views.**

Across the harbor on the Kowloon side, the pier is a convenient starting point for touring Tsim Sha Tsui. As you face the bus station, Ocean Terminal, where luxury cruise ships berth, is on your left. Inside this terminal, and in the adjacent Harbour City complex, are miles of air-conditioned shopping arcades. Across the street, the Peninsula hotel is the classic destination for afternoon tea. Or simply stroll eastward along the waterfront to the Avenue of Stars and an extended view of the famous Hong Kong skyline. ✉ *Central Ferry Pier, Pier 7, Man Kwong St., Central* ☎ *2367–7065* 🌐 *www.starferry.com.hk* 🎫 *Upper deck from HK$5; lower deck from HK$4* Ⓜ *Hong Kong.*

Statue Square

PLAZA/SQUARE | The neoclassical building on Statue Square's east side, completed in 1912, originally served as the Supreme Court and now houses the **Court of Final Appeal.** In front of this building stands the **Cenotaph,** a monument honoring those who lost their lives in the First and Second World Wars. The plot of land on which this public square stands was gifted by HSBC, whose headquarters dominate the southern end, with the stipulation that no building constructed there could block the bank's view of the harbor. ✉ *Central* ✢ *Between Chater Rd. and Des Voeux Rd. Central* Ⓜ *Central, Exit K.*

★ Tai Kwun

OTHER ATTRACTION | Hong Kong's colonial-era police HQ has been reborn as a stylish cultural complex, where you can browse law-and-order museum exhibits and contemporary art exhibitions, as well as drink and dine at glam restaurants and cocktail bars. Tai Kwun, meaning "big station" in Cantonese, is a sprawling complex and one of Central's top sights. The best place to start is the **Barracks Block,** the handsome colonial building on the south side of the central parade ground. Here you'll find the visitor centre and an exhibition on Tai Kwun's history. Then explore the **Central Magistracy** with its restored courtrooms, before heading to the claustrophobic concrete cells of **Victoria Prison.** Art fans should make a beeline for **JC Contemporary** at the rear of the complex, a three-story art gallery by architects Herzog de Meuron. Among the many places to eat and drink are the upscale **Magistracy Dining Room,** housed in a beautifully restored courtroom, and stylish speakeasy **001.** Free English-language guided tours of Tai Kwun can be reserved online via the website. ✉ *10 Hollywood Rd., Central* 🌐 *www.taikwun.hk* Ⓜ *Central, Exit D1.*

★ Victoria Peak

MOUNTAIN | Whatever the time, whatever the weather, be it your first visit or your 50th, Victoria Peak is Hong Kong's one unmissable sight. Soaring just over 1,805 feet above sea level, Hong Kong Island's highest hill looks out over a forest of skyscrapers, the glittering harbor beyond and—on a clear day—Kowloon's eight mountains. On rainy days wisps of clouds catch on the buildings' pointy tops, and at night both sides of the harbor burst into color. The best views are to be had from **Sky Terrace 428,** a ticketed attraction on top of the **Peak Tower** (the anvil-shape building, which also serves as the upper terminus of the Peak Tram). But you get almost as good a view for free from Lion Pavilion outside, a short walk along Findlay Path.

Well-signed nature walks around Victoria Peak offer wonderful respites. You'll be treated to spectacular views in all directions on the **Peak Circle Walk,** an easygoing 40- to 60-minute paved path that begins and ends at the Peak Tram Upper Terminus. Before buying a return ticket on the tram or on a bus, consider walking back downhill to Central, either along the tree-shared **Morning Trail** or via the short and steep Old Peak Road.

The **Peak Tram,** Asia's first funicular railway, has been rumbling up the steep

Victoria Peak offers a stunning view of the Hong Kong skyline.

inclines of Victoria Peak since it opened in 1888; before that, the only way up was to walk or take a bumpy ride in a sedan chair. The **Lower Terminus** starts just up past St. John's Cathedral on the opposite side of Garden Road. Sit on the right hand side of the tram carriage for the best views. Several buses go direct from the Central Bus Terminal near the Star Ferry Pier to the Peak Tram Lower Terminus. Bus 15 goes all the way to the top of the Peak, and is a good option on busy weekends when wait times for the Peak Tram can be over an hour. ✉ *Central* ✣ *Between Garden Rd. and Cotton Tree Dr.* ☎ *2522–0922* 🌐 *www.thepeak.com.hk* 🎫 *HK$76 one-way, HK$108 round-trip.*

Restaurants

Central is a gastronomic wonderland, offering up a peerless array of mouth-watering meals that run the gamut from simple wonton noodles to fine-dining Cantonese, Japanese, French, and so much more. Some of the fanciest establishments are found in Central's five-star hotels, while less formal feeds can be had up the hill in stylish SoHo. Booking ahead is advised for dinner, and you can avoid the queues of hungry office workers at lunchtime by eating after 2 pm.

Amber

$$$$ | **MODERN FRENCH** | This contemporary French fine-dining stalwart in the Landmark Mandarin Oriental has put a greater focus on sustainability in recent years, earning a Michelin green star for its efforts. Interiors are light and refreshed, while Netherlands-born head chef Richard Ekkebus has introduced an entirely dairy-free menu in an effort to emulate the comparative lightness of Asian cooking that does without cream, butter, and heavily reduced sauces. **Known for:** contemporary and playful modern European cooking; well-heeled diners; only prix-fixe menus, including vegetarian, dairy-, and gluten-free. $ *Average main: HK$1,600* ✉ *Landmark Mandarin Oriental, 7th fl., 15 Queen's Rd., Central* ☎ *2132–0066* 🌐 *www.mandarinoriental.com/en/hong-kong/the-landmark/dine/amber* Ⓜ *Central.*

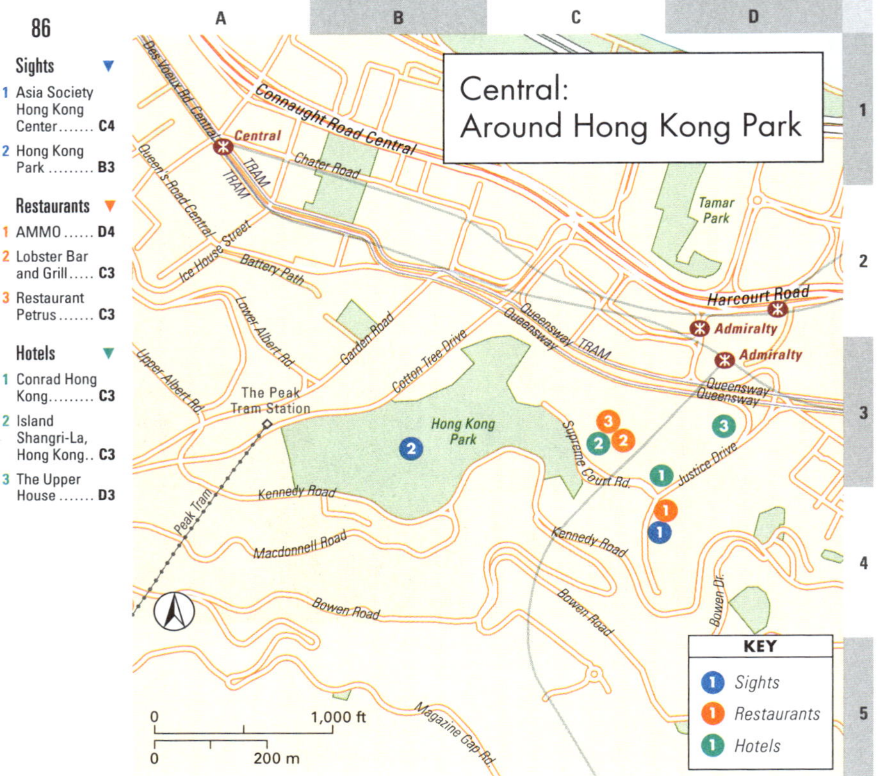

AMMO

$$$ | **MODERN ITALIAN** | Though a bit out of the way, few places in Hong Kong have the kind of stunning garden views that you'll find at AMMO. Housed in a former ammunition compound (hence the name) that was converted into the Asia Society Hong Kong Center, the restaurant's interiors and menus blend the old with the new resulting in an impressive and dynamic dining experience. **Known for:** Italian culinary techniques with Asian flourishes; sleek interior design in a heritage building; beautifully presented afternoon tea. *Average main: HK$350 ✉ Asia Society Hong Kong Center, 9 Justice Dr., Admiralty, Central ☎ 2537–9888 🌐 www.ammo.com.hk Ⓜ Admiralty.*

★ Bo Innovation

$$$$ | **CANTONESE** | Known as the "Demon Chef," Alvin Leung ripped up the rule book to create Bo Innovation, which wowed diners in Wan Chai for half a decade before moving to Central in 2022. Dishes tend to be clever reworkings of Cantonese classics using molecular techniques, and the nightly set menus are themed to help create a unique and thought-provoking dining experience unlike any other. **Known for:** molecular gastronomy; celebrity chef-owner; signature molecular xiao long bao (soup dumpling). *Average main: HK$1,280 ✉ 1st fl., H Code, 45 Pottinger St., Central ☎ 2850–8371 🌐 www.boinnovation.com ⏲ Closed Sun. No lunch Mon. and Tues. Ⓜ Central.*

Caprice

$$$$ | **FRENCH** | Only prix-fixe menus are served at this ultra-luxe French restaurant in the Four Seasons, a Hong Kong fine-dining institution which has retained either two or three Michelin stars every year since opening in 2008. The dining room, with its floor-to-ceiling windows framing harbor views, is as spectacular as the food, masterminded with passion and precision by executive chef Guillaume Galliot. **Known for:** luxe interiors with crystal chandeliers; delicious desserts; French haute cuisine. *Average main: HK$2,980* *Four Seasons Hotel Hong Kong, 6th fl., 8 Finance St., Central* *3196–8860* *www.fourseasons.com* *Closed Mon.* *Hong Kong.*

Chôm Chôm

$$$ | **VIETNAMESE** | Tapas-style sharing plates of Vietnamese-inspired cuisine pair with inventive cocktails at this sleek, industrial-styled restaurant in SoHo. The vibe is tailor-made for a casual date or dinner with friends, and the dishes, like rice-paper rolls bursting with soft-shell crab, or sticky, tender tamarind pork ribs, are unfailingly likable, if on the small side. **Known for:** cool vibe with great music and fun staff; bold, zingy, spicy flavors; great cocktails and mixed drinks. *Average main: HK$230* *58 Peel St., Central* *2810–0850* *www.chomchom.com.hk* *No lunch* *Central.*

Cuisine Cuisine

$$$ | **CANTONESE** | This Cantonese restaurant in IFC Mall impresses with a premium offering of dim sum alongside upscale banquet dishes made with pricy ingredients like bird's nest, king prawns, and wagyu beef. **Known for:** stunning harbor views from the dining room; signature of crisp suckling pig with foie gras; slow service during busy periods. *Average main: HK$330* *International Finance Centre Mall, 3rd fl., 8 Finance St., Central* *2393–3933* *www.miradining.com/cuisine-cuisine-ifc* *Hong Kong.*

Duddell's

$$$ | **CANTONESE** | Art and food come together in this beautiful two-story establishment, which encompasses a bar, garden terrace, and dining room. The interiors are sophisticated yet inviting, and the Cantonese cuisine has garnered plenty of praise from locals and visitors alike. **Known for:** regular art exhibitions and screenings hosted at the restaurant; Sunday brunch with free-flowing champagne; Cantonese tasting menus with premium ingredients. *Average main: HK$330* *Shanghai Tang Mansion, 3rd fl., 1 Duddell St., Central* *2525–9191* *www.duddells.co* *Central.*

8½ Otto e Mezzo Bombana

$$$$ | **ITALIAN** | Spearheaded by Umberto Bombana (the former executive chef of the Ritz-Carlton Hong Kong), this glitzy haunt is for many the best Italian fine-dining restaurant in Asia. The service is crisp, the wine list is extensive, and the interior is nothing less than glamorous. **Known for:** first Italian restaurant outside Italy to earn three Michelin stars; celebrity chef-owner Umberto Bombana, the "king of white truffles"; a degustation menu that offers a sampling of Bombana's best. *Average main: HK$600* *Landmark Alexandra, 2nd fl., Shop 202, 18 Chater Rd., Central* *2537–8859* *www.ottoemezzobombana.com* *Closed Sun.* *Central.*

Fiata Pizza

$$ | **PIZZA** | This modish SoHo spot packs out nightly with devoted foodies chasing a taste of chef-owner Salvatore Fiata's famous Neapolitan-style pizzas, revered for their beautifully charred crusts and quality toppings like mozzarella di bufala, truffle pesto, and spicy sausage from Fiata's home city of Caserta in southern Italy. The tables fill up fast, so book well in advance online. **Known for:** Hong Kong's best Neapolitan pizzas; compact but thoughtful drink selection; deliciously rich and boozy tiramisu. *Average main: HK$200* *2*

China's Cuisines

China is a vast country with many regional styles of cooking. The following is a primer to help you navigate the abundance of restaurant menus that you'll encounter during your trip.

Cantonese: From southern Guangdong province, a cuisine that roasts, stir-fries, braises, and steams. Spices are used in moderation and the emphasis is on freshness. Notable dishes include dim sum, roasted goose, claypot rice and steamed scallops with ginger and garlic.

Chiu chow: Also from Guangdong province and known for its vegetarian and seafood dishes, which are mostly poached, steamed, or braised. Signature dishes include oyster congee and fish ball noodle soup.

Hunan: Stewing, frying, braising, and smoking are featured cooking methods. Flavors are spicy and sour, incorporating chili peppers, shallots, and garlic, along with dried and preserved condiments. Signatures includes Mao's red-braised pork and steamed fish head with shredded chilies.

Macanese: An eclectic blend of southern Chinese and Portuguese cooking, featuring the use of salted dried fish, coconut milk, turmeric, and other spices. Common dishes include African-style barbecued chicken with spicy piri piri sauce and curried baked chicken.

Beijing: China's capital city, Beijing, features northern-style cuisine and dishes that once graced imperial tables. Regional specialties include Peking duck, *zha jiang mien* (noodles with soybean paste), and quick-fried tripe.

Northern Chinese: Staples are lamb and mutton, preserved vegetables, and noodles, steamed breads, pancakes, stuffed buns, and dumplings.

Sichuan: Famed for bold flavors and spiciness resulting from liberal use of chilies and mouth-numbing Sichuan peppercorns. Regional dishes include *dan dan* spicy noodles, twice-cooked pork, and *mapo* tofu.

Shanghainese: Cuisine characterized by rich flavors produced by braising and stewing, and the use of alcohol in cooking. Signature dishes include baby hairy crabs stir-fried with rice-cake slices, *xiao long bao* soup dumplings, and "drunken chicken."

Taiwanese: Diverse cuisine owing to its history and subtropical location. Seafood, pork, rice, soy, and fruit form the backbone of the cuisine. Specialties include "three cup chicken" with a sauce made of soy, rice wine, and sugar; oyster omelets; cuttlefish soup; and dried tofu.

Yunnan: In China's far southwest, Yunnanese cuisine is noted for its use of vegetables, mushrooms, bamboo shoots, and flowers in its spicy preparations. Signature dishes include "over the bridge" rice noodle soup and fried fish with lemongrass.

Staunton St., Central ☎ 6032–6626 🌐 www.fiatapizza.com Ⓜ Central.

Ho Lee Fook

$$$ | **CHINESE** | As the tongue-in-cheek name suggests, the food at this funky eatery is nothing like your average Chinese restaurant. Dishes are bold and playful, inspired by old-school Chinatown classics but with a decidedly modern twist; standout creations include Cantonese roast goose and wagyu short-rib. **Known for:** fortune cat and mah-jongg tile design motifs; being as much about the drinks as the food; fusion desserts with local ingredients. *$ Average main: HK$278 ✉ 3–5 Elgin St., Soho, Central ☎ 2810–0860 🌐 www.holeefook.com.hk ⏲ No lunch Ⓜ Central.*

Kau Kee

$ | **CANTONESE** | This bustling, no-frills restaurant that has been around since the 1930s offers some of the best beef brisket noodles in town. Expect a line when you arrive, though solo diners can sometimes jump ahead. **Known for:** brisket noodles with juicy, tender beef; brisk service; strict minimum spend per person. *$ Average main: HK$90 ✉ Ground fl., 21 Gough St., Central ☎ 2850–5967 ▭ No credit cards ⏲ Closed Sun. Ⓜ Sheung Wan.*

La Rambla by Catalunya

$$$ | **SPANISH** | Named after Barcelona's most bustling boulevard, the Catalan-inspired recipes are the brainchild of Netflix celebrity chef Rafa Gil. Highlights from the tapas menu include the *bombas* (deep-fried smoked potato and meat balls covered in bread crumbs and spicy sauce) and the famous ham, cheese, and truffle "bikini" sandwiches. **Known for:** authentic and refined Spanish food; photo-worthy Gaudi-inspired interiors; sherry-forward beverage program. *$ Average main: HK$285 ✉ IFC Mall, 3071–73 Level 3, 8 Finance St., Central ☎ 2866–7900 🌐 www.catalunya.hk Ⓜ Hong Kong.*

La Vache!

$$$ | **STEAK HOUSE** | In homage to the iconic Relais de Venise restaurant in Paris, this intimate neighborhood brasserie offers only one entrée: steak frites. A meal here includes a green salad, a perfectly grilled entrecôte steak, and unlimited refills of crispy, stick-thin fries. **Known for:** doing one dish and doing it to perfection; decent value for the quality; French wines and classic cocktails. *$ Average main: HK$398 ✉ 48 Peel St., SoHo, Central ☎ 2880–0248 🌐 www.lavache.com.hk Ⓜ Central.*

Liberty Exchange Kitchen & Bar

$$$ | **MODERN AMERICAN** | Popular with corporate types for its Exchange Square location, this two-level restaurant and bar serves modern American food with a Pan-Asian twist. Steaks, burgers, and stone-oven pizzas share the menu with miso black cod, zingy Asian-inspired salads, and char sui pork belly. **Known for:** bankers pitching up for after-work drinks; in the same complex as the Hong Kong stock exchange; tasty rectangular Neapolitan-style pizzas. *$ Average main: HK$300 ✉ 2 Exchange Sq., 8 Connaught Pl., Central ☎ 2810–8400 🌐 www.lex.hk ⏲ Closed Sun. Ⓜ Hong Kong.*

Lobster Bar and Grill

$$$$ | **SEAFOOD** | Lobster and steaks top the bill at this classy grill in the Shangri-La Hotel. With a vibe that is at once formal and cozy, the restaurant features live jazz performances Tuesday to Saturday evenings and Sunday afternoons. **Known for:** lobster bisque with chunks of succulent poached lobster; Sunday roasts with two-hour freeflow drinks; luxurious beef wellington to share. *$ Average main: HK$798 ✉ Island Shangri-La, 6th fl., Supreme Court Rd., Admiralty, Central ☎ 2820–8560 🌐 www.shangri-la.com Ⓜ Admiralty.*

★ Lung King Heen

$$$$ | **CHINESE** | A Hong Kong legend, this Four Seasons stalwart was the first Chinese restaurant in the world to be

awarded 3 Michelin stars back in 2009, an accolade it retained for 14 years. The elevated Cantonese cuisine on offer emphasizes seasonality and showcases masterful techniques. **Known for:** exquisite seafood and dim sum; extensive premium tea and wine list; harbor views and handsome interiors. *Average main: HK$600 ✉ Four Seasons Hotel Hong Kong, 4th fl., 8 Finance St., Central ☎ 3196–8880 🌐 www.fourseasons.com Ⓜ Hong Kong.*

Magistracy Dining Room

$$$$ | BRITISH | In the running for Hong Kong's most gorgeously-attired restaurant, this elegant eatery is named for its singular location in a grand old courthouse, part of the Central Magistracy block at Tai Kwun, Central's former police compound-turned-lifestyle hotspot. Serving elegant, old-world British fare with elevated ingredients, meals at Magistracy might open with fresh oysters, smoked salmon or dressed crab, and progress to rare rib of beef, carved tableside and served with Yorkshire puddings. **Known for:** heritage and history of its setting; Botanical Garden, a hidden-gem terrace bar; elevated British classics including pies and roasts. *Average main: HK$750 ✉ Tai Kwun, 1 Arbuthnot Rd., Central Magistracy Block, Central ☎ 2252–3177 🌐 www.themagistracyhongkong.com ⏲ No lunch Mon.–Wed. Ⓜ Central.*

Mak's Noodles

$ | CHINESE | The real test of a good Cantonese noodle shop is its wontons, and at Mak's they're fresh, plump, and generously filled with whole shrimp. What started as a stall in Central in 1968 is now a small Hong Kong chain, selling not only wonton noodles but noodles with beef brisket, fish balls, and dumplings in soup. **Known for:** famous wonton noodles; sauce-tossed noodles with pork; sui kau dumplings, filled with diced mushrooms and shrimp. *Average main: HK$48 ✉ 77 Wellington St., Central ☎ 2854–3810 🌐 www.maksnoodle.com ▭ No credit cards Ⓜ Central.*

Mandarin Grill + Bar

$$$$ | CONTEMPORARY | This Terence Conran–designed dining room at the Mandarin Oriental mixes old-school elegance with elevated grill offerings like New Zealand grass-fed wagyu beef and even whole roasted pheasant. Start with fresh oysters and caviar, and finish with classic indulgent desserts. **Known for:** clean, minimalist interiors; prime rib of roast beef carved tableside; sourcing fish and seafood from sustainable suppliers. *Average main: HK$750 ✉ Mandarin Oriental, 5 Connaught Rd. Central, Central ☎ 2825–4004 🌐 www.mandarinoriental.com Ⓜ Central.*

Mott 32

$$$ | CHINESE | One of Hong Kong's most successful high-end restaurant exports, Mott 32 has locations in cities worldwide. But this is the original, serving its trademark refined take on Chinese cuisine since 2014. **Known for:** named after a convenience store in New York's Chinatown district; classy evening dim sum like iberico pork soup dumplings; stunning interiors that marry industrial chic elements, elegant Chinese motifs, and luxurious detailing. *Average main: HK$500 ✉ Standard Chartered Bldg., Basement fl., 4–4A Des Voeux Rd., Central ☎ 2885–8688 🌐 www.mott32.com Ⓜ Central.*

Restaurant Petrus

$$$$ | FRENCH | From atop the Island Shangri-La Hong Kong, Petrus scales the upper Hong Kong heights of prestige, formality, and price. Luxe French fare is served in a clubby dining room decked out with heavy curtains and glittering chandeliers—this may be one for the dealmakers. **Known for:** grand design and breathtaking harbor views; memorable wine list with rare vintages; exceptional foie gras. *Average main: HK$688 ✉ Island Shangri-La Hong Kong, 56th fl., Supreme Court Rd., Admiralty, Central*

☎ *2820–8590* ⊕ *www.shangri-la.com* ⏲ *Closed Mon.* Ⓜ *Admiralty.*

Shui Kee

$ | **CHINESE** | Fold-up tables and stools are scattered around this small stall, which specializes in cow offal served with noodles in broth. Tender beef brisket and deep-fried wontons are also popular options. **Known for:** being one of Central's few remaining dai pai dong (outdoor food stalls); refreshing chilled chrysanthemum tea; sharing tables with other diners. *Average main: HK$35* ✉ *2 Gutzlaff St., Central* ☎ *2541–9769* ▭ *No credit cards* ⏲ *Closed weekends. No dinner* Ⓜ *Central.*

Sing Heung Yuen

$ | **CHINESE** | This outdoor stall has been in operation here since the 1970s and the canopied tables are pretty much always packed from 8 am to 3:30 pm. The iconic dishes are the instant ramen noodles or beef and macaroni served in a sweet tomato broth, as well as the toasted, crispy buns drizzled with condensed milk. **Known for:** sitting outside at plastic tables and chairs; affordable, old-style Hong Kong cooking; refreshing iced lemon tea. *Average main: HK$35* ✉ *2 Mee Lun St., Central* ☎ *2544–8368* ▭ *No credit cards* ⏲ *Closed Sun. No dinner.*

Sing Kee

$ | **CHINESE** | This is one of the rare *dai pai dong* food stalls in the area that stays open late into the evening. Cheap and cheerful, the seafood-centric menu is nevertheless pretty extensive. **Known for:** hot stir-fries paired with icy beers; no restrooms; eating on the street after dark. *Average main: HK$70* ✉ *63 Stanley St., Central* ☎ *2541–5678* ▭ *No credit cards* Ⓜ *Central.*

22 Ships

$$$ | **SPANISH** | Enjoy a fun dining experience at this buzzing tapas bar run by Madrid native Antonio Oviedo, who has worked in some of Spain's most well-known Michelin-starred kitchens. Expect a creative and contemporary menu with to-share dishes like black octopus paella and sea urchin toast, served in a funky space that includes an outdoor terrace. **Known for:** lively communal dining; no service charge; relaxed outdoor seating area. *Average main: HK$230* ✉ *PMQ, S109–113, Block A, Staunton St., Central* ☎ *2555–0722* ⊕ *www.22ships.hk* Ⓜ *Sheung Wan.*

Yung Kee

$$$ | **CHINESE** | **FAMILY** | Close to Central's nightlife district of Lan Kwai Fong, this three-story restaurant has been a Hong Kong institution since it first opened as a food stall in 1942. The food is authentic Cantonese, served amid writhing gold dragons and phoenixes. **Known for:** signature charcoal-roasted goose with beautifully crisp skin and tender meat; excellent dim sum in an upscale environment; thousand-year-old preserved eggs for more adventurous palates. *Average main: HK$450* ✉ *32–40 Wellington St., Central* ☎ *2522–1624* ⊕ *www.yungkee.com.hk* Ⓜ *Central.*

Coffee and Quick Bites

Bakehouse

$ | **BAKERY** | This hip, homegrown Hong Kong bakery chain has a handy branch just off the Central–Mid-Levels Escalator at Staunton Street, where you can line up to grab an order of signature sourdough egg tarts (you'll want at least two), which pair beautifully with a single-origin coffee to go. Other treats include buttery croissants, cookies, doughnuts, savory pastries, and sourdough loaves. **Known for:** much-hyped sourdough egg tarts; locations popping up all over Hong Kong; French founder Grégoire Michaud. *Average main: HK$25* ✉ *5 Staunton St., Central* ✥ *Just off Central–Mid-Levels Escalator* ⊕ *www.bakehouse.hk* Ⓜ *Central.*

Leaf Dessert

$ | **CHINESE** | Visit this retro outdoor stall for authentic Chinese desserts. Sweet soups made with red bean or ground black sesame are served in both hot and chilled versions. **Known for:** traditional Hong Kong sweet treats; gruff and surly service; also serving savory dishes like wonton noodles. *Average main: HK$14* *2 Elgin St., SoHo, Central* *2544–3795* *No credit cards* *Closed Sat.*

Tai Cheong Bakery

$ | **BAKERY** | Loved for their crumbly pastry and custard-rich centers, the egg tarts (*dan ta*) steal the show at this long-running Hong Kong bakery. Tai Cheong sells all sorts of packaged and oven-fresh baked goods including BBQ pork buns, crunchy egg biscuit rolls, and sugar-dusted Chinese doughnuts. **Known for:** a personal favorite of Chris Patten, the last-serving British governor of Hong Kong; above-average prices; central location. *Average main: HK$12* *35 Lyndhurst Terr., Central* *8300–8301.*

Hotels

Prepare to pay top dollar for a spacious harbor-view room at Central's international hotels, which include ultraluxe icons like the original Mandarin Oriental and the palatial Four Seasons on the waterfront. In Admiralty, a cluster of five-star tower hotels offers swank sanctuaries above Pacific Place, though staying here puts you slightly out of the action. For more affordable options, head to the Mid-Levels, where you'll need to rely on the Central–Mid-Levels Escalator (or taxis) to navigate the slopes.

★ Bishop Lei International House

$ | **HOTEL** | Up in the exclusive Mid-Levels above Central, this long-standing tower hotel offers unbeatable value, especially if you book its compact harbor-facing suites which offer impressive views and a more sensible amount of space than the standard rooms. **Pros:** unique perch near Central–Mid-Levels Escalator, saving you countless steps up and down to SoHo and Central; spotless, well-maintained rooms; shuttle-bus service to and from Hong Kong station. **Cons:** Central–Mid-Levels Escalator runs upward-only after 10 am, so lots of steps down in the morning; rather dated decor; relatively small rooms. *Rooms from: HK$750* *4 Robinson Rd., Mid-Levels, Central* *2868–0828* *www.bishopleihtl.com.hk* *227 rooms* *No Meals* *Central.*

Conrad Hong Kong

$$$ | **HOTEL** | A gleaming-white, oval-shape tower rising from the Pacific Place complex, this luxury chain-hotel offers dramatic views of the harbor and the Peak, along with super convenience for mall shopping, high-end restaurants, and transport to other parts of Hong Kong. **Pros:** open-air pool area is dramatically backed by towering skyscrapers; elevator whisks guests down to Pacific Place shopping mall; directly connected to Admiralty MTR station. **Cons:** has a bit of a chain hotel feel; rooms are due for a revamp; some might find glitzy Pacific Place soulless. *Rooms from: HK$2,500* *Pacific Place, 88 Queensway, Admiralty, Central* *2521–3838* *www.hilton.com* *512 rooms* *No Meals* *Admiralty.*

★ Four Seasons Hotel Hong Kong

$$$$ | **HOTEL** | One of Hong Kong's finest ultraluxe hotels, the Four Seasons wows with knockout harbor views from its sumptuous guest rooms, world-class restaurants, a gorgeous infinity pool, and legendary service. **Pros:** elite service and attention to detail; direct access to Hong Kong station and the Central Ferry Piers; superb restaurants and bars. **Cons:** breakfast not included in high rates; cheaper rooms have views of Victoria Peak; lobby can be busy and crowded. *Rooms from: HK$5,500* *International Finance Centre, 8 Finance St., Central* *3196–8888* *www.fourseasons.com/*

hongkong 399 rooms No Meals Ⓜ *Central.*

Garden View Hong Kong

$ | **HOTEL** | Though somewhat out of the action, rooms in this high-rise hotel affiliated with the YWCA overlook the peaceful Hong Kong Zoological and Botanical Gardens and are clean, well designed, and affordable. **Pros:** value for money; kitchenettes in some suites; impressive views from guestrooms. **Cons:** traffic can get bad during rush hours; limited amenities; bit of a trek uphill from Central. *Rooms from: HK$700* *1 MacDonnell Rd., Mid-Levels* *2877–3737* *hotel.ywca.org.hk* 141 rooms No Meals Ⓜ *Central.*

Island Shangri-La, Hong Kong

$$$$ | **HOTEL** | Towering above Pacific Place, this Hong Kong icon opened in 1991 and continues to charm with renovated, design-forward guest rooms and suites offering stunning harbor views and a refreshed, creative take on the brand's trademark Asian high-end hospitality. **Pros:** truly grand lobby; beautiful pool deck with a great up-close skyline view; elevator access to Pacific Place Mall. **Cons:** need to travel to either Central or Wan Chai for nightlife; atmosphere can be rather business-like; very expensive restaurants. *Rooms from: HK$3,920* *Pacific Place, Supreme Court Rd., Admiralty, Central* *2877–3838* *www.shangri-la.com* 565 rooms No Meals Ⓜ *Admiralty.*

★ Mandarin Oriental Hong Kong

$$$$ | **HOTEL** | First opened in 1963, the flagship of the Mandarin Oriental hotel group has lost little of its opulence, colonial charm, or shine: it still features impeccable service and sumptuous rooms levelled up with goose-down bedding, silk kimonos, and acres of marble in the bathrooms. **Pros:** beautifully designed rooms with harbor views; old-world ambience at its finest; high-end spa, salon, and barber. **Cons:** land reclamation has moved the harbor further away; small indoor pool; rooms slightly smaller than similarly priced hotels. *Rooms from: HK$4,600* *5 Connaught Rd., Central* *2522–0111* *www.mandarin-oriental.com* 501 rooms No Meals Ⓜ *Central.*

★ The Murray

$$$$ | **HOTEL** | Next to Hong Kong Park and the lower terminus of the Peak Tram, this 25-story office tower was converted into a lavishly minimalist luxury hotel in 2018, and boasts elegantly appointed harbor-view rooms, a swimming pool, spa and five restaurants, including one on the rooftop. **Pros:** adjacent to St John's Cathedral, Hong Kong Park, and Peak Tram lower terminus; generously sized bathrooms with Japanese toilets; floor-to-ceiling windows. **Cons:** 10-minute uphill walk from Central MTR station; indoor pool only; rather small fitness center. *Rooms from: HK$3,458* *22 Cotton Tree Dr., Central* *3141–8888* *www.niccolohotels.com* 336 rooms No Meals Ⓜ *Admiralty.*

Ovolo Central

$$ | **HOTEL** | Perfect for urban explorers, this tech-forward boutique hotel is mere steps from Central's hottest dining and nightlife, and comes with boldly styled, art-filled guest rooms, a fitness center, and Veda, a casual restaurant specializing in vegetarian and vegan Indian fare. **Pros:** next door to Tai Kwun and a short hop to Lan Kwai Fong; free drinks in lobby during evening Social Hour; feel-good pop music in public areas. **Cons:** some rooms due a refresh; steep uphill walk from Central MTR station; street noise on lower floors. *Rooms from: HK$1,850* *2 Arbuthnot Rd., Central* *3755–3000* *www.ovolohotels.com* 42 rooms No Meals Ⓜ *Central.*

The Pottinger Hong Kong

$$$ | **HOTEL** | Overlooking the historic "ladder street" from which it takes its name, The Pottinger weaves romantic elements of local heritage into its chic chinoiserie-inspired guest rooms furnished with

Lan Kwai Fong is a hotspot for Hong Kong nightlife.

delicate silkscreen headboards and floral motifs. **Pros:** just steps from shops, bars, and restaurants; thoughtful local touches in the art, amenities, and decor; reasonably big bathrooms. **Cons:** no swimming pool; standard rooms not particularly spacious; underwhelming views in some rooms. *Rooms from: HK$2,378* *21 Stanley St., Central* *2308–3188* *www.sino-hotels.com* *68 rooms* *No Meals.*

★ The Upper House

$$$$ | **HOTEL** | A tranquil haven of designer luxury, even the lowest tier rooms at Upper House clock in at a palatial 70 square meters (about 750 square feet) and come with huge window-side bathtubs, walk-in rain showers, and free minibars (or Maxi-Bars as they call them). **Pros:** minimalist design with works by contemporary Asian artists; superb harbor or mountain views; incredibly personalized service. **Cons:** no spa or pool (but in-room spa treatments available); can be difficult to get a taxi; no reception so check-in can be confusing. *Rooms from: HK$4,250* *Pacific Place, 88 Queensway, Admiralty, Central* *2918–1838* *www.thehousecollective.com* *117 rooms* *No Meals* *Admiralty.*

Nightlife

Since the 1980s, Central's nightlife has been synonymous with Lan Kwai Fong, a square of sloping streets lined with open-fronted bars, where touts tempt revelers with drinks deals. Though the global pandemic and Hong Kong protests have dampened some of its former raucous energy, it remains a hotspot for partygoers, especially those drawn to its late-night clubs. For a more urbane experience, head to the bars of SoHo, where the atmosphere leans sophisticated, and the focus is on quality drinks and bar snacks. Central also hosts a smattering of live music venues, catering to jazz aficionados and indie music fans alike.

BARS

★ Argo

COCKTAIL BARS | Regularly ranked in the top 10 of Asia's best bars, Argo in the Four Seasons is known for its highly creative and environmentally conscious approach to mixology, celebrating sustainable ingredients such as cacao husks, bamboo, and coffee flowers. The design scheme features sweeping architectural curves and warm brass accents, best appreciated by taking a seat at the bar. ✉ *Four Seasons Hotel, 8 Finance St., Central* ☎ *3196–8882* 🌐 *www.fourseasons.com* Ⓜ *Hong Kong.*

Cardinal Point

BARS | Book ahead for an outdoor table to enjoy stunning skyline views from this bar on the 45th-floor roof terrace of The Landmark. Cocktails are expensive and err on the sweet side, so stick to wine, beer, or mixed drinks and savor the city lights to a soundtrack of DJ beats. ✉ *The Landmark, Gloucester Tower, 45th fl., 15 Queen's Rd., Central* ☎ *3501–8560* 🌐 *www.cardinalpoint.com.hk* Ⓜ *Central.*

Foxglove

LIVE MUSIC | This speakeasy tucked behind an umbrella shopfront holds one of the best jazz nights in town. The upscale, maritime-inspired decor is a pleasant backdrop to cocktails inspired by ingredients from around the globe, as well as a list of dependable classics. ✉ *Printing House, 2nd fl., 6 Duddell St., Central* ☎ *2116–8949* 🌐 *www.mingfathouse.com/foxglove* Ⓜ *Central.*

The Globe

PUB | This British-style SoHo pub is known for having one of Hong Kong's best selections of local and international craft brews. It's a fun and convivial spot, with a mix of ages and a pretty even split between expats and locals. Other draws include televised sport and hearty, gastropub-style grub: fish and chips, sausage and mash, and homemade pies. ✉ *45–53 Graham St., SoHo, Central* ☎ *2543–1941* 🌐 *www.theglobe.com.hk* Ⓜ *Central.*

Did You Know? 

Statue Square took its name from bronze figures of British royalty that stood here before the Japanese occupation, when they were removed and melted down. The only figure exempt was stern Sir Thomas Jackson (1841–1915), who looks over the square toward HSBC—he was the chief manager for almost 30 years.

★ Honky Tonks Tavern

BARS | A hit with the happy hour crowd (5–7 pm, all night long on Wednesday), Honky Tonks is a highly polished SoHo watering hole posing as an American-style dive bar. Classic and signature cocktails, Hong Kong craft beers, and a wide choice of bourbon can be paired with elevated bar snacks like crisp fried chicken and "big ass" pizzas—available by the slice for a steal during happy hour. ✉ *Pak Tsz Lane Park, Man Hing La., SoHo, Central* 🌐 *www.honkytonkstavern.com* Ⓜ *Sheung Wan.*

Kinsman

BARS | This moody bar behind a nondescript door is infused with stylish old Hong Kong decor. The drinks are equally inspiring, with a focus on Chinese and Cantonese spirits. Try the Kowloon Dairy, a smooth mix of amaro and monkfruit spirit. ✉ *65 Peel St., Central* ☎ *2865–5011* 🌐 *www.singularconcepts.com/kinsman* Ⓜ *Central.*

La Cabane Wine Bistro

WINE BAR | A cozy, intimate refuge for Hong Kong oenophiles, La Cabane specializes in natural, organic, and low-intervention wines. French and New World wines are on offer, and can be paired with French-influenced fare like steak frites, beef tartare, and cheese selections. ✉ *62 Hollywood Rd., Central* ☎ *2776–6070* 🌐 *www.lacabane.hk* Ⓜ *Central.*

Racks City

SPORTS BARS | This grungy pool hall turned late-night boozer is good for a game of pool, darts, or beer pong, played to a hip hop soundtrack. ✉ *Winning Centre, 46–48 Wyndham St., Central* ☎ *2868–0400* Ⓜ *Central.*

Staunton's Gastropub

PUB | Adjacent to Hong Kong's famous outdoor escalator, this SoHo stalwart relaunched postpandemic as an all-day gastropub, pairing wines, beers, and cocktails with British classics like all-day breakfast and shepherd's pie. As the weekend approaches the place gets crowded, but the upstairs balcony is still the perfect perch from which to people-watch. ✉ *10–12 Staunton St., SoHo, Central* ☎ *2973–6611* 🌐 *stauntonshk.com* Ⓜ *Central.*

DANCE CLUBS

Dragon-i

DANCE CLUB | Around since 2002, Dragon-i made its name as a hotspot for the glitterati, hosting globe-trotting celebs like David Beckham and featuring intimate live shows from the likes of Snoop Dogg and Jamiroquai. It remains the domain of the city's young, rich, and beautiful (if not necessarily classy) crowd, and still attracts international acts and DJs. Have a drink on the deck, or step inside the vivid red playroom, which doubles as a Chinese restaurant earlier in the day. ✉ *The Centrium, 60 Wyndham St., Central* ☎ *3110–1222* 🌐 *www.dragon-i.com.hk* Ⓜ *Central.*

Oma

DANCE CLUB | This dark and dingy techno bunker boasts a top-of-the-line sound system and strong drinks. Expect great tech house music and parties that go all night. ✉ *Harilela House, Lower basement fl., 79 Wyndham St., Central* ☎ *2521–8815* Ⓜ *Central.*

Varga Lounge

COCKTAIL BARS | Named after the Peruvian painter of pinup girls, this is a colorful, eclectic little spot for a cocktail with its bright walls and 1950s-inspired art. The downstairs bar opens onto the street, while large groups can take over the upstairs lounge. ✉ *36 Staunton St., SoHo, Central* ☎ *2104–9697* 🌐 *www.vargaloungehk.com* Ⓜ *Central.*

Shopping

It can feel like you're never more than a few steps from an air-conditioned shopping arcade in Central, a district that rules the roost when it comes to high-end designer shopping in Hong Kong. Glitzy malls like IFC, Landmark, and Pacific Place often stock Hong Kong exclusives from big-name designer labels, and you can usually count on impeccable customer service. To experience a different side of Central, swap the malls for stalls on Li Yuen streets East and West for cheap souvenirs like silk dressing gowns; Pottinger Street for fancy dress; or Graham Street for foodstuffs.

ANTIQUES AND COLLECTIBLES

Arch Angel Antiques

ANTIQUES & COLLECTIBLES | Specializing in Chinese antiques, this shop stocks a respectable collection of fine ceramics, furniture, ancestor portraits, and more. ✉ *70 Hollywood Rd., Central* ☎ *2851–6848* Ⓜ *Central.*

Teresa Coleman Fine Arts Ltd.

ANTIQUES & COLLECTIBLES | British collector Teresa Coleman specializes in finely woven and embroidered costumes and textiles from the imperial courts of the Qing and Ming dynasties (circa 1368–1912). Her upstairs showroom also displays a wide collection of Tibetan rugs, Himalayan Buddhist art, antique painted and carved fans, lacquered boxes, prints, and paintings. By appointment only. ✉ *Yu Yuet Lai Bldg., Room 405, 54 Wyndham St., Central* ☎ *2526–2450* 🌐 *www.teresa-coleman.com* Ⓜ *Central.*

Wattis Fine Art

ANTIQUES & COLLECTIBLES | Run by affable expert Jonathan Wattis and his wife Vicky since 1988, Wattis Fine Art specializes in antique maps, prints, and photographs of Hong Kong, China, and Southeast Asia. ✉ *2nd fl., 20 Hollywood Rd., Central* ☎ *2524–5302* 🌐 *www.wattis.com.hk* Ⓜ *Central, Exit D2.*

ART

10 Chancery Lane Gallery

ART GALLERY | Tucked behind Tai Kwun, this white-walled gallery spotlights emerging artists from all over the world, with a primary focus on artists from the Asia Pacific area. Owner-curator Katie de Tilly has a particularly keen eye for photography, and the gallery has regularly featured the works of Vietnamese-American fine arts photographer Dinh Q. Lê and pioneering Chinese artist Wang Keping. ✉ *Ground fl., 10 Chancery La., SoHo, Central* ☎ *2810–0065* 🌐 *www.10chancerylanegallery.com* Ⓜ *Central, Exit D2.*

BOOKS AND STATIONERY

Lok Man Rare Books

ANTIQUES & COLLECTIBLES | Stocking a hand-picked selection of antiquarian tomes, this cozy bookshop is the place to browse for centuries-old first editions on subjects as diverse as wine, food, history, and sport. Lok Man Rare Books relocated in 2023 to the stunning Pedder Arcade, the renovated fifth floor of the Art Deco Pedder Building. ✉ *Pedder Bldg., 5th fl., 12 Pedder St., Central* ☎ *2868–1056* 🌐 *www.lokmanbooks.com* Ⓜ *Central, Exit D2.*

CLOTHING

Sonjia

CLOTHING | Korean-English ex-lawyer Sonjia Norman crafts quietly luxurious, one-of-a-kind pieces and modified vintage clothing under the Sonjia label. Her clothes span occasions from yoga classes to dinner parties; plus, the boutique also offers an array of jewelry, scarves, and home accessories. ✉ *Western Commercial Bldg., 6th fl., 31 Des Voeux Rd. W, Sheung Wan* ☎ *2529–6223* 🌐 *www.sonjiaonline.com* Ⓜ *Sheung Wan.*

Spy Henry Lau

CLOTHING | Local bad boy Henry Lau brings an edgy attitude to his fashion for men and women. Bold and often dark, with a touch of bling, his clothing and accessories lines are not for the faint-hearted. ✉ *125 Wellington St., Central* ☎ *2530–3128* 🌐 *www.spyhenrylau.com* Ⓜ *Central.*

CLOTHING: TAILORS

Jantzen Tailor

COUTURE | Catering to expatriate bankers since 1972, this reputable tailor specializes in classic shirts in various fabrics and styles, from herringbone to houndstooth, with hand-sewn button shanks, customizable interlinings, and a selection of complementary neckties. ✉ *Lok Yuen Bldg., 5th fl., Room 504–505, 25–27 Des Voeux Rd. Central, Central* ☎ *2570–5901* 🌐 *www.jantzentailor.com* Ⓜ *Central, Exit B.*

Linva Tailors

COUTURE | In operation since 1965, this old-fashioned tailor makes cheongsam, the elegant, form-fitting Chinese dresses known for their high collars and side slits. Prices are affordable but vary according to fabric, which ranges from basics to special brocades and beautifully embroidered silks. ✉ *38 Cochrane St., Central* ☎ *2544–2456* Ⓜ *Central, Exit D2.*

W. W. Chan & Sons Tailors Ltd.

COUTURE | Chan is known for excellent-quality suits and shirts in classic cuts and has an array of fine European fabrics. The store features a mirrored, hexagonal changing room so you can check every angle. ✉ *Entertainment Bldg., 8th fl., Unit B, 30 Queen's Rd. Central, Central* ☎ *2366–9738* 🌐 *www.wwchan.com* Ⓜ *Central.*

DEPARTMENT STORES

Lane Crawford

DEPARTMENT STORE | Hong Kong's most prestigious department store started

Tailor-Made

Hong Kong's renowned tailors have long offered residents and visitors the unique opportunity to enjoy the precision and craftsmanship of a custom-made suit. Whether for business, special occasions, or simply the pleasure of a perfect fit, these expert tailors will have the finished garments ready for your departure.

Tailoring Tips

■ **Set Your Style.** Be clear about what you want. Bring samples—a favorite piece of clothing or magazine photos. Hong Kong tailors were once trained in classic, structured garments but now accommodate modern, casual, or experimental styles. Classic suit styles include the American cut, which has a jacket with notched lapels, a center vent, and two or three buttons. The trousers are lean, with flat fronts. The British cut also has notched lapels and two- or three-button jackets, but it features side vents and pleated trousers. The double-breasted Italian cut has wide lapels and pleated trousers.

■ **Choose Your Fabric.** You're getting a deal on workmanship, so consider splurging on, say, a luxurious blend of cashmere and wool. When having something copied, though, choose a fabric similar to the original. Take your time selecting: fabric is the main cost factor. Examine fabric on a large scale; small swatches are deceiving.

■ **Measure Up.** Meticulous measuring is the mark of a superior craftsman, so be patient. And for accuracy, stand as you normally would (you can't suck in the gut forever).

■ **Place Your Order.** Most tailors require a deposit of 30%–50% of the total cost. Request a receipt detailing price, fabric, style, measurements, fittings, and production schedule. Ask for a swatch to compare with the final product.

■ **Get Fit.** There should be at least two fittings. The first is for major alterations. Subsequent fittings are supposed to be for minor adjustments, but don't settle for less than perfect: Keep sending it back until they get it right. Bring the correct clothes, such as a dress shirt and appropriate shoes, to try on a suit. Try jackets buttoned and unbuttoned. Examine every detail. Are shoulder seams puckered or smooth? Do patterns meet? Is the collar too loose or tight? (About two fingers' space is right.)

Finding a Tailor

■ As soon as you arrive, visit established tailors to compare workmanship and cost.

■ Ask if the work is bespoke (made from scratch) or made-to-measure (based on existing patterns but handmade according to your measurements).

■ You get what you pay for. Assume the workmanship and fabric will match the price.

■ A fine suit may require six or more days to create, though many tailors can deliver a faster service.

out as a makeshift provisions shop back in 1850. This branch in the IFC Mall is one of Hong Kong's four Lane Crawford locations, divided up into small gallery-like spaces for different luxury brands and designers. In addition to fashion, the store stocks everything from beauty to homewares. ✉ *IFC Mall, Podium 3, 8 Finance St., Central* ☎ *2118–3388, 2118–7777 Lane Crawford concierge* 🌐 *www.lanecrawford.com.hk* Ⓜ *Hong Kong, Exit A1.*

HOME DECOR

★ G.O.D.

SOUVENIRS | The name of this pioneering lifestyle brand stands for "Goods of Desire," which translates to imaginative yet functional homewares, fashion, and more, much of it vintage-style and emblazoned with playful Hong Kong iconography. Perfect for trendy, Hong Kong–themed gifts for the folks back home. ✉ *48 Hollywood Rd., Central* ☎ *2805–1876* 🌐 *www.god.com.hk* Ⓜ *Central, Exit D2.*

JEWELRY AND ACCESSORIES

Chow Tai Fook

JEWELRY & WATCHES | Jade is not the only thing you'll see from this local chain founded in 1929. It also has fine jewelry in diamond, jadeite, ruby, sapphire, emerald, 18K gold, and more-traditional pure gold. And don't worry about tracking one down; Chow Tai Fook has more than 60 Hong Kong locations. ✉ *Aon China Bldg., Ground fl., 29 Queen's Rd. Central, Central* ☎ *2523–7128* 🌐 *www.chowtaifook.com* Ⓜ *Central, Exit D2.*

MALLS AND SHOPPING CENTERS

IFC Mall

MALL | Packed with designer boutiques and the department store Lane Crawford, IFC Mall sits above the Hong Kong MTR station with its in-town airport check-in desks, and connects to the Four Seasons Hotel. Leisure facilities include a plush cinema multiplex and a roof terrace with stunning harbor views. ✉ *8 Finance St., Central* ☎ *2295–3308, 2295–3308 hotline* 🌐 *www.ifc.com.hk* Ⓜ *Hong Kong, Exit F.*

Landmark

MALL | Central's most prestigious shopping site is home to a bevy of big-name upscale fashion brands. Even if your credit-card limit isn't up to a spree here, swanky Café Landmark is a great place to watch moneyed fashionistas on a retail therapy kick. A pedestrian bridge links the mall with shopping arcades in Landmark Prince's, Landmark Alexandra, Landmark Chater, and the Mandarin Oriental Hotel. ✉ *15 Queen's Rd. Central, Pedder St. and Des Voeux Rd., Central* ☎ *2500–0555 Customer Service* 🌐 *www.landmark.hk* Ⓜ *Central, Exit G.*

Pacific Place

MALL | Quieter and more exclusive than most competitors, this marble-clad mall is popular with well-to-do residents. High-end fashions, a Lane Crawford department store, and several excellent restaurants share the floor space, while some of Hong Kong's swankiest hotels cluster around it, including JW Marriott, the Island Shangri-La, Conrad, and the Upper House.

High-end international prêt-à-porter fills most of its four floors. When your bags are weighing you down, sandwiches, sushi, and Starbucks are on hand, as is a multiplex cinema. The JW Marriott, the Island Shangri-La, the Conrad, and the Upper House hotels are connected to this plaza, all with enticing afternoon tea options. Elevated walkways join Pacific Place with four arcades: the Admiralty Centre, United Centre, Queensway Plaza, and fashion-forward Lab Concept. ✉ *88 Queensway, Admiralty, Central* ☎ *2844–8900* 🌐 *www.pacificplace.com.hk* Ⓜ *Admiralty, Exit F.*

SPECIALTY STORES

Fook Ming Tong Tea Shop

SPECIALTY STORE | A local favorite established in 1987, Fook Ming Tong is known for excellent service and high-quality longjing, oolong, and jasmine teas that have been painstakingly sourced by tea masters. ✉ *IFC Mall, 3rd fl., Shop 3015, 8 Finance St., Central* ☎ *2295–0368* 🌐 *www.fookmingtong.com* Ⓜ *Hong Kong.*

Kowloon Soy Co.

FOOD & DRINK | Enhance your wok cooking by picking up a bottle of soy sauce made the traditional way—brewed for months in ceramic vats under the hot Hong Kong sun. The owner speaks English and can guide you through the shop's other artisanal food products, which include fermented bean paste and pickled tofu, all made locally without using industrial processes. ✉ *9 Graham St., Central* ☎ *2544–3697* Ⓜ *Central.*

Activities

SPAS

Four Seasons Spa

SPA | Pamper yourself in high style at one of Hong Kong's most glamorous spas, with opulent treatment rooms, a serene steam and sauna complex, and divine harbor views. ✉ *Four Seasons Hotel, 6th fl., 8 Finance St., Central* ☎ *3196–8900* 🌐 *www.fourseasons.com* Ⓜ *Central.*

The Mandarin Spa

SPA | Inspired by Traditional Chinese Medicine, bespoke treatments are designed to cleanse and nourish both body and soul at this ultraluxe spa, while the on-site Mandarin Salon and Barber offer yet more ways to get you looking and feeling your best. ✉ *The Landmark Mandarin Oriental, 15 Queen's Rd. Central, Central* ☎ *2132–0011* 🌐 *www.mandarinoriental.com* Ⓜ *Central.*

Southside

For all the unrelenting urbanity of Hong Kong Island's north coast, the south coast is a rolling landscape of green hills dropping down to picturesque bays and sandy beaches. With beautiful sea views, Southside is a breath of fresh air—literally and figuratively—and coveted turf for some of Hong Kong's wealthiest residents. The pace is slower than it is in more congested parts of the city, and there are lots of sea breezes and opportunities to take sampan rides, play a round of golf, swim, or simply enjoy the scenery.

Sights

The quieter south side of Hong Kong Island is geared up for family fun, whether that's beach jaunts to Repulse Bay, Stanley or Shek O, or traditional sampan cruises through the iconic "floating village" of Aberdeen Harbour. Ocean Park, Hong Kong's beloved original theme park, combines rides with water slides, giant pandas and marine life, while for nature enthusiasts, the area boasts some of the city's most scenic hiking trails. The Dragon's Back is a must for its breathtaking ridge-top views, while the Wilson Trail, starting in Stanley and stretching all the way to the New Territories, is a worthy challenge for dedicated trekkers.

Aberdeen Harbour

MARINA/PIER | Until the 1970s, Aberdeen's harbor was home to a flotilla of junks, sampans, and houseboats sheltering a community of thousands of water-dwelling fisherfolk. You'll still see a handful of houseboats moored along Aberdeen Promenade, some selling locally caught fish. Head to Pier 6 on the promenade to visit a houseboat turned harbor history museum and gift shop. Sign up for a sampan tour of the harbor inside the museum, or eat a tasty bowl of "sampan noodles" served by a roving kitchen boat. You can also take a ferry from Aberdeen Harbour to Lamma and Cheung Chau islands. ✉ *Southside.*

Ap Lei Chau Island

ISLAND | A road bridge connects Aberdeen with Ap Lei Chau (Duck's Tongue

Island), a residential area where many of the former boat-dwellers have been rehoused. You can also cross by sampan from Aberdeen Promenade. A small Tin Hau temple and the Ap Lei Chau Cooked Food Market, known for its seafood feasts, are the main reasons to visit. On the south side of the island, Horizon Plaza is an outlet mall selling cut-price designer homewares and fashion. ✉ *Southside.*

Béthanie

HISTORIC SIGHT | One of Hong Kong's few examples of French colonial architecture, Béthanie was built in 1875 by the French Mission as a sanatorium for priests and missionaries recovering from tropical diseases. The Hong Kong Government took over the building in the 1970s and leased it to the University of Hong Kong; and at the turn of the 21st century, the property was extensively restored and was subsequently declared a historic monument. Béthanie houses a photogenic neo-Gothic chapel—a popular wedding venue—a theater, a small basement museum, an exhibition hall, and facilities for the School of Film and Television. Guided tours are available for booking via Cityline (🌐 *www.cityline.com*) and last about 30 minutes. ✉ *139 Pok Fu Lam Rd., Pok Fu Lam, Southside* ☎ *2584–8633* 🌐 *www.hkapa.edu* 🎫 *Tour HK$37.*

★ Dragon's Back

TRAIL | The eighth, final, and most famous stage of the 50-km (31-mile) Hong Kong Trail is known as the Dragon's Back, and is easily done as a day hike, taking around three hours to cover the 7.5-km (4.7-mile) route, which climbs over a mountain ridge with glorious sea views on both sides. The trail starts at the Tei Wan bus stop on SheK O Road (take Bus 9 from Shau Kei Wan MTR station) and finishes at Big Wave Bay, where you can grab refreshments then hire a bodyboard and hit the waves. ✉ *SheK O Rd., Southside* 🎫 *Free.*

★ Ocean Park

THEME PARK | **FAMILY** | Built on 170 hilly acres overlooking the sea just east of Aberdeen, this theme park, water park, zoo, and aquarium complex has something for all ages. Older thrill-seekers can take on the gravity-defying Hair Raiser coaster, while younger kids are catered for with slower rides and a huge adventure playground. Pandas are the highlight of the zoo area, and the Grand Aquarium is home to over 5,000 marine animals. ⚠ **Be aware that the Ocean Theatre has performing dolphins and seals.** Water World (open seasonally; check website for exact dates) comes with slides and an all-weather indoor wave pool, and requires a separate ticket. Ocean Park has its own dedicated MTR stop, taking around 10 minutes to reach from Admiralty station. ✉ *Ocean Park Rd., Aberdeen, Southside* ☎ *3923–2323* 🌐 *www.oceanpark.com.hk* 🎫 *HK$498.*

Shek O

TOWN | This seaside locale is Southside's easternmost village, home to a few beach shops and casual restaurants selling Southeast Asian fare. The main reason to make the trip is Shek O Beach, an enticing crescent of golden sand facing rocky offshore islands. You can also cut through town and cross a bridge to the "island" of Tai Tau Chau, which is really a large rock with a lookout over the South China Sea. Hikers should head to nearby Shek O Country Park, known for its bird-watching and coastal views. To get here from Central, take the MTR to Shau Kei Wan (Exit A3), then take Bus 9 to the last stop (about 30 minutes). ✉ *Southside.*

Stanley

TOWN | **FAMILY** | This easygoing peninsula town lies south of Deep Water and Repulse bays. You'll find a row of waterfront pubs and restaurants, and great shopping in Stanley Market, full of casual clothes, cheap souvenirs, and cheerful bric-a-brac. Stanley's beach is the site

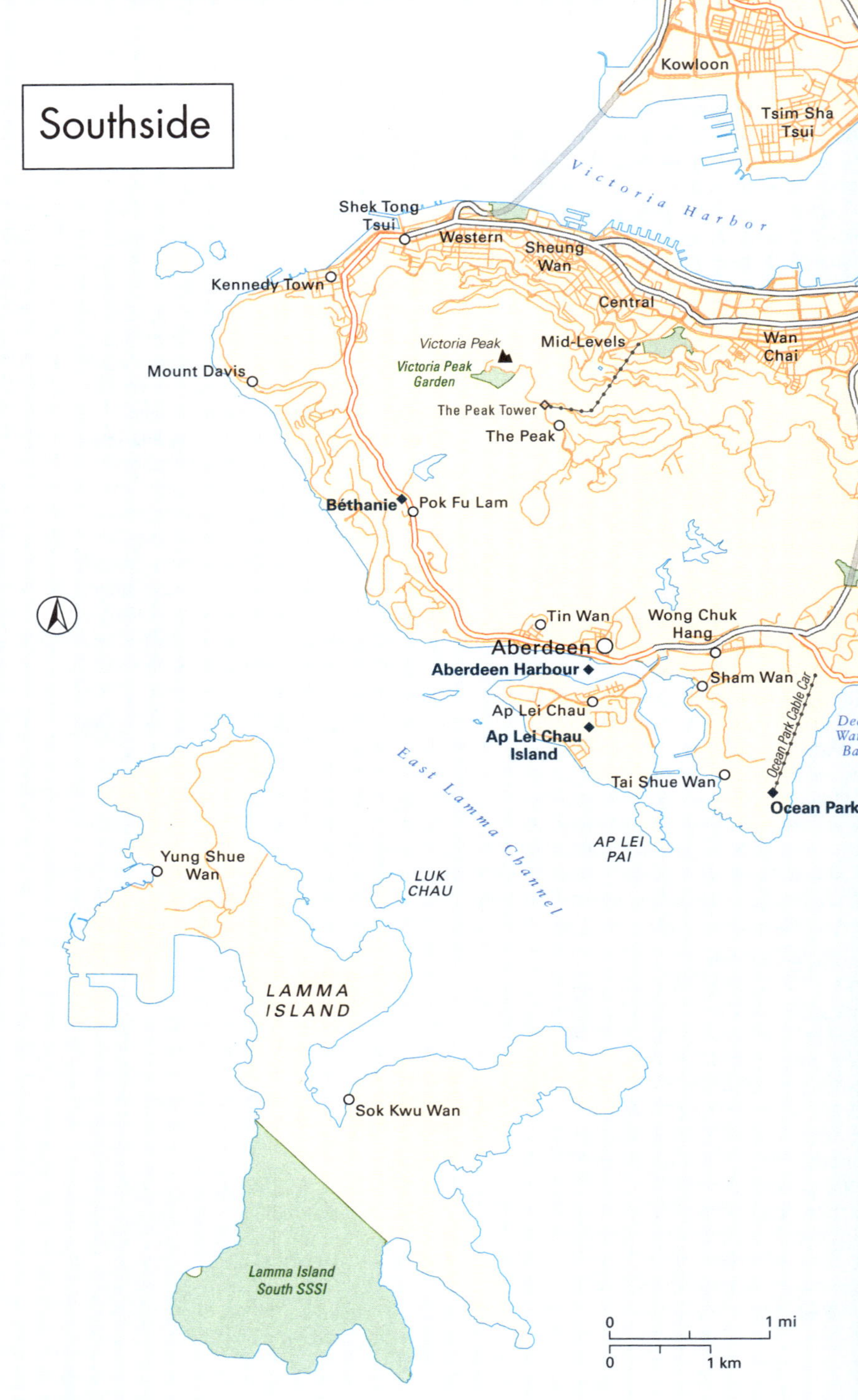
Southside
Kowloon
Tsim Sha Tsui
Victoria Harbor
Shek Tong Tsui
Western
Sheung Wan
Kennedy Town
Central
Victoria Peak
Mid-Levels
Wan Chai
Victoria Peak Garden
Mount Davis
The Peak Tower
The Peak
Béthanie
Pok Fu Lam
Tin Wan
Wong Chuk Hang
Aberdeen
Aberdeen Harbour
Sham Wan
Ap Lei Chau
Ap Lei Chau Island
Ocean Park Cable Car
Deep Water Bay
East Lamma Channel
Tai Shue Wan
Ocean Park
AP LEI PAI
Yung Shue Wan
LUK CHAU
LAMMA ISLAND
Sok Kwu Wan
Lamma Island South SSSI
0
1 mi
0
1 km

Cha Kwo Ling
Yau Tong
Kowloon Bay
North Point
Quarry Bay
Junk Bay
Causeway Bay
Tai Hang
Sai Wan Ho
Shau Kei Wan
Happy Valley
HONG KONG ISLAND
Chai Wan
Siu Sai Wan
Wilson Trail
Tathong Channel
Deep Water Bay
Tai Tam Waterworks Heritage Trail
Deep Water Bay Beach
Tai Long Wan
Tai Tam
Dragon's Back
MIDDLE ISLAND
Repulse Bay
Repulse Bay Beach
Shek O
Repulse Bay
Shek O Beach
Tai Tam Bay
Stanley Main Beach
ROUND ISLAND
Stanley
Stanley Bay
Cape D'Aguilar
Sheung Sze Mun

of the Dragon Boat Races every June. For war buffs, Stanley Military Cemetery has graves of British and other Commonwealth soldiers who died during the Japanese occupation of Hong Kong in World War II. To get here from Exchange Square Bus Terminus in Central, take Bus 6, 6A, 66, or 260. ✉ *Southside.*

Tai Tam Waterworks Heritage Trail

TRAIL | One of Hong Kong's most unusual and rewarding hikes is this 5 km (3.1 mile) downhill ramble that reveals a side of the island most people never see. A series of beautifully preserved reservoirs, bridges, aqueducts, and dams, designed by British engineers during the early colonial era to provide clean drinking water to Hong Kong's rapidly expanding population, are surrounded by rolling hills and a whole lot of serenity. To reach the trailhead, take a taxi to Wong Nai Chung Gap, by the residences of Hong Kong Parkview, from where it's about a 1.6 km (1 mile) walk. ✉ *Tai Tam, Tai Tam Reservoir Rd., Southside* 🎫 *Free.*

Wilson Trail

TRAIL | The 78-km (48-mile) trail runs from Stanley Gap on the south end of Hong Kong Island, through rugged peaks that have a panoramic view of Repulse Bay and the nearby islands, and to Nam Chung in the northeastern New Territories. You have to cross the harbor by MTR at Quarry Bay to complete the entire walk. The trail is smoothed by steps paved with stone, and footbridges aid with steep sections and streams. Clearly marked with signs and information boards, this popular walk is divided into 10 sections, and you can easily take just one or two (figure on three to four hours per section); traversing the whole trail takes about 31 hours.

Section 1, which starts at Stanley Gap Road, is only for the very fit. Much of it requires walking up steep mountain grades. For an easier walk, try Section 7, which begins at Sing Mun Reservoir and takes you along a greenery-filled, fairly level path that winds past the eastern shore of the reservoir in the New Territories and then descends to Tai Po, where there's a sweeping view of Tolo Harbour. Other sections will take you through the monkey forest at the Kowloon Hill Fitness Trail, over mountains, and past charming villages. To reach Section 7, take the MTR to Tsuen Wan, then catch Minibus 82. Get off at the bus terminus and walk for 15 minutes toward the main eastern dam. Turn left where the dam ends and you'll find the start of the trail. ✉ *Stanley Gap Rd., Southside* 🎫 *Free.*

Beaches

Deep Water Bay

BEACH | Just east of Ocean Park is this lovely beach that sees fewer crowds than Repulse Bay, though weekends can get a bit more crowded. It's a good place to have a barbecue or swim under the watchful eye of a lifeguard. Leafy trees provide ample shade, and there's a great view of the Ocean Park cable car. To get here, take Bus 6, 6A, or 260 from Exchange Square Bus Terminus in Central. **Amenities:** food and drink; lifeguards; showers; toilets; water sports. **Best for:** sunset; swimming; walking. ✉ *Southside* ☎ *2812–0228.*

Repulse Bay

BEACH | **FAMILY** | The beach in this upscale neighborhood is large and wide, and can get very crowded on summer weekends. Two huge statues, of the goddesses Tin Hau and Kwun Yam, stand at the east end of the beach, part of a kitsch collection of shrines and statues built in the 1970s. Look for a famous apartment building with a hole through it—following the principles of feng shui, the opening allows the dragon that lives in the mountains behind to readily drink from the bay. To get here, take Bus 6, 6A, or 260 from Exchange Square Bus Terminus in Central. **Amenities:** food and drink; lifeguards; showers; toilets; water sports. **Best for:** sunset; swimming; walking. ✉ *Beach Rd.*

at Seaview Promenade, Repulse Bay, Southside ☎ *2812–2483.*

Restaurants

The south side of Hong Kong Island is a string of beaches, rocky coves, and luxury developments. The Repulse Bay complex has some good restaurants, most of which boast alfresco seating so diners can take full advantage of the sea breeze. Stanley Village has a row of restaurants and pubs squeezed between the sea and its famous market. Also on Southside, Shek O is a tiny seaside village with a few decent open-air restaurants that skew toward Southeast Asian flavors.

Cococabana

$$$ | **MEDITERRANEAN** | With a prime spot right on the golden sand of Shek O Beach, this sunny terrace restaurant dishes up Mediterranean seafood classics like *bouillabaisse* (traditional Provençal fish soup), steamed mussels, and salad niçoise, alongside well-charred Neapolitan pizzas and pasta. With its charming maritime-theme interior and a smattering of outdoor tables, it's a lovely spot to simply relax with a drink and listen to the rolling waves. **Known for:** beach umbrellas and loungers ($150 per day for two people); only restaurant on Shek O Beach itself; warm, laid-back service. *Average main: HK$280* ✉ *Shek O Beach, Shek O Rd., Southside* ☎ *2812–2226* *www.toptables.com.hk/cococabana.*

The Verandah

$$$$ | **EUROPEAN** | From the well-spaced tables overlooking the bay to the unobtrusive service to the menu of delicious French-inspired classics, this is an unabashedly regal experience that delivers with finesse at every turn. The beautiful colonial setting pays homage to the former Repulse Bay Hotel, and is also the perfect place to enjoy a traditional English afternoon tea. **Known for:** a reasonably priced wine list; views of Repulse Bay; classic European cuisine. *Average main: HK$600* ✉ *The Repulse Bay, 109 Repulse Bay Rd., Repulse Bay, Southside* ☎ *2292–2822* *www.therepulsebay.com* *Closed Mon. and Tues.*

Coffee and Quick Bites

Classified, Repulse Bay

$$ | **INTERNATIONAL** | The nicest spot for a drink or casual meal at Repulse Bay, Classified has two highly coveted swing sofas hanging from its open frontage, which offer glorious beach and sea views. The brunch-centric menu riffs around bacon and eggs, avocado on toast, and eggs Benedict, along with smoothies, fresh juice, and freshly brewed coffee—or you can go for healthy salads, pasta, and tartines at lunch or dinner. **Known for:** unbeatable beach views; delicious smoothies; occasionally slow service. *Average main: HK$175* ✉ *The Pulse, Shop 107, 28 Beach Rd., Repulse Bay, Southside* ☎ *2351–3454* *www.classifiedfood.com.*

Hotels

Being largely residential and far removed from the touristy northern coast of Hong Kong Island, Southside has relatively few recommendable lodgings. That said, prices in Southside are considerably lower than elsewhere, taxis are a cinch thanks to Uber, and you're more likely to enjoy unimpeded sea views. For travelers who prize space, value for money, and quiet, the area might be an option worth considering.

Le Méridien Hong Kong, Cyberport

$$ | **HOTEL** | Located in a business and technology hub, this mid-century styled, pet-friendly lifestyle hotel on the island's quieter southern shore might be an option if you fancy staying far from the crowds and you don't mind taking taxis to get around. **Pros:** vast sunset views over bay and sea; multiple restaurants; outdoor pool and fitness center. **Cons:** isolated location on south side of island;

Did You Know?

Once a thriving fishing village, Shek O is known for its lush scenery and beautiful beaches, which serve as frequent backdrops to Cantopop music videos.

no MTR so you're relying on taxis and buses; little to see or do in the immediate area. *Rooms from: HK$1,350* *100 Cyberport Rd., Pok Fu Lam, Southside* *2980–7788* *le-meridien.marriott.com* *170 rooms* *No Meals* *Pok Fu Lam.*

Southside by Ovolo

$ | **HOTEL** | Converted from a warehouse, this design-savvy hotel mixes bold urban artwork, mood lighting, and friendly common spaces for a very cool industrial-chic result, working hard to account for its gritty location in an industrial area beside a traffic overpass. **Pros:** floor-to-ceiling windows; fun social areas; 24-hour gym. **Cons:** small entry-level rooms; design not for everyone; far from the bright lights of Central. *Rooms from: HK$935* *64 Wong Chuk Hang Rd., Aberdeen, Southside* *3460–8100* *www.marriott.com* *162 rooms* *Free Breakfast.*

The T Hotel

$ | **HOTEL** | Overlooking the quiet west coast of Hong Kong Island, this unusual hotel has a devoted following of returning guests who appreciate the service, comfort, and value it offers, on account of it being a part of a vocational training school for hospitality professionals. **Pros:** great rooms and facilities for the price; stunning sea views; warm, enthusiastic service. **Cons:** far from Hong Kong's sights, dining, and nightlife; no MTR station nearby; 30 minutes by bus to Central. *Rooms from: HK$980* *VTC Pokfulam Complex, 6th fl., 145 Pok Fu Lam Rd., Southside* *3717–7388* *www.thotel.edu.hk* *30 rooms* *No Meals.*

Shopping

The eponymous market in Stanley Village is the main reason shoppers might stray south. Trawling its bazaar-like lanes for clothes, toys, souvenirs, and homewares is a fun way to pass the time between sea-swimming and drinking cold beer in a Stanley pub. Other Southside shopping spots include Horizon Plaza, a vast furniture and fashion warehouse on the islet of Ap Lei Chau, and Wong Chuk Hang, with its scattered selection of art and design stores in the area's old warehouses.

ANTIQUES AND COLLECTIBLES

Manks Ltd.

ANTIQUES & COLLECTIBLES | Established by London-born antiques dealer Susan Man, this spot in the Wong Chuk Hang industrial district stocks 20th-century decorative arts, European antiques, and Scandinavian furniture. *Heung Wah Industrial Bldg., The Factory, 18th fl., 46 Heung Yip Rd., Wong Chuk Hang, Southside* *2522–2115* *www.manks.com.*

MALLS AND SHOPPING CENTERS

Horizon Plaza

OUTLET | With multiple floors of high-end fashion and housewares, though skewing more to the latter, the huge Horizon Plaza is an outlet mall for local and international designer brands. *2 Lee Wing St., Ap Lei Chau, Southside* *2554–9089.*

MARKETS

★ **Stanley Market**

MARKET | Set back from the waterfront at Stanley Village, this covered market has the look and vibe of a middle-eastern bazaar. You can pick up some good buys in sportswear, casual clothing, textiles, and paintings if you comb through the stalls, which line a main street so narrow that awnings from each side meet in the middle. One of the best things about Stanley Market is getting here: the winding bus ride from Central takes you over the top of Hong Kong Island, with fabulous views along on the way. *Stanley, Southside* *www.hk-stanley-market.com.*

Chapter 4

WAN CHAI, CAUSEWAY BAY, AND EASTERN

Updated by
Audrey Phoon

NEIGHBORHOOD SNAPSHOT

TOP REASONS TO GO

- **Have a tipple:** Wan Chai is perhaps most famous for its world-class nightlife. Whether you're looking for a rooftop bar, a live-music speakeasy, or a buzzy pub, you'll find it here.
- **Visit historical landmarks:** Some of Hong Kong's most famous buildings are clustered in this district, like the beautifully preserved Blue House and the ornate Pak Tai Temple.
- **Experience the arts:** The Hong Kong Arts Centre, Hong Kong Academy for Performing Arts, and Comix Home Base are great spots to discover local up-and-coming talent.
- **Snap the perfect Victoria Harbour photo:** Wan Chai's harborfront is one of the best places to take in views of Victoria Harbour and the city skyline.
- **Go high-low shopping:** From designer outfits to cheap home decor items and local produce, the area surrounding Lee Tung Avenue and Wan Chai Market has it all.

MAKING THE MOST OF YOUR TIME

Wan Chai's trams run mostly along Hennessy Road, with a detour along Johnston Road at the neighborhood's western end. Queen's Road East runs parallel to these two streets to the south, and a maze of lanes connects it with Hennessy. The thoroughfares north of Hennessy are laid out in a grid. Causeway Bay's diagonal roads make the neighborhood hard to navigate, but it's small; wander around and before long you'll hit something familiar.

Rattle to Wan Chai by tram along roads dense with signs. Get off at Southorn Playground, and wander the lanes south of Johnston Road before heading up Luard Road and over walkways to the Hong Kong Academy for Performing Arts and Hong Kong Arts Centre, in adjacent buildings. The Hong Kong Convention and Exhibition Centre is a few minutes away—wander its harborside promenade. If you're here at dusk, Wan Chai's drinking holes will be lighting up as you walk back to the MTR along Fleming Road.

GETTING HERE

- Both Wan Chai and Causeway Bay have their own MTR stops, but a pleasant way to arrive from Central is on the tram along Hennessy Road. If you're going beyond Wan Chai, check the sign at the front: some continue to North Point and Shau Kei Wan, via Causeway Bay, while others go south to Happy Valley.
- The underground MTR stations are small labyrinths, so read the signs carefully to find the best exit. Traffic begins to take its toll on journey times to places beyond Causeway Bay, and the MTR is often the quickest way to travel.

Explore beyond Western and Central and you'll discover that Wan Chai, Causeway Bay, Happy Valley, and the fast-gentrifying neighborhoods of the Eastern District are equally as vibrant—revealing another facet of Hong Kong. While Wan Chai—the neighborhood made famous in *The World of Suzie Wong*—is still remembered for its nightlife (think raunchy entertainment and rowdy expats), it's now better known for its rich food and beverage scene and creative local businesses.

It's also home to the Convention Centre, beautiful colonial buildings, and a handful of arts institutions. Causeway Bay, one of the territory's liveliest areas, is a shopping and dining destination, and the Happy Valley horse races, a big part of Hong Kong life, are just a short walk away. Just east of Causeway Bay, the formerly residential and industrial Eastern District is blossoming into an arts hub, with plenty of chic cafés and restaurants taking root here, too.

Wan Chai

All in all, Hong Kong's notorious center of lowlife is fairly tame these days, with a bustling mix of hotels, shops, and convention facilities. The area's reformation is best observed from Starstreet Precinct, where cool fashion boutiques and perfumeries jostle with trendy cafés and independent art galleries. But this doesn't mean the old neighborhood has lost all its character. A few streets back from Wan Chai's new office blocks are crowded alleys where you can still experience old Hong Kong and stumble across a wet market, a tiny furniture-maker's shop, an age-old temple, and yes, some of the remaining strip joints, dive bars, and gambling dens that have long made the quarter popular with denizens of the night.

Sights

Lively Wan Chai is home to several historic cultural and religious monuments as well as some of the territory's newer landmarks—a range that reflects Hong Kong's dynamic evolution. If you can, the best way to move around is on foot

A
B
C
D
E
F
1
2
3
4
5
6
7
8
9
KEY
Sights
Restaurants
Quick Bites
Hotels
Victoria Harbor
Central and Western District Promenade
Expo Drive
Expo Drive Central
Expo Dr. East
Wan Chai Promenade
Central Wan Chai Bypass
Lung Wo Road
Hung Hing Road
Convention Avenue
Lung Hop St.
Fenwick Pier St.
Tim Mei Ave.
Exhibition Centre
Tonnochy Road
Marsh Road
Harbour Road
Fleming Road
Harcourt Road
Harbour Drive
Gloucester Road
Admiralty
Jaffe Road
Arsenal Street
Fenwick Street
Lockhart Road
Stewart Road
Queensway
TRAM
Luard Road
Hennessy Road
Wan Chai
Morrison Hill Road
Heard
Wan Chai Rd.
Anton
Landale
Johnston Road
Queen's Road East
WAN CHAI
Thomson Road
Oi Kwan Rd.
Gresson
Lun Fat
Ship St.
Star Street
Cross Ln.
Tai Yuen Street
Lee Tung Ave.
Wan Chai Park
Kennedy Road
Bowen Road
Wan Chai Gap Road
Shiu Fai Terrace
Stubbs Road
Peak Road
Lover's Stone Garden
Bowen Road Park
Aberdeen Tunnel

Wan Chai

Sights

1 Blue House D7
2 Central Plaza D5
3 Comix Home Base E6
4 Hong Kong Arts Centre C5
5 Hong Kong Convention and Exhibition Centre D4
6 Johnston Road D6
7 Lovers' Rock E9
8 Wan Chai Pak Tai Temple D8

Restaurants

1 Bengal Brothers B6
2 DiVino Patio E5
3 Dynasty Restaurant D4
4 Han Ga Ram C7
5 Hee Kee Fried Crab Expert F5
6 La Crêperie B6
7 Liu Yuan Pavilion C6
8 Megan's Kitchen E6
9 One Harbour Road C4
10 Sang Kee F5
11 Ta Pantry B7
12 Trattoria Felino C6
13 Tung Po Kitchen F5
14 Yixin Restaurant C6

Quick Bites

1 Capital Café E6
2 Cheung Fun Wong E6
3 Kam Fung C7

Hotels

1 Aki Hong Kong - MGallery E5
2 Dorsett Wanchai F7
3 Grand Hyatt Hong Kong C4
4 The Harbourview C5
5 The Hari Hong Kong F5
6 Hotel Indigo Hong Kong Island, an IHG Hotel D7
7 Mira Moon Hong Kong F5
8 Novotel Century Hong Kong E5
9 Renaissance Harbour View Hotel Hong Kong D4
10 The St. Regis Hong Kong D5

The Blue House is one of the few remaining examples of tenement housing built with wide balconies.

as most sights are within easy walking distance of each other.

Blue House

HISTORIC SIGHT | A rare example of Lingnan-style architecture, this historic 1920s tenement painted an eye-catching cobalt blue once housed a clinic and martial arts school. Now a community hub and museum, it offers a glimpse into old Hong Kong. Nearby are other similar houses in bright orange and yellow. ✉ *72, 72A, 74, and 74A Stone Nullah La., Wan Chai* ☎ *2833–4608* 🌐 *vivabluehouse.hk/en* Ⓜ *Wan Chai, Exit A3.*

Central Plaza

NOTABLE BUILDING | Clad in reflective gold, silver, and copper-colored glass, this glitzy triangular building was built in 1992, at the height of Hong Kong's success. At the time it was briefly the territory's tallest building, but Two IFC soon beat it by 130 feet and, later, ICC by 360 feet. Note the colorful fluorescent lights atop the building; they actually are a clock that indicates time by changing colors every 15 minutes. ✉ *18 Harbour Rd., Wan Chai* ☎ *2586–8111* 🌐 *www.centralplaza.com.hk.*

Comix Home Base

ARTS CENTER | Devoted to the creative and quirky world of comics and animation, this center celebrates local artists by offering up ample space to create, exhibit, and sell their work. The complex is also a great example of Hong Kong's historic East-meets-West architecture, as it's housed in a cluster of revitalized prewar tenement-style buildings with cantilevered balconies, high ceilings, and staircases made of China fir wood. ✉ *7 Mallory St., Wan Chai* ☎ *2824–5303* 🌐 *www.comixhomebase.com.hk.*

Hong Kong Arts Centre

ARTS CENTER | The 19-story Hong Kong Arts Centre houses a branch of the Hong Kong Art School, several contemporary art galleries, interactive workshops, multimedia installations, art studios, a cinema, and performing arts venues. There are also a handful of eateries. It has been a longtime champion of up-and-coming artists and diverse genres, and also operates the comic and animation hub Comix Home Base, on nearby Mallory Street. There are free guided tours every Wednesday and Saturday at 3 pm, lasting about 45 minutes. ✉ *2 Harbour Rd., Wan Chai* ☎ *2582–0200* 🌐 *www.hkac.org.hk* 🎫 *Free* Ⓜ *Wan Chai, Exit C.*

Hong Kong Convention and Exhibition Centre

CONVENTION CENTER | Land is so scarce in Hong Kong that developers usually only build skyward, but the HKCEC juts into the harbor instead. Curved-glass walls and a swooping roof make it look like a tortoise lumbering into the sea or a gull taking flight, depending on who you ask. Of all the international trade fairs, regional conferences, and other events held here, by far the most famous was the 1997 Handover Ceremony. An obelisk commemorates it on the waterfront promenade, which also affords great views of Kowloon.

Outside the center stands the *Golden Bauhinia*. This gleaming sculpture of the bauhinia flower, Hong Kong's symbol, was a gift from China. The police hoist the flag daily at 8 am; on the first of every month, there is an enhanced flag-raising ceremony with musical accompaniment by police bands. ✉ *1 Expo Dr., Wan Chai* ☎ *2582–8888* 🌐 *www.hkcec.com* Ⓜ *Wan Chai, Exit A.*

Johnston Road

STREET | Trams clatter along this busy road, which is choked with traffic day and night. It's also packed with shops selling food, cell phones, herbal tonics, and bargain-basement clothes. Rattan furniture, picture frames, paper lanterns, and Chinese calligraphic materials make up the more traditional assortment at Queen's Road East, which runs parallel to Johnston Road. The lanes that stretch between the two roads are also lined with stalls, forming a minimarket of clothing and accessories. ✉ *Johnston Rd., between Heard and Gresson Sts., Wan Chai* Ⓜ *Wan Chai, Exit A3.*

Did You Know?

Wan Chai was once one of the five *wan*—areas the British set aside for Chinese residences—but it developed a reputation for vice and attracted sailors on shore leave during the Vietnam War. How times have changed: Wan Chai is still as risqué an area as Hong Kong has to offer, but that says more about the territory's overall respectability than it does about the available indulgences. Today many venture to the area for arts and culture at the Hong Kong Academy for Performing Arts and the Hong Kong Arts Centre, or to shop at the many stylish boutiques that dot the newly gentrified neighborhood.

Lovers' Rock

PUBLIC ART | High above Wan Chai sits the suggestively shaped monolith known as Lovers' Rock, or Yan Yuen Shek. It's often visited by local single women, who burn joss sticks and make offerings in hope of finding a husband. Not in the market? The walk along Bowen Road offers excellent views over the city, particularly at dusk. The easiest way up is on Minibus 24A from the Admiralty MTR station. ✉ *Bowen Rd., between Wan Chai Gap and Stubbs Rds., Wan Chai.*

Wan Chai Pak Tai Temple

TEMPLE | Pak Tai Temple in Wan Chai (not to be confused with Pak Tai Temple in Cheung Chau) is the largest temple on Hong Kong Island and a reminder of Wan Chai's early development. Built in 1863 by the local community, the Taoist shrine honors Pak Tai, the Supreme Emperor of the Dark Heaven. Its colorful, intricate carvings, imposing statues of deities, and handcrafted ceramics roof make it well worth a visit. Conveniently, the temple is located close to other attractions like Blue House and

Bright lanterns hang from the Pak Tai Temple in Wan Chai.

Wan Chai Market. ✉ *2 Lung On St., Wan Chai* Ⓜ *Wan Chai, Exit A3.*

Restaurants

The range of dining options in Wan Chai is extreme—from five-star luxury to noodle-shop dives open into the wee hours.

Bengal Brothers

$$$ | **INDIAN** | The effervescent Tanvir Bhasin and Vidur Yadav (who aren't actually brothers but friends who met in New York) run this wildly popular modern Indian canteen, which serves up street-style bites that are as lively they are. Think tasty kathi rolls wrapped in Indian flatbreads, and fries showered in a house-made spice mix. **Known for:** elevated versions of Indian street food; colorful, funky interiors; wide-ranging alcohol menu. $ *Average main: HK$300* ✉ *6 Johnston Rd., Wan Chai* ☎ *9245–8774* 🌐 *www.bengal-brothers.com* Ⓜ *Wan Chai.*

DiVino Patio

$$$ | **ITALIAN** | Located along a stretch of semi-alfresco eateries known as Brim 28 (named after its waterside location on 28 Harbour Road), DiVino Patio touts rustic, homestyle Italian fare to match its laid-back surroundings. The expansive space is designed like a retro grocery store, and you can purchase gourmet condiments, salumi, and cheeses to enjoy on the go. **Known for:** Italian comfort food; alfresco dining on the patio; value-for-money lunch sets. $ *Average main: HK$230* ✉ *Causeway Centre, 28 Harbour Rd., Wan Chai* ☎ *2877–3552* 🌐 *www.divinogroup.com* Ⓜ *Wan Chai.*

Dynasty Restaurant

$$$ | **CHINESE** | Dining on haute Cantonese cuisine at this stunning restaurant with panoramic views over Victoria Harbour is a memorable experience. The chefs here are famed for adapting family-style recipes into elegant dishes, and the service is impeccable yet friendly. **Known for:** seasonal Cantonese menu heavy on seafood; Victoria Harbour views; one of the

best versions of char siu in Hong Kong. $ *Average main: HK$340* ✉ *Renaissance Harbour View Hotel, 3rd fl., 1 Harbour Rd., Wan Chai* ☎ *2584–6971* Ⓜ *Wan Chai.*

Han Ga Ram

$$$ | **KOREAN** | Come here for a refined, modern rendition of quintessential Korean cuisine. Barbecued meats are a must, and we especially recommend the *sam gyup sal* (thick slabs of pork belly). **Known for:** a more sophisticated experience than your typical Korean barbecue restaurant; reliably tasty Korean classics and innovative creations; warm and friendly service. $ *Average main: HK$250* ✉ *QRE Plaza, 27th fl., 202 Queen's Rd., Wan Chai* ☎ *2891–5090* Ⓜ *Wan Chai.*

Hee Kee Fried Crab Expert

$$$ | **CANTONESE** | Hee Kee's claim doesn't ring hollow—it's indeed one of Hong Kong's culinary crab experts. Order the spicy chili crab with garlic and the fried rice, and you're all set for a tasty feast. **Known for:** great typhoon shelter cuisine; loud and local atmosphere; live seafood kept in tanks. $ *Average main: HK$500* ✉ *Ground fl., Shop 1–4, 379 Jaffe Rd., Wan Chai* ☎ *2893–7565* Ⓜ *Causeway Bay, Exit C.*

La Crêperie

$$ | **FRENCH** | This French-owned spot specializes in thin Breton crepes filled with all sorts of sweet or savory fillings. Most of the clientele is French, which is a good indication of the authenticity of the food. **Known for:** Hong Kong's most authentic French crepes; affordable set menus at lunch and tea time; rustic Breton-inspired interiors. $ *Average main: HK$100* ✉ *100 Queen's Rd. E, 1st fl., Wan Chai* ☎ *2529–9280* 🌐 *www.lacreperie.com.cn* ⏲ *Closed Mon.* Ⓜ *Wan Chai.*

★ Liu Yuan Pavilion

$$ | **CHINESE** | **FAMILY** | Often regarded as one of the best Shanghainese restaurants in town, Liu Yuan's cooking style stays loyal to tradition with a no-fuss mentality that has worked in their favor for years. Easy favorites include sweet strips of crunchy eel, pan-fried meat buns, and steamed *xiao long bao* dumplings plumped up with minced pork and broth. **Known for:** being favored by Hong Kong's Shanghainese community; elegant interiors with comfortable booths; hard-to-get reservations. $ *Average main: HK$120* ✉ *The Broadway, 3rd fl., 54–62 Lockhart Rd., Wan Chai* ☎ *2804–2000* Ⓜ *Wan Chai.*

Megan's Kitchen

$$$ | **CANTONESE** | Among Hong Kong's hundreds of hot pot restaurants, Megan's Kitchen stands out for its innovative soup bases that include tom yum cappuccino and Japanese miso tofu broths, as well as its handmade treats like kimchi dumplings and rainbow-hued cuttlefish balls. The corporate-looking decor is nothing to shout about, but the excellent service and lively vibe keep fans coming back. **Known for:** unique soup flavors; impressive selection of beef from around the world; complimentary rice and dessert. $ *Average main: HK$350* ✉ *Lucky Centre, 5th fl., 165–171 Wan Chai Rd., Wan Chai* ☎ *2866–8305* 🌐 *meganskitchen.com* Ⓜ *Wan Chai.*

One Harbour Road

$$$ | **CHINESE** | It's hard to say what's more impressive at the Grand Hyatt's Cantonese showpiece—the interior design (two terraced levels boasting an incredible sense of space and motion), or the view over the harbor from the floor-to-ceiling windows. Unlike many harborside establishments, though, you don't need a window seat to catch the view. **Known for:** scenic Victoria Harbour views from almost every table; creative and unusual alcohol pairings with signature barbecued meat and seafood; top-notch food and service in an elegant but unpretentious environment. $ *Average main: HK$360* ✉ *Grand Hyatt Hong Kong, 7th and 8th fl., 1 Harbour Rd., Wan Chai* ☎ *2584–7722* 🌐 *www.hongkong.grand.hyattrestaurants.com* Ⓜ *Wan Chai.*

Sang Kee

$$$$ | **CANTONESE** | A Wan Chai institution, this old faithful spot has churned out Cantonese classics like its signature salt-baked chicken since 1976. It started off as a dai pai dong—street-food stall—but moved into a shop space in the 1980s when the government began closing these stalls to make way for the MTR. **Known for:** excellent salt-baked chicken; reliably tasty dim sum at lunchtime; easy-to-get tables. *Average main: HK$1,000 Sunshine Plaza, 3rd–4th fl., 353 Lockhart Rd., Wan Chai 2575–2239 www.sangkee.com.hk Causeway Bay.*

Ta Pantry

$$ | **ECLECTIC** | What started out as a one-table private kitchen in a quiet Wan Chai neighborhood has blossomed into a larger location in the Starstreet Precinct due to popular demand. Decked out like a stylish Parisian apartment, the newer space accommodates 20 guests, and there are different menus from which to choose, ranging from Japanese-inspired meals to Shanghai-style dinner. **Known for:** private, homey atmosphere that's perfect for small group celebrations; innovative cooking like foie gras dumplings from a chef who used to work at Michelin-starred restaurants; free corkage. *Average main: HK$200 Hang Tak Bldg., Underground fl., Shop B, 1 Electric St., Wan Chai 2521–8121 www.ta-pantry.com Closed Sun. Wan Chai.*

Trattoria Felino

$$$ | **ITALIAN** | Run by a chef from Naples, this casual, slightly cramped space has earned a reputation for authentic, well-priced Italian fare. Think honest, hearty plates of pasta and tender stews. **Known for:** affordable prices; being booked out weeks in advance; somewhat rushed service. *Average main: HK$350 Pao Yip Bldg., Ground fl., Shop 3 and 4, 1–7 Ship St., Wan Chai 5697–4477 www.trattoriafelino.com Closed Mon. Wan Chai, Exit B2.*

★ Tung Po Kitchen

$$ | **CANTONESE** | **FAMILY** | Dining at arguably Hong Kong's most famous indoor *dai pai dong* food stall is a riot, with owner Robby Cheung frequently coming out to hold singalong sessions and toast guests. The food is Hong Kong cuisine with fusion innovations, and you should wash everything down with a cold beer (served here in Chinese soup bowls). **Known for:** spaghetti with cuttlefish and fresh squid ink; seafood dishes and stir-fries; owner Robby Cheung, who's known to blast pop songs and moonwalk;. *Average main: HK$110 KONNECT, 2nd fl., 303 Jaffe Rd., Wan Chai 2880–5224, 2880–9399 No credit cards No lunch Causeway Bay, Exit C.*

Yixin Restaurant

$$$$ | **CANTONESE** | This family-run restaurant has been around for over 50 years and is now run by the daughter of the original chef. Except for a refresh of the interiors, little has changed in that time—the kitchen still serves up nostalgic dishes like minced pork and chive patties and braised pipa-style duck, and the dining room is filled with local families and corporate executives who've been going for years. **Known for:** some of the best char siu and lemon chicken in Hong Kong; old-school dim sum; exclusive private rooms and wine cellar in the basement. *Average main: HK$1,200 Shanghai Industrial Investment Bldg., Ground fl., Shop 2–4, 50 Hennessy Rd., Wan Chai 2365–2106 www.yixinrestaurant.com Wan Chai.*

Coffee and Quick Bites

Capital Café

$ | **CHINESE** | It's a blast from the past at this retro Hong Kong café, done up in period '70s decor, complete with autographed Cantopop idol posters from that era. The food is old-school as well, and you'll find hearty local specialties like elbow macaroni with barbecued pork, milk tea, and toasted sandwiches filled with fluffy scrambled eggs. **Known for:** pop star clientele; vintage Hong Kong–style interiors; wide range of cha chaan teng fare, including classics and more modern creations. *Average main: HK$35* *6 Heard St., Wan Chai* *2666–7766* *No credit cards.*

Cheung Fun Wong

$ | **CANTONESE** | You'll recognize this nondescript street stall from the others around it by the crowds in front, especially during lunchtime. The silky rice rolls drenched in a tasty peanut sauce draw Hong Kongers from across town. **Known for:** cheap, tasty meals; local vibes; standing room only. *Average main: HK$20* *Pao Woo Mansion, Ground fl., Shop D, 177–179 Wan Chai Rd., Wan Chai* *8202–7207* *No credit cards* *Closed Sun.* *Wan Chai, Exit A3.*

Kam Fung

$ | **BAKERY** | The space is dingy, the tables are cramped, and the staff is brash—but the food makes it all worth it. Kam Fung has been around for more than five decades, serving traditional Hong Kong café fare such as crumbly crusted freshly baked egg tarts, and pineapple buns wedged with a thick slab of butter. **Known for:** some of Hong Kong's best pineapple bolo buns and milk tea; long queues but fast turnovers; local vibes. *Average main: HK$25* *41 Spring Garden La., Wan Chai* *2572–0526* *No credit cards* *No dinner* *Wan Chai.*

Hotels

Hotels around the Hong Kong Convention and Exhibition Centre offer great views, although there isn't a lot happening in the area in the evenings. Staying in Wan Chai's heart, around Lockhart Road, is noisier but buzzier.

Aki Hong Kong – MGallery

$$ | **HOTEL** | A minimalist Japandi design hotel with light, bright rooms that come with lovely city or Victoria Harbour views, this hotel even has a few tatami rooms, a first for Hong Kong. **Pros:** rooms have lots of natural light; easy walk to many of Wan Chai's main attractions; warm and friendly service. **Cons:** in a very busy area; rooms are on the small side; no proper work desk or chair. *Rooms from: HK$1,200* *239 Jaffe Rd., Wan Chai* *2121–5000* *www.aki-hongkong-mgallery.com* *173 rooms* *No Meals* *Wan Chai.*

Dorsett Wanchai

$ | **HOTEL** | This comfortable, if older, hotel occupies a prime spot between Wan Chai and Causeway Bay opposite the popular Happy Valley Racecourse, yet its rates are surprisingly reasonable—perhaps because many rooms look onto Sai Wan War Cemetery, where more than 1,500 soldiers who died during World War II are buried. **Pros:** good value; family suites accommodate larger groups; self-service laundry. **Cons:** many rooms face the cemetery; tired decor; low-floor rooms susceptible to road noise. *Rooms from: HK$900* *387–397 Queen's Rd. E, Wan Chai* *3552–1111* *www.wanchai.dorsetthotels.com* *454 rooms* *No Meals* *Wan Chai.*

Favorite Places

Audrey Phoon: Even when I'm not in Hong Kong, I dream about the cheung fun (steamed rice rolls) at Cheung Fun Wong. This street stall is so unassuming and un-fancy it doesn't have a seating area, but the constant stream of locals swinging by marks it out as something special. Here, the rice rolls are so silky they melt in the mouth, and the magic sauce they're bathed in (a mix of peanut butter, chilli sauce and sesame sauce) is frighteningly addictive—a must-visit.

Grand Hyatt Hong Kong

$$$$ | **HOTEL** | **FAMILY** | A direct connection to the Hong Kong Convention and Exhibition Centre makes this a business-first hotel, but leisure travelers also enjoy the elegant rooms, with sweeping harbor views and luxurious touches such as an oversize square bathtub and mirror TV. **Pros:** delicious dining options; extensive sports facilities; Plateau spa is a beautiful sanctuary. **Cons:** quiet outside the hotel at night; hotel pool is packed on summer days; rooms are starting to look a little tired. *Rooms from: HK$3,300* *1 Harbour Rd., Wan Chai* *2588–1234* *www.hyatt.com/grand-hyatt* *542 rooms* *No Meals* *Wan Chai, Exit A1.*

The Harbourview

$$ | **HOTEL** | This waterfront property, run by a company affiliated with the Chinese YMCA of Hong Kong, has small but relatively inexpensive rooms near the Wan Chai Star Ferry pier. **Pros:** views of Victoria Harbour; free Wi-Fi; affordable rates for the location. **Cons:** rooms are a bit tired and dated; no free toiletries; no bottled water in room. *Rooms from: HK$1,250* *4 Harbour Rd., Wan Chai* *2802–0111* *www.theharbourview.com.hk* *320 rooms* *No Meals* *Wan Chai.*

★ The Hari Hong Kong

$$ | **HOTEL** | Owned by a family of art lovers and collectors, this elegant hotel brings understated chic to a street dominated by bathroom fittings stores. **Pros:** rooms have character and a sense of place; thoughtfully designed layouts; beautiful common spaces. **Cons:** many rooms are on the small side; lobby not on the ground floor; not many dining options in the immediate vicinity. *Rooms from: HK$1,600* *330 Lockhart Rd., Wan Chai* *2129–0388* *www.thehari.com/hong-kong* *210 rooms* *No Meals* *Wan Chai.*

Hotel Indigo Hong Kong Island, an IHG Hotel

$$$ | **HOTEL** | This standout boutique hotel has serious architectural chops—the exterior resembles a circling dragon—as well as photogenic interiors, where exquisitely designed guest rooms have dramatic floor-to-ceiling windows, colorful contemporary decor, and funky tiled-wall murals. **Pros:** eclectic neighborhood near nightlife and restaurants; panoramas from the higher floors; convenient location near MTR and major bus routes. **Cons:** pricey drinking and dining options; over-air-conditioned public spaces; tiny fitness center. *Rooms from: HK$2,000* *242–246 Queen's Rd. E, Wan Chai* *3926–3888* *www.ihg.com/hotelindigo* *138 rooms* *No Meals* *Wan Chai.*

Mira Moon Hong Kong

$$$ | **HOTEL** | If you get a little nostalgic for *Alice in Wonderland* at Mira Moon hotel, you're not totally off the mark: the hypermodern, abstract interiors are meant to depict the legend behind the Mid-Autumn moon festival—a fairy-tale-like Chinese legend revolving around the Moon Goddess of Immortality and a space-traveling jade rabbit. **Pros:** local flavor; free mobile Wi-Fi and minibar; neighborhood nightlife means lots of late-night eateries nearby. **Cons:** some rooms look into nearby apartments; cab desert; entry-level rooms on small side. *Rooms from: HK$2,100* *388 Jaffe Rd., Wan Chai* *2643–8888* *www.miramoonhotel.com* *89 rooms* *No Meals* *Causeway Bay, Exit B.*

Novotel Century Hong Kong

$$ | **HOTEL** | Decent harbor views from some rooms compensate for sparse furnishings and the lack of any personality, while the business center is handy for those with work to do. **Pros:** near the subway, Wan Chai bars and clubs, and Hong Kong Convention and Exhibition Centre; unaffiliated but delicious Shanghainese restaurant in the basement; 24-hour fitness center. **Cons:** dull rooms with small bathrooms; can get crowded with tour groups and during business conventions; interiors are showing their age. *Rooms from: HK$1,050* *238*

Jaffe Rd., Wan Chai ☎ 2598–8888 ⊕ www.novotelhongkongcentury.com ⇨ 509 rooms 🍽 No Meals Ⓜ Wan Chai.

Renaissance Harbour View Hotel Hong Kong
$$ | HOTEL | FAMILY | The modest guest rooms in this Hong Kong Convention and Exhibition Centre hotel are simply outfitted with attractive modern decor; although many have harbor views, some overlook a sprawling outdoor pool, a driving range, a jogging trail, and a playground that should help keep the kids busy. **Pros:** great harbor views; harborside recreational garden; spacious lobby for working or relaxing. **Cons:** lobby can be packed with corporate cats at lunchtime; quiet at night; slow elevators. *Ⓢ Rooms from: HK$1,350 ✉ 1 Harbour Rd., Wan Chai ☎ 2802–8888 ⊕ www.renaissance-harbourviewhk.com ⇨ 858 rooms 🍽 No Meals Ⓜ Wan Chai.*

The St. Regis Hong Kong
$$$$ | HOTEL | The most luxurious stay in Wan Chai, this André Fu–designed hotel features posh touches in each of its spacious rooms, from plush bathrobes and Frette bed linens to St. Regis–branded bottles of gin in the minibar. **Pros:** sophisticated dining options; 24-hour butler service; champagne served in The Drawing Room every evening. **Cons:** area is quiet in the evening; not all rooms have harbor views; inconsistent service standards. *Ⓢ Rooms from: HK$3,400 ✉ 1 Harbour Dr., Wan Chai ☎ 2138–6888 ⊕ www.marriott.com ⇨ 129 rooms 🍽 No Meals Ⓜ Exhibition Centre.*

Nightlife

Wan Chai is the pungent night flower of the nocturnal scene, where the way of life served as inspiration for the novel *The World of Suzie Wong*. It now shares the streets with hip wine bars, salsa sessions, and after parties that continue past sunrise. The seedy "hostess bars" in this neighborhood are easy to spot, with curtained entrances guarded by old ladies on stools and suggestive names in neon—though their numbers are quickly dwindling. But some things never change: the busiest nights are still when there's a navy ship in the harbor on an R&R stopover.

BARS

Mizunara: The Library
BARS | This sophisticated speakeasy is tucked away on the fourth floor of a commercial building. It specializes in whisky, with a collection that spans 700 bottles from Japan to Scotland, though cocktails meticulously made with hand-cut ice are available, too. A Zen garden that shades the bar from the surrounding buildings makes the place feel like an oasis amid the urban chaos. *✉ Kiu Yin Commercial Bldg., 4th fl., 361–363 Lockhart Rd., Wan Chai ☎ 3571–9797 ⊕ www.mizunarathelibrary.com Ⓜ Causeway Bay.*

The Stage
COCKTAIL BARS | In the heritage building where dinner-and-drinks institution The Pawn used to be, and under the umbrella of the new multiconcept space Sophia Loren Hong Kong, is this opulent 1970s-style cocktail bar. From Wednesday to Sunday, live entertainment performances ranging from jazz acts to drag shows take center stage. The outdoor terrace that faces busy Luard Road is a lovely place to take in the buzz of the streets. *✉ 2nd fl., 60–66 Johnston Rd., Wan Chai ☎ 3594–6302 ⊕ heritage1888.com/stage-bar Ⓜ Wan Chai.*

Tai Lung Fung
BARS | Stepping into this unpretentious retro bar feels like you're entering an old Wong Kar-wai movie, with its neon-lit signs, vintage cinema seats for chairs, and dingy-chic, graffiti'd walls. The drinks are just as rich in local character—order the homemade plum wine or the lemongrass martini for something unique. *✉ 5 Hing Wan St., Wan Chai ☎ 2572–0055 ⊕ tailungfungbar.com Ⓜ Wan Chai.*

The Wanch

LIVE MUSIC | The Wanch is a pillar of Hong Kong's live-music scene—from up-and-coming local acts to cover bands across music genres from folk to rock, it's supported them all over the years. The vibe is dive bar, but the operation is slick: the drinks and bar snacks are great, service is friendly and efficient, and prices are reasonable. Performances run all week, but the best time to go is on Friday and Saturday, when the place really begins buzzing. ✉ *Henan Bldg., 1st fl., 90 Jaffe Rd., Wan Chai* ☎ *3692–5933* Ⓜ *Wan Chai.*

DANCE CLUBS

Dusk Till Dawn

DANCE CLUB | Loud, energetic cover bands get the dance floor jumping on Wednesday to Saturday night. Popular with expats, it can get crowded, but patrons are usually having too much fun to care. ✉ *76–84 Jaffe Rd., Wan Chai* ☎ *2528–4689* Ⓜ *Wan Chai.*

Joe Bananas

LIVE MUSIC | Considered a Hong Kong landmark—at least, on the nightlife circuit—Joe Bananas is known for its live bands and handsome interiors. It tends to draw an after-hours crowd, since the doors stay open until 5 am almost every day of the week. During the day, this is also a popular spot to watch sports games and enjoy comfort foods with a cold beer. ✉ *23 Luard Rd., Wan Chai* ☎ *2537–4618* 🌐 *www.joebananas.hk* Ⓜ *Wan Chai.*

Shopping

No malls, no international chains—Wan Chai provides a change of pace when shopping in Central starts to feel a bit repetitive. Try out your Cantonese at the rock-bottom no-name clothing outlets on the lanes between Johnston Road and Queen's Road East, where everything from underwear to evening wear is available. On Johnston Road itself, shops selling bamboo birdcages and kung fu gear pay homage to Wan Chai's traditional side, in contrast to the stylish modern furniture stores and fashion boutiques that have mushroomed here. The small, meandering Starstreet Precinct behind Three Pacific Place is a great place to discover some of these new, independent local businesses. Rosewood furniture and camphor wood chests are two of the specialties of the mid-range furniture shops on Queen's Road East and Wan Chai Road, near Admiralty. The Suzy Wong stereotype lives on in the marine-filled tattoo parlors lining Lockhart Road. Techno-happy modern Hong Kong is alive and well at the Wan Chai Computer Centre, a collection of dozens of computing outlets on Hennessy Road.

ART

Kiang Malingue

ART GALLERY | It feels like a Brutalist museum, but this beautiful space is actually a commercial contemporary art gallery. Founders Edouard Malingue and Lorraine Kiang Malingue represent both established and emerging international artists across different disciplines, from video to sound and painting. Even if you're not looking to buy anything, the on-site exhibitions and talks are worth a visit. ✉ *10 Sik On St., Wan Chai* ☎ *2810–0317* 🌐 *kiangmalingue.com* Ⓜ *Wan Chai.*

CAMERAS AND ELECTRONICS

Wanchai Computer Centre

ELECTRONICS | You can find decent deals on computer goods and accessories in the labyrinth of shops spanning several floors. It's not as easy to negotiate prices here as it once was, but there are technicians who can help you put together a computer in less than a day if you're rushed; otherwise, two days is normal. The starting price is around HK$3,250 depending on the hardware, processor, and peripherals you choose. This is a great resource, whether you're a techno-buff who's interested in assembling your own computer (a popular pastime in Hong Kong) or a technophobe looking for high-quality headphones. ✉ *130 Hennessy Rd., Wan Chai* ☎ *2834–7685* Ⓜ *Wan Chai, Exit A5.*

CLOTHING

45R

CLOTHING | Around since 1978, Japanese brand 45R has garnered a reputation for ultracomfortable, exquisitely crafted jeans. Following the successes of outposts in Paris and New York, a flagship store opened on Star Street in 2008. Amid the minimalist surroundings, find heaps of its famous hand-dyed denim as well as breezy button-downs, wooly sweaters, and understated frocks. ✉ *Vincent Mansion, Ground fl., 7 Star St., Wan Chai* ☎ *2861–1145* 🌐 *45rglobal.com* Ⓜ *Wan Chai.*

kapok

DESIGN | Hip utilitarian bags, soft fabrics, minimalist watches, comfy kicks, music, stationery—kapok is a one-stop shop for lifestyle products and accessories from independent brands. Meanwhile, the boutique's café serves up steamy French coffee that you're welcome to sip while browsing. If you're lucky, you'll catch one of the store's many exhibitions and pop-up collaborations. ✉ *8 Sun St., Wan Chai* ☎ *2549–9254* 🌐 *www.ka-pok.com* Ⓜ *Admiralty.*

Vivienne Tam

CLOTHING | Hong Kong–bred, New York–based designer Vivienne Tam is known for her colorful modern Chinese designs, like denim jackets styled after kung fu tops and T-shirts that resemble cheongsam blouses. This boutique (she has several across Hong Kong, China, and Macau) is unique because it's in the middle of Lee Tung Avenue, a photo-worthy redeveloped pedestrian street that was formerly home to wedding-card printing businesses but is now packed with shops and cafés. ✉ *Shop G17, 200 Queen's Rd. E, Wan Chai* ☎ *2265–8808* 🌐 *www.viviennetam.com* Ⓜ *Wan Chai.*

HOME DÉCOR

Lala Curio

HOME DECOR | Laura Cheung's grandfather spent a lifetime hand-carving rosewood tables, and her father helmed a wildly successful ceramic manufacturing company, so it's only natural that she carry on the tradition with Lala Curio, an eclectic home-ware store in the heart of Wan Chai. Cheung's collections tip a hat to ancient Chinese craftsmanship, albeit with a whimsical modern spin; offerings range from pretty lacquer boxes to mosaic-tiled trays and bespoke upholstery. ✉ *333 Lockhart Rd., Wan Chai* ☎ *2295–6263* 🌐 *www.lalacurio.com* Ⓜ *Wan Chai.*

OVO

FURNITURE | This atmospheric, high-ceiling showroom feels like a cross between a shop and an art gallery. Designed by an in-house team, the home furnishings and accessories here are smart and rarely fussy. Beautiful, unvarnished blocks of wood, for example, are proposed as side tables. The store also carries a more European mix of in-house and international contemporary designs from brands like Tom Dixon, Fritz Hansen, and Andreu World. ✉ *1 Wan Chai Rd., Wan Chai* ☎ *2527–6088* 🌐 *www.ovo.com.hk* Ⓜ *Wan Chai.*

JEWELRY AND ACCESSORIES

Wing On Jewelry Ltd.

JEWELRY & WATCHES | There's a nostalgic charm to the butterflies, birds, and natural forms fashioned from jade, pearls, precious stones, and gold here. Everything looks like an heirloom inherited from your grandmother. With on-site gemologists and artisans, and a commitment to post-sale service, this store has a long list of repeat customers. If, however, you lean toward Scandinavian aesthetics and clean lines, this probably isn't the place for you. Wing On Jewelry also has a Causeway Bay branch at 459 Hennessy Road. ✉ *146 Johnston Rd., Wan Chai* ☎ *2572–2332* 🌐 *www.wingon-jewelry.com.hk* Ⓜ *Wan Chai.*

Hope that luck will be a lady and stick with you at Happy Valley Racecourse.

SPECIALTY STORES

Monocle

SPECIALTY STORE | As if running a magazine, website, and radio station weren't enough, Monocle also has a handful of retail outlets, and Hong Kong devotees of the London-based media brand rejoiced when its store-cum-office opened on Star Street's St. Francis Yard in 2010. Whether shopping for excellent reading material or stylish accessories (picture trendy totes, linen-bound notebooks, greeting cards, and embossed card cases), you'll be in good company. ✉ *Bo Fung Mansion, Shop 1, 1–4 St. Francis Yard, Wan Chai* ☎ *2804–2323* 🌐 *www.monocle.com* Ⓜ *Wan Chai, Exit A3.*

TOYS

Tai Yuen Street Market

TOYS | More popularly known as Toy Street, this lively market is a fun stroll for both kids and adult toy collectors. Vintage collectibles and modern playthings line the stalls from floor to ceiling, so prepare to dig around a bit for what you want. It's also a great spot to buy local produce like dried seafood and festive decorative items. ✉ *Tai Yuen St., Wan Chai* Ⓜ *Wan Chai.*

Causeway Bay

Shoppers crowd the streets of Causeway Bay, the area east of Wan Chai, seven days a week. The action happens within a five-block radius of the intersection of Hennessy Road and Percival Street, where you'll find pockets of maze-like malls full of clothing, jewelry, and gadgets. There are also lots of restaurants in the area, as well as upstairs cafés (inside commercial and residential buildings) that are often populated by teens and twenty-somethings. The more recently developed area to the east of the intersection, around Yun Ping Road and Hysan Avenue, offers a more sophisticated selection of shops, with the nearby Lee Garden malls popular with celebrities and wealthy residents of the neighborhood.

Sights

Beyond its glitzy malls and bustling streets, Causeway Bay offers a surprising mix of historical and cultural landmarks. Hidden among the high-rises, ornate traditional temples provide a glimpse into Hong Kong's spiritual heritage, with quiet courtyards offering respite from the crowds. Colonial-era relics stand as reminders of the past, while the legendary Happy Valley Racecourse continues to be a unique draw even for those who don't gamble.

Causeway Bay Typhoon Shelter

MARINA/PIER | Hong Kong's maritime past and present are much in evidence on Causeway Bay's waterfront. Beginning in 1883, those who lived on sampans and old-fashioned junks gathered during bad weather in the Causeway Bay Typhoon Shelter, the first of its kind in the territory. Most boat-dwellers have moved to dry land, so these days yachts and speedboats moor here. A few traditional sampans, crewed primarily by elderly women, still ferry owners to their sailboats. ✉ *Near entrance of Cross Harbour Tunnel, Causeway Bay* Ⓜ *Causeway Bay, Exit D1.*

★ Happy Valley Racecourse

SPORTS VENUE | The biggest attraction east of Causeway Bay for locals and visitors alike is this local legend, where millions of Hong Kong dollars make their way each year. The exhilarating blur of galloping hooves under jockeys dressed in bright silk jerseys is a must-see. The races make great Wednesday nights out on the town. Aside from the excitement of the races, there are restaurants, bars, and even a racing museum to keep you amused. The public entrance to the track is a 20-minute walk from Causeway Bay MTR Exit A (Times Square), or simply hop on the Happy Valley tram, which terminates right in front.

■ TIP→ Every Wednesday night during race season (September to mid-July), the first of about eight races kicks off at 7:15. ✉ *Sports Rd. at Wong Nai Chung Rd., Happy Valley, Causeway Bay* 🎫 *HK$10* Ⓜ *Causeway Bay, Exit A.*

Noonday Gun

HISTORIC SIGHT | A block east of the Royal Hong Kong Yacht Club stands the Noonday Gun, which Noël Coward made famous in his song *Mad Dogs and Englishmen*. It's still fired by a Jardine Matheson employee at noon every day. It is said that the tradition began when a Jardine employee fired a gun in salute of the company's head arriving at the port, angering an officer of the Royal Navy. ✉ *Victoria Park Rd., Causeway Bay* Ⓜ *Causeway Bay, Exit D1.*

Victoria Park

CITY PARK | Hong Kong Island's largest park is a welcome breathing space on the edge of Causeway Bay. It's beautifully landscaped and has recreational facilities for soccer, basketball, swimming, lawn bowling, and tennis. At dawn every morning hundreds practice tai chi chuan here. During the Mid-Autumn Festival it's home to the Lantern Carnival, when the trees are a mass of colorful lights. Just before Chinese New Year (late January to early February), the park hosts a huge flower market. On the eve of Lunar New Year, after a traditional family dinner at home, much of Hong Kong happily gathers here to shop and wander into the early hours of the first day of the new year. ✉ *1 Hing Fat St., Causeway Bay* ☎ *2890–5824* 🌐 *www.lcsd.gov.hk* 🎫 *Free* Ⓜ *Tin Hau, Exit A2.*

Restaurants

Causeway Bay is one of Hong Kong's busiest shopping districts and has some of the trendiest restaurants in town. It's popular with the younger crowd and is often compared with Tokyo's Shibuya district—and this is also where you'll find some of Hong Kong's best Japanese food, as well as many midprice eateries. The area behind the giant Sogo

KEY
Sights
Restaurants
Quick Bites
Hotels
Victoria Harbor
Cross-Harbour Tunnel
Wan Chai Promenade
Central Wan Chai Bypass
Expo Drive
Expo Drive Central
Expo Dr East
Convention Avenue
Hung Hing Road
Exhibition Centre
Fleming Road
Tonnochy Road
Marsh Road
Gloucester Rd.
CAUSEWAY BAY
Harbour Road
Harbour Drive
Jaffe Road
Lockhart Road
Causeway Bay
Gloucester Road
Hennessy Road
Stewart Road
Luard Road
Wan Chai
WAN CHAI
Thomson Road
TRAM
Johnston Road
Heard St.
Wan Chai Rd.
Cross Ln.
Morrison Hill Road
Oi Kwan Rd.
Canal Road West
Canal Road East
Russell Street
Yiu Wa St.
Matheson Street
Leighton Road
Percival Street
Lee Garden Road
Hysan Avenue
Tai Yuen Street
Lee Tung Ave.
Wan Chai Park
Queen's Road East
Wong Nai Chung Road
HAPPY VALLEY
Happy Valley Recreation Ground
Kennedy Road
Bowen Road
Stubbs Road
Shiu Fai Terrace
Wan Chai Gap Road
Lover's Stone Garden
Bowen Road Park
Aberdeen Tunnel
Ventris Road
Yik Yam St.
Shan Kwong Road

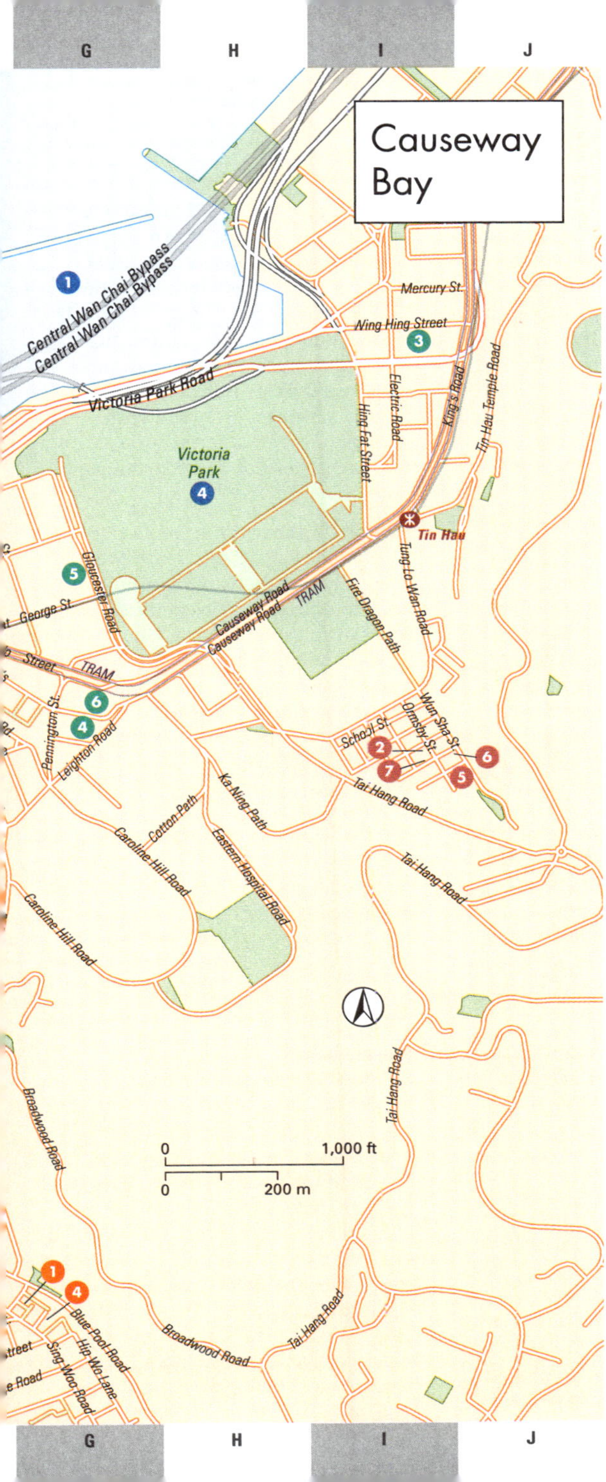

Causeway Bay

Sights

1 Causeway Bay Typhoon Shelter G2
2 Happy Valley Racecourse E8
3 Noonday Gun F3
4 Victoria Park H3

Restaurants

1 Hong Kong Cuisine 1983 ..... G9
2 Hotpot Instinct E4
3 Mother of Pizzas E6
4 Nan Tei G9
5 Pak Loh Chiu Chow Restaurant E5
6 Sushi Hiro F5
7 Tonkichi Tonkatsu Seafood F4
8 Under Bridge Spicy Crab D4

Quick Bites

1 agnès b. café E5
2 Bing Kee I5
3 Café Matchbox F4
4 Cheung Hing Coffee Shop F9
5 Chin Jor Fan Tong I5
6 Man Sing I5
7 Plumcot I5

Hotels

1 Cosmo Hotel D6
2 Crowne Plaza Hong Kong Causeway Bay E6
3 Empire Hotel Hong Kong, Causeway Bay I2
4 Lanson Place Causeway Bay, Hong Kong G5
5 The Park Lane Hong Kong, Autograph Collection G4
6 Regal Hongkong Hotel G5

Shark's Fin Soup

It makes sense that soup made from a shark's fin—said to be an aphrodisiac—costs so much. Only the promise of increased virility would lead someone to pay HK$1,000 or more for a bowl of the stuff. It actually consists of cartilage from the great beast's pectoral, dorsal, and lower tail fins that has been skinned, dried, and reconstituted in a rich stock form. This cartilage has almost no taste on its own, and is virtually indistinguishable from *tun fun* (cellophane) noodles that are used to create "mock shark's-fin soup."

Selling sharks' fins is a big business, and Hong Kong is said to be responsible for 50% of the global trade. The soup is a fixture at banquets, weddings, and state dinners here. Love potion, elixir, vitality booster, or not, at the very least the dish is high in protein. Recently, however, conservation groups have pointed out that it's also high in mercury. But of even greater concern is the practice of "finning." Since shark meat as a whole isn't valuable, fishermen often clip the fins and dump the rest of the animal back into the sea, and an increasing number of diners—especially the younger crowd—and restaurants are foregoing this dish for environmental reasons.

So, is eating shark's-fin soup a not-to-be-missed Hong Kong experience or a morally reprehensible act? Well, we don't need to take sides in the debate to warn you away from it. Let us repeat: the shark's-fin cartilage *has no taste*. This makes it—and bird's-nest soup, that other tasteless Cantonese delicacy—a waste of money in the culinary universe.

department store has some great street snacking options. If you fancy a cup of milk tea dotted with black tapioca pearls, this is the place to go, though Causeway also has its fair share of high-end eateries, which are concentrated in the area surrounding Lee Gardens Two, home to many luxury fashion stores.

Some of the most exciting dining options in the area are the upstairs eateries. Hidden away from street view, these venues rely mainly on foodies in the know, but house some of the best eats in the neighborhood.

Hong Kong Cuisine 1983
$$$ | CHINESE FUSION | Run by a former private chef to one of Hong Kong's richest tycoons, this contemporary Chinese restaurant serves elevated classics with a twist, like chicken wings stuffed with braised boneless duck web (deboned duck feet), and steamed egg white and crabmeat pudding served in an eggshell. A wine sommelier is on hand to recommend pairings from the in-house cellar. **Known for:** elevated Cantonese cuisine; private club atmosphere; refined dim sum. *Average main: HK$500* ✉ *1st fl., 2 Tsoi Tak St., Happy Valley* ☎ *2893–3788* 🌐 *www.1983hkc.com* Ⓜ *Causeway Bay.*

Hotpot Instinct
$$ | CHINESE | Hot pot cooking is immensely popular in Hong Kong, and places like Hotpot Instinct are packed even during the steamy summer months. The large menu offers thinly sliced beef, pork, seafood, and a range of house-made fish balls and meatballs, which diners then dip into a boiling vat of broth at their table. **Known for:** premium seafood like lobster, geoduck, and abalone; good selection of Chinese-style hot pot soup bases; extremely fresh ingredients. *Average main: HK$120* ✉ *The L. Square,*

6th fl., 459 Lockhart Rd., Causeway Bay ☎ 2573–2844 Ⓜ Causeway Bay.

Mother of Pizzas

$$$ | **PIZZA** | With a Hong Konger who trained in pizza-making in Canada at the helm, a piano in the middle of the dining room, and a chunky cocktail list, this isn't your usual pizza parlor. The pies are made with top-grade Italian flour that's fermented for 48 hours and come in imaginative flavors like the Summer of Love 1967 piled with San Marzano tomatoes, Italian sausage, fresh sliced pineapples, and chili-infused honey. **Known for:** pizza flavors you won't find elsewhere; Neapolitan meets New York–style dough; small but tasty selection of pasta. *$ Average main: HK$300 ✉ 13 Leighton Rd., Causeway Bay ☎ 2891–2221 ⊕ www.motherofpizzas.com Ⓜ Causeway Bay.*

Nan Tei

$ | **JAPANESE** | This *izakaya* offers plate upon plate of *yakitori* and *kushiyaki* (Japanese-style skewered and grilled items) in a relaxed atmosphere. The ox tongue is exceptional—succulent, soft, and flavored with just the right amount of salt. **Known for:** simple, authentic Japanese grilling; late-night dining; cozy neighborhood atmosphere. *$ Average main: HK$95 ✉ 10 Yuen Yuen St., Happy Valley ☎ 3118–2501 ⊙ No lunch Sun. Ⓜ Causeway Bay.*

Pak Loh Chiu Chow Restaurant

$$$$ | **CHIU CHOW** | Chiu Chow cuisine is known for its delicate flavors, with light seasoning that showcases fresh ingredients, and this elegant restaurant is one of the top spots in Hong Kong to try it. An institution that's been around for more than 50 years, it serves both traditional Chiu Chow dishes and more modern creations; must-orders include the cold crab and marinated goose. **Known for:** rarely found Chiu Chow dishes; tasty dim sum at lunchtime; sleek, stylish interiors. *$ Average main: HK$600 ✉ 23–25 Hysan Ave., Causeway Bay ☎ 2576–8886 ⊕ pakloh.com Ⓜ Causeway Bay, Exit F1.*

Sushi Hiro

$$$ | **JAPANESE** | *Uni* (sea urchin), *ikura* (salmon roe), *o-toro* (the fattiest of fatty tuna) … if these dishes make you drool, then make a beeline for Sushi Hiro, hidden in an office building but quite possibly the best place in town for raw fish. Dinner can be pricey, but lunch sees some fantastic deals. **Known for:** fresh fish filleted in front of you; truly Japanese minimalist interior; intimate seating perfect for couples and small groups. *$ Average main: HK$350 ✉ Henry House, 10th fl., 42 Yun Ping Rd., Causeway Bay ☎ 2882–8752 Ⓜ Causeway Bay.*

Tonkichi Tonkatsu Seafood

$$ | **JAPANESE** | This restaurant specializes in *tonkatsu*—pork cutlets that are dipped in panko and deep-fried. When it's done right, as it is here, the pork is crispy on the outside but remains tender and juicy on the inside. **Known for:** quality pork options that include kurobuta from Japan; great-value set meals; child-friendly environment. *$ Average main: HK$200 ✉ The World Trade Centre, Shop 1302, 280 Gloucester Rd., Causeway Bay ☎ 2310–8806 ⊕ tonkichi.com.hk Ⓜ Causeway Bay.*

Under Bridge Spicy Crab

$$$ | **CANTONESE** | This Anthony Bourdain–approved restaurant doles out typhoon shelter cuisine, and its specialty is sweet, fleshy crabs showered in crispy fried garlic. It started decades ago as a street stall but has become so successful, it now occupies three different units along the same street. **Known for:** Hong Kong's most famous typhoon shelter cuisine restaurant; deep-fried crab and mantis shrimp; comfortable, if loud, late-night dining environment. *$ Average main: HK$350 ✉ Golden Jubilee House, Ground fl. and 1st fl., 391 Lockhart Rd., Causeway Bay ☎ 2893–1289 Ⓜ Causeway Bay, Exit C.*

Coffee and Quick Bites

agnès b. café

$ | CAFÉ | This café is a great spot to rest your heels after a day of shopping, and enjoy a cup of tea and a slice of cake. Some of the cakes are marked with the brand's iconic "b." logo to reel in the fashionista-foodies. **Known for:** fairly peaceful environment in a busy mall; decent coffee; takeaway boxed chocolates that make great souvenirs. *$ Average main: HK$40 ✉ Times Square, Level 6, Kiosk D, 1 Matheson Rd., Causeway Bay ☎ 2506–3822 🌐 cafefleuriste.agnesb.com.hk Ⓜ Causeway Bay.*

Bing Kee

$ | FAST FOOD | Dining in Hong Kong doesn't get more local than having a meal at this open-air stall, where you'll be wedged among taxi drivers and office workers slurping up their food. The menu is full of café favorites like pork chop sandwiches and beef brisket noodles, but the most popular items by far are the thick milk tea and cloyingly sweet Hong Kong–style French toast. **Known for:** one of Hong Kong's most famous and long-standing street stalls; affordable cha chaan teng fare, in particular the French toast and milk tea; no-frills dining. *$ Average main: HK$75 ✉ 5 Shepherd St., Causeway Bay ☎ 2577–3117 ▭ No credit cards Ⓜ Tin Hau.*

Café Matchbox

$ | CHINESE | The decor, staff uniforms, and—of course—the food all capture the retro vibe of the 1960s Hong Kong *cha chaan teng* (local café). Cantonese pop songs from that era play over the sound system while diners relish bowls of elbow macaroni served in soup and topped with ham and eggs. **Known for:** nostalgic old Hong Kong atmosphere; cute photo spots around the café; inclusive environment with kid- and pet-friendly areas. *$ Average main: HK$55 ✉ Fashion Walk, Ground fl., Shop C and D, 57 Paterson St., Causeway Bay ☎ 2868–0363 🌐 www.cafematchbox.com.hk Ⓜ Causeway Bay.*

Cheung Hing Coffee Shop

$ | FUSION | This quaint *cha chaan teng* has been a local favorite since it opened in 1951. You can't go wrong with one of their famous, crispy-on-the-outside, fluffy-inside pineapple buns stuffed with a slab of butter alongside a cup of creamy milk tea. **Known for:** some of Hong Kong's best pineapple bolo buns and egg tarts; one of Hong Kong's oldest cha chaan tengs; slightly more expensive than other teahouses. *$ Average main: HK$80 ✉ 9 Yik Yam St., Happy Valley ☎ 2572–5097 Ⓜ Causeway Bay, Exit A.*

Chin Jor Fan Tong

$$ | CHINESE | At this hip noodle shop in the quietly cool Tai Hang neighborhood next to Causeway Bay, you can mix and match your order according to the soup base, noodle type, spice level, and toppings that you want. The braised beef sweet potato noodles that marry light, chewy noodles with a bold, beefy broth are recommended. **Known for:** healthy, natural cooking methods and ingredients; fully customizable noodle bowls; cozy, homey feel. *$ Average main: HK$150 ✉ 39 Sun Chun St., Causeway Bay ☎ 5118–1869 ⏲ Closed Mon. Ⓜ Tin Hau.*

Man Sing

$ | CHINESE | Hong Kong's top foodies swear by the steamed meat cake from this cheap and cheerful roadside eatery—the trademark dish consists of a towering mound of minced fatty pork that's been drizzled in soy sauce and topped with a golden orb of salted egg yolk. But the meat cake is not the only thing that makes this place a worthwhile visit; also try the spicy "saliva" chicken (a classic Sichuan poultry dish named after its complex, mouthwatering flavors), spice-tossed lamb rack, and silken steamed egg with fresh crab. **Known for:** homestyle cooking; being popular with local celebrities; long lines and limited seating. *$ Average main: HK$60 ✉ 16*

Wun Sha St., Tai Hang, Causeway Bay ☎ *6902–2688* 💳 *No credit cards* ⏲ *No lunch* Ⓜ *Tin Hau.*

Plumcot

$ | **BAKERY** | From croissants to caneles, Plumcot makes all manner of pastries—and very well. This is one of Hong Kong's most popular patisseries and sells out nearly every day, so go early if you want a bite. **Known for:** Parisian-style pastries made with French ingredients; seasonal bakes like brioche with homemade jam; stylish, minimalist packaging. 💲 *Average main: HK$50* ✉ *10A Sun Chun St., Causeway Bay* 🌐 *plumcot.co* ⏲ *Closed Mon. and Tues.* Ⓜ *Tin Hau.*

Hotels

Once dominated by business hotels, Causeway Bay now caters to diverse travelers, with accommodation options that range from sleek, luxurious spaces to hidden guesthouses. The best stays are clustered near the waterfront along Gloucester Road, where you get skyline views, or tucked in quieter streets like Yun Ping Road and Leighton Road behind the shopping hub. With easy transport links and endless dining, this is a prime base for exploring Hong Kong's energy.

Cosmo Hotel

$ | **HOTEL** | This youthful design hotel should appeal to guests who appreciate clean lines and bright, cheery interiors. **Pros:** cheerful rooms in one of three mood colors—orange, green, or yellow; outdoor terrace with free coffee and tea round the clock; free daily shuttle bus. **Cons:** surrounded by busy streets; no free toiletries; some rooms face a cemetery. 💲 *Rooms from: HK$600* ✉ *375–377 Queen's Rd. E, Wan Chai* ☎ *3552–8388* 🌐 *www.cosmohotel.com.hk* 🛏 *142 rooms* 🍽 *No Meals* Ⓜ *Causeway Bay.*

Crowne Plaza Hong Kong Causeway Bay

$$ | **HOTEL** | Overlooking Happy Valley and the surrounding hillsides through floor-to-ceiling double-glazed windows, the superior rooms are sleek, but suites afford especially panoramic views through three walls of windows. **Pros:** older but spacious rooms; short walk from Times Square and shopping streets; great outdoor pool with a view. **Cons:** racing fans get better track views at nearby Dorsett Wanchai; inconsistent housekeeping standards; rooms look dated. 💲 *Rooms from: HK$1,500* ✉ *8 Leighton Rd., Causeway Bay* ☎ *3980–3980* 🌐 *www.cphongkong.com* 🛏 *263 rooms* 🍽 *No Meals* Ⓜ *Causeway Bay.*

Empire Hotel Hong Kong, Causeway Bay

$$ | **HOTEL** | A quiet locale just east of Victoria Park is enhanced by soothingly decorated guest rooms, where the amenities include glass-walled showers. **Pros:** quiet neighborhood; beautiful west-facing views; some rooms have free access to the spa. **Cons:** small rooms and windows; no pool or gym; situated away from the action. 💲 *Rooms from: HK$1,400* ✉ *8 Wing Hing St., Causeway Bay* ☎ *3692–2333* 🌐 *www.empirehotel.com.hk* 🛏 *280 rooms* 🍽 *No Meals* Ⓜ *Tin Hau.*

★ Lanson Place Causeway Bay, Hong Kong

$$$ | **HOTEL** | Formerly focused on longer stays, this boutique luxury hotel re-launched in 2024 with a complete makeover featuring elegant interiors by the award-winning French designer Pierre-Yves Rochon. **Pros:** attractive, distinctive accommodations; in a quiet area but steps from the center of Causeway Bay; free self-service laundry. **Cons:** no harbor views; some rooms have an odd pillar in them; no proper drop-off area for taxis. 💲 *Rooms from: HK$2,500* ✉ *133 Leighton Rd., Causeway Bay* ☎ *3477–6888* 🌐 *hongkong.lansonplace.com* 🛏 *188 rooms* 🍽 *No Meals* Ⓜ *Causeway Bay.*

The Park Lane Hong Kong, Autograph Collection

$$ | **HOTEL** | Guest rooms are as airy as the views at this elegant landmark, where glass-top furnishings and glass

walls accent the open outlooks over Victoria Park greenery, the harbor, and the skyline. **Pros:** excellent views; close to Causeway Bay shopping; rooftop bar and restaurant. **Cons:** tired rooms; no pool; no central heating. *$ Rooms from: HK$1,500 ✉ 310 Gloucester Rd., Causeway Bay ☎ 2839–3366 🌐 www.parklane.com.hk 820 rooms 🍽 No Meals Ⓜ Causeway Bay.*

Regal Hongkong Hotel

$$ | HOTEL | The baroque-style guest rooms at this local chain hotel may be a little too opulent for the average traveler's taste, but the location—just two minutes' walk from Causeway Bay's hottest shops, and three minutes from the nearest MTR station—can't be beat. **Pros:** rooftop pool; spacious rooms; dining discounts for hotel guests. **Cons:** damp smell in rooms and corridors; cleaning standards are inconsistent; room decor is dated. *$ Rooms from: HK$1,000 ✉ 88 Yee Wo St., Causeway Bay ☎ 2890–6633 🌐 www.regalhotel.com/en/regal-hong-kong-hotel 481 rooms 🍽 No Meals Ⓜ Causeway Bay.*

Nightlife

Though not as wild as other districts, the nightlife in Causeway Bay continues to draw a mix of locals and visitors. From intimate whiskey dens to buzzing beer halls, there's something for every night owl.

BARS

Second Draft

BREWPUBS | This contemporary gastropub is run by Young Master, Hong Kong's top craft beer group. What's nice is that you don't just get beers from the brand here—nearly every local brewer is represented in this comfortable space, which has 23 taps kept at specific temperatures. Flavors are fresh and Asian-inspired, from pineapple-infused ales to beers brewed with yuzu peel and sansho peppers. There's a menu of local light bites too, so you don't have to drink on an empty stomach. *✉ Fashion Walk, Shop H01, 9 Kingston St., Causeway Bay ☎ 5648–0770 🌐 www.seconddraft.hk Ⓜ Causeway Bay.*

Takumi Mixology Salon

COCKTAIL BARS | Run by a rising bar star who has piloted several other bars to award-winning success, this intimate bar specializes in bespoke Japanese-style cocktails. As you might expect, prices are on the high side, but the tailored tipples—like sakura liqueur paired with fresh Japanese fruit and roasted tea—are just as elevated. *✉ Cubus, 3rd fl., 1 Hoi Ping Rd., Causeway Bay ☎ 5394–3681 🌐 www.instagram.com/takumihk Ⓜ Causeway Bay.*

Shopping

Hong Kong fashionistas hungry for new labels choose Causeway Bay over Central any day. Quirky-but-cool Asian brands that won't arrive stateside for years are the pull at Japanese department store Sogo and micromalls like the Island Beverley Centre. The low-profile storefronts on Yiu Wa Street belie its *hot* reputation for homegrown clothing and housewares. Similar up-and-coming boutiques are scattered along Vogue Alley, at the intersection of Paterson and Kingston streets. Megamall Times Square soars behind all this—its mix of designer and mid-range gear makes it a good one-stop shopping destination. Other good bets for clothing are the big branches of local chains. Garment prices in the stalls and poky shops along Jardine's Crescent and Jardine's Bazaar are unbeatable; and you can see how real Hong Kongers do their food shopping at the "wet market" (so called because the vendors are perpetually hosing down their produce) at the end of these streets.

Causeway Bay is one of the most trendy shopping areas in Hong Kong.

BEAUTY

Aroma Natural Skin Care

SKINCARE | This store has been the secret weapon of skin regime enthusiasts for years, with stock from some of the industry's most venerated brands, many of them hard to track down. Find your Bioderma, Obagi, and Skin Ceuticals here, as well as the mandatory spectrum of whitening products. ✉ *Island Beverley, Shop 863, 1 Great George St., Causeway Bay* ☎ *2506–0699* Ⓜ *Causeway Bay.*

Sa Sa Cosmetics

COSMETICS | The fuchsia-pink signs that announce Hong Kong's best and largest cosmetic discounter will become familiar sights on any shopping expedition. Look for deals on everything from cheap glittery makeup to sleek designer lines. Fragrances are a particularly good buy; prices are usually even lower than those at airport duty-free shops. ✉ *Leighton Centre, Ground fl. and 2nd fl., 77 Leighton Rd., Causeway Bay* ☎ *2555–0806* 🌐 *www.sasa.com* Ⓜ *Causeway Bay.*

Two Girls

COSMETICS | This shop carries Hong Kong's first local cosmetics line, also known as Two Girls Brand. The colorful, old-fashioned packaging, which is reminiscent of traditional Chinese medicines, is more remarkable than the products. That said, the line's classics—including hair oil, talcum powder, and soap—make interesting gifts. ✉ *Causeway Place, Shop 283, 2–10 Great George St., Causeway Bay* ☎ *2504–1811* 🌐 *www.twogirls.hk* Ⓜ *Causeway Bay, Exit E.*

CAMERAS AND ELECTRONICS

Broadway

ELECTRONICS | Like its more famous competitor, Fortress, Broadway is a large electronic-goods chain. There isn't a lot to differentiate between the two, although Broadway's staff are better known for being knowledgeable about their products. Look for familiar name-brand cameras, computers, sound systems, home appliances, and mobile phones. ✉ *Times Square, 8th fl., Shop 814, 1 Matheson St., Causeway Bay*

2506–0228 *www.broadwaylifestyle.com* *Causeway Bay.*

DG Lifestyle Store

ACCESSORIES | Hong Kong's first Apple Authorized Reseller is still going strong when it comes to the latest iPhone, iPad, Mac, and Apple Watch products. But it's perhaps most well-known for its eye-opening range of third-party Apple accessories and gadgets, from crystal-studded phone cases to diamond-encrusted versions in real gold. *Times Square, 9th fl., Shop 917, 1 Matheson St., Causeway Bay* *2506–1338* *Causeway Bay.*

★ **Fortress**

ELECTRONICS | Part of billionaire Li Ka-shing's empire, this extensive chain of shops sells electronics with warranties—a safety precaution that draws the crowds. It also has good deals on printers and accessories, although selection varies by shop. You can spot a Fortress by looking for the big castle logo. For the full list of outlets, visit the website. *Times Square, Shop 914–915, 1 Matheson St., Causeway Bay* *9820–0115* *www.fortress.com.hk* *Causeway Bay.*

CLOTHING

G2000

CLOTHING | This inexpensive chain carries men's and women's business wear. It's a great place to look for suits with matching shirts (and ties) for a good price. Expect a mix of city-chic and casual, and especially good fits for anyone petite. *Excelsior Plaza, Shop 25–30, 24–26 E. Point Rd., Causeway Bay* *2972–2576* *www.g2000.com.hk* *Causeway Bay, Exit E.*

I.T Hysan One

CLOTHING | Championing fashion innovation, this avant-garde men's and women's concept store carries a vast selection of top international and local designers. Walking through its sprawling four floors is an experience in itself—it's divided by brands, and each brand has a distinct, artistic space. Whether you're looking for a wild new ensemble from Comme des Garçons, or funky sunglasses from in-house brand Neith, you're likely to find something special here. *1 Hysan Ave., Causeway Bay* *2972–2572* *www.ithk.com* *Causeway Bay.*

Olivia Couture

COUTURE | The surroundings are functional, but the gowns, wedding dresses, and cheongsams by local designer Olivia Yip are lavish. With a growing clientele—including socialites looking to stand out—Yip is quietly making a name for herself and her Parisian-influenced pieces. *Redana Centre, Ground fl., Shop 3, 25 Yiu Wa St., Causeway Bay* *2838–6636* *www.oliviacouture.com* *Causeway Bay.*

Vein

CLOTHING | Modern and minimalist, Vein's decor is in perfect harmony with its Nordic apparel. The lineup of Scandinavian luxury labels and home accessories is updated regularly, but you can usually find at least a dozen stalwart, simple-yet-elegant brands, including Filippa K and Rodebjer. Expect clean lines, a muted palette, and unexpected splashes of color. *Lee Garden Two, Shop 118, 28 Yun Ping Rd., Causeway Bay* *2528–4988* *veinthe-store.com* *Causeway Bay.*

DEPARTMENT STORES

★ **City'super**

SUPERMARKET | Wherever you're from and whatever you're looking for—whether it's fresh oysters from France or quirky products like bottled water for pets—this gourmet supermarket and variety-store chain is the place to begin your search. In addition to edibles, it carries gadgets, inexpensive jewelry, accessories, and cosmetics. The Times Square location often has international-theme food festivals. Be sure to check out the Japanese imported sweets like Royce's unusual chocolate-covered potato chips. *Times Square, Basement One, 1 Matheson St., Causeway Bay* *2429–8588* *www.citysuper.com.hk* *Causeway Bay, Exit A.*

Sogo

DEPARTMENT STORE | A lynchpin of the Causeway Bay shopping scene, Japanese brand Sogo's main branch has 16 floors of clothing, housewares, and personal-care items. The selection of street wear, makeup, and accessories is particularly strong, with a dazzling variety of Asian and international labels represented. A vast basement-level grocery store keeps the Japanese expat community happily fed. ✉ *555 Hennessy Rd., Causeway Bay* ☎ *2833–8338* 🌐 *www.sogo.com.hk* Ⓜ *Causeway Bay, Exit D.*

HOME DECOR

Franc Franc

HOUSEWARES | This Japanese home and living store has everything you'd need to equip your downtown apartment, from bookshelves to bubble bath. The funky, colorfully modern designs and intriguing gadgets will keep all types of shoppers entertained, and it's quite a feat to leave the store with empty hands. ✉ *Fashion Walk, Ground fl. and 1st fl., Shop B, 8 Kingston St., Causeway Bay* ☎ *3583–2528* 🌐 *hk.francfranc.net* Ⓜ *Causeway Bay.*

Muji

DEPARTMENT STORE | Those familiar with this Japanese brand are often delighted to find one of its stores, and Hong Kong now has more than a dozen branches. The full name is Mujirishi Ryohin (meaning "no-brand quality goods"), which only partly describes the sleek minimalism of everything from household items and stationery to clothing and simply packaged snacks. ✉ *Lee Theatre Plaza, 3rd and 4th fl., 99 Percival St., Causeway Bay* ☎ *3971–3120* 🌐 *www.muji.com.hk* Ⓜ *Causeway Bay, Exit A.*

JEWELRY AND ACCESSORIES

City Chain Co. Ltd.

JEWELRY & WATCHES | Hong Kong–founded City Chain Co. Ltd. was Hong Kong's first watch retail chain. These days it has hundreds of shops in Asia and offers a wide selection of watches for various budgets, including ones by Ellesse, Cyma, and Armani. ✉ *Times Square, 9th fl., Shop 911, 1 Matheson St., Causeway Bay* ☎ *2897–1666* 🌐 *www.citychain.com.hk* Ⓜ *Causeway Bay.*

Elegant Watch & Jewellery Company Limited

JEWELRY & WATCHES | With luxury watch collectors in mind, Elegant Watch is an authorized dealer of more than 35 top brands such as Tag Heuer, Breitling, and Franck Muller. ✉ *Times Square, Shop 302–303, 1 Matheson St., Causeway Bay* ☎ *2111–9128* 🌐 *www.elegantwatch.net* Ⓜ *Causeway Bay, Exit A.*

MALLS AND SHOPPING CENTERS

Hysan Place

MALL | Across the street from Causeway Bay's popular Sogo looms neighborhood newcomer Hysan Place. This gleaming 17-story mall devotes the fourth and fifth floors to Japanese and Korean designers. Try on urban-chic garb from Beams, Dickies, or Rains, then head up to the sixth floor for pampering. Dubbed the Garden of Eden, this level is overflowing with name-brand beauty products, lingerie shops, dessert counters, and nail salons. For a fix of fresh air, step out onto the Sky Garden on the fourth level, or slip into the three-level Eslite bookstore to relax with a book and a cuppa. ✉ *500 Hennessy Rd., Causeway Bay* ☎ *2886–7222* 🌐 *www.leegardens.com.hk* Ⓜ *Causeway Bay, Exit F2.*

Island Beverley

MALL | This hip micromall played a big part in putting Causeway Bay on the fashion map. Shoe-box-size boutiques fill its four cramped floors—some showcase small, local designers; others stock Japanese and Korean brands hard to find overseas. Edgy club wear competes for the space with cutesy numbers for girls who just don't want to grow up. Indeed, many of the clothes look like they'll only fit local schoolgirls, but not to worry: Island Beverley has a great selection of bags, accessories, and jewelry. ✉ *1 Great George St., Causeway Bay* ☎ *2890–6823* Ⓜ *Causeway Bay, Exit E.*

Lee Gardens One and Two

MALL | These two adjacent malls are a firm favorite with local celebrities. They come as much for the mall's low-key atmosphere—a world away from the bustle of Central—as for the clothes. And with so many big names under one small roof—Dior, Louis Vuitton, and Hermès, to name but a few—who can blame them? The second floor of Lee Gardens Two is taken up with designer kiddie wear. The two buildings, one on either side of Hysan Avenue, are linked by a second-floor footbridge. ✉ *33 Hysan Ave., Causeway Bay* ☎ *2907–5227* 🌐 *www.leegardens.com.hk* Ⓜ *Causeway Bay, Exit F.*

★ Times Square

MALL | This gleaming mall packs most of Hong Kong's best-known stores into 16 frenzied floors, organized thematically. Lane Crawford and Marks & Spencer both have branches here, as does favored local gourmet grocer City'super. Many beauty brands are located in the basement, giving way to names like Bottega Veneta and Cartier on the second floor, and midrange options like Zara higher up. The electronics, sports, and outdoors selection is particularly good. An indoor atrium hosts everything from rock bands to fashion shows to local movie stars.

■ TIP→ **Among the dozen or so eateries, classic Lei Garden is a good pick, thanks to its excellent dim sum menu and Zen interior.** ✉ *1 Matheson St., Causeway Bay* ☎ *2118–8900* 🌐 *www.timessquare.com.hk* Ⓜ *Causeway Bay.*

Windsor House Computer Plaza

ELECTRONICS | Clean, wide corridors distinguish this less frantic computer arcade from the others. It has two floors of products with a wide selection of Mac and PC computer games, video games, laptops, desktops, and accessories. This is a reputable center with competitive prices. ✉ *Windsor House, 10th fl., 311 Gloucester Rd., Causeway Bay* ☎ *2895–0668* 🌐 *www.windsorhouse.hk* Ⓜ *Causeway Bay, Exit E.*

MARKETS

Jardine's Bazaar and Jardine's Crescent

MARKET | These two small parallel streets are so crammed with clothing stalls it's difficult to make your way through. Most offer bargains on the usual clothes, children's gear, bags, and cheap souvenirs like chopstick sets. The surrounding boutiques are also worth a look for local and Korean fashions, though the sizes are small. ✉ *16 Jardine's Cres., Causeway Bay* Ⓜ *Causeway Bay, Exit F.*

SHOES, HANDBAGS, AND LEATHER GOODS

Hana Vintage

VINTAGE | This shop is chock-full of luxury secondhand bags, all of them in excellent condition. Chanel lovers will appreciate their collection of vintage Chanel bags. ✉ *47 Lee Garden Rd., Causeway Bay* 🌐 *hk.hanavtgsys.com* Ⓜ *Causeway Bay.*

Milan Station

HANDBAGS | Even if you're willing to shell out for an Hermès Kelly bag, how can anyone expect you to survive the wait-list? Milan Station resells the "it" bags of yesterday that have been retrieved from Hong Kong's fickle fashionistas. Inexplicably, the shop entrances (there are more than half a dozen here) were designed to look like MTR stations. The concept has been so successful, unimaginatively named copycats have sprung up, such as Paris Station. Discounts vary according to brand and trends, but the merchandise is in good condition. ✉ *Percival House, Ground fl., 77–83 Percival St., Causeway Bay* ☎ *2504–0128, 2730–8037 customer service* 🌐 *www.milanstation.com.hk* Ⓜ *Causeway Bay, Exit A.*

Prestige Shoe Co. Ltd.

SHOES | Local maker Prestige does fashion-forward, acceptable-quality, reasonably priced shoes that will take wearers to work or around town. It's conveniently located in the Island Beverley mall, where you can buy an equally stylish and affordable outfit to match your new shoes. ✉ *Island Beverley, Underground fl., Shop 86, 1 Great George St., Causeway Bay* ☎ *2915–6813* Ⓜ *Causeway Bay, Exit E.*

Activities

Causeway Bay is a haven for wellness lovers because of its many spas and fitness studios, which are popular with the corporate executives working in the area. Its parks and waterfront promenades offer plenty of green spaces for a stroll or morning tai chi, too.

SPAS

SPA by MTM

SPA | At this soothing Japanese spa, the aesthetic is as important as the physical treatments; each room has a specific identity and products are custom blended on-site. ✉ *16F Soundwill Plaza, 38 Russell St., Causeway Bay* ☎ *2923–7888* 🌐 *www.spabymtm.com* Ⓜ *Causeway Bay, Exit A.*

Eastern

From North Point to Quarry Bay and Taikoo Shing, the densely populated neighborhoods east of Causeway Bay are largely residential and industrial, with a good number of shopping malls and restaurants that cater to residents. But the area is fast becoming an arts and culture hub—you'll find art galleries and bookshops installed in converted industrial buildings, hip cafés wedged between older businesses, and some fascinating museums that are well worth seeking out.

Sights

Hong Kong's newest arts hub, the Eastern District, blends heritage with modern creativity. While it's still primarily an industrial and residential enclave, it boasts a growing number of museums, from restored historical sites to cutting-edge contemporary spaces. Art galleries and cultural centers showcase local talent, while public installations bring creativity to the streets. With new venues opening alongside established institutions, this district is quickly becoming a must-visit for culture lovers.

Hong Kong Museum of the War of Resistance and Coastal Defence

HISTORY MUSEUM | FAMILY | The Lei Yue Mun Fort makes for an appropriate home for this museum that focuses on Hong Kong's military history and coastal defense. It's in the redoubt, a high area of land overlooking the narrowest point of the harbor; you take an elevator and cross an aerial walkway to reach it. As well as the fascinating displays indoors, there's a historical trail complete with tunnels, cannons, and observation posts. Free guided tours are available on Wednesday, weekends, and public holidays. ✉ *175 Tung Hei Rd., Shau Ki Wan, Eastern* ☎ *2569–1500* 🌐 *hk.waranddefence.museum* 🎟 *Free* 🕒 *Closed Thurs.* Ⓜ *Shau Ki Wan, Exit B2.*

Law Uk Folk Museum

CULTURAL MUSEUM | This restored Hakka house was once the home of the Law family, who arrived here from Guangdong in the mid-18th century. It's the perfect example of a triple- *jian,* double- *lang* residence. Jian are enclosed rooms—here, the bedroom, living room, and workroom at the back. The front storeroom and kitchen are the *lang,* where the walls don't reach up to the roof, and thus allow air in. Although the museum is small, informative texts outside and displays of rural furniture and farm implements inside give a powerful idea of what rural Hong Kong was

Shopping Hong Kong's Markets

Chinese markets are hectic and crowded, but great fun for the savvy shopper. The intensity of the bargaining and the variety of goods available are well worth the detour.

Nowadays Hong Kongers may prefer to flash their cash in department stores and designer boutiques, but generally, markets still offer the most competitive prices. Parents and grandparents, often toting children, go to their local neighborhood wet market almost daily to pick up fresh items such as tofu, fish, meat, fruit, and vegetables.

Some markets have a mishmash of items; others are more specialized, dealing in one particular ware. Prices paid are always a great topic of conversation. A compliment on a choice article will often elicit the price paid in reply, and a discussion may ensue on where to get the same thing at an even lower cost.

Great Finds

The prices we list below are meant to give you an idea of what you can expect to pay for certain items. Actual post-bargaining prices will of course depend on how well you haggle, while prebargaining prices are often based on how much the vendor thinks he or she can get out of you.

Jade. A symbol of purity and beauty for the Chinese, jade comes in a range of colors. Subtle and simple bangles vie for attention with large sculptures in markets. A lavender jade Guanyin (Goddess of Mercy) pendant runs about HK$260 and a green jade bangle about HK$300 before bargaining.

Silk. You'll find silk items, from purses to slippers to traditional dresses, at certain markets. A meter of silk brocade (that's slightly more than a yard) costs around HK$35, and the price is generally negotiable only if you buy large quantities.

Mah-jongg Sets. The clack-clack of mah-jongg tiles can be heard late into the night in many public-housing estates during the summer. Cheap plastic sets go for about HK$40. Far more aesthetically pleasing are ceramic sets in slender drawers of painted cases. These run about HK$250 after bargaining, from a starting price of HK$450.

"Maomorabilia." The Chairman's image is available on badges, bags, lighters, watches, ad infinitum. Pop art–like figurines of Mao and his Red Guards clutching red books are kitschy but iconic. For sound bites and quotes from the Great Helmsman, buy the Little Red Book itself. Prebargaining, a badge costs HK$30, a bag HK$50, and a ceramic figurine HK$400. Just keep in mind that many posters are fakes.

Pearls. Many freshwater pearls are grown in Taihu; seawater pearls come from Japan or the South Seas. Some have been dyed and others mixed with semiprecious stones. Designs can be pretty wild, and the clasps are not of high quality, but necklaces and bracelets are cheap. Postbargaining, a plain, short strand of pearls should cost around HK$50.

Propaganda and Comic Books. Follow the adventures of Master Q, or look for scenes from Chinese history and lots of *gongfu* (Chinese martial arts) stories, like *Longfumun* (Dragon Tiger Gate). Most titles are in Chinese and often in black and white, but can be bargained down to around HK$15.

Retro Finds. Odd items from the prewar '30s to the booming '70s include treasures like antique furniture, wooden toys, and tin advertising signs. Small items such as teapots can be bought for around HK$250. Retro items are harder to haggle for than mass-produced items.

Shopping Know-How

At the Markets: Make sure to put money and valuables in a safe place. Pickpockets and bag slashers aren't common, but they exist. When purchasing, watch out for fake materials (for example, synthetic silk).

Bringin' Home the Goods: Although that faux-Gucci handbag is tempting, remember that some countries have heavy penalties for the import of counterfeit goods. Likewise, that animal fur may be cheap, but you may get fined a lot more at your home airport than what you paid for it. Counterfeits are generally prohibited in the United States, but there's some gray area regarding goods with a "confusingly similar" trademark. Each person is allowed to bring in one such item, as long as it's for personal use and not for resale.

When to Go: Avoid weekends if you can and try to go early in the morning, from 8 am to 10 am, or early evening for the night markets. Rainy days are also good bets for avoiding the crowds and getting better prices.

How to Bargain

Successful bargaining requires knowing your prices and never losing your cool. Here's a step-by-step guide to getting the price you want and having fun at the same time.

DO'S

- Start by deciding how much you're willing to pay for an item.
- Let the vendor know you're interested.
- The vendor will quote you a price, sometimes using a calculator.
- At this point it's up to you to express either incredulity or loss of interest. But be forewarned, the vendor plays this game, too.
- Name a price that's around 50%–60% of the original price—lower if you feel daring.
- Pass the calculator back and forth until you reach an agreement.

DON'TS

- Don't enter into negotiations if you aren't seriously considering the purchase.
- Don't haggle over small sums of money.
- If the vendor isn't budging, walk away; he'll likely call you back.
- It's better to bargain if the vendor is alone. He's unlikely to come down on the price if there's an audience.
- Saving face is everything in Hong Kong. Remain pleasant and smile often.
- Buying more than one of something can get you a better deal.
- Dress down and leave your jewelry and watches in the hotel safe on the day you go marketing. You'll get a lower starting price if you don't flash your wealth.

like. It's definitely worth a trip to bustling industrial Chai Wan, at the eastern end of the MTR, to see it. Photos show what the area looked like in the 1930s—these days a leafy square is the only reminder of the woodlands and fields that once surrounded this buttermilk-color dwelling. ✉ *14 Kut Shing St., Chai Wan, Eastern* ☎ *2896–7006* 🌐 *www.lcsd.gov.hk* 🎫 *Free* ⏲ *Closed Tues.* Ⓜ *Chai Wan, Exit B.*

Oi!

ARTS CENTER | **FAMILY** | A lovely Craftsman-style historic complex that originally housed the Royal Hong Kong Yacht Club back when the area was close to the shoreline is now home to Oi!, a relaxed, government-run community art space. It showcases fun, accessible art from internationally recognized and upcoming artists, like twirling trees on giant turntables. The indoor-outdoor layout and large lawn—where kids can run about—make this a popular spot for families. ✉ *12 Oil St., North Point* ☎ *2512–3000* 🌐 *www.apo.hk/en/web/apo/oi.html* 🎫 *Free* Ⓜ *North Point, Exit A.*

Para Site

ARTS CENTER | Located next to Hong Kong's oldest funeral home, this two-story contemporary art center showcases cutting-edge exhibitions exploring social and political themes. It was founded in 1996 by seven artists and is one of the island's few non-profit art spaces. The intimate setting encourages interaction with the art, and the views of the surrounding skyscrapers from here are spectacular, especially at dusk. ✉ *Wing Wah Industrial Bldg., 22nd fl., 677 King's Rd., Quarry Bay* ☎ *2517–4620* 🌐 *www.para-site.art* ⏲ *Closed Mon. and Tues. and public holidays* Ⓜ *Fortress Hill, Exit B.*

Quarryside

ARTS CENTER | This creative community hub is representative of several such spaces popping up in Hong Kong that encourage community interaction. The design of the building is a nod to the industrial heritage of the neighborhood, where the world's largest sugar refinery once stood. The space houses a theater, a workshop, and a community kitchen, where activities like educational tours and culinary lessons are regularly held. ✉ *20 Hoi Shin La., Quarry Bay* 🌐 *quarryside.hk* 🎫 *Free* Ⓜ *Quarry Bay, Exit B.*

Tai Tam Country Park (Quarry Bay Extension)

CITY PARK | This 670-acre extension of Hong Kong's largest park is packed with challenging trails, like the Mount Parker Trail and Sir Cecil's Ride, that reward hardworking hikers with stunning views of Hong Kong's skyline. Another interesting sight is the Wartime Stoves, relics of cooking ranges built by the government in 1938 in anticipation of war. Since Hong Kong fell soon after the start of the Battle of Hong Kong on 8 December 1941, it's thought that the stoves have never been used. The densely forested park is also home to rich wildlife, including the elusive Chinese leopard and the Hong Kong newt, making this a compelling stop for both history and nature lovers. ✉ *Tai Tam Country Park (Quarry Bay Extension), Quarry Bay.*

Restaurants

In culinary terms, the Eastern District has really upped its game in recent years, with the opening of a slew of international restaurants, bars, and even a fine-dining establishment. But the area is still rooted in local flavor—whether you're after Chiu Chow classics or a bowl of snake soup, you'll find it here.

Chiu Chow Delicacies

$$ | **CHIU CHOW** | Chiu chow cuisine is known for its delicate flavors and healthier style of cooking, and this no-frills joint serves up authentic dishes at reasonable prices. The braised goose and oyster congee are must-tries. **Known for:** crowds who come for affordable Chiu Chow; casual ambience; shared tables when busy. *Average main: HK$200* *Gain Yu Bldg., Ground fl., Shop 4, 96 Wharf Rd., North Point* *3568–5643* *North Point, Exit A1.*

Fung Shing Restaurant

$$$ | **CANTONESE** | This all-day restaurant is perpetually packed with locals and tourists who come for breakfast baskets of dim sum and Cantonese classics at lunch and dinner. The retro interiors—that look like they haven't been refreshed since the 1970s—and no-nonsense service only add to the authentic experience. **Known for:** classic recipes and traditional cooking methods; table sharing; brusque service. *Average main: HK$300* *62–28 Java Rd., North Point* *2578–4898* *North Point, Exit A1.*

Grand Cuisine Shanghai Kitchen

$$ | **CHINESE** | There's usually a queue and the service is often brusque, but the extraordinarily tasty Shanghai-style dumplings are worth the chaotic experience at this traditional Chinese restaurant. The hand-pulled noodles are good, too. **Known for:** traditional Shanghai dishes, in particular the xiaolongbao; cramped but cozy interiors; extra charges for takeaways and credit card payments. *Average main: HK$150* *Po On Mansion, Ground fl., G510–511, 1 Tai Yue Ave., Quarry Bay* *2568–9989* *Tai Koo, Exit B.*

She Wong Leung

$$$ | **CANTONESE** | One for adventurous eaters, this casual restaurant is known for its snake soup, which is believed to boost immunity and improve joint health. But there are tamer, equally tasty dishes, too, if you chicken out while ordering. **Known for:** a different snake soup for each season; homestyle, nonsnake Chinese dishes; snake wine that's supposed to be beneficial for health. *Average main: HK$300* *Ground fl., Shop A, 298 Electric Rd., North Point* *2578–8135* *Fortress Hill, Exit A.*

Té Bo

$$$ | **FRENCH FUSION** | Inside the posh 1880 members' club within a slick corporate building, Té Bo offers a rare fine-dining experience in the Eastern District. It's helmed by French-trained, Swiss-Filipino chef Sebastian Lorenz, and as you might expect, the elevated dishes here draw inspiration from different regions. **Known for:** interactive fine dining worth traveling for; chef who used to work at a Michelin-starred restaurant; a peek into a private club. *Average main: HK$500* *Two Taikoo Place, 2nd fl., 979 King's Rd., Quarry Bay* *3610–8185* *www.1880.com.hk/1880social/dining* *Closed weekends* *Quarry Bay, Exit A.*

Coffee and Quick Bites

Camper's

$ | **JAPANESE FUSION** | This cozy, Japanese-inspired diner is popular with locals for its fresh, wholesome comfort food. Its menu is packed with hearty rice bowls and flavorful curries, all made with healthy ingredients. **Known for:** healthy, home-style comfort food; vegetable-forward dishes that can be made vegan on request; quick service and laid-back vibes. *Average main: HK$80* *13A Pan Hoi St., Quarry Bay* *2668–6613* *Quarry Bay, Exit A.*

Coffeelin

$$ | **ITALIAN** | It looks like a sleek trattoria, but this Milanese-inspired coffee shop is 100% homegrown. The stunning interiors with details like custom-made cups and hand-painted mirrors reflect the local owner's love of Italian coffee culture. **Known for:** gorgeous handcrafted

interiors; robust Italian coffee; cool, quirky merchandise designed in-house. *Average main: HK$100* *Ground fl., Shop 2, 228 Electric Rd., North Point* *6891–1200* *www.instagram.com/coffeelin_hk* *Fortress Hill, Exit A.*

Master Low-Key Food Shop

$ | DESSERTS | This takeout-only snack shop is extremely popular for its flavorful egg puffs that are crispy on the outside and heavenly soft and chewy on the inside. Wait time varies, though it usually averages around 30 minutes. **Known for:** egg puffs in a variety of flavors; little far from main tourist draws; consistent line, rain or shine. *Average main: HK$38* *Shop B3, 76A Shau Kei Wan Main St., Shau Kei Wan, Eastern* *5592–4100* *No credit cards* *Shau Kei Wan.*

Hotels

There aren't as many hotels in the Eastern District as there are in the more touristed spots, but what the area lacks in quantity, it makes up for in quality. The hotels in this neighborhood are generally newer and more willing to go all in to draw guests, with comfortable, value-for-money rooms, swanky amenities, and multiple food and drink options.

East Hong Kong

$$ | HOTEL | The younger, funkier sibling to Hong Kong's posh Upper House, this spot has photo-worthy, minimalist-chic guest rooms, some with modernist swing seats and bathtubs facing the harbor, that are hot favorites with influencers. **Pros:** excellent harbor views; adjacent to Tai Koo MTR station; 24-hour gym and pool. **Cons:** quiet residential surroundings; lobby can get crowded because it doubles as a community co-working space; somewhat open bathrooms which may not suit everyone. *Rooms from: HK$1,200* *29 Taikoo Shing Rd., Tai Koo, Eastern* *3968–3968* *www.east-hong-kong.com* *331 rooms* *No Meals* *Tai Koo.*

Hyatt Centric Victoria Harbour Hong Kong

$$ | HOTEL | Harbor-facing rooms without the eye-watering price tags and big crowds are exactly what this sleek, contemporary hotel off the tourist track offers. **Pros:** close to North Point MTR station and ferry pier; modern, comfortable rooms; 23rd-story restaurant and bar with a view. **Cons:** windows have colored glazing; neighboring mall is rather quiet; check-in and-out can be slow. *Rooms from: HK$1,050* *1 N. Point Estate La., North Point* *3762–1234* *www.hyatt.com* *665 rooms* *No Meals* *North Point, Exit A1.*

Shopping

Shopping options in the Eastern District reflect the area's make-up—it's a largely residential precinct with a few industrial pockets. In the condominium-dense areas of Taikoo Shing and Kornhill, family-friendly malls with multiplex cinemas, numerous food options, and popular chain stores jostle for space with soaring residential buildings. The older, shabbier sections of Quarry Bay and North Point offer a more characterful experience. While there's no specific area where the best shops are clustered, it's worth wandering through the streets to discover independent stores that have stood the test of time and newer boutiques by young entrepreneurs, wedged between wet markets, traditional Chinese pharmacies, and sundry stores.

DEPARTMENT STORES

Marks & Spencer

DEPARTMENT STORE | Classic, good-quality clothing is what this British retailer has built an empire on—its underwear, in particular, is viewed as a national treasure. Although basics are on the staid side, the newer Per Una, Autograph, and Limited collections are decidedly trendier. Marks & Spencer is also one of the few stores in town to stock a full range of sizes, which includes women's shoes up to a U.S. size 10 and men's up to U.S. size 12. There are branches in many of Hong Kong's malls, the biggest of which is in Cityplaza; most have a British specialty food section, too, with a good range of wines. ✉ *Cityplaza Two, 1st fl., Shop 130, 18 Taikoo Shing Rd., Eastern* ☎ *2921–8721* 🌐 *www.marks-and-spencer.hk* Ⓜ *Tai Koo, Exit A.*

MALLS AND SHOPPING CENTERS

Cityplaza

MALL | An ice-skating rink and a multiplex theater are two of the reasons Cityplaza is the territory's most popular family mall—so popular, in fact, that it's best to steer clear on weekends, when you have to fight through the crowds. Toys and children's clothing labels are well represented, as are mid-range local and international adult brands. Cityplaza also has branches of Marks & Spencer (the largest in Hong Kong) and Japanese supermarket APiTa. There are also nearly 100 food outlets in the mall where you can get everything from a snack to a fancy meal. ✉ *18 Tai Koo Shing Rd., Tai Koo, Eastern* ☎ *2568–8665* 🌐 *www.cityplaza.com.hk* Ⓜ *Tai Koo, Exit D1.*

MARKETS

Chun Yeung Street Market

MARKET | Come evening, this sprawling market in a Hokkien neighborhood gets as busy as the popular Ladies Market in Mong Kok. It specializes in produce from China's Fujian (Hokkien) province that you won't find at many other places in Hong Kong, although you'll also find a few dry goods stalls peddling clothing, bags, and even jewelry. Because it's close to a tram terminus, local trams—"*ding dings*"—frequently clatter down the center of the market, adding to the bustle and color. ✉ *Chun Yeung St., North Point* Ⓜ *North Point, Exit A3.*

SHOES, HANDBAGS, AND LEATHER GOODS

Brand Off Tokyo

HANDBAGS | This Japanese chain, like Milan Station, carries secondhand goods from luxury brands like Louis Vuitton, Hermès, Chanel, and Prada. The shop is also a member of the Association Against Counterfeit Product Distribution, a Japanese organization that uses scientific evidence to determine whether items are genuine or knockoffs. ✉ *Cityplaza, 1st fl., Shop 120, 18 Tai Koo Shing Rd., Tai Koo, Eastern* ☎ *2967–6137* 🌐 *www.brandoff.com.hk* Ⓜ *Tai Koo, Exit D1.*

SPECIALTY STORES

AO: The Photo Book Center

BOOKS | Run by Hong Kong's foremost arts printer, this space combines an appointment-only exhibition area with a bookshop filled with thousands of rare, collectible art and photography books. It's located under the same roof as the printing presses, in an industrial building. ✉ *Asia One Tower, 13th fl., 8 Fung Yip St., Chai Wan* 🌐 *www.asiaonebooks.com* Ⓜ *Chai Wan, Exit C.*

Sam Kee Book Co.

BOOKS | It's a local institution, a bookstore, and a cat sanctuary, all rolled into one. This longstanding shop in the basement of an unassuming mall has a vast range of mostly Chinese books and foreign-language tomes that span Japanese manga and Nordic thrillers, among which a collection of rescued felines sprawl. While you're free to browse the books, don't touch the cats—the owner is adamant that this isn't a petting zoo. ✉ *King's Centre, Shop 19, 193 King's Rd., North Point* ☎ *2578–5956* Ⓜ *Fortress Hill, Exit B.*

Wander Kagu

SPECIALTY STORE | Hong Kong has a surprisingly strong outdoor culture given its many hiking trails, and this independent store with a Japanese aesthetic will ensure you're stylishly dressed to tackle them. It's packed with chic camping gear sourced from around the world, and it has a section of vintage clothing, too. ✉ *405 Eastern Centre, 1065 King's Rd., Quarry Bay* ☎ *6899–9622* 🌐 *www.wanderkagu.com* ⏲ *Closed Wed.* Ⓜ *Tai Koo, Exit B.*

Woo Ping Optical Co.

SPECIALTY STORE | If you've seen a notable pair of spectacles on a Hong Kong celebrity, chances are they're from this retro shop that's been around for more than 50 years. Woo Ping has a reputation for stocking unusual, statement-making vintage eyewear that often can't be found anywhere else. Prices run affordable, and they do regular prescriptions, too. ✉ *276 King's Rd., North Point* ☎ *2571–7810* Ⓜ *Fortress Hill, Exit B.*

Chapter 5

KOWLOON PENINSULA

Updated by
Doris Lam

NEIGHBORHOOD SNAPSHOT

TOP REASONS TO GO

■ Explore Mong Kok: Favored by the city's youth, this area teems with a maze of narrow shopping streets.

■ Stroll the West Kowloon Promenade: The grassy promenade lined with restaurants, cafés, and major art venues is the perfect place to spend your afternoon.

■ Watch "A Symphony of Lights": Every evening at 8 pm from the Tsim Sha Tsui waterfront, you can witness the city's skyline erupting into a visual spectacle of color.

■ Visit the Temple Street Night Market: Walking through the neon-lit street lined with stalls that sell affordable souvenirs, quirky toys, snacks, and clothing, is a must-do.

MAKING THE MOST OF YOUR TIME

Kowloon is alive most of the day, with shops opening around 10 am in the morning and closing in early-to-late evening. Prices are generally cheaper in the Kowloon side compared to Hong Kong island, and a more local, down-to-earth fare can be spotted here. The most populated and bustling areas for eating, wandering, and shopping in Kowloon are Tsim Sha Tsui and Mong Kok.

In general, Kowloon is safe to explore. The only places that may need slightly more caution would be Jordan, where the famed Temple Street Night Market is based, and Sham Shui Po, a predominately lower-income neighborhood filled with markets, cheap eateries, and modern cafés. If possible, avoid these two areas late at night.

GETTING HERE

■ The most romantic passage from Hong Kong Island to the Kowloon side is via Star Ferry from Central Pier to Tsim Sha Tsui (TST) pier. There are crossings from Central every 6 to 12 minutes and a little less often from Wan Chai.

■ MTR and buses are your best bet for getting around Kowloon. Underground walkways connect the Tsim Sha Tsui station with the East Tsim Sha Tsui station on the East Rail Line, where trains depart every 10 to 15 minutes for the eastern New Territories. The Kowloon Airport Express station connects with Austin station on the West Rail.

■ For sights in far-flung parts of Kowloon, including Kowloon City, Wong Tai Sin Temple, and Chi Lin Nunnery, find the closest MTR station for the area and make your way on foot, or search for bus or minibus routes that will lead you there directly.

Just across the harbor from Central, Kowloon takes its name from the string of mountains that bound it in the north: *gau lung*, "nine dragons" (there are actually eight mountains; the ninth represents the boy emperor who named them). Kowloon may be the less glamorous part of the city compared to its island-side counterpart, but its dense, gritty, urban fabric feels more authentically local.

It's also the backdrop for Hong Kong's best museums and most interesting spiritual sights, as well as street upon street of hard-core consumerism in every imaginable guise.

Parts of Kowloon are among the most densely populated areas on the planet and support a corresponding abundance of restaurants. Many hotels, planted here for the view of Hong Kong Island (spectacular at night), also have excellent restaurants, though they're uniformly expensive. Some of the best food in Kowloon is served in streetside eateries, where dishes are served family-style, seats are unfussy, beers are cheap, and the atmosphere is loud.

If you enjoy rubbing elbows with the locals in chatty all-day noodle stalls just as much as shuffling through touristy pedestrian night markets and malls, Kowloon is the place to be. Postcard skyline views abound from harbor-front hotels in Tsim Sha Tsui, a 10-minute ferry ride away from Hong Kong Island, with a calmer atmosphere heading eastward toward Hung Hom.

Kowloon is home to famous Nathan Road, the postcard image of a busy Hong Kong street, where bright neon lights adorn every building. But Kowloon is also the place for old-school outdoor markets, drawing locals and adventurous visitors who are willing to bargain for their bargains. In addition to good sales at outdoor vending areas like the evocative Temple Street Night Market and the Ladies' Market, cultural shopping experiences abound in places such as the Bird Garden or the Jade Market.

Tsim Sha Tsui

You'll probably come to this district hugging the waterfront at the southern tip of Kowloon (in Chinese the name means "pointed sandy mouth") to see one or more of Hong Kong's top museums. These collections are within easy reach

A
B
C
D
E
F
1
2
3
4
5
6
7
8
9
Man Wai St.
Man Yuen Street
Man Ying Street
Man Wui St.
Ferry Street
Wai Ching Street
Canton Road
Battery Street
Reclamation Street
Shanghai St.
Temple Street
Woosung Street
Parkes Street
Saigon Street
Pak Hoi St.
Nanking Street
Nathan Road
Saigon St.
Cheong Lok St.
Nanking St.
Chi Wo Street
Gascoigne Road Flyover
Gascoigne Road
Jordan Road
Wui Man Road
King George V Memorial Park
Kwun Chung Street
Shanghai Street
Temple Street
Woosung Street
Parkes Street
Pilkem Street
Bowring Street
Jordan
Tak Hing Street
Tak Shing Street
Cox's Road
Austin
Hong Kong West Kowloon High Speed Rail Station
Austin Road West
Lin Cheung Road
Austin Road
Hillwood Road
Austin Avenue
Observatory Rd.
Kimberley Road
Kimberley Street
Carnarvon Road
Granville Road
Cameron Road
Prat Avenue
Hart Ave.
Kowloon Park
Haiphong Road
Tsim Sha Tsui
Hanoi Road
Bristol
Kowloon Park Drive
Ashley Road
Hankow Road
Lock Road
Mody Road
Minden Row
Chatham Road South
Peking Road
Middle Rd.
Signal Hill Garden
Salisbury Road
Salisbury Road Underpass
Star Ferry Pier
Tsim Sha Tsui Public Pier
Avenue of the Stars
Victoria Harbor
0
1,000 ft
0
200 m

Tsim Sha Tsui

Sights

1 Avenue of Stars G7
2 Hong Kong Museum of Art D8
3 Hong Kong Museum of History G4
4 Kowloon Mosque and Islamic Centre D6
5 Kowloon Park D5
6 Nathan Road D5

Restaurants

1 Aqua E7
2 Bubbly Feast Hotpot F4
3 Carna by Dario Cecchini F6
4 CHAAT F8
5 Check-In Taipei C5
6 Din Tai Fung C6
7 Dong Lai Shun G6
8 EN Tsim Sha Tsui F5
9 Felix D7
10 Gaylord D7
11 Hoi King Heen H5
12 Hutong E7
13 Ko Lau Wan Hotpot and Seafood Restaurant F6
14 Ladies Sik Faan F7
15 Lai Ching Heen E8
16 The Legacy House F8
17 Outdark Korean Restaurant F5
18 Oyster & Wine Bar E7
19 Sabatini G6
20 The Steak House E8
21 Tai Ping Koon F5
22 WHISK E5
23 Wu Kong D7

Quick Bites

1 Bakehouse D6
2 The Butterfly Room F8
3 Lee Keung Kee D3
4 Mammy Pancake, Tsim Sha Tsui C8
5 Shari Shari Kakigori House G4

Hotels

1 BP International C3
2 FWD House 1881 .... C7
3 Harbour Grand Kowloon I6
4 Holiday Inn Golden Mile E7
5 Hop Inn F6
6 Hotel ICON I5
7 Hyatt Regency Hong Kong, Tsim Sha Tsui F6
8 InterContinental Grand Standford Hong Kong H5
9 K11 Artus E8
10 Kowloon Shangri-La G6
11 The Langham C7
12 The Luxe Manor E4
13 Marco Polo Hongkong Hotel C7
14 The Mira E5
15 Mondrian Hong Kong F6
16 The Peninsula Hong Kong D7
17 Rosewood Hong Kong F8
18 Royal Garden G6
19 Sheraton Hong Kong Hotel & Towers E7
20 Stanford Hillview Hotel F4

of one another amid high-rises, hotels, shops, and Kowloon Park, a coveted parcel of green space.

One of the best things to see in Tsim Sha Tsui (often referred to simply as TST) is Central: there are fabulous cross-harbor views from the **Star Ferry Pier** as well as from the ferries themselves. The sweeping pink-tile **Hong Kong Cultural Centre** and the Former Kowloon–Canton Railway clock tower are the first landmarks along the breezy pedestrian **TST East Promenade,** which starts at the Avenue of Stars and stretches a couple of miles east.

Sights

Tsim Sha Tsui is home to Hong Kong's most iconic promenade. The walk along the promenade not only offers stunning views of Central, but also guides visitors past several landmarks, including the Avenue of Stars, the Clock Tower, and the Hong Kong Cultural Centre. The district is also home to some of the city's best museums, such as the Hong Kong Museum of Art and the Hong Kong Museum of History.

Avenue of Stars

PROMENADE | FAMILY | You have to look down to appreciate the city's walk of fame. Countless local film stars have pawed the wet concrete—you may not recognize many names unless you're a fan of Hong Kong films, but the homage shows how big the local film industry is. **■TIP→ Visit the avenue at 8 pm for the Symphony of Lights, a quirky show in which more than 40 skyscrapers light up on cue as a commentator introduces them in time to a musical accompaniment.** ✉ *TST East Promenade, Tsim Sha Tsui* ✣ *Outside InterContinental Hong Kong* 🌐 *www.avenueofstars.com.hk* Ⓜ *Tsim Sha Tsui, Exit E.*

★ Hong Kong Museum of Art

ART MUSEUM | An extensive collection of Chinese art is packed inside this landmark art museum, which emerged from a years-long face-lift with new exhibitions and experiences. The collections include a heady mix of Qing ceramics, ancient calligraphic scrolls, bronze, jade, lacquerware, textiles, and contemporary canvases. It's all well organized into thematic galleries. The museum sits on the Tsim Sha Tsui waterfront in Kowloon, a few minutes from the Star Ferry and Tsim Sha Tsui MTR stop. ✉ *10 Salisbury Rd., Tsim Sha Tsui* ☎ *2721–0116* 🌐 *hk.art.museum* 🎫 *Free (except special exhibitions)* ⏲ *Closed on Thurs. (except public holidays) and the first 2 days of the Lunar New Year* Ⓜ *Tsim Sha Tsui MTR, Exit F.*

Hong Kong Museum of History

CULTURAL MUSEUM | FAMILY | For a comprehensive hit of history, this museum's popular Hong Kong Story should do the trick. The exhibit starts 400 million years ago in the Devonian period and makes its way all the way through to the 1997 Handover, with spectacular life-size dioramas that include village houses and a colonial-era shopping street. The ground-floor Folk Culture section offers an introduction to the history and customs of Hong Kong's main ethnic groups. Upstairs, gracious stone-walled galleries whirl you through the Opium Wars and the beginnings of colonial Hong Kong. Don't miss the chilling account of conditions during the Japanese occupation or the colorful look at Hong Kong life in the '60s.

Allow at least two hours to stroll through—more if you linger in every gallery and make use of the interactive elements. Pick your way through the gift shop's clutter to find local designer Alan Chan's T-shirts, shot glasses, and notebooks. His retro-kitsch aesthetic is based on 1940s cigarette-girl images. To get here from the Tsim Sha Tsui MTR walk along Cameron Road, then left for a block along Chatham Road South. A signposted overpass takes you to the museum. ✉ *100 Chatham Rd. S, Tsim Sha Tsui* ☎ *2724–9042* 🌐 *hk.history.*

museum 🎫 *Free (except special exhibitions)* ⏲ *Closed on Tues. (except public holidays) and the first 2 days of the Lunar New Year* Ⓜ *Tsim Sha Tsui, Exit B2.*

Kowloon Mosque and Islamic Centre

MOSQUE | Hong Kong's largest Islamic worship center stands in front of Kowloon Park. Visitors can call ahead to arrange for a tour or simply drop by the building, which was designed by noted Indian architect I. M. Kadri. In addition to prayer halls, the complex includes a medical clinic and a library. ✉ *105 Nathan Rd., Tsim Sha Tsui* ☎ *2724–0095* 🌐 *islamictrusthk.org/kowloon-masjid* 🎫 *Free* Ⓜ *Tsim Sha Tsui, Exit A1.*

Kowloon Park

NATURE SIGHT | **FAMILY** | These 33 acres, crisscrossed by paths and meticulously landscaped, are a refreshing retreat after a bout of shopping. There are children's playgrounds, a fitness trail, a soccer field, an aviary, a Chinese garden, and a sculpture garden featuring 19 works by local artists. On Sunday and public holidays, there are stalls with arts and crafts, as well as a kung fu corner. ✉ *22 Austin Rd., Tsim Sha Tsui* ☎ *2724–3344* 🌐 *www.lcsd.gov.hk* 🎫 *Free* Ⓜ *Tsim Sha Tsui MTR, Exit A1; Jordan, Exit C1.*

Nathan Road

STREET | Running for several miles, this street is filled with hotels, restaurants, malls, and boutiques—retail space is so costly that the southern end is dubbed the Golden Mile. The mile's most famous tower block is ramshackle Chungking Mansions, packed with cheap hotels and Indian restaurants. The building was a setting for local director Wong Kar-Wai's film *Chungking Express.* To the left and right are mazes of narrow streets with even more shops selling jewelry, electronics, clothes, souvenirs, and cosmetics. ✉ *Nathan Rd., Tsim Sha Tsui* ✣ *Between Salisbury Rd. and Boundary St.* Ⓜ *Tsim Sha Tsui.*

Restaurants

Tsim Sha Tsui is a foodie's paradise. The high density of hotels here—from the legendary Peninsula Hotel to Rosewood—means that there is no shortage of luxury dining options, many with Michelin stars. This district also has several large shopping malls, all filled with restaurants, some better than others. The area is also known for its authentic Korean and Indian cuisine.

Aqua

$$$ | **ECLECTIC** | The menu at this trendy restaurant and bar brings together the East and the West—the Japanese kitchen plates up fresh sashimi, tempura, and innovative sushi rolls, while the restaurant's Italian side offers traditional risottos and pastas with a modern twist. The Japanese offerings usually fare better than the Italian ones, but the thing really worth going to Aqua for is the superb view of the Hong Kong skyline. **Known for:** panoramic harbor views; Western-Japanese fusion dishes; upscale ambience. [$] *Average main: HK$380* ✉ *H Zentre, 17th fl., 15 Middle Rd., Tsim Sha Tsui* ☎ *3427–2288* 🌐 *www.aqua.com.hk* Ⓜ *Tsim Sha Tsui.*

Bubbly Feast Hotpot

$$$ | **CHINESE** | This restaurant specializes in coconut chicken hot pot made from fresh coconut water, with tender chickens raised on coconut meat. Open 24 hours a day, the shop also offers a wide range of beef, meat balls, noodles, and other hot pot bites—all at a reasonable price. **Known for:** sweet and nourishing coconut chicken hot pot; sashimi menu available on the side; modern interiors. [$] *Average main: HK$300* ✉ *Kimbry Court, Ground fl., Shop A, 58–60 Kimberley Rd., Tsim Sha Tsui* ☎ *6528–1828* Ⓜ *Tsim Sha Tsui, Exit B1.*

Carna by Dario Cecchini

$$$$ | **ITALIAN** | Created by Dario Cecchini, a celebrity butcher famed for championing the nose-to-tail cooking philosophy

Kowloon Park, not to be confused with Kowloon Walled City Park, is a green respite in the bustle of Tsim Sha Tsui.

of utilizing all cuts of meat, Carna is a luxurious Italian steak house located in Mondrian Hong Kong. Its sumptuous, leather-filled space was designed by renowned designer Joyce Wang and offers stunning views of the harbor (reserve window seats, if possible). **Known for:** attentive service; family-style Tuscan Menu (available on select days via preorder); tasty Wagyu and Tuscan steaks. *Average main: HK$1,000* *Mondrian Hong Kong, 39th fl., 8A Hart Ave., Tsim Sha Tsui* *3550–0339* *www.mondrianhotels.com* *No lunch weekdays* *Tsim Sha Tsui.*

CHAAT

$$$ | **INDIAN** | A table at this Michelin-starred Indian restaurant is notoriously hard to get, but if you manage to snag one, try the ice cream cone-shaped baked samosa and the juicy and flavorful black pepper chicken tikka. Be sure to pair your meal with one of the craft cocktails that utilize fragrant spices like cumin, cardamom, and chai masala. **Known for:** refined Indian street food flavors; occasional celebrity chef pop ups; lesser known sea-view terrace for happy hour. *Average main: HK$470* *Rosewood Hong Kong, 5th fl., 18 Salisbury Rd., Tsim Sha Tsui* *3891–8732* *www.rosewoodhotels.com* *Closed Mon.* *Tsim Sha Tsui, Exit J.*

Check-In Taipei

$$$ | **TAIWANESE** | For Taiwanese cuisine that blends tradition with modernity, head to Check-In Taipei. Tucked inside Harbour City mall, the restaurant offers eye-catching and comfortable interiors while serving up unique twists on Taiwanese classics, such as the Japanese eel on top of a cheesy egg crepe and dan dan beef noodles. **Known for:** modern Taiwanese cuisine; value weekday lunch sets; experimental mochi desserts. *Average main: HK$250* *Harbour City, Shop 2204–6, 2 Gateway Blvd., Tsim Sha Tsui* *3595–0995* *www.checkintaipei.hk* *Tsim Sha Tsui, Exit L5.*

Din Tai Fung

$$$ | **CHINESE** | Originally from Taiwan, this global restaurant chain is most famous for its expertly made dumplings. The place is serious about its craft—each dumpling is made from a specified amount of dough and kneaded to a uniform thinness to ensure maximum quality control. **Known for:** perfected Taiwanese classics; xiao long bao with paper-thin skin; silky smooth drunken chicken. *Average main: HK$250* *Silvercord, 3rd fl., 30 Canton Rd., Tsim Sha Tsui* *2730–6928* *www.dintaifung.com.hk* *Tsim Sha Tsui.*

Dong Lai Shun

$$$$ | **CHINESE** | **FAMILY** | This buzzing Chinese restaurant specializes in Beijing and Huaiyang cuisine and draws a following for its upscale atmosphere, Mongolian mutton hot pot, and stellar appetizers (the smoked eggs and crispy eel). Try the hand-cut noodles, traditional Peking duck, and award-winning combo dishes such as wok-fried crabmeat, rock lobster, and salted egg yolk served on rice crackers. **Known for:** inner Mongolian shuan yang rou (mutton hot pot); having more than 100 restaurants across China; special hairy crab menu (only available in the fall). *Average main: HK$600* *The Royal Garden, 69 Mody Rd., Tsim Sha Tsui* *2733–2020* *www.rghk.com.hk* *Tsim Sha Tsui.*

EN Tsim Sha Tsui

$$$ | **JAPANESE** | Unlike some of the more common Japanese eateries, Rakuen serves authentic Okinawan cuisine. Start with the *umi-budo*—an interesting variety of sea kelp shaped like bunches of grapes (the bubble-like appearance has also won it its "green caviar" nickname). **Known for:** ambience that transports you to Japan; all-you-can-eat wagyu; luxurious snow crab. *Average main: HK$500* *Golden Dragon Center, 38–40 Cameron Rd., Tsim Sha Tsui* *3428–2500* *www.en.com.hk* *No lunch* *Tsim Sha Tsui.*

Felix

$$$$ | **EUROPEAN** | This Philippe Starck–designed, preposterously fashionable scene atop the Peninsula boasts breathtaking floor-to-ceiling views of Hong Kong. The dinner menu is equally stunning, and while rooted in European cooking, includes bright Asian touches as demonstrated by items such as the grilled wagyu beef tenderloin. **Known for:** unfaultable service; stunning harbor views; classy and upscale ambience. *Average main: HK$1,000* *The Peninsula Hong Kong, 28th fl., 19–21 Salisbury Rd., Tsim Sha Tsui* *2696–6778* *hongkong.peninsula.com* *No lunch* *Tsim Sha Tsui.*

Gaylord

$$ | **INDIAN** | This was one of the first Indian restaurants on the Hong Kong dining scene, and the atmosphere is still intimate and fun, especially on nights when there's live music. The food is packed with authentic spices, and there's an extensive menu for vegetarians. **Known for:** heritage Indian restaurant; elevated classics like chicken tikka masala; atmospheric dining. *Average main: HK$200* *Prince Tower, 5th fl., 12A Peking Rd., Tsim Sha Tsui* *2376–1001* *Tsim Sha Tsui.*

Hoi King Heen

$$$ | **CHINESE** | If you're looking for stellar Cantonese cuisine, this is the place for you. The chefs serve a range of modern classics made from the freshest ingredients and influenced by their reverence for natural flavors. **Known for:** beautiful VIP private dining rooms; tableside cutting of peking duck; glossy and flavorful char siu. *Average main: HK$500* *InterContinental Grand Stanford, 70 Mody Rd., Tsim Sha Tsui* *2731–2883* *www.hongkong.intercontinental.com* *East Tsim Sha Tsui.*

★ Hutong

$$$$ | **CHINESE** | It's easy to see why Hutong is a hot spot: it has some of the most imaginative northern Chinese cuisine in town. What's more, the beautifully decorated dining room sits atop H Zentre, overlooking the entire festival of lights that is the Hong Kong island skyline. **Known for:** a sensational selection of regional Chinese creations; a Sunday brunch with 18 specialties and free-flowing Veuve Clicquot; amazing Victoria Harbour and skyline views. *Ⓢ Average main: HK$1,000 ✉ H Zentre, 18th fl., 15 Middle Rd., Tsim Sha Tsui ☎ 3428–8342 ⊕ www.hutong.com.hk Ⓜ Tsim Sha Tsui.*

Ko Lau Wan Hotpot and Seafood Restaurant

$$$ | **CHINESE** | Anyone seeking an authentic hot pot experience need look no farther than Ko Lau Wan. Locals flock here for the tender beef and seafood that you cook at your table in a piping-hot pot of broth. **Known for:** hot pot beloved by locals; high-quality seafood; beef with beautiful marbling. *Ⓢ Average main: HK$500 ✉ Winfield Commercial Bldg., 2nd fl., 6–8 Prat Ave., Tsim Sha Tsui ☎ 3520–3800 ⏲ No lunch Ⓜ Tsim Sha Tsui.*

Ladies Sik Faan

$$ | **CANTONESE** | **FAMILY** | Celebrate the romance of old Hong Kong at Ladies Sik Faan, an elevated dai pai dong–style experience. "Sik faan" translates to "let's eat" or, more literally, "eat rice"—which isn't a bad idea if you order any of their sauce-heavy dishes like scallops with vermicelli, black bean clams, and sweet and sour pork. Their bite-size prawn toast, topped with a dollop of black truffle, is a must-order when visiting. **Known for:** prawn toast with black truffle for sharing; colorful old Hong Kong vibes; classic dai pai dong dishes. *Ⓢ Average main: HK$200 ✉ The Pinnacle, Basement fl., Shop A, 8 Minden Ave., Tsim Sha Tsui ☎ 2388–6111 ⊕ www.instagram.com/ladies_street_sikfaan ⏲ No lunch Ⓜ Tsim Sha Tsui, Exit N3.*

Lai Ching Heen

$$$$ | **CHINESE** | Previously named Yan Toh Heen, this renowned Cantonese restaurant located in the Regent Hong Kong has an elegant dining room against expansive harbor views and food that is at the top of its class. Exquisite is hardly the word for the decor, which mixes contemporary with the traditional and encompasses gorgeous details like jade-color place settings. **Known for:** Peking duck transformed into 3 dishes; excellent dim sum; two Michelin-starred dining. *Ⓢ Average main: HK$1,000 ✉ InterContinental Hong Kong, 18 Salisbury Rd., Tsim Sha Tsui ☎ 2313–2323 ⊕ hongkong.regenthotels.com/dining-destination Ⓜ Tsim Sha Tsui.*

The Legacy House

$$$$ | **CHINESE** | **FAMILY** | This Michelin-starred Chinese restaurant in Rosewood Hong Kong is spacious and glamorous, serving beloved classics such as Peking duck and char siu, as well as regional Cantonese delicacies like deep-fried pigeon and minced fish soup. Three different eight-course tasting menus are available, as well as a set dim sum menu. **Known for:** cool and moody atmosphere; friendly, professional, and accommodating staff; art-filled private dining rooms. *Ⓢ Average main: HK$700 ✉ Rosewood Hong Kong, 5th fl., 18 Salisbury Rd., Tsim Sha Tsui ☎ 3891–8732 ⊕ www.rosewoodhotels.com Ⓜ Tsim Sha Tsui, Exit J.*

Outdark Korean Restaurant

$$ | **KOREAN** | Tsim Sha Tsui is sometimes called Little Korea due to the number of Korean restaurants in the district; and while the number of Korean restaurants has dwindled after COVID-19, a few stalwarts remain, one of which is Outdark. This fried-chicken outpost from Busan, South Korea dishes out all the Korean classics, but the spicy cheesy chicken served on a stone platter is particularly tasty. **Known for:** a wide range of Korean alcoholic drinks; stone platter dishes; big

menu and big servings. $ *Average main: HK$140 ✉ H8 Bldg., 17th fl., Hau Fook St., Tsim Sha Tsui ☎ 2722–0831 ⏲ No lunch except Sun. Ⓜ Tsim Sha Tsui, Exit B2.*

Oyster & Wine Bar

$$$ | SEAFOOD | Against the romantic backdrop of Hong Kong's twinkling harbor, this is the top spot in town for oyster lovers. More than 20 varieties are flown in daily and displayed around the horseshoe oyster bar, ready for shucking. **Known for:** Victoria Harbour views; free-flow oyster brunch on Sunday; cool oyster display. $ *Average main: HK$500 ✉ Sheraton Hong Kong Hotel & Towers, 18th fl., 20 Nathan Rd., Tsim Sha Tsui ☎ 2369–1111 ⏲ No lunch Mon.–Sat. Ⓜ Tsim Sha Tsui.*

Sabatini

$$$$ | ITALIAN | Opened by the acclaimed Sabatini restaurateur brothers, this small corner of Italy with sponge-painted walls and wooden furnishings has a cult following among those who crave authentic Italian cuisine. Linguine Sabatini, the house specialty, is their take on *linguine al frutti di mare*. **Known for:** seasonal truffle menu; Italian-esque interiors and ambience; old-school, white-tablecloth dining. $ *Average main: HK$800 ✉ The Royal Garden, 3rd fl., 69 Mody Rd., Tsim Sha Tsui ☎ 2733–2000 🌐 www.rghk.com.hk Ⓜ East Tsim Sha Tsui.*

The Steak House

$$$$ | STEAK HOUSE | This restaurant, with its lively, informal atmosphere and gleaming harbor views, serves one of the best steaks in the city. You can choose from among 10 steak knives and more than a dozen mustards and rock salts—gimmicky, but fun—but the main event is the perfectly cooked, char-grilled meats. **Known for:** sweeping sea views; lush ambience and furnishings; beautifully plated dishes. $ *Average main: HK$1,000 ✉ Regent Hong Kong, Ground fl., 18 Salisbury Rd., Tsim Sha Tsui ☎ 2313–2323 🌐 hongkong.regenthotels.com/dining-destination ⏲ No lunch weekends Ⓜ Tsim Sha Tsui.*

Tai Ping Koon

$$ | CHINESE | This is one of the oldest restaurants in Hong Kong and also one of the first places to serve "soy sauce" Hong Kong–style Western cuisine. The decor, staff, and menu seem to have remained unchanged since day one, adding to the nostalgic charm of the place. **Known for:** roasted pigeon; old Hong Kong ambience; dramatic baked soufflé. $ *Average main: HK$200 ✉ 40 Granville Rd., Tsim Sha Tsui ☎ 2721–3559 🌐 www.taipingkoon.com.hk Ⓜ Tsim Sha Tsui.*

WHISK

$$$ | EUROPEAN | At the Mira Hotel's flagship restaurant, seasonal ingredients are turned into creative European dishes designed to impress. The half roasted yellow chicken—a mainstay in the rotating menu—is a must-try. **Known for:** elegant yet casual for fine-dining; French techniques with Japanese influences; seasonal promotions available. $ *Average main: HK$500 ✉ The Mira Hotel, 5th fl., 118 Nathan Rd., Tsim Sha Tsui ☎ 2315–5999 🌐 www.themirahotel.com Ⓜ Tsim Sha Tsui.*

Wu Kong

$$ | CHINESE | This restaurant serves good Shanghainese fare at reasonable prices. The signature xiao long bao (soup dumplings) are great, and the honey ham with crispy bean-curd skin wrapped in soft bread is delicious and authentic. **Known for:** some of the best soup dumplings in Hong Kong; good-value set menus featuring seasonal ingredients; noisy environment. $ *Average main: HK$150 ✉ Leung Chi Bldg., Basement fl., 27 Nathan Rd., Tsim Sha Tsui ☎ 2366–7244 🌐 www.wukong.com.hk Ⓜ Tsim Sha Tsui.*

A Spot of Tea

Legend has it that the first cup dates from 2737 BC, when *Camellia sinensis* leaves fell into water being boiled for Emperor Shenong. He loved the result, tea was born, and so were many traditions.

Historically, when a girl accepted a marriage proposal she drank tea, a gesture symbolizing fidelity (tea plants die if uprooted). Betrothal gifts were known as "tea gifts," engagements as "accepting tea," and marriages as "eating tea." Traditionally the bride and groom kneel before their parents, offering cups of tea in thanks.

Serving tea is a sign of respect. Young people proffer it to their parents or grandparents; subordinates do the same for their bosses. When you're served tea, show your thanks by tapping the table with your index and middle fingers.

Even modern medicine acknowledges that tea's powerful antioxidants reduce the risk of cancer and heart disease. It's also thought to be such a good source of fluoride that Mao Zedong eschewed toothpaste for a green-tea rinse.

Tea Types

Pu'er tea, which is known here as *Bo Lei*, is the beverage of choice at dim sum places. In fact, another way to say dim sum is *yum cha*, meaning "drink tea."

Afternoon tea is another local fixation—neighborhood joints with Formica tables, grumpy waiters, and often, menus written only Chinese. Most people go for *nai cha* made with evaporated milk. A really good cup is smooth, sweet, and hung with drops of fat. An even richer version, *cha chow*, is made with condensed milk. If *yuen yueng* (yin yang, half milk tea and half instant coffee) sounds a bit much, *ling-mun cha* (lemon tea) is also on hand. Don't forget to order a side of french toast or a pineapple bun, often served with a thick slab of butter sandwiched in the middle.

The bubble (or *boba*) tea craze may have died down a bit, but you'll still find plenty street stalls selling the popular Taiwanese drink. These cold brews contain pearly balls of tapioca or other types of jelly. Traditional herbal tea shops can also be found across the city, offering dark-hued liquid remedies for an array of health issues. These teas are typically Traditional Chinese Medicine-backed, and intensely potent. Modern herbal tea chains such as Healthworks also offer convenient health blends in MTR stations all over town.

Coffee and Quick Bites

Bakehouse

$ | **DESSERTS** | Come to Bakehouse for its freshly baked egg tarts with buttery, crispy shells and creamy custard filling. Expect to stand in line whenever you go, and don't be surprised if it's sold out early in the afternoon. **Known for:** arguably one of the best egg tarts in the city; selection of excellent desserts like tarts, danishes, croissants; preorder recommended. *Average main: HK$60* *44 Hankow Rd., Tsim Sha Tsui* *www.bakehouse.hk* *Tsim Sha Tsui.*

The Butterfly Room

$$$$ | **BRITISH** | Rosewood Hong Kong's lush afternoon tea experience at The Butterfly Room will make you feel as though you're a Disney princess. The

fixed set comes with creative welcome bites, finger sandwiches, baked scones, and sweets—not to mention the dramatic chocolate trolley that'll roll by the table when you think you can't physically stomach another pastry. **Known for:** ultraluxurious high tea experience; chocolate trolley; Instagram-worthy ambience. *$ Average main: HK$568 ✉ Rosewood Hong Kong, 2nd fl., 18 Salisbury Rd., Tsim Sha Tsui ☎ 3891–8732 🌐 www.rosewoodhotels.com Ⓜ Tsim Sha Tsui, Exit J.*

Lee Keung Kee

$ | **CHINESE** | Bubble-shaped egg waffles are a local specialty in Hong Kong, and Lee Keung Kee offers a delicious version. The waffles here are crisp on the outside but soft and cottony on the inside. **Known for:** long but fast-moving line; original flavor egg waffle that isn't too sweet; small stall with take-out only. *$ Average main: HK$30 ✉ 178 Nathan Rd., Tsim Sha Tsui 💳 No credit cards Ⓜ Tsim Sha Tsui.*

Mammy Pancake, Tsim Sha Tsui

$ | **CANTONESE** | This Tsim Sha Tsui takeaway spot for bubble-shape egg waffles is positioned right by the Star Ferry, making it the perfect breakfast or mid-day snack as you step off the boat. You can choose from a huge variety of sweet or savory fillings, from banana chocolate-chip to salted seaweed and corn. **Known for:** many popular branches throughout the territory; unique savory flavors; grab-and-go by Star Ferry. *$ Average main: HK$35 ✉ 1st fl., Shop KP–13, 29 and 30, Tsim Sha Tsui Star Ferry Pier, Tsim Sha Tsui 🌐 www.mammypancake.com Ⓜ Tsim Sha Tsui, Exit L5.*

Shari Shari Kakigori House

$$ | **JAPANESE** | For the best Japanese kakigori (shaved ice dessert), head to Shari Shari where ice is imported from Japan and shaved in-store into airy, flakey pieces. The snowflake-textured shaved ice is then mixed or topped with a range of delicious flavors, such as Earl Grey, pistachio, tiramisu, and mango. **Known for:** long waiting times after dinner hours; low calorie dessert option; authentic kakigori made from Japanese ice. *$ Average main: HK$150 ✉ Golden Mansion, Ground fl., 83–85A, Chatham Rd. S, Tsim Sha Tsui ☎ 2661–2347 Ⓜ Tsim Sha Tsui, Exit P3.*

 Hotels

The southern tip of the Kowloon peninsula is the birthplace of the Golden Mile, and upholding its reputation is a cluster of luxury hotels around the southern end of Nathan Road. Postcard skyline views from posh suites overlooking Victoria Harbour provide an oasis of serenity above the bustling and boisterous neighborhood below.

BP International

$ | **HOTEL** | Though guest rooms in this modern town on the north side of Kowloon Park have few frills and vary in size considerably (ask for a larger one), they do have one bonus: views over an extensive swath of greenery or the harbor. **Pros:** on-site coffee shop, restaurant, and lounge; self-service coin laundry; glorious green views from most rooms. **Cons:** can get crowded with business and tour groups; few amenities; small rooms with dated decor. *$ Rooms from: HK$750 ✉ 8 Austin Rd., Tsim Sha Tsui ☎ 2376–1111 🌐 www.bpih.com.hk 529 rooms No Meals Ⓜ Tsim Sha Tsui.*

FWD House 1881

$$$$ | **HOTEL** | Formerly named Hullet House, this hotel offers 10 huge suites at a former colonial marine police headquarters dating back to the 1880s. **Pros:** historic surroundings; notable restaurants and bars on the ground floor; Bentley transfer included. **Cons:** public areas can get crowded; photo taking hotspot decreases privacy; limited rooms available. *$ Rooms from: HK$6,500 ✉ 2A Canton Rd., Tsim Sha Tsui ☎ 3988–0000 🌐 www.fwdhouse1881.com 10 suites Free Breakfast Ⓜ Tsim Sha Tsui.*

The Dim Sum Experience

Dim sum restaurants have always been associated with noise, so don't be dissuaded by the boisterous throngs of locals gathered around large round tables. At one time big metal carts filled with bamboo baskets were pushed around the restaurant by ladies who would shout out the names of the dishes and stamp a mark onto a table's check when it ordered a basket of this or that. This is still the typical dim sum experience outside of China, but in Hong Kong most restaurants require you to order off a form, creating a more sedate and efficient dining experience. Thankfully, many places offer English-translated order forms or menus, although you should ask your waiter about daily specials that might not appear in translation, as those are often some of the most exciting dim sum options. And never forget that most basic principle of Hong Kong ordering: simply point to something you see at a nearby table.

Although dim sum comes in small portions, it's still intended for sharing among several diners. When all is said and done, a group can expect to sample about 10 or 12 dishes, but don't order more than one of any single item. Most dim sum restaurants prepare between 15 and 100 varieties of the more than 2,000 kinds of dim sum in the Cantonese repertoire, daily. These can be dumplings, buns, crepes, cakes, pastries, or rice; they can be filled with beef, shrimp, pork, chicken, bean paste, or vegetables; and they can be bamboo-steamed, pan-fried, baked, or deep-fried. More esoteric offerings vary vastly from place to place. Abandon any squeamish tendencies and try at least one or two unusual plates, like marinated chicken's feet or steamed rice rolls filled with pork liver.

You'll be able to find dim sum from before dawn to around 5 or 6 pm, but it's most popular for breakfast (from about 7:30 to 10 am) and lunch (from about 11:30 am to 2:30 pm). Dim sum is served everywhere from local teahouses to high-concept restaurants, but it's often best at casually elegant, blandly decorated mid-range spots that cater to Chinese families.

The following is a guide to some of our favorite common dim sum items, but don't let it narrow your mind. It's almost impossible to find a bite of dim sum that's anything less than delicious, and the more unique house specialties can often be the best.

Buns

■ **Cha siu so:** baked barbecued pork pastry buns; they're less common than the steamed cha siu bao, but arguably even better.

■ **Cha siu bao:** steamed barbecued pork buns are an absolute must. With the combination of soft and chewy textures and sweet and salty tastes, you might forget to remove the paper underneath before eating.

Dumplings

■ **Har gau:** steamed dumplings with a light translucent wrap that conceals shrimp and bamboo shoots.

■ **Siu mai:** steamed pork dumplings are the most common dumplings, and you'll find them everywhere, easily recognizable by their bright yellow wrappers; some are stuffed with shrimp as an additional filling.

Meats

■ **Ngau yuk yuen:** steamed beef balls, like meatballs, placed on top of thin bean-curd skins and served with vinegar; not the most flavorful option, but a good one for kids or picky eaters.

■ **Pie gwat:** bite-size pieces of succulent pork spare ribs in a black-bean and chili-pepper sauce.

Rice creations

■ **Har cheong fun:** shrimp-filled rice rolls, whose dough is made in a rice-noodle style; the thick, flat rice rolls are drowned in soy sauce. Other versions include ngau yuk cheong fun (beef filled) and char siu cheong fun (barbecued pork filled).

■ **Ja leung:** similar to Cheong Fun, but filled with a deep-fried dough pastry and wrapped in a thin layer of rice roll. It's often dotted with chopped scallions and served with soy sauce, but should also be dunked in sweet sauce and peanut paste.

■ **Ho yip fan:** delicious sticky rice, which is usually cooked with chopped Chinese mushrooms, Chinese preserved sausage, and dried shrimp, and wrapped and steamed in a lotus leaf to keep it moist (don't eat the leaf).

Don't be afraid of ...

■ **Woo tao go:** a glutinous pan-fried taro cake, sweet enough for dessert but eaten as a savory dish, with delicate undertones that come from preserved Chinese sausage, preserved pork belly, and dried shrimp. Another version of this is *lau bak go*, which is made with turnip instead of taro.

■ **Foong jow:** marinated chicken feet, whose smooth, soft texture is unlike any other. Once you get past the idea that you're sucking the cartilage off a foot, the sensation is wonderful.

■ **Gam cheen to:** cow's stomach served with chunks of daikon and doused in an addictive black-bean sauce with chili.

Sweets

■ **Dan taht:** tarts with a custard filling, generally served for dessert.

■ **Mong gwor bo deen:** mango pudding that has a consistently glassy texture. The pudding itself is not too sweet and needs to be eaten with condensed milk.

■ **Ma lai go:** this soft and spongy steamed cake is served warm and is popular for its eggy, custardy aroma.

Harbour Grand Kowloon
$$ | **HOTEL** | **FAMILY** | This hotel offers a long list of amenities: most of the large, comfortable, contemporary rooms have harbor views, and the year-round outdoor pool, spa, gym, and array of lounges and restaurants are spectacular. **Pros:** harborfront location on the peaceful side of the promenade; extensive business center; three-minute walk to the subway. **Cons:** slightly away from tourist attractions; designs are a bit dated; hospitality is a hit or miss. *$ Rooms from: HK$1,500 ✉ Whampoa Garden, 20 Tak Fung St., Hung Hom, Tsim Sha Tsui ☎ 2621–3188 ⊕ www.harbourgrand.com/kowloon 554 rooms No Meals M Hung Hom.*

Holiday Inn Golden Mile
$$ | **HOTEL** | Most views from the basic, medium-size rooms involve an up-close look at your neighbors, but being in the heart of Tsim Sha Tsui is the main attraction, along with such perks as a refreshing outdoor pool area with sauna and steam rooms. **Pros:** multiple dining options include a Cantonese restaurant, Italian restaurant, and popular buffet; in the heart of TST; located right by a metro station. **Cons:** no views; can get crowded with groups; designs are a bit dated. *$ Rooms from: HK$1,300 ✉ 50 Nathan Rd., Tsim Sha Tsui ☎ 2369–3111 ⊕ holidayinn.com/hongkong-gldn 614 rooms No Meals M Tsim Sha Tsui.*

★ **Hop Inn**
$ | **B&B/INN** | One of the city's most charming and personable budget hotels exudes loads of character in tidy, comfortable rooms that are well organized and clean. **Pros:** fun, beautifully original decor for budget lodgings; friendly staff; beds for every budget. **Cons:** not too many amenities, but the price is right; decor in need of refurbishment; rooms near elevators or reception can be noisy. *$ Rooms from: HK$650 ✉ Lyton Building, 5th fl., 36 Mody Rd., Tsim Sha Tsui ☎ 2881–7331 ⊕ www.hopinn.hk 15 rooms No Meals M Tsim Sha Tsui.*

★ **Hotel ICON**
$$ | **HOTEL** | The interiors throughout this hotel are designed to make a statement, from the vertical garden hanging above the lobby café to the stylish, panoramic, top-floor lounge—and, in between, are gorgeous, view-filled guest rooms outfitted with cozy woods, natural fabrics, and high-tech amenities. **Pros:** a designer's dream; dedication to guest experience; famous dinner buffet. **Cons:** surrounding area is thick with crowds at times; long walk from the MTR; lobby can feel busy when small tour groups arrive. *$ Rooms from: HK$1,800 ✉ 17 Science Museum Rd., Tsim Sha Tsui ☎ 3400–1000 ⊕ www.hotel-icon.com 262 rooms No Meals M Tsim Sha Tsui East.*

Hyatt Regency Hong Kong, Tsim Sha Tsui
$$ | **HOTEL** | At this location boxed in by high-rises, only the upper-floor rooms have memorable views, but all are cozy retreats done in olive and brown tones with burgundy armchairs and classic photos of Hong Kong on the walls. **Pros:** close to the action and Minden Street bar scene; good dining options; complimentary smartphones with unlimited data and local calls. **Cons:** busy shopping-mall surroundings; partial harbor views; details feel dated. *$ Rooms from: HK$2,000 ✉ 18 Hanoi Rd., Tsim Sha Tsui ☎ 2311–1234 ⊕ www.hyatt.com/hyatt-regency 381 rooms No Meals M Tsim Sha Tsui.*

★ **InterContinental Grand Standford Hong Kong**
$$ | **HOTEL** | Its location at the tip of the Kowloon peninsula ensures panoramic, front-row harbor views from most of the restaurants and contemporary guest rooms. **Pros:** exceptional views; impeccable service; extravagant spa and good restaurant lineup. **Cons:** most rooms don't have bathtubs; can be hard to get reservations at the popular restaurants; long walk from the MTR. *$ Rooms from: HK$1,900 ✉ 70 Mody Rd., Tsim Sha Tsui ☎ 2721–5161 ⊕ www.hongkong-ic.*

intercontinental.com 🛏 *572 rooms* 🍽 *No Meals* Ⓜ *Tsim Sha Tsui.*

K11 Artus

$$$$ | HOTEL | FAMILY | A luxury hotel residence designed for small families in mind, K11 Artus offers ultrastylish accommodations that range from spacious studios to one- to three-bedroom residences to penthouses, all equipped with kitchens, balconies, and modern interiors. **Pros:** 24-hour digital concierge; art-focused decor throughout the entire hotel; connected to K11 Musea. **Cons:** more expensive than other five-star hotels; just one on-site dining option; more suited to longer-term stays. 💲 *Rooms from: HK$5,500* ✉ *18 Salisbury Rd., Tsim Sha Tsui* ☎ *5100–1788* 🌐 *www.artus.com.hk* 🛏 *287 rooms* 🍽 *No Meals* Ⓜ *Tsim Sha Tsui, Exit J.*

Kowloon Shangri-La

$$$ | HOTEL | You might feel like a '70s tycoon amid murals, fountains, and crystal chandeliers in the lobby, and the feeling extends to the spacious rooms decorated in warm colors with armchairs, rich wooden furniture, bay windows, and nice marbled bathrooms. **Pros:** warm hospitality; excellent business facilities; quality Chinese restaurant. **Cons:** less exciting garden views on lower floors; hotel and amenities feel dated; service is a hit or miss. 💲 *Rooms from: HK$2,200* ✉ *64 Mody Rd., Tsim Sha Tsui* ☎ *2721–2111* 🌐 *www.shangri-la.com/kowloon* 🛏 *688 rooms* 🍽 *No Meals* Ⓜ *Tsim Sha Tsui East.*

The Langham

$$$ | HOTEL | Attractive luxury is apparent everywhere, from the opulent, European-baroque-style lobby to warmly decorated guest rooms, each finished with hardwood floors and silk drapes, and many with such touches as separate sitting areas and marble bathrooms with deep tubs and walk-in showers. **Pros:** one of the better buffet breakfasts in Hong Kong (included in some room rates); excellent dining options; modern room designs. **Cons:** limited city views; surrounded by heavy traffic; standard rooms are on the smaller size. 💲 *Rooms from: HK$2,600* ✉ *8 Peking Rd., Tsim Sha Tsui* ☎ *2375–1133* 🌐 *www.hongkong.langhamhotels.com* 🛏 *499 rooms* 🍽 *No Meals* Ⓜ *Tsim Sha Tsui.*

The Luxe Manor

$$ | HOTEL | In the absence of views, rooms are a show in themselves, with audacious design, artsy decor, and plenty of luxury and comfort. **Pros:** a trippy experience for art and design lovers; close to nightlife and shopping; live music at the hotel's bar and lounge. **Cons:** no views; lobby feels deserted at times; the over-the-top design is not for everyone. 💲 *Rooms from: HK$1,000* ✉ *39 Kimberley Rd., Tsim Sha Tsui* ☎ *3763–8888* 🌐 *www.theluxemanor.com* 🛏 *159 rooms* 🍽 *No Meals* Ⓜ *Tsim Sha Tsui.*

Marco Polo Hongkong Hotel

$$ | HOTEL | FAMILY | Spacious rooms with sweeping views of Hong Kong Island are near the shopping hub along Canton Road and linked to Harbour City's immense shopping complex. **Pros:** westward views; convenient to Star Ferry and other transport; easy access to Harbour City shopping. **Cons:** full in late March during the Hong Kong Rugby Sevens tournament; boisterous crowds during German Bierfest; busy atmosphere. 💲 *Rooms from: HK$2,000* ✉ *Harbour City, Canton Rd., Tsim Sha Tsui* ☎ *2113–0088* 🌐 *www.marcopolohotels.com* 🛏 *665 rooms* 🍽 *No Meals* Ⓜ *Tsim Sha Tsui.*

The Mira

$$ | HOTEL | Streamlined-sleek guest rooms have touches of modern buzz everywhere (glass-pod showers, laptop safes, free smartphones), but the excellent service and guest-friendly facilities make this much more than a design showplace. **Pros:** hip, seen-and-be-seen vibe; good in-house dining; great spa with pool. **Cons:** lobby can be a little too active at times; rooms are on the smaller size; overly strong perfume in the lobby. $ *Rooms from: HK$1,500 ✉ 118 Nathan Rd., Tsim Sha Tsui ☎ 2368–1111 🌐 www.themirahotel.com 492 rooms No Meals Ⓜ Tsim Sha Tsui.*

Mondrian Hong Kong

$$ | **HOTEL** | Opened in late 2023, this art-forward hotel offers rooms accented with stylish, colorful furniture. **Pros:** luxury with a hint of playfulness; convenient location; excellent on-site cocktail bar. **Cons:** rooms are on the smaller side; some rooms are not completely soundproof; surrounding buildings block some seaside views. $ *Rooms from: HK$1,800 ✉ 8A Hart Ave., Tsim Sha Tsui ☎ 3550–0388 🌐 www.mondrianhotels.com 324 rooms No Meals Ⓜ Tsim Sha Tsui, Exit N3.*

★ The Peninsula Hong Kong

$$$$ | **HOTEL** | Even in a city with so many world-class hotels, The Peninsula—opened in 1928 and the luxury brand's flagship—stands apart from the rest, an oasis of old-world glamour, with Kowloon and harbor views that'll make you feel like you own Hong Kong and high-ceiling, apartment-like rooms furnished with chic, residential-style elegance and updated with guest-oriented technology. **Pros:** legendary dining and service; state-of-the-art room facilities; extensive on-site facilities. **Cons:** rooms are pricey; the lobby feels like a tourist trap in the afternoon; no outdoor pool. $ *Rooms from: HK$5,080 ✉ Salisbury Rd., Tsim Sha Tsui ☎ 2920–2888 🌐 hongkong.peninsula.com 300 rooms No Meals Ⓜ Tsim Sha Tsui, Exit L3.*

Rosewood Hong Kong

$$$$ | **HOTEL** | **FAMILY** | Opened in 2019, this harborside outpost of the Rosewood is polished, tasteful, and luxurious, with modern rooms and bathrooms with gorgeous checkered-marble floors. **Pros:** high-quality hotel restaurants; thoughtful spa offerings; connects to K11 Musea. **Cons:** facilities and restaurants can get crowded; have to go through K11 Musea to access MTR; service can be improved. $ *Rooms from: HK$4,000 ✉ Victoria Dockside, 18 Salisbury Rd., Tsim Sha Tsui ☎ 3891–8888 🌐 www.rosewoodhotels.com 413 rooms No Meals Ⓜ Tsim Sha Tsui, Exit J.*

Royal Garden

$$ | **HOTEL** | A comfortable business hotel built around a towering garden atrium happens to be a particularly good place for world-class dining, with four notable restaurants on-site, though the spacious, sleek, and soothing guest rooms do not have views. **Pros:** excellent pool; distinguished restaurants; full spa. **Cons:** no views from rooms; crowded lobby area; rooms are dated. $ *Rooms from: HK$2,000 ✉ 69 Mody Rd., Tsim Sha Tsui ☎ 2721–5215 🌐 www.rghk.com.hk 420 rooms No Meals Ⓜ Tsim Sha Tsui East.*

Sheraton Hong Kong Hotel & Towers

$$ | **HOTEL** | Such perks as good dining and the chance to sip champagne in a bubbling rooftop Jacuzzi enhance the warm and modern guest rooms, many with city and harbor views. **Pros:** beautiful art-filled lobby and public spaces; classy shopping arcade; excellent business and fitness facilities. **Cons:** at the dense and congested southern end of Nathan Road; slower service and check in; service can be spotty. $ *Rooms from: HK$1,900 ✉ 20 Nathan Rd., Tsim Sha Tsui ☎ 2369–1111 🌐 www.sheraton.com/hongkong 782 rooms No Meals Ⓜ Tsim Sha Tsui.*

Stanford Hillview Hotel

$ | **HOTEL** | Straightforward and relatively no-frills rooms are set above busy Tsim Sha Tsui on a hillside below the Hong Kong Observatory, providing a nice retreat and pleasant views. **Pros:** excellent all-day buffet in the Hillview Cafe; quiet; stately renovated building. **Cons:** small, simple rooms; requires a short uphill walk to entrance; limited food offerings. $ *Rooms from: HK$700 ✉ Knutsford Terrace, Observatory Rd., Tsim Sha Tsui ☎ 2722–7822 🌐 www.stanfordhotels.com.hk 177 rooms No Meals Ⓜ Tsim Sha Tsui.*

K11 Musea is an experiential retail destination filled with art, exclusive luxury shops, and restaurants.

Nightlife

Central and Wan Chai are undoubtedly the king and queen of nightlife in Hong Kong. If you're staying in a hotel, however, or having dinner across the water in Kowloon, Ashley Road and Knutsford Terrace, both in Tsim Sha Tsui, still make for a fun night out. If cocktails on the water with a view of the harbor sounds like your kind of thing, check out the *Aqua Luna*, a cruise experience organized by Aqua Restaurant Group.

BARS

All Night Long

LIVE MUSIC | This Knutsford Terrace staple hosts a talented Filipino cover band that mainly works hits from the '80s and '90s. Drinks are a little overpriced, but there's an impressive sound system that prompts a loud sing-along from the crowd. Spanish-style artwork adorns the red-and-yellow walls. ✉ *9 Knutsford Terr., Tsim Sha Tsui* ☎ *2367–9487* Ⓜ *Tsim Sha Tsui.*

Aqua Luna

SOUND/LIGHT SHOW | As one of the city's last traditionally crafted vessels, or junks, the plush *Aqua Luna*'s dramatic appearance and red sails make her easy to spot. Step off dry land from the piers in Kowloon, Central, or Stanley, order a gin and tonic, and take in the shimmering harbor sights for 45 minutes. The price tag includes one drink, and a snack menu is available. Choose from several evening sails, or the dim sum and afternoon tea cruises. They also offer package options which include dinner at Aqua or Hutong. ✉ *Hong Kong Cultural Centre, Public Pier No. 1, Tsim Sha Tsui* ☎ *2116–8821* 🌐 *www.aqua.com.hk.*

★ Aqua Spirit

BARS | Inside an impressive curvaceous skyscraper, this very cool bar sits on the mezzanine level of the top floor. The high ceilings and glass walls offer up unrivaled views of Hong Kong and the surrounding harbor filled with ferries and ships. Tables are placed in front of the windows so you never have to crane your neck to see the skyline. ✉ *H Zentre, 17th fl., 15 Middle Rd., Tsim Sha Tsui* ☎ *3427–2288* 🌐 *www.aqua.com.hk* Ⓜ *Tsim Sha Tsui.*

Avoca
COCKTAIL BARS | Mondrian Hotel's cocktail bar offers creative, Hong Kong–inspired tipples such as lap yuk (Chinese cured pork belly) old fashioned and mango pomelo colada. Snag a seat by the window for a gorgeous sea view. ✉ *Mondrian Hong Kong, 38th fl., 8A Hart Ave., Tsim Sha Tsui* ☎ *3550–0338* 🌐 *www.mondrianhotels.com* Ⓜ *Tsim Sha Tsui, Exit N3.*

Bar Buonasera
COCKTAIL BARS | This Japanese-style cocktail and whiskey bar offers some of the classiest drinks in Tsim Sha Tsui. They have an extensive whiskey-based cocktail menu, as well as highballs and tea-forward drinks. ✉ *Mody House, 7th fl., 30 Mody Rd., Tsim Sha Tsui* ☎ *2111–4444* 🌐 *www.barbuonasera.com* Ⓜ *Tsim Sha Tsui, Exit N3.*

The Cell
BARS | This unique bar is set in the reporting room of a former police station, with three cells that used to hold pirates and smugglers now converted into private drinking rooms. The specialty here is whiskey, but they also have an interesting cocktail menu and tasty bar bites. ✉ *FWD House 1881, Main Bldg., Ground fl., 2A Canton Rd., Tsim Sha Tsui* ☎ *3988–0138* 🌐 *www.fwdhouse1881.com* Ⓜ *Tsim Sha Tsui, Exit L5.*

Dada
BARS | This bar in the eccentric Luxe Manor hotel is a tribute to surrealism: a side gallery boasts two original etchings by Salvador Dalí. References to that artist and other greats like Magritte abound. A dark and spacious bar area is anchored by a central counter, from which bottles of absinthe glimmer. ✉ *2nd fl., Luxe Manor, 39 Kimberly Rd., Tsim Sha Tsui* ☎ *3763–8778* 🌐 *www.dadalounge.com.hk* Ⓜ *Tsim Sha Tsui.*

★ DarkSide
LIVE MUSIC | Head to Rosewood's DarkSide for aged spirits, cigars, and cocktails, complemented by live jazz every night. Drinks are enjoyed in a dark and velvet-adorned space, perfect for a cozy date. ✉ *Rosewood Hong Kong, 2nd fl., 18 Salisbury Rd., Tsim Sha Tsui* ☎ *3891–8732* 🌐 *www.rosewoodhotels.com* Ⓜ *Tsim Sha Tsui, Exit J.*

Delaney's The Irish Pub
PUB | This Irish pub has interiors that were shipped here from the Emerald Isle, and the mood is as authentic as the furnishings. Guinness and Delaney's ale (a specialty microbrew) are on tap, and there's a traditional Irish menu. The crowd includes some Irish regulars, so get ready for spontaneous outbursts of fiddling and other Celtic traditions. ✉ *Mary Bldg., Basement fl., 71–77 Peking Rd., Tsim Sha Tsui* ☎ *2301–3980* 🌐 *www.instagram.com/delaneys_kowloon* Ⓜ *Tsim Sha Tsui.*

★ Felix
BARS | High up in the Peninsula Hong Kong, this bar is immensely popular with visitors. It not only has a brilliant view of the island, but the dramatic interiors are by the visionary designer Philippe Starck. Another memorable feature: tthe women's bathroom overlooks the harbor, while the men's has great city views. ✉ *Peninsula Hong Kong, 28th fl., Salisbury Rd., Tsim Sha Tsui* ☎ *2696–6778* 🌐 *hongkong.peninsula.com* Ⓜ *Tsim Sha Tsui.*

Ned Kelly's Last Stand
LIVE MUSIC | Come to this boisterous Australian watering hole, named for the continent's notorious bushranger, for an exuberant Dixieland jazz outfit that often leads the crowd in a rowdy sing-along. The band plays from 9:30 pm to 1 am nightly. ✉ *11A Ashley Rd., Tsim Sha Tsui* ☎ *2376–0562* Ⓜ *Tsim Sha Tsui.*

Qura Bar

LOUNGES | Lit up by mood lighting and decorated with plush sofas, Regent Hotel's Qura Bar oozes glam and mystery. It also offers a wide selection of wines and interesting cocktails infused with flavors like wasabi, tomato, feta cheese, and leather. For bar bites, they do more than just fries—try their beef tartare, stuffed chicken wings with chorizo rice, or tuna tacos. ✉ *Regent Hong Kong, 18 Salisbury Rd., Tsim Sha Tsui* ☎ *2313–2313* 🌐 *hongkong.regenthotels.com/dining-destination* Ⓜ *Tsim Sha Tsui, Exit J.*

Woobar

BARS | This fashionable space is in keeping with the W Hong Kong's chic and fun aesthetic. Wednesday night you can opt for free-flowing wine and a selection of tasty cheeses. The lychee martinis are excellent. ✉ *W Hong Kong, 1 Austin Rd. W, Tsim Sha Tsui* ☎ *3717–2222* 🌐 *www.woobar-whongkong.com* Ⓜ *Kowloon.*

Performing Arts

Hong Kong Cultural Centre

CONCERTS | The Hong Kong Cultural Centre's 2,000-seat concert hall, an oval-shape space fitted with an adjustable acoustic canopy and curtains, houses an 8,000-pipe Austrian organ, one of the world's largest. The Grand Theatre often hosts visiting Broadway musicals, opera, and ballet, while cozier plays take place in the Studio Theatre. Exhibitions are occasionally mounted in the atrium. ✉ *10 Salisbury Rd., Tsim Sha Tsui* ☎ *2734–2009* 🌐 *www.hkculturalcentre.gov.hk* Ⓜ *Tsim Sha Tsui.*

Shopping

Lit up in neon and jam-packed with shops, Nathan Road is Tsim Sha Tsui's main drag—but sky-high prices, overcrowded streets, and aggressive street hawkers bent on ripping you off may leave you wishing you'd gone elsewhere. Slip down the side streets and things get better. Granville and Cameron roads are home to cheap clothing outlets, while Asian imports and young designers fill the boutiques at the funky Rise Shopping Arcade.

On the other end of the spectrum, the glamorous K11 Musea mall is worth a visit, even just for window shopping. By the pier, Harbour City is another expansive shopping mall decked with all the big designer names. Bespoke tailoring is another Tsim Sha Tsui specialty; however, it pays to choose a well-established place because quality varies enormously.

BEAUTY

FACES

COSMETICS | This sprawling one-stop shop, just a stone's throw from the Kowloon Star Ferry terminal, carries a long list of high-profile and niche beauty brands. It can get overwhelmingly packed with tourists, so be prepared to rub elbows with other shoppers as you pick out your new lippie. ✉ *Harbour City, Ocean Terminal, Shop 202, 5 Canton Rd., Tsim Sha Tsui* ☎ *2118–5622* Ⓜ *Tsim Sha Tsui, Exit L6.*

Don Don Donki

COSMETICS | From obscure Japanese snacks and fatty wagyu beef to Japanese cosmetics and household products, Don Don Donki has it all. This Japanese chain is built like a maze, and its theme song blasts on repeat throughout the day; but if you're able to power through the overstimulation, the range of cosmetics offerings here is unmatched. From fake lashes, face masks, and makeup to curry-flavored toothpastes, there's something for everyone. Plus, this particular branch closes in the early hours of the morning, perfect for night owls who are itching for a stroll. ✉ *Mira Place 2, B1 fl., Shop B161, 163, and B165–173, 118 Nathan Rd., Tsim Sha Tsui* ☎ *2650–0411* 🌐 *www.dondondonki.com* Ⓜ *Tsim Sha Tsui, Exit B1.*

BOOKS AND MUSIC

eslite spectrum Tsim Sha Tsui

BOOKS | This bookstore spans two floors and has a good selection of English books and magazines. Lifestyle shops from small local businesses dot around the space and sell everything from jewelry to snacks. The store can be accessed at street level or via Harbour City. ✉ *Star House, 2nd and 3rd fl., 3 Salisbury Rd., Tsim Sha Tsui* ☎ *9820–0254* 🌐 *meet.eslite.com* Ⓜ *Tsim Sha Tsui, Exit L6.*

CAMERAS AND ELECTRONICS

DJI

ELECTRONICS | From drones and professional microphones to action cameras, the DJI shop offers everything you may need to record your adventures. ✉ *Park Lane Shopper's Blvd., Ground fl. and 1st fl., 129 Nathan Rd., Tsim Sha Tsui* ☎ *2616–9128* 🌐 *www.dji.com* Ⓜ *Tsim Sha Tsui.*

Fortress

ELECTRONICS | Fortress is a trusted staple when it comes to electronics shopping in Hong Kong. You can find the latest tech from computers, cameras, smartphones, and TVs to drones and beauty appliances here. ✉ *Harbour City, Ocean Centre, 3rd fl., Shop 333A, 333B and 335–337, Canton Rd., Tsim Sha Tsui* ☎ *9820–0254* 🌐 *www.fortress.com.hk* Ⓜ *Tsim Sha Tsui.*

CLOTHING

Giordano

CLOTHING | Hong Kong's version of the Gap is the most established and ubiquitous local source for basic T-shirts, jeans, and casual wear. Like its U.S. counterpart, the brand now has a bit more fashion sense, but prices are still reasonable. Although the flagship store is in Manson House on Nathan Road, you'll have no problem finding one on almost every major street. ✉ *Manson House, Ground fl., 74–78 Nathan Rd., Tsim Sha Tsui* ☎ *2926–1028* 🌐 *www.giordano.com.hk* Ⓜ *Tsim Sha Tsui, Exit B1.*

giordano ladies

CLOTHING | If Giordano is the Gap, giordano ladies is the Banana Republic, albeit with a more Zen aesthetic. Find clean-line modern classics in neutral black, gray, white, and beige; each collection is brightened by a soft highlight color, such as leafy green, indigo, or rusty orange. Everything is elegant enough for the office and comfortable enough for the plane. ✉ *Manson House, 1st fl., 74–78 Nathan Rd., Tsim Sha Tsui* ☎ *2926–1331* 🌐 *www.giordanoladies.com* Ⓜ *Tsim Sha Tsui.*

Initial

CLOTHING | This team of local designers creates simple but whimsical clothing with a trendy urban edge. The bags and accessories strike a soft vintage tone, fitting the store's fashionably worn interiors, casually strewn secondhand furniture, and sultry jazz soundtrack. ✉ *Harbour City, Gateway Arcade, 2nd fl., Shop 2402, Canton Rd., Tsim Sha Tsui* ☎ *3427–9006* 🌐 *www.initialfashion.com* Ⓜ *Tsim Sha Tsui.*

CLOTHING: TAILORS

Maxwell's Clothiers Ltd.

CLOTHING | After you've found a handful of reputable, high-quality tailors, one way to choose between them is price. Maxwell's is known for its competitive rates. It's also a wonderful place to have favorite men's and women's shirts and suits copied. It was founded by third-generation tailor Ken Maxwell in 1961 and follows Shanghai tailoring traditions, while also providing the fabled 24-hour suit upon request. The showroom and workshop are in Kowloon, but son Andy and his team take appointments in the United States, Canada, Australia, and Europe twice annually. ✉ *Maxwell Centre, 13th fl., 39–41 Hankow Rd., Tsim Sha Tsui* ☎ *2366–6658* 🌐 *www.maxwells-clothiers.com* Ⓜ *Tsim Sha Tsui, Exit A1.*

Mode Elegante

CLOTHING | Don't be deterred by the somewhat dated mannequins in the windows. Mode Elegante is a favorite source for custom-made suits among women and men in the know. Tailors here specialize in European cuts. You'll have your choice of fabrics from the United Kingdom, Italy, and elsewhere. Your records are put on file so you can place orders from abroad. It'll even ship the completed garment to you almost anywhere on the planet. Alternatively, you can make an appointment with director Gary Zee, one of Hong Kong's traveling tailors, who makes regular visits to North America, Australia, Europe, and Japan. ✉ *Hankow Centre, Ground fl., Shop 22B, 5–15 Hankow Rd., Tsim Sha Tsui* ☎ *2366–8153* 🌐 *www.modeelegante.com* Ⓜ *Tsim Sha Tsui.*

★ **Sam's Tailor**

CLOTHING | Unlike many famous Hong Kong tailors, you won't find the legendary Sam's in a chic hotel or sleek mall. But don't be fooled. These digs in humble Burlington Arcade, a tailoring hub, have hosted everyone from U.S. presidents (back as far as Richard Nixon) to performers such as the Black Eyed Peas, Kylie Minogue, and Blondie. This former uniform tailor to the British troops once even made a suit for Prince Charles in a record hour and 52 minutes. The men's and women's tailor does accept 24-hour suit or shirt orders, but will take about two days if you're not in a hurry. Founded by Naraindas Melwani in 1957, "Sam" is now his son, Manu Melwani, who runs the show with the help of his own son, Roshan, and about 57 tailors behind the scenes. In 2004 Sam's introduced a computerized bodysuit that takes measurements without a tape measure (it uses both methods, however). These tailors also make biannual trips to Europe and North America: schedule updates are listed on the website. ✉ *Burlington Arcade, 94 Nathan Rd., Tsim Sha Tsui* ☎ *9883–5727* 🌐 *www.samstailor.com* Ⓜ *Tsim Sha Tsui.*

Spotting Jade

Authentic jade can be tricky for the casual shopper to spot, but a couple of simple tricks can help discern genuine from ersatz. When lifted, jade should be heavier than a similarly sized stone. Hold it to the light, and it should look fibrous, not homogenous. A more full-proof technique relies on the shopkeeper's cooperation. Scratch the surface of the stone in question with a knife, scissors, or whatever is on hand, and it shouldn't leave a mark.

DEPARTMENT STORES

LCX

DEPARTMENT STORE | This spacious store combines local and international fashion, beauty products, and dining under one roof. Youthful clothing brands like American Eagle, Vans, Fred Perry, Havaianas, and Initial all have their own areas here, as do Lush, and other cosmetics lines. LCX also has a handful of restaurants, including Gyu-Kaku Japanese and Pizza Maru. ✉ *Harbour City, Ocean Terminal, 3rd fl., 2–27 Canton Rd., Tsim Sha Tsui* ☎ *3102–3668, 3102–3668 customer service hotline* 🌐 *www.lcx.com.hk* Ⓜ *Tsim Sha Tsui, Exit A.*

JEWELRY AND ACCESSORIES

Prince Jewellery and Watch Company

JEWELRY & WATCHES | This shop carries timepieces made by more than 60 international brands, including Omega, Chopard, Breguet, and IWC. There's other jewelry on sale as well, which may entertain those accompanying the avid watch shopper. ✉ *Prestige Tower, Basement fl. and Ground fl., 23–25 Nathan Rd., Tsim Sha Tsui* ☎ *2739–2333* 🌐 *www.princejewellerywatch.com* Ⓜ *Tsim Sha Tsui, Exit L5.*

Rabeanco

HANDBAGS | Locally based Rabeanco has a reasonably priced line of beautiful, quality bags in Italian leather. Expect designs that are contemporary and colorful, but never flashy or absurd. ✉ *The One, Shop UG215, 100 Nathan Rd., Tsim Sha Tsui* ☎ *3409–9930* 🌐 *www.rabeanco.com* Ⓜ *Tsim Sha Tsui, Exit A.*

TSL Jewellery

JEWELRY & WATCHES | One of the big Hong Kong chains, TSL (Tse Sui Luen) specializes in diamond jewelry, and manufactures, retails, and exports its designs. Its range of 100-facet stones includes the Estrella cut, which reflects nine symmetrical hearts and comes with international certification. Although its contemporary designs use platinum settings, TSL also sells pure, bright, yellow-gold items targeted at Chinese customers. ✉ *Park Lane Shopper's Blvd., Nathan Rd., Tsim Sha Tsui* ☎ *2375–2661* 🌐 *www.tslj.com* Ⓜ *Tsim Sha Tsui.*

MALLS AND SHOPPING CENTERS

Elements

MALL | This upscale shopping mall is in the Kowloon West residential and commercial district, just above Kowloon's Airport Express train and check-in station. Beautifully designed, it's divided into five different zones based on the titular elements: metal, wood, water, earth, and fire. This is one-stop shopping as far as international luxury brands are concerned, with Valentino, Prada, and Gucci, just to name a few. ✉ *1 Austin Rd. W, Tsim Sha Tsui* ☎ *2735–5234* 🌐 *www.elementshk.com* Ⓜ *Kowloon, Exit C2.*

★ Harbour City

MALL | The four interconnected complexes that make up Harbour City contain almost 500 shops between them—if you can't find it here, it probably doesn't exist. Pick up a map on your way in, as it's easy to get lost. **Ocean Terminal,** the largest section, runs along the harbor and is divided thematically, with kids' wear and toys on the ground floor, and sports and cosmetics on the first. The top floor is home to white-hot department store LCX. Near the Star Ferry pier, the **Marco Polo Hong Kong Hotel Arcade** has branches of the department store Lane Crawford. Louis Vuitton, Chanel, and Burberry are some of the posher boutiques that fill the **Ocean Centre** and **Gateway Arcade,** parallel to Canton Road. Most of the complex's restaurants are here, too—including the popular American import, The Cheesecake Factory. A cinema and three hotels round out Harbour City's offerings.

■ TIP→ Free Wi-Fi is available. ✉ *3–27 Canton Rd., Tsim Sha Tsui* ☎ *2377–2100* 🌐 *www.harbourcity.com.hk* Ⓜ *Tsim Sha Tsui.*

★ K11 Musea

MALL | This may just be the most dramatic and luxurious shopping mall ever built in Hong Kong. Composed of curved, sculptural shapes, the building is an architectural stunner even from the outside; inside, bronze-color waves, walls swathed in greenery, and contemporary art installations elevate the experience even further. The washrooms are equally theatrical, with gorgeous powder spaces. Shopping gears towards the pricier side, with well-known luxury brands populating the floors. Check out MoMA Design Store—affiliated with New York's Museum of Modern Art—for curated artistic gifts, houseware, and lifestyle goods. ✉ *18 Salisbury Rd., Tsim Sha Tsui* ☎ *3892–3890* 🌐 *www.k11musea.com* Ⓜ *East Tsim Sha Tsui.*

Mira Place

MALL | Not to be confused with the neighboring Miramar Shopping Centre, this mall targets Hong Kong's young elite and has offerings like agnès b. and Coach. ✉ *118 Nathan Rd., Tsim Sha Tsui* ☎ *2730–5300* 🌐 *www.mira-mall.com* Ⓜ *Tsim Sha Tsui.*

Rise Shopping Arcade

MALL | Many a quirky Hong Kong streetwear trend is born in this fabulous micromall. Don't let its grubby exterior

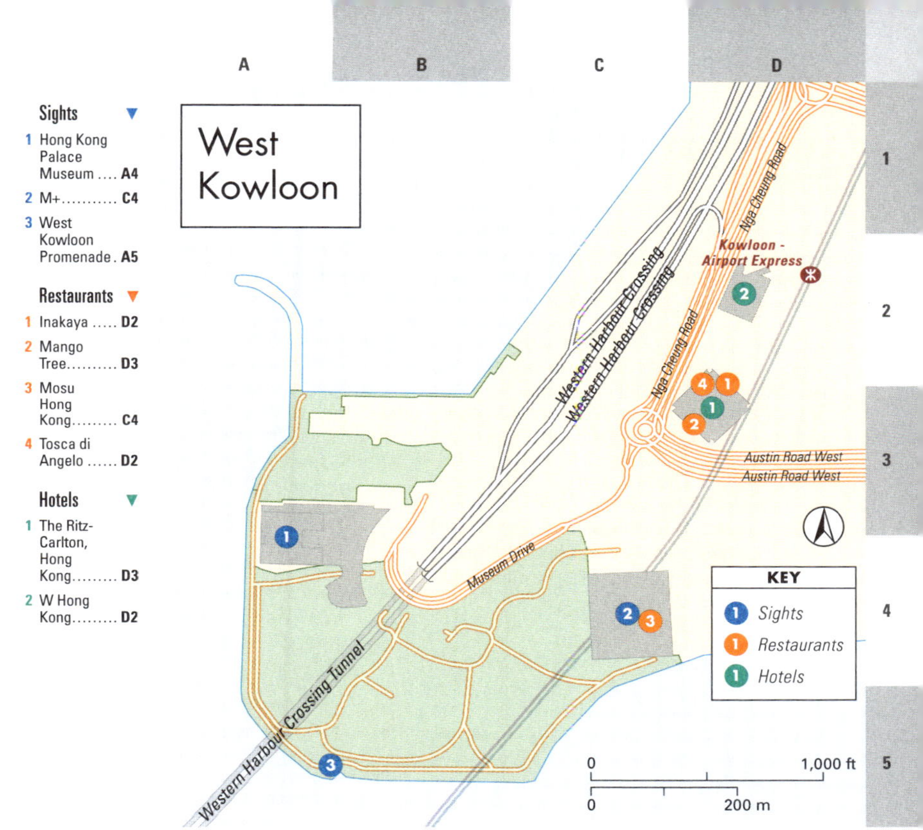

West Kowloon

A B C D

1 2 3 4 5

Sights

1 Hong Kong Palace Museum A4

2 M+........... C4

3 West Kowloon Promenade . A5

Restaurants

1 Inakaya D2

2 Mango Tree.......... D3

3 Mosu Hong Kong......... C4

4 Tosca di Angelo D2

Hotels

1 The Ritz-Carlton, Hong Kong......... D3

2 W Hong Kong......... D2

Nga Cheung Road
Kowloon - Airport Express
Western Harbour Crossing
Austin Road West
Museum Drive
Western Harbour Crossing Tunnel

KEY
Sights
Restaurants
Hotels

0 1,000 ft
0 200 m

put you off: the arcade is a haven of Asian cool. Japanese designers are particularly well represented. Handmade shoes and oversize retro jewelry are other fixtures, all at bargain prices. ✉ *5–11 Granville Circuit, off Granville Rd., Tsim Sha Tsui* Ⓜ *Tsim Sha Tsui, Exit B2.*

Activities

SPAS

Asaya

SPA | The Rosewood Hotel's wellness space and brand, Asaya, will make you feel as though you've been transported to Bali. Designed entirely differently from the rest of the hotel, the Asaya space offers the perfect zen backdrop to massages and yoga classes, as well as niche wellness offerings like art therapy, astrology sessions, and projective drawing analysis. ✉ *Rosewood Hong Kong, 6th fl., 18 Salisbury Rd., Tsim Sha Tsui* ☎ *3891–8588* 🌐 *www.rosewoodhotels.com* Ⓜ *Tsim Sha Tsui, Exit J.*

The Peninsula Spa

SPA | Here's another excuse to visit Hong Kong's grande-dame hotel—as if you needed one. Even the aromatic hand soaps in the bathrooms soothe the senses at this lavish East-meets-West sanctuary, which has separate facilities for men and women. You'll enjoy a range of therapies such as massages, chakra balancing, and facials in rooms overlooking the harbor; the view from the sauna must rank among the best in the world. ✉ *The Peninsula, 7th fl., Salisbury Rd., Tsim Sha Tsui* ☎ *2696–6682* 🌐 *www.peninsula.com* Ⓜ *Tsim Sha Tsui, Exit L3.*

West Kowloon

Just a little bit farther west than Tsim Sha Tsui's main attractions, West Kowloon makes for a nice change of pace. Occupying the harborfront greenspace is the West Kowloon Cultural District, home to a host of excellent museums and performance venues. The waterfront is lined with mid-range restaurants and cafes. On sunny weekends, it's a popular dog-friendly picnic spot.

Stroll north and you'll find the International Commerce Centre, Hong Kong's tallest skyscraper. It houses a number of upscale restaurants and the Ritz-Carlton Hong Kong, which offer remarkable views of Victoria Harbour.

Sights

Hong Kong Palace Museum

CULTURAL MUSEUM | FAMILY | This museum showcases over 900 artifacts from the National Palace Museum at Beijing's Forbidden City. In addition to its regular showings, the museum regularly hosts special exhibitions across six floors. There is also a number of on-site eateries, including a dim sum restaurant and a pleasant teahouse. ✉ *8 Museum Dr., West Kowloon, Tsim Sha Tsui* ☎ *2200–0217* 🌐 *www.hkpm.org.hk* 🎫 *HK$90* 🕓 *Closed Tues.* Ⓜ *Kowloon, Exit E4.*

★ M+

ART MUSEUM | FAMILY | Located in the West Kowloon Cultural District, M+ is Hong Kong's first global art museum. With 17,000 square meters of exhibition space across 33 galleries, three cinema houses, a roof garden, and other state-of-the-art facilities, M+ has undoubtedly been *the* most highly anticipated art addition of this decade. There are four permanent collections, as well as an ongoing roster of special exhibits spanning Chinese, Asian, and international art across different media and genres. There are multiple onsite dining options, including Mosu Hong Kong, a sophisticated Korean restaurant. The M+ Shop is an excellent place to pick up an artsy souvenir. ✉ *38 Museum Dr., West Kowloon, Tsim Sha Tsui* ☎ *2200–0217* 🌐 *www.mplus.org.hk* 🎫 *HK$160* 🕓 *Closed Mon.* Ⓜ *Kowloon, Exit C1 or D1.*

West Kowloon Promenade

PROMENADE | FAMILY | This spacious promenade overlooks Victoria Harbour and offers a dazzling view of Hong Kong Island's skyline. The promenade is grass-lined—a rare sight in the city—and has ample space for walking, jogging, biking, and picnicking. Though it's a lot quieter than the Avenue of Stars and the TST East Promenade, it does get crowded on the weekends. ✉ *West Kowloon, Tsim Sha Tsui* ☎ *2200–0217* 🌐 *www.westkowloon.hk* 🎫 *Free* Ⓜ *Kowloon, Exit C1 or D1.*

Restaurants

Inakaya

$$$$ | JAPANESE | On the 101st floor of the ICC building, Inakaya flaunts a jaw-dropping, bird's-eye city view and an equally extravagant interior, the highlight of which is a *robatayaki* (Japanese equivalent of barbecue) room, where a long counter is adorned with baskets of fresh ingredients. Because robatayaki is served in bite-size morsels, prices can add up, but it's a fun and unique experience. **Known for:** unforgettable grilled dishes prepared on long wooden paddles in front of your eyes; top-notch whiskies, wines, and sakes to sip among the clouds; teppanyaki A5 Wagyu, multicourse kaiseki meals, deluxe sushi platters. 💲 *Average main: HK$800* ✉ *International Commerce Centre, 101st fl., 1 Austin Rd. W, Kowloon* ☎ *2972–2666* 🌐 *www.jcgroup.hk* Ⓜ *Austin.*

Mango Tree

$$ | THAI | This eatery has won rave reviews since the first outlet opened in Bangkok. The Hong Kong branch lives up to its predecessor's reputation and boasts a winning formula of slick decor, friendly service, and tasty, refined takes on authentic regional Thai dishes. **Known for:** reliably good Thai food; chic yet unpretentious atmosphere; potent tropical cocktails. *Average main: HK$180* *Shop 2032, 1 Austin Rd. W, Tsim Sha Tsui* *2668–4884* *www.mangotree.com.hk* *Kowloon.*

★ Mosu Hong Kong

$$$$ | **KOREAN** | Named after the Korean pronunciation of cosmos—a flower that reminds executive chef Sung Anh of his childhood—Mosu is a Korean fine-dining restaurant located in the M+ museum. The tasting menus are populated with dishes that refined and creative, with a clear Korean flair. **Known for:** acorn noodles with black truffle; abalone tart; sister restaurant of three-Michelin starred Mosu Seoul. *Average main: HK$2,000* *M+ Tower, 3rd fl., 38 Museum Dr., West Kowloon Cultural District, Tsim Sha Tsui* *2398–0291* *hk.restaurantmosu.com* *Closed Mon. No lunch Tues. and Wed.* *Kowloon, Exit B.*

Tosca di Angelo

$$$ | **ITALIAN** | Stuck high up the clouds on the 102nd floor of the towering International Commerce Centre, Tosca di Angelo is a fine-dining restaurant helmed by a Sicilian chef who expertly dishes out Southern Italian fare. The views can be hit-or-miss, depending on how clear the skies are on the day you visit; regardless, you'll be preoccupied with the stunning interiors (complete with pretty fountains) and plates bursting with flavor. **Known for:** sea view from the sky; Michelin-starred dining; impeccable service. *Average main: HK$470* *International Commerce Centre, 102nd fl., 1 Austin Rd. W, Tsim Sha Tsui* *2263–2270* *www.ritzcarlton.com* *Closed Mon.* *Kowloon.*

Favorite Places

Doris Lam: I've watched the Kowloon West promenade transform over the years, going from empty land with patchy grass to the vibrant art and cultural district it is today. It's now home to several museums, including Hong Kong's renowned art museum, M+, a stunning promenade overlooking Hong Kong Island, hip restaurants, and plenty of grass-lined picnic space. It's a bit out of the way from everything else, but well worth the extra effort.

Hotels

★ The Ritz-Carlton, Hong Kong

$$$$ | **HOTEL** | **FAMILY** | At the world's third highest hotel, occupying the 102nd through the 118th floors of West Kowloon's ICC skyscraper, every large, luxurious guest room enjoys a stupendous vantage point. **Pros:** earth-shattering views; top-class service and amenities; sanctuary of a spa. **Cons:** pricey rates and food; surrounding Kowloon area lacks nightlife; famous Ozone bar feels overpriced and touristy. *Rooms from: HK$4,700* *International Commerce Centre, 1 Austin Rd. W, Kowloon* *2263–2270* *www.ritzcarlton.com* *312 rooms* *No Meals* *West Kowloon.*

★ W Hong Kong

$$$$ | **HOTEL** | A hip, young vibe prevails, though guest rooms are veritable urban oases—soundproof and spacious; alternately colorful or sleek on even and odd floors; and equipped with mood lighting, surround audiovisual systems, big mirrors, and even bigger harbor views. **Pros:** spacious and colorful rooms; panoramic views; exciting bars and restaurants.

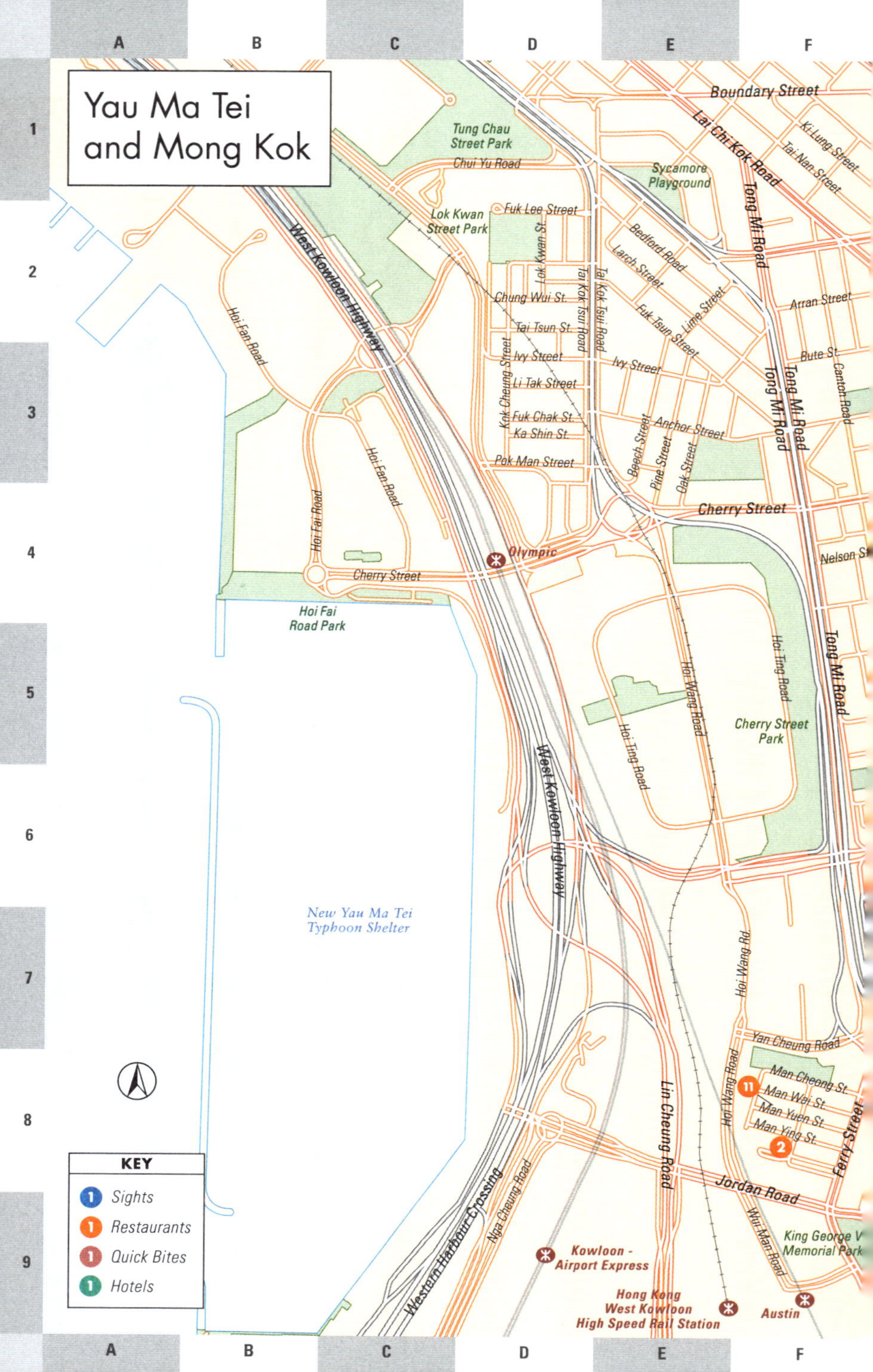

Yau Ma Tei and Mong Kok
A
B
C
D
E
F
1
2
3
4
5
6
7
8
9
Boundary Street
Lai Chi Kok Road
Ki Lung Street
Tai Nan Street
Tung Chau Street Park
Chui Yu Road
Sycamore Playground
Tong Mi Road
Lok Kwan Street Park
Fuk Lee Street
Lok Kwan St.
Bedford Road
Larch Street
West Kowloon Highway
Hoi Fan Road
Tai Kok Tsui Road
Arran Street
Chung Wui St.
Fuk Tsun Street
Lime Street
Tai Tsun St.
Ivy Street
Bute St.
Canton Road
Kok Cheung Street
Li Tak Street
Fuk Chak St.
Ka Shin St.
Anchor Street
Beech Street
Pine Street
Oak Street
Pok Man Street
Cherry Street
Hoi Fai Road
Olympic
Nelson St
Hoi Fai Road Park
Hoi Ting Road
Hoi Wang Road
Cherry Street Park
New Yau Ma Tei Typhoon Shelter
Hoi Wang Rd
Yan Cheung Road
Man Cheong St.
Man Wai St.
Man Yuen St.
Man Ying St.
Lin Cheung Road
Ferry Street
Jordan Road
KEY
Sights
Restaurants
Quick Bites
Hotels
Western Harbour Crossing
Nga Cheung Road
Wui Man Road
King George V Memorial Park
Kowloon - Airport Express
Hong Kong West Kowloon High Speed Rail Station
Austin

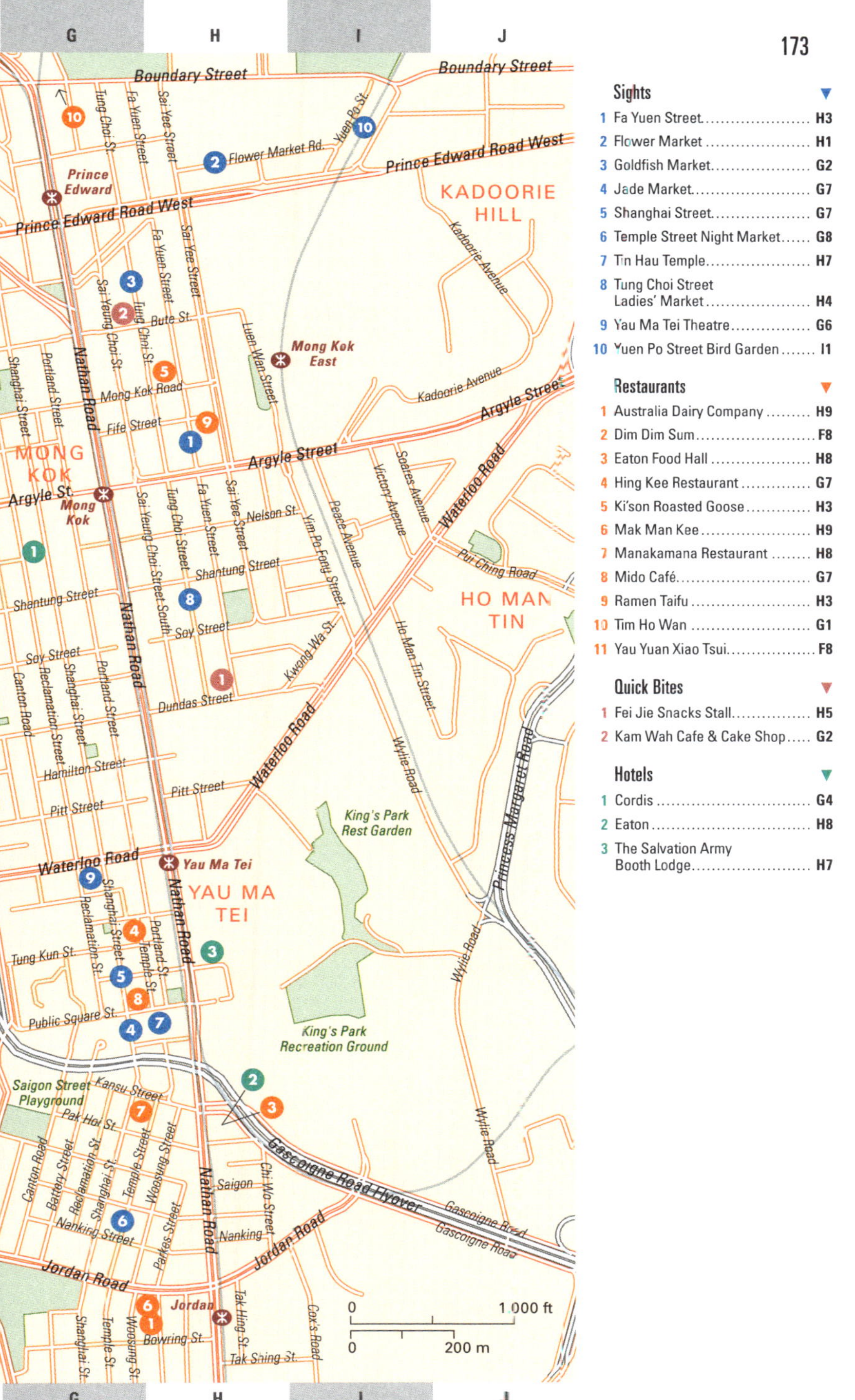

Sights

1. Fa Yuen Street H3
2. Flower Market H1
3. Goldfish Market G2
4. Jade Market G7
5. Shanghai Street G7
6. Temple Street Night Market G8
7. Tin Hau Temple H7
8. Tung Choi Street Ladies' Market H4
9. Yau Ma Tei Theatre G6
10. Yuen Po Street Bird Garden I1

Restaurants

1. Australia Dairy Company H9
2. Dim Dim Sum F8
3. Eaton Food Hall H8
4. Hing Kee Restaurant G7
5. Ki'son Roasted Goose H3
6. Mak Man Kee H9
7. Manakamana Restaurant H8
8. Mido Café G7
9. Ramen Taifu H3
10. Tim Ho Wan G1
11. Yau Yuan Xiao Tsui F8

Quick Bites

1. Fei Jie Snacks Stall H5
2. Kam Wah Cafe & Cake Shop G2

Hotels

1. Cordis G4
2. Eaton H8
3. The Salvation Army Booth Lodge H7

Cons: noisy atmosphere outside rooms; construction nearby; long walk from the MTR through the mall. *Rooms from: HK$6,000* *1 Austin Rd. W, Kowloon Station, Kowloon* *3717–2222* *www.w-hongkong.com* *393 rooms* *No Meals* *West Kowloon.*

Yau Ma Tei

Located north of Tsim Sha Tsui, the vibrant area of Yau Ma Tei teems with people and is home to several street markets. The area of Yau Ma Tei around Jordan Road—known as Jordan—blends into the neighboring district, and the Jordan MTR stop is a good place to start your exploring. Restaurants here are on the cheaper side, with numerous local gems at every turn.

Sights

Jade Market

MARKET | Jade in every imaginable shade of green, from the milkiest apple tone to the richest emerald, fills the stalls of this Kowloon market. Quality and prices at the stalls vary hugely, which means that if you know your stuff and haggle insistently, you can get fabulous finds. ⚠ **Beware that some of the so-called jade sold here is actually aventurine, bowenite, soapstone, serpentine, or Australian jade—all inferior to the real thing.** Look out for stalls with authentic jade certifications for a better chance of finding real jade. *251 Shanghai St., Yau Ma Tei* *Free* *Yau Ma Tei, Exit C.*

★ Temple Street Night Market

MARKET | Each evening, as darkness falls, the lamps strung between the stalls of this Yau Ma Tei street market slowly light up, and the air fills with aromas wafting from myriad food carts. Hawkers try to catch your eye by flinging up clothes; Cantonese opera competes with swelling pop music and the sounds of spirited haggling; fortune-tellers and street performers add another element to the sensory overload. Granted, neither the garments nor the cheap gadgets sold here are much to get excited about, but it's the atmosphere people come for—any purchases are a bonus. The market stretches for almost a mile and is one of Hong Kong's liveliest nighttime shopping experiences. Fortune-tellers, open-air cafés, and street doctors also offer their services here. *Temple St., Yau Ma Tei* *Between Jordan Rd. and Kansu St.* *Yau Ma Tei, Exit C; Jordan, Exit A.*

Tin Hau Temple

TEMPLE | **FAMILY** | This incense-filled site is dedicated to Taoist sea goddess Tin Hau, queen of heaven and protector of seafarers. The crowds here testify to her being one of Hong Kong's favorite deities—indeed, this is one of over 100 temples dedicated to her. Like all Tin Hau temples, this one once stood on the shore. Kowloon reclamation started in the late 19th century, and now the site is more than 3 km (2 miles) from the harbor. The main altar is hung with gold-embroidered cloth and usually piled high with offerings. There are also two smaller shrines inside the temple honoring earth god Tou Tei and city god Shing Wong. Surrounding Temple Street night market is a fortune-telling hot spot: you may well be encouraged to have a try with the chim. Each stick is numbered, and you shake them in a cardboard tube until one falls out. A fortune-teller asks you your date of birth and makes predictions from the stick based on numerology. Alternatively, you could have a mystically minded bird pick out some fortune cards for you.

TIP→ Agree on a price before your fortune, as bargaining with fortune-tellers is common. *56–58 Temple St., Yau Ma Tei* *Between Temple St. and Nathan Rd.* *2385–0759* *Yau Ma Tei, Exit C.*

Shanghai Street

STREET | Traditional trades are plied along this street. There are blocks dominated by tailors or shops selling Chinese cookware or everything you need to set up a household shrine. Nearby Ning Po Street is known for its paper kites and for the colorful paper and bamboo models of worldly possessions (boats, cars, houses) that are burned at Chinese funerals. ✉ *Shanghai St. between Jordan Rd. and Argyle St., Yau Ma Tei* Ⓜ *Yau Ma Tei, Exit C.*

Yau Ma Tei Theatre

ARTS CENTER | The government transformed this former movie theater (which screened adult films for years before being abandoned) into a 300-seat venue for Chinese opera performances. Some of the shows have English supertitles. A historic redbrick building around the corner on Shanghai Street serves as the theater's administration building. ✉ *6 Waterloo Rd., Yau Ma Tei* ☎ *2264–8108* 🌐 *www.lcsd.gov.hk/ymtt* Ⓜ *Yau Ma Tei, Exit B2.*

Restaurants

Yau Ma Tei has some of the best cheap eats in town, especially in the area around Jordan Road, which houses a large Nepalese population and a corresponding number of authentic Nepalese and Indian food spots. The famed Temple Street is also a good place to start: The street hides dai pai dongs and wallet-friendly noodle shops amid the many DVD shops and souvenir stores.

Australia Dairy Company

$ | CANTONESE | You can dine on a range of Hong Kong classics at this no-frills cha chaan teng. The service is curt and the turnover is fast, but the scrambled egg sandwich is moist and pillowy soft. **Known for:** Hong Kong–style buttered French toast; steamed milk pudding; busy, bustling atmosphere. Ⓢ *Average main: HK$80* ✉ *47 Parkes St., Jordan* ☎ *2730–1356* 💳 *No credit cards* ⏲ *Closed Thurs.* Ⓜ *Jordan.*

Dim Dim Sum

$ | CHINESE | Hidden away near the old Jordan pier, this little sit-down restaurant has excellent dim sum without the insane queues that plague its more famous competitors. That's not to say that it doesn't get packed during mealtimes; thankfully, the venue stays open until 10 pm, so you can sneak in for a late-night dinner when the crowds have dissipated. **Known for:** affordable dim sum; minipineapple buns; decent classics. Ⓢ *Average main: HK$80* ✉ *Man Kin Bldg., Ground fl., 28 Man Wui St., Jordan, Yau Ma Tei* ☎ *2771–7766* 🌐 *www.instagram.com/dimdimsumhk* 💳 *No credit cards* Ⓜ *Austin.*

Eaton Food Hall

$ | INTERNATIONAL | Eaton Hotel's jazzy food hall is as hip as the hotel. The spacious and well-designed modern food court offers a handful of dining options, from Japanese curry and Cantonese beef noodles to burgers and tacos—all hearty and delicious at reasonable prices. **Known for:** creative workshops and events; occasional buskers; plenty of seating. Ⓢ *Average main: HK$100* ✉ *Eaton HK, Ground fl., 380 Nathan Rd., Yau Ma Tei* ☎ *2710–1818* 🌐 *www.eatonfoodhall.com* Ⓜ *Jordan, Exit B2.*

Hing Kee Restaurant

$$ | CHINESE | Located on a boisterous stretch of Temple Street, this crowded, open-air eatery is the perfect spot to soak in the local atmosphere. The food isn't amazing, but it's cheap and offers a wide range of choices. **Known for:** stir-fried crab with black beans; glossy morning glory (water spinach); an array of stone pot flavors. Ⓢ *Average main: HK$150* ✉ *14–19 Temple St., Yau Ma Tei* ☎ *2384–3647* 💳 *No credit cards* Ⓜ *Yau Ma Tei.*

Mak Man Kee

$ | CANTONESE | This 60-year-old restaurant is a Michelin Bib Gourmand joint known for its Cantonese wonton noodles and dry mixed noodles. The noodles are

Did You Know?

The Temple Street Night Market is also known as Men's Street for the inexpensive men's jeans, watches, and shoes that overflow from carts. The market opens around 2 pm, becoming a lively pedestrian mall closer to dusk. Come in the evening for a partylike feel and to practice your bargaining skills.

ultraspringy, while the broth is deeply fragrant and the prawn-filled wontons have the thinnest dumpling skin. **Known for:** generous meat portions; gelatinous pork knuckles; very good noodles. *$ Average main: HK$80 ✉ 51 Parkes St., Yau Ma Tei ☎ 2736–5561 🌐 www.mmk.hk Ⓜ Jordan, Exit C2.*

Manakamana Restaurant

$$ | **NEPALESE** | For a dose of Indian and Nepalese food, head to Manakamana. The restaurant serves the essentials, like brightly colored curries and meat-filled steamed *momo* dumplings, as well as plenty of vegetarian options. **Known for:** open until midnight; flavor-packed grilled meats; Nepali family-style cooking. *$ Average main: HK$100 ✉ 107 Temple St., Jordon, Yau Ma Tei ☎ 2385–2070 💳 No credit cards Ⓜ Jordan.*

Mido Café

$ | **CHINESE** | This old-school cha chaan teng (local café) has plenty of charm, since the decor hasn't changed much since the '60s. Try the famous baked-pork-chop rice or enjoy a slice of crispy French toast with a cup of milk tea. **Known for:** nostalgic Hong Kong interiors; saucy porkchop rice; no photo policy. *$ Average main: HK$60 ✉ 63 Temple St., Yau Ma Tei ☎ 2384–6402 💳 No credit cards Ⓜ Yau Ma Tei.*

★ Yau Yuan Xiao Tsui

$ | **CHINESE** | It might look like any other tiny, storefront noodle joint, but its humble appearance belies its culinary prowess. The restaurant serves authentic Shaanxi snacks, which can be best described as some of the heartiest and delicious chow that China has to offer. **Known for:** signature biang biang mien (long, wide, al dente noodles with chili oil and marinated spareribs); brusque yet efficient service; handmade dumplings with lamb and scallion oil. *$ Average main: HK$50 ✉ Man Yiu Bldg., 36 Man Yuen St., Jordon, Jordan ☎ 5300–2682 💳 No credit cards Ⓜ Austin.*

Hotels

As you venture up and off Kowloon's central artery of Nathan Road through Yau Ma Tei, accommodations tend to be older and cheaper—though many provide excellent value.

Eaton

$$ | **HOTEL** | Rooms above a theater and shopping complex come in a variety of welcoming styles, from an East-meets-West decor in some to airy, bright, functional contemporary design in others—all are set up for maximum comfort and relaxation. **Pros:** comfortable rooms in a relatively convenient location; free Wi-Fi; hip events attract a younger crowd. **Cons:** Nathan Road can be overwhelming with traffic, crowds, and noise; area is slightly sketchier at night; rooms show wear. *$ Rooms from: HK$1,500 ✉ 380 Nathan Rd., Yau Ma Tei ☎ 2782–1818 🌐 hongkong.eatonhotels.com 465 rooms No Meals Ⓜ Yau Ma Tei.*

The Salvation Army Booth Lodge

$ | **HOTEL** | At this surprisingly pleasant budget retreat operated by the Salvation Army, everything is bright and clean, from the walls to the starched sheets on the firm double beds in the Spartan but large rooms. **Pros:** clean but no-frills lodgings at a bargain price; small but pleasant breakfast available; renovated modern finishes. **Cons:** noisy vehicle and foot traffic on the main street; toiletries must be purchased; spotty heat insulation. *$ Rooms from: HK$600 ✉ 11 Wing Sing La., Yau Ma Tei ☎ 2771–9266 🌐 salvationarmy.org.hk/our-work/booth-lodge 44 rooms No Meals Ⓜ Yau Ma Tei, Exit C.*

Shopping

The bright-lights–big-city look of Tsim Sha Tsui gives way to housing blocks and tenements hung with aging signs north of Jordan Road. Streets are crowded and traffic is manic, but this down-to-earth chaos is what makes shopping in these north Kowloon neighborhoods rewarding. Well, that and all the bargains at the area's markets. Yau Ma Tei has jade and pearls on Kansu Street; clothing, bric-a-brac, and domestic appliances fill atmospheric Temple Street nightly. If you prefer fixed prices, Yue Hwa's seven-story flagship store is one of the best places in Hong Kong for cheap gifts.

It's Good to Be Jaded

The Chinese believe that jade brings luck, and it's still worn as a charm in amulets or bracelets. A jade bangle is often presented to newborns, and homes are frequently adorned with jade statues or other carved decorative items.

BOOKS AND MUSIC

Kubrick

BOOKS | Stocking alternative-spirited books, graphic novels, magazines, and music in a variety of foreign languages, Kubrick is the closest thing to a bilingual community bookshop you're likely to find in Hong Kong. Coming here will give you a good, if slightly unpolished, sense of the city's contemporary culture. As an added bonus, the store is attached to a cinema that regularly shows art-house flicks and a casual café that occasionally hosts poetry readings or music gigs. When seeking directions, ask for the Broadway Cinemateque. ✉ *Prosperous Garden, Shop H2, 3 Public Square St., Yau Ma Tei* ☎ *2384–8929* 🌐 *www.kubrick.com.hk* Ⓜ *Yau Ma Tei, Exit C.*

DEPARTMENT STORES

★ Yue Hwa Chinese Products Emporium

DEPARTMENT STORE | This popular purveyor of Chinese goods has 12 stores across Hong Kong, and the flagship one features seven floors laden with everything from clothing and housewares to traditional medicine. The logic behind its layout is hard to fathom, so go with time to rifle around. As well as the predictable tablecloths, silk pajamas, and chopsticks, there are cheap and colorful porcelain sets and offbeat local favorites like mini-massage chairs. The fifth floor has a selection of tea—you can pick up a HK$50 packet of leaves or an antique Yixing teapot stretching into the thousands. ✉ *301–309 Nathan Rd., Jordan, Yau Ma Tei* ☎ *3511–2222* 🌐 *www.yuehwa.com* Ⓜ *Jordan.*

JEWELRY AND ACCESSORIES

Sandra Pearls

JEWELRY & WATCHES | You might be wary of the lustrous pearls hanging at this little Jade Market stall. But the charming owner does, in fact, sell genuine cultured and freshwater pearl necklaces and earrings at reasonable prices. Some pieces are made from shell, which Sandra is always quick to point out, and could pass muster among the snobbiest collectors. ✉ *Jade Market, Stall 437 and 447, Kansu St., Yau Ma Tei* ☎ *9485–2895* Ⓜ *Jordan, Exit A.*

Mong Kok

Mong Kok lives up to its Chinese name, which translates roughly as "busy corner." Long city blocks here are known for bustling markets that sell clothing, flowers, pets, and temple goods. The neighborhood is the epicenter of Hong Kong street fashion—the trends that originate from these bustling streets are known as "MK style." Mong Kok is technically the last district of Kowloon: Boundary Street marks the beginning of the New Territories, though these days the urbanized areas are known as New Kowloon.

Sights

Fa Yuen Street

STREET | FAMILY | Parallel to Tung Choi Street Ladies' Market, this street is sneaker central, lined with shoe shops selling some brands you know and lots more you don't. If you're not sporty, the stretch between Mongkok Road and Nullah Road offers cheap versions of the latest clothing fashion trends. ✉ *Fa Yuen St. between Mongkok Rd. and Shan Tung St., Mong Kok* 🎫 *Free* Ⓜ *Mong Kok, Exit D3.*

Flower Market

MARKET | Huge bucketfuls of roses and gerbera spill out onto the sidewalk along Flower Market Road, a collection of street stalls selling cut flowers and potted plants. Delicate orchids and vivid birds of paradise are some of the more exotic blooms. During Lunar New Year, there's a roaring trade in narcissi, poinsettias, and bright yellow chrysanthemums—all auspicious flowers. Head there in the morning or in the afternoon, as most of the market closes in the early evening. ✉ *Flower Market Rd., Mong Kok* ✣ *Between Yuen Ngai St. and Yuen Po St.* 🎫 *Free* Ⓜ *Mong Kok East, Exit C; Prince Edward, Exit B1.*

Goldfish Market

STORE/MALL | FAMILY | Goldfish are thought to bring good luck in Hong Kong (though aquariums have to be properly positioned for maximum benefit), and this small collection of sellers is a favorite local source. Shop fronts are decorated with bags of glistening, pop-eyed creatures, waiting for someone to take them home. Some of the fish for sale inside are serious rarities and fetch unbelievable prices. There are other types of animals as well. ✉ *Tung Choi St. and Nullah Rd., Mong Kok* 🎫 *Free* Ⓜ *Mong Kok East, Exit C; Prince Edward, Exit B2.*

Tung Choi Street Ladies' Market

MARKET | Block upon block of tightly packed stalls overflow with clothes, bags, and knickknacks along Tung Choi Street in Mong Kok. Despite the name, items for women, men, and children are for sale. Most offerings are imitations or no-name brands; rifle around enough and you can often pick up some cheap, cheerful basics. Haggling is the rule here: a poker face and a little insistence can get you dramatic discounts. At the corner of each block and behind the market are stands and shops selling the street snacks Hong Kongers can't live without. Pick a place where locals are munching and point at whatever takes your fancy. Parallel **Fa Yuen Street** is Mong Kok's unofficial sportswear market. ✉ *Tung Choi St., Mong Kok* ✣ *Between Dundas St. and Argyle St.* 🎫 *Free* Ⓜ *Mong Kok.*

Yuen Po Street Bird Garden

STORE/MALL | FAMILY | Though mostly built as a neighborhood park in which bird-owning residents can meet and "walk" their caged pets, the Urban Renewal Authority also included some 70 stalls to be used by those who lost trade when the famous Hong Lok Street songbird stalls were demolished in a revitalization project in the late 1990s. Though it sells various kinds of feathered creatures, you can also pick up the picturesque, empty carved cages and put them to better (empty) use in your home decor. Access the main entrance from Boundary Street, a short walk from the Prince Edward MTR station. ✉ *Yuen Po St., Mong Kok* ✣ *Between Boundary St. and Prince Edward Rd. W* Ⓜ *Mong Kok East, Exit C; Prince Edward, Exit B1.*

Restaurants

For the best street snacks in town, look no further than Mong Kok, where you'll find curry fish balls, among other snacks. The Tung Choi Street vicinity is especially rich in eateries of this type, selling everything from regional specialties like spicy Chongqing noodles to curry fish balls on bamboo skewers and fragrant egg waffles.

Stroll through the flower market for a dose of color.

Ki'son Roasted Goose

$$ | **CANTONESE** | Hong Kong roast meats are famous for a reason, and roast goose is one of the must-try dishes. This is a good place to sample the roasted bird with a side of rice or noodles—the goose skin is crispy, while the meat remains tender and flavorful. **Known for:** unfussy all-day dining restaurant; excellent roast meats; budget-friendly. *Average main: HK$100* ✉ *34 Mong Kok Rd., Mong Kok* ☎ *2812–1889* ▭ *No credit cards* Ⓜ *Mong Kok, Exit B3.*

Ramen Taifu

$$ | **RAMEN** | This quirky ramen shop lined with loud anime posters and drawings offers outstanding tsukemen (dipping ramen) for lunch until 4:30 pm, after which it switches to soup ramen. Customers are given a little paper to note down their ramen preferences, from the type of ramen, soup intensity level, amount of ramen noodles, and toppings. **Known for:** big portions; attentive and friendly service; small space, so expect to wait. *Average main: HK$100* ✉ *Kin Wong Mansion, Ground fl., 39 Fife St., Mong Kok* ☎ *2487–4488* Ⓜ *Mong Kok, Exit B2.*

★ Tim Ho Wan

$$ | **CHINESE** | This award-winning eatery serves some of the city's best dim sum at dirt-cheap prices. Opened by a former Four Seasons Hotel chef, this humble spot makes all of its shrimp dumplings, rice rolls, and baked cha siu buns fresh to order. **Known for:** very popular, so expect a line; golden pineapple buns; international dim sum franchise, with Michelin-starred flagship. *Average main: HK$100* ✉ *9–11 Fuk Wing St., Sham Shui Po, Mong Kok* ☎ *2788–1226* ▭ *No credit cards* Ⓜ *Sham Shui Po.*

Coffee and Quick Bites

Fei Jie Snacks Stall

$ | **CHINESE** | Dundas Street in Mong Kok is filled with street vendors. The Fei Jie Snacks Stall is one of the best, with its dizzying selection of skewered choices ranging from chewy squid to duck gizzard to pig intestine (best eaten with a squirt of mustard). **Known for:** innard combos; juicy pig intestines; beloved by locals. $ *Average main: HK$20* ✉ *Shop 4A, 55 Dundas St., Mong Kok* ☎ *8489–2326* ▭ *No credit cards* Ⓜ *Mong Kok.*

Kam Wah Cafe & Cake Shop

$$ | **CANTONESE** | This classic cha chaan teng serves some of the best Hong Kong classic dishes. Sample both their baked treats and carb-focused mains—try the beef hor fun, a savory and aromatic stir-fry noodle dish, followed by a pineapple bun with a slab of cold butter or an egg tart (or both). **Known for:** Hong Kong cha chaan teng classics; quick and unfussy service and seating; egg tarts straight from the oven. $ *Average main: HK$100* ✉ *47 Bute St., Mong Kok* ☎ *2392–6830* ▭ *No credit cards* Ⓜ *Prince Edward, Exit B2.*

Hotels

Cordis

$$ | **HOTEL** | **FAMILY** | At this sleek glass-and-steel box that transformed a once seedy block, whimsical sculptures of Mao's Red Guards greet you at the entrance, and luxurious guest rooms feature floor-to-ceiling windows, mirrored walls, mood lighting, and glass-walled marble bathrooms. **Pros:** great spa and pool; loads of shopping at adjoining high-end mall; good choice of in-house bars and restaurants. **Cons:** very busy surroundings; loud neighborhood; busy check-in. $ *Rooms from: HK$1,600* ✉ *555 Shanghai St., Mong Kok* ☎ *3552–3388* 🌐 *www.cordishotels.com/en/hong-kong* *665 rooms* *No Meals* Ⓜ *Mong Kok.*

Shopping

Here you'll discover blocks and blocks of brandless garments and accessories at the Fa Yuen Street Ladies' Market. Parallel Tung Choi Street has cut-price sporting goods. Goldfish, flowers, and birds each have their own dedicated market in Prince Edward. By comparison, the cavernous Langham Place megamall feels like an alternate universe.

CLOTHING

Me & George

VINTAGE | Anyone who loves a good thrift-store rummage will delight in the messy abandon of Me & George (also known as Mee & Gee), not to mention the rock-bottom prices. Clothing here start at HK$10. Yes, you heard right! Expect a mix of poorly made factory rejects and vintage dresses, shoes, and handbags. Fitting is not usually allowed (as is the case with most small fashion import outlets), but staff are often tolerant of quick try-ons in front of a mirror. ✉ *64 Tung Choi St., Mong Kok* Ⓜ *Mong Kok, Exit E2.*

MALLS AND SHOPPING CENTERS

Langham Place

MALL | The light beige sandstone of Langham Place stands in stark contrast to the pulsating neon signs and crumbling residential blocks around it. Yet the mall—with nearly 200 shops packed into 15 floors—has fast become a fixture on Mong Kok's chaotic shopping scene. It is especially popular with youngsters, who are drawn by the Asian labels in offbeat boutiques ranged around a spiral walkway from the 9th to 12th floors. Extra-long escalators—dubbed "Xpress-calators"—whisk you quickly up four levels at a time. The elegant glass-and-steel skyscraper across the road is the Langham Place Hotel; its stylish dining patio, The Backyard, offers the serenest of outdoor sanctuaries in one of the region's most congested neighborhoods. ✉ *8 Argyle St., Mong Kok* ☎ *3520–2800* 🌐 *www.langhamplace.com.hk* Ⓜ *Mong Kok, Exit C3.*

SHOES, HANDBAGS, AND LEATHER GOODS

Sportshouse

SPORTING GOODS | Check out the Sporthouse chain for trendy sneakers and other casual footwear by brands like Nike, Puma, Adidas, Converse, and

Birkenstock. ✉ *Ground fl., 64–68 Fa Yuen St., Mong Kok* ☎ *2388–0190* 🌐 *www.sportshouse.com* Ⓜ *Mong Kok, Exit E2.*

Activities

SPAS

Chuan Spa

SPA | If it's a quiet moment you're after, your best bet is Chuan Spa, which overlooks the city from the top floor of the Cordis hotel. In five-star spa surroundings, you can try cupping (an ancient Chinese acupressure technique), gua sha (a scraping practice to improve blood flow), or acupuncture—all of which aim to promote health and balance by distributing chi (energy) throughout the body. ✉ *Cordis, 555 Shanghai St., Mong Kok* ☎ *3552–3510* 🌐 *www.chuanspa.com.hk* Ⓜ *Mong Kok, Exit C3.*

Northern Kowloon

There's much to do in Kowloon beyond Tsim Sha Tsui and Mong Kok. Wong Tai Sin Temple and Chi Lin Nunnery, just a few subway stops to the east of Mong Kok, are two of Hong Kong's must-do spiritual sights. The Kowloon Walled City Park and Cattle Depot Artist Village are surrounded by fairly uninspiring residential and commercial districts but still worth a trip.

Sights

Cattle Depot Artist Village

ARTS CENTER | A former slaughterhouse has been transformed into an artistic hub, housing a number of artists' studios, galleries, and theater groups, including 1a Space, an experimental art venue, and On & On Theatre Workshop, a professional theater company. Individual artists and galleries keep erratic hours, and what you see will depend on who's open to the public at any given time. ✉ *63 Ma Tau Kok Rd., To Kwa Wan, Kowloon* ☎ *2848–6230* 🌐 *www.heritage.gov.hk* 🎫 *Free* Ⓜ *To Kwa Wan; Bus 101.*

Sham Shui Po

Two stops from Mong Kok on the MTR is Sham Shui Po, a labyrinth of small streets teeming with flea markets and wholesale shops where you can buy anything from electronics to computers to clothing. The Golden Computer Arcade, filled with small computer hardware shops, is favored by locals. Prices are competitive, but parts usually come without a warranty.

★ Chi Lin Nunnery

HISTORIC PARK | This nunnery was founded in 1934 as a retreat for Buddhist nuns. In the 1990s, the complex was rebuilt with traditional Tang Dynasty architectural techniques involving wooden dowels and brackets, which work to hold everything together without a single nail. Most of the 15 cedar halls house altars to bodhisattvas (those who have reached enlightenment)—bronze plaques explain each one. The Main Hall is the most imposing—and inspiring—part of the monastery. Overlooking the smaller second courtyard, it honors the first Buddha, known as Sakyamuni. The soaring ceilings are held up by cedar columns that support the roof. The principles of feng shui governed all construction: buildings face south toward the sea, to bring abundance; they're backed by the mountain, a provider of strength and good energy. The temple's clean lines are a vast departure from most of Hong Kong's colorful religious buildings. **■ TIP→ If there's time, take a stroll around nearby Nan Lian Garden.** ✉ *5 Chi Lin Dr., Diamond Hill, Kowloon* 🎫 *Free* Ⓜ *Diamond Hill, Exit C2.*

Founded as a retreat for Buddhist nuns, Chi Lin Nunnery remains an active monastery and residence for about 60 nuns today.

Kowloon Walled City Park

CITY PARK | One of Hong Kong's most beautiful parks, Kowloon Walled City Park is designed in Qing-dynasty style. In previous centuries it was a walled military site, then a notorious slum filled with unlicensed doctors and dentists, opium dens, brothels, gambling houses, and worse, until it was demolished in 1994. Today the major attraction is the Yamen—the imperial government administrative building—the only remaining structure from the original Walled City and an example of southern Chinese architecture of the 19th century. There are also a number of traditional gardens on the grounds, and eight zones showcasing different flora that you can see on free 45-minute guided tours on weekends. Hong Kong's Thai community is based in the streets south of the park, and there are countless hole-in-the-wall Thai restaurants. ✉ *Tung Tau Tsuen Rd., Kowloon* ✣ *Between Junction Rd. and Tung Tsing Rd.* ☎ *2716–9962* 🌐 *www.lcsd.gov.hk* 🎫 *Free* Ⓜ *Sung Wong Toi; Bus 113.*

Lion Rock

TRAIL | The easiest way to access the trail to Lion Rock, a spectacular summit, is from Kowloon. The hike passes through dense bamboo groves along the Eagle's Nest Nature Trail and up open slopes to Beacon Hill for 360-degree views over hills and the city. The contrasting vistas of green hills and the cityscape are extraordinary. There's a climb up the steep, rough track to the top of Lion Rock, a superb vantage point for appreciating Kowloon's setting between hills and sea. The trail ends at Wong Tai Sin Taoist Temple, where you can have your fortune told. To start, catch the MTR to Choi Hung (25 minutes from Tsim Sha Tsui) and a 10-minute taxi ride up Lion Rock to Gilwell Campsite. At the end of the road you'll see a sign indicating the start of the trail. From Wong Tai Sin, return by MTR. ✉ *Lion Rock Country Park, Sha Tin, New Territories* 🎫 *Free.*

Dumplings—both steamed and fried—are popular street snacks in Hong Kong.

★ Sik Sik Yuen Wong Tai Sin Temple

TEMPLE | There's a practical approach to prayer at one of Hong Kong's most exuberant places of worship. Here the territory's three major religions—Taoism, Confucianism, and Buddhism—are all celebrated under the same roof. You'd think that ornamental religious buildings would look strange with highly visible vending machines and LCD displays in front of them, but Wong Tai Sin pulls it off in cacophonous style. The temple was established in the early 20th century, on a different site on Hong Kong Island, when two Taoist masters arrived from Guangzhou with the portrait of Wong Tai Sin—a famous monk who was born around AD 328—that still graces the main altar. In the '20s the shrine was moved here and expanded over the years.

Start at the incense-wreathed main courtyard, where the noise of many people shaking out *chim* (sticks with fortunes written on them) forms a constant rhythm. After wandering the halls, take time out in the Good Wish Garden—a peaceful riot of rockery—at the back of the complex. At the base of the complex is a small arcade where soothsayers and palm readers are happy to interpret Wong Tai Sin's predictions for a small fee. At the base of the ramp to the Confucian Hall, look up behind the temple for a view of Lion Rock, a mountain in the shape of a sleeping lion.

■ TIP→ If you feel like acquiring a household altar of your own, head for Shanghai Street in Yau Ma Tei, the Kowloon district north of Tsim Sha Tsui, where religious shops abound. ✉ *Wong Tai Sin Rd., Kowloon* ☎ *2327–8141* 🌐 *www.siksikyuen.org.hk* 🎫 *Free (donations welcomed)* Ⓜ *Wong Tai Sin, Exit B2 or B3.*

Restaurants

Dubbed Little Thailand, Kowloon City is home to some of the best Thai restaurants in town, as well as a handful of affordable eateries dishing out regional cuisines across Asia.

Islam Food

$$ | CHINESE | This might not be the prettiest restaurant you've ever seen, but its pan-fried beef patties (translated as "veal goulash" on the menu) are incredibly delicious. The browned pastry packets arrive at the table piping hot and bursting with tender minced beef—good luck stopping after just one. **Known for:** tasty halal food; tender lamb brisket curry, pan-fried mutton dumplings, hot-and-sour soup; lines out the door at peak hours. *Average main: HK$100* *Ground fl., 33–35 Tak Ku Ling Rd., Kowloon City, Kowloon* *2382–1882* *www.islamfood.com.hk* *No credit cards* *Sung Wong Toi.*

Lung Jie Thai Restaurant

$$ | THAI | Lung Jie is one of the more popular Thai restaurants in Kowloon City, and for good reason—the food is excellent and the flavors are authentic. They've got two branches in Kowloon City alone, with each one attracting a line during dinner hours. **Known for:** refreshing papaya salad; well-done Thai classics; unfussy interiors. *Average main: HK$150* *2A–B Nga Tsin Long Rd., Kowloon City, Kowloon* *2383–5382* *No credit cards* *Sung Wong Toi.*

Tso Choi Restaurant

$$ | CHINESE | If you have a delicate constitution, take a pass on this home-style Cantonese restaurant. Tso Choi (which literally translates as "rough dishes") is not everyone's cup of tea. **Known for:** offals galore; soy braised pigeon; down-to-earth ingredients that produce big flavors. *Average main: HK$100* *17A Nga Tsin Wai Rd., Kowloon City, Kowloon* *2383–7170* *No credit cards* *Sung Wong Toi, Exit B3.*

Coffee and Quick Bites

Pâtisserie Tony Wong

$ | BAKERY | Opened by one of Hong Kong's best-known pastry chefs, this takeaway bakery offers a gorgeous collection of French-style pastries and gâteaux (layered cakes). The most famous creation here is the Rose—an elaborate layered cake decorated with edible chocolate petals. **Known for:** playful, artlike pastries; multiple locations around the territory; special occasion cakes. *Average main: HK$80* *65 Fuk Lo Tsun Rd., Kowloon City, Kowloon* *2382–6639* *www.patisserietonywong.com* *Sung Wong Toi, Exit B3.*

Shopping

CAMERAS AND ELECTRONICS

Golden Computer Arcade

ELECTRONICS | It's the most famous—some would say infamous—computer arcade in town. Know what you want before you go to avoid being dazed by the sheer volume of computer equipment and software. *146–152 Fuk Wa St., Sham Shui Po, Kowloon* *Sham Shui Po, Exit D.*

CLOTHING

Lu Lu Cheung

CLOTHING | A fixture on the Hong Kong fashion scene for decades, Lu Lu Cheung creates designs that exude comfort and warmth. In both daytime and evening wear, natural fabrics and forms are represented in practical yet imaginative ways. *Festival Walk, Shop LG1–60, 80 Tat Chee Ave., Kowloon Tong, Kowloon* *3188–1287* *www.lulucheung.com.hk* *Kowloon Tong.*

MALLS AND SHOPPING CENTERS

★ Festival Walk

MALL | Located in residential Kowloon Tong, about 20 minutes from Central on the MTR, Festival Walk stretches across six floors, with Marks & Spencer, an Apple store, MUJI, and H&M serving as anchors. Vivienne Tam and PS by Paul Smith draw the elite crowds; ba&sh and Club Monaco keep the trend spotters happy. If you want a respite from the sometimes scorching-hot weather, Festival Walk also has one of the city's largest ice rinks, a multiplex cinema, and numerous restaurants and cafés. ✉ *80 Tat Chee Ave., Kowloon Tong, Kowloon* ☎ *2844–2200* 🌐 *www.festivalwalk.com.hk* Ⓜ *Kowloon Tong.*

Mega Box

MALL | This 18-story mall is a great option for family shopping expeditions: those with minimal retail stamina can amuse themselves at IKEA, the IMAX theater, or the skating rink, and there are also numerous on-site eateries. However, unlike other malls that are in walking distance from MTR stations, visitors need to take a free shuttle here from the Kowloon Bay MTR station. To catch it, exit the MTR station at Exit A and go through Telford Plaza; you can always ask the Plaza concierge if you're confused. Shuttles run about every 10 minutes. ✉ *38 Wang Chiu Rd., Kowloon Bay* ☎ *2989–3000* 🌐 *www.megabox.com.hk* Ⓜ *Kowloon Bay, Exit A.*

Chapter 6

LANTAU ISLAND AND THE NEW TERRITORIES

Updated by
Jonathan DeLise

NEIGHBORHOOD SNAPSHOT

TOP REASONS TO GO

■ **See the Big Buddha:** One of Lantau Island's most popular attractions and also one of its most refreshing, Po Lin Monastery and Big Buddha are set in the green hill zone overlooking the airport. Visitors ascend a large series of steps and enter the Big Buddha to learn more about its construction and to admire some Buddhist art.

■ **Soar above the Hillside:** Ride the Ngong Ping 360 cable car up toward Po Lin Monastery and the Big Buddha, while taking in some scenic views of Hong Kong's airport, the verdant hillsides of Lantau, and the ever-expanding airport suburb of Tung Chung.

■ **Visit Hong Kong Disneyland:** Although it is by far the smallest of Disney's theme parks, there are still a number of hits that are either exclusive to the park or first introduced here. Namely, Mystic Manor, a fun house ride with 3-D video, Ant-Man and The Wasp: Nano Battle! with its own curious video effects, and Frozen Ever After, inspired by the eponymous movie.

■ **Explore a fishing village:** Tai O, one of the last remaining fishing villages, is known for houses built on stilts, boat rides, and seafood restaurants.

■ **Hike green trails:** Stretching 70 km (43 miles) along the midsection of the island, Lantau Trail has about 12 different sections, all with their own levels of difficulty. Hike up to Sunset Peak (860 meters/2,851 feet) for some excellent vistas at dusk.

MAKING THE MOST OF YOUR TIME

The New Territories region borders mainland China to the north and Sai Kung Peninsula to the east. Places worth visiting are a fair distance from each other, so day trips here take some planning. It's best to choose two or three sights to visit in a day, allowing 15–30 minutes of travel time between each, depending on whether you're going by bus or taxi. Note that fewer people speak English away from the city center.

Despite the distances between population centers, the range covered by the MTR, buses, and minibuses can get you close to many sights.

GETTING HERE

■ Lantau is connected via Tsing Yi to Kowloon by the lengthy Tsing Ma Bridge. Most Lantau roads lead to and from Tung Chung, the new high-rise town on the north shore, just west of the bridge and close to Hong Kong International Airport. The Tung Chung Road winds through the mountains and connects northern Lantau with the southern coast. Here the South Lantau Road stretches from the town of Mui Wo (where ferries from Central arrive) in the east to Tai O in the west, passing Cheung Sha Beach and Ngong Ping.

■ The speediest way to get to Lantau from Central is the MTR's Tung Chung line, which takes about half an hour. Far more pleasant is the 35-minute ferry from Central to Mui Wo.

■ In 2020, to benefit residents and travelers going between Hong Kong International Airport and the Hong Kong–Zhuhai–Macau Bridge terminus, a new Tuen Mun–Chek Lap Kok Link tunnel opened, connecting the western New Territories districts of Tuen Mun and Yuen Long.

Beyond all the towering skyscrapers and bustling markets, nearly 70% of Hong Kong's land is rural, rugged, and relatively unspoiled. Easy day trips from one of the most startlingly busy and modern metropolises in the world take you to pristine beaches, hillside forests, incense-filled temples, and still-quiet fishing villages.

No matter what sort of experience you crave, Hong Kong's vast and efficient transport network makes it easy to get around. Even still, some buses to more rural parts of the New Territories might only operate on weekends and public holidays, so try and review the bus schedules in advance.

Lantau is the largest of Hong Kong's more than 260 islands, and has long been a favorite getaway for city dwellers who want to escape to the forested landscapes and mountain vistas. The island is home to the world's favorite mouse, at Hong Kong Disneyland, as well as one of the world's largest Buddhas, the Tian Tan Buddha at Ngong Ping. Near these sights are towering peaks offering mountain hikes, and nice beaches backed by quiet fishing villages. You can take in the scenery from the Ngong Ping 360 cable car, a 5¾-km (3½-mile) ride filled with fantastic views of Lantau's steep northern coast.

Many of Hong Kong's lush, trail-laced parks are tucked away in the New Territories, on the eastern side of Kowloon. Sha Tin, Tuen Mun, and other "new towns" house more than half a million residents apiece, making them feel like their own cities. Even so, it's still easy to get away from the urban congestion.

Lantau Island

Manic development is changing Lantau, but the island is still known as the "lungs of Hong Kong" because of the abundant forests, relative dearth of skyscrapers (save for near the airport), and laid-back attractions—beaches, fishing villages, and hiking trails. At Ngong Ping, a minitheme park sits at the base of the island's most famous local attraction, the Tian Tan Buddha. Hong Kong Disneyland sits on the northeast coast, close to the massive Tsing Ma bridge. At 147 square km (57 square miles), Lantau is almost twice the size of Hong Kong Island, so there's room for all this development, yet the island mostly remains a welcome green getaway.

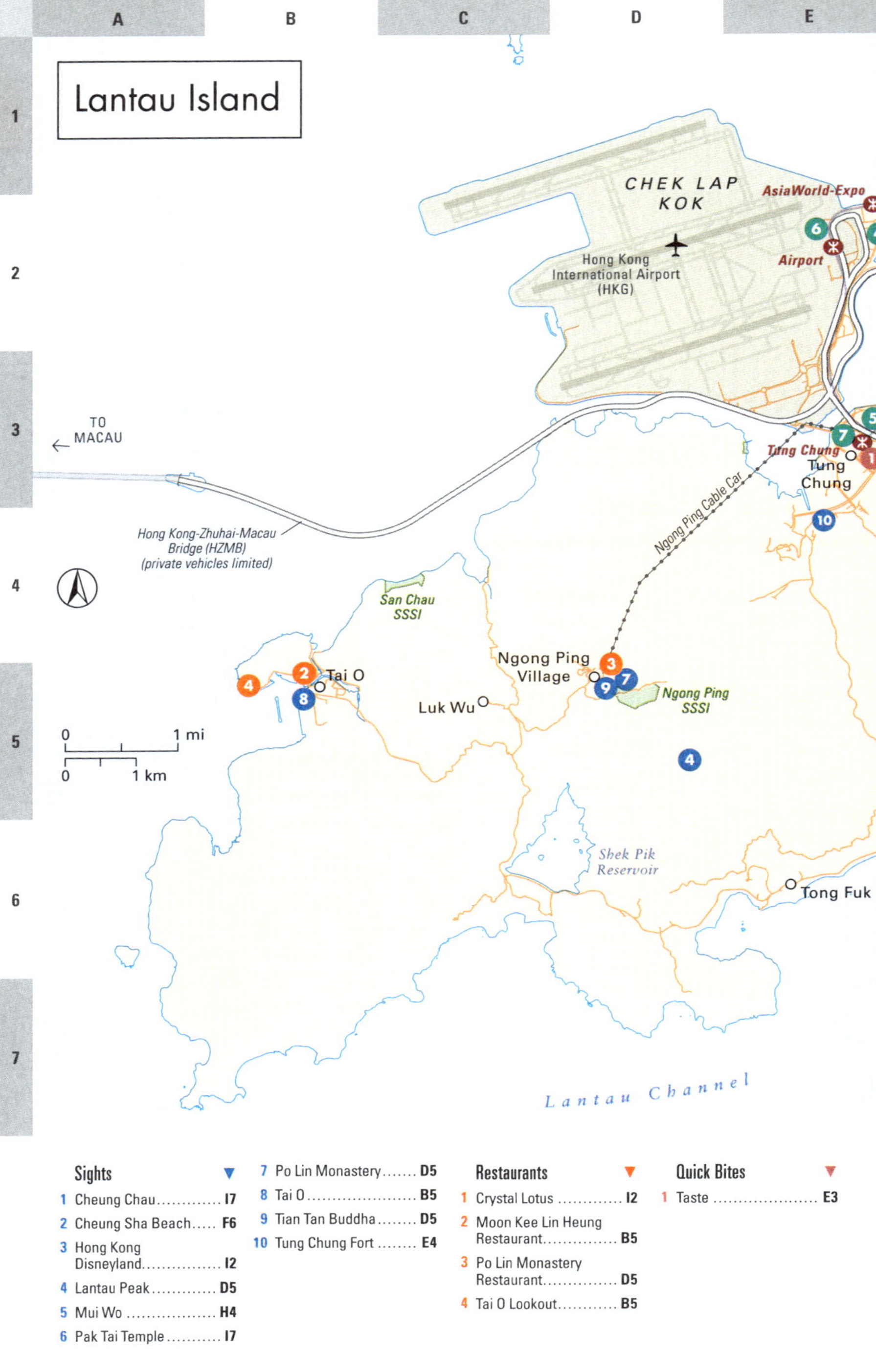

A
B
C
D
E
1
2
3
4
5
6
7
Lantau Island
CHEK LAP KOK
AsiaWorld-Expo
Hong Kong International Airport (HKG)
Airport
TO MACAU
Tung Chung
Tung Chung
Ngong Ping Cable Car
Hong Kong-Zhuhai-Macau Bridge (HZMB) (private vehicles limited)
San Chau SSSI
Ngong Ping Village
Ngong Ping SSSI
Tai O
Luk Wu
0
1 mi
0
1 km
Shek Pik Reservoir
Tong Fuk
Lantau Channel
Sights
1 Cheung Chau I7
2 Cheung Sha Beach F6
3 Hong Kong Disneyland I2
4 Lantau Peak D5
5 Mui Wo H4
6 Pak Tai Temple I7
7 Po Lin Monastery D5
8 Tai O B5
9 Tian Tan Buddha D5
10 Tung Chung Fort E4
Restaurants
1 Crystal Lotus I2
2 Moon Kee Lin Heung Restaurant B5
3 Po Lin Monastery Restaurant D5
4 Tai O Lookout B5
Quick Bites
1 Taste E3

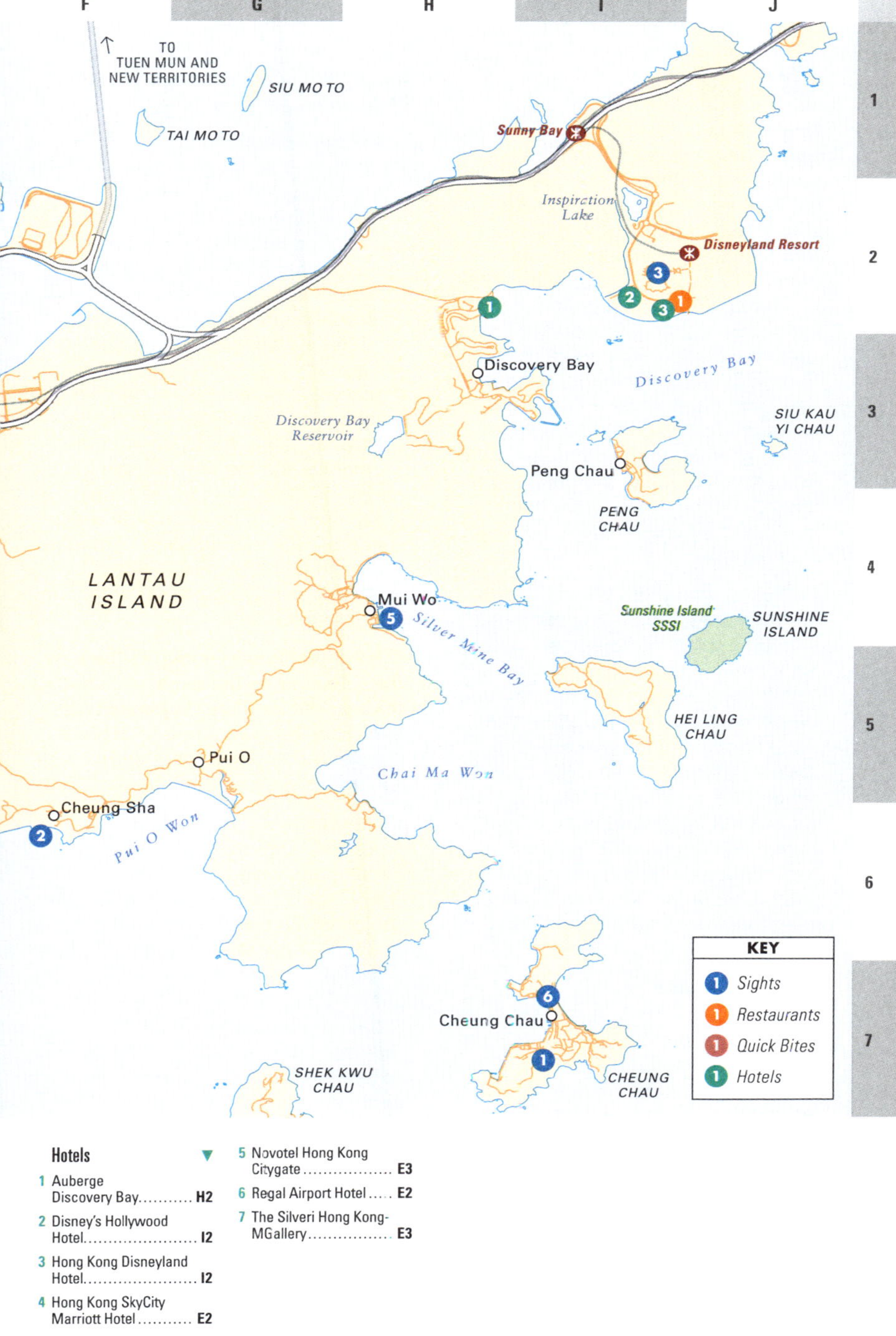

Hotels

1 Auberge Discovery Bay........... **H2**
2 Disney's Hollywood Hotel....................... **I2**
3 Hong Kong Disneyland Hotel....................... **I2**
4 Hong Kong SkyCity Marriott Hotel........... **E2**
5 Novotel Hong Kong Citygate.................. **E3**
6 Regal Airport Hotel..... **E2**
7 The Silveri Hong Kong-MGallery................. **E3**

Sights

Cheung Chau

ISLAND | Located just off the southern coast of Lantau Island, the 2½-km-long (1½-mile-long) Cheung Chau Island was once a haven for pirates like the notorious Cheung Po Tsai, whose treasure cave is reportedly on the island's southwest tip. These days, it is most famous for the centuries-old tradition called the Bun Festival, which celebrates Buddha's purported birthday in April/May. Residents live mostly on the sandbar connecting the two hilly tips of this dumbbell-shape island. The town harbor is lined with seafood restaurants and shops. A 35-minute fast ferry departs from Central's Pier 5 outside Two IFC shopping plaza.

On sunny weekends, Cheung Chau's Tung Wan beach is so crowded that its sweep of golden sand is barely visible. At one end of the beach is the Warwick Hotel, and plenty of nearby restaurants offer food, refreshments, and shade. Apart from emergency vehicles, no private cars are allowed on this island. Among the tourist attractions, find the striking Pak Tai Temple, one of the oldest in Hong Kong, as well as a cave that allegedly housed the hidden treasures of pirate Cheung Po Tsai. 🌐 *www.discoverhongkong.com/us/explore/great-outdoor/wellness/cheung-chau.html.*

Cheung Sha Beach

BEACH | **FAMILY** | Three kilometers (2 miles) of golden sand make Cheung Sha Beach one of Hong Kong's longest stretches of sand. It gets breezy at this spot 8 km (5 miles) southwest of Mui Wo, so it's popular with windsurfers. From April through October, there are also lifeguards around, so you can swim with a bit more peace of mind. Upper Cheung Sha Beach is equipped for barbecues, and there is also a refreshment stand. Witnessing a sunset here is a swell end to a sun-drenched day. ✉ *South Lantau Rd., Lantau Island* ☎ *2980–2114* Ⓜ *Tung Chung.*

Hong Kong Disneyland

AMUSEMENT PARK/CARNIVAL | **FAMILY** | Though Hong Kong's home to Mickey Mouse is lower-key compared with other Magic Kingdoms, there are still plenty of diversions to occupy one's time. Younger kids will find plenty of amusement at Sleeping Beauty Castle and Toy Story Land, while older siblings and parents will probably gravitate to the more-thrilling Space Mountain. Inside the dedicated Marvel area, daredevils will also enjoy the multisensory, immersive Iron Man Experience and the Ant-Man theme attraction. Plus, The World of Frozen, based on the animated musical, opened in late 2023 to much acclaim. It's highly recommended to purchase tickets online, as there's usually a crush of humanity by the main gate.

■ TIP→ Keen to stay overnight? There are three thematic on-site hotels, including the travel-theme Disney Explorers Lodge. ✉ *Fantasy Rd., Lantau Island* ☎ *3550–3388* 🌐 *www.hongkongdisneyland.com* 🎫 *HK$669* Ⓜ *Disneyland Resort.*

Lantau Peak

VIEWPOINT | The most glorious views of Lantau—and beyond—are from atop the 3,064-foot Lantau Peak. The ascent up the mountain that locals call Fung Wong Shan requires a strenuous 7½-mile hike west from Mui Wo, or you can begin at the Po Lin Monastery—from where the voyage is still a demanding two hours. The most striking views are at sunrise, particularly between December and February, when the air is dry and the sky is clear. ✉ *Lantau Island* ☎ *2988–8927 Lantau ranger's office* Ⓜ *Tung Chung.*

Mui Wo

TOWN | Mui Wo is a sleepy little town, but it has some good waterfront restaurants. Silvermine Bay Beach, a pleasant sandy stretch, is a half-mile northeast of the ferry pier. It has lifeguards every month

Busier than Upper Cheung Sha Beach, Lower Cheung Sha Beach is an ideal place for beachside dining and watersports.

save for December–February. A gentle uphill trail leads to the Silvermine Caves and Waterfall, the small 19th-century mine that gave the bay its English name. Given its relatively secluded location, and lower-than-expected vehicular traffic, it's a quality area to go for a bike ride. ✉ *Lantau Island* ☎ *2984–8229 connects to Silvermine Beach.*

Pak Tai Temple

TEMPLE | This temple (also known as Yuk Hui Temple) on Cheung Chau is dedicated to Pak Tai, the god of the sea, who is supposed to have rid the island of pirates. The renovated temple originally dates to 1783, when an image of Pak Tai was brought to appease the spirits of people killed by pirates, thought to be the source of bubonic plague outbreaks. According to legend, he did the trick: he remains the island's favorite deity. Beside the main altar are four whale bones salvaged from nearby. ✉ *End of Pak She St., Cheung Chau Island, New Territories* ☎ *2981–0663* 🌐 *www.ctc.org.hk* 🎫 *Free.*

Po Lin Monastery

TEMPLE | Built in 1906, this peaceful Buddhist monastery is located adjacent to the Tian Tan Buddha. The grounds feature stately halls with many intricate statues, carvings, and paintings, as well as landscaped gardens with koi fish ponds. The Grand Hall of Ten Thousand Buddhas houses, like its name, 10,000 golden buddha statues and is a sight to behold. There is a popular vegetarian restaurant on-site. ✉ *Ngong Ping, Lantau Island* ☎ *2985–5248* 🌐 *plm.org.hk* 🎫 *Free* Ⓜ *Tung Chung.*

Tai O

TOWN | Tucked away on the western end of Lantau, this fishing village inhabited largely by the *shuishangren,* literally "people on the water," some of whom continue to live in stilts houses. There's a temple dedicated to Kwan Tai, god of war, that was established in the 15th century. Remains of salt pans line part of the shoreline, and a glance beyond the coast sometimes rewards you with a sighting of a rare Hong Kong pink dolphin. The

1902 Tai O Police Station, on the village's southwest tip, has been restored and converted into the Tai O Heritage Hotel, a great place for tea, or a continental meal. ✉ *Lantau Island.*

★ **Tian Tan Buddha** (*Big Buddha*)
RELIGIOUS BUILDING | The Tian Tan Buddha, also known as the Big Buddha, is the world's largest seated, outdoors bronze Buddha. It's fair to say that the vast silhouette is impressive. Its 268 steep steps lead to the lower podium, allowing you to stare up at all 202 tons of Buddha as you ascend. At the summit, cool breezes and fantastic views over Lantau Island await. Nearby, the Wisdom Path runs beside 38 halved tree trunks arranged in a hillside infinity loop. Each trunk is carved with Chinese characters that make up the Heart Sutra, a 5th-century Buddhist prayer that expresses the doctrine of emptiness. The idea is to walk around the path—which takes five minutes—and reflect. Follow the signposted trail to the left of the Big Buddha. ✉ *Ngong Ping, Lantau Island* ☎ *2985–5248* 🌐 *plm.org.hk* 🎫 *Free* Ⓜ *Tung Chung.*

Tung Chung Fort
MILITARY SIGHT | All that remains of the old Tung Chung village is the hulking granite Tung Chung Fort. Considering how this neighborhood has become absolutely overcome with housing developments and shopping, that any vestige of pre-British remains makes it that much more fascinating. The first fortification on this spot was built during the Song Dynasty, some time in the late 1100s CE; the current structure dates from 1832, although it was refurbished in 1988. ✉ *Tung Chung Rd., Lantau Island* ☎ *2208–4488 Hong Kong Heritage DIscovery Centre* ⏲ *Closed Tues.* Ⓜ *Tung Chung.*

Restaurants

Although the airport is close by, you'll also wind up on Lantau Island if you're visiting the Big Buddha at Ngong Ping, Tai O fishing village, or Disneyland Hong Kong. There are several restaurants within the Disneyland park itself, none of them distinguished, but good if you're traveling with children. The best restaurants are in the Disney hotels. You can reach Lantau by ferry or by one of the many airport-bound buses. Otherwise, Lantau doesn't have the most diverse food options, save for a few seafood places in Tai O, some ho-hum Western options in Discovery Bay, and the casual eateries at shopping centers like Citygate.

Crystal Lotus
$$$ | **CHINESE** | **FAMILY** | The first thing you'll notice here is the most Disney-ish touch: a computer-animated koi pond, where electronic fish dart out of the way as you walk by. Once inside the crystal-studded space, your focus will turn to the food on the pan-Chinese menu. **Known for:** Sichuanese dan dan noodles; honey-glazed barbecue pork; double-boiled pear with mandarin peel. $ *Average main: HK$400* ✉ *Hong Kong Disneyland Hotel, Lantau Island* ☎ *3510–6000* 🌐 *www.hongkongdisneyland.com* ☞ *For Disney dim sum, reservations required 24–48 hours in advance* Ⓜ *Disneyland Resort.*

Moon Kee Lin Heung Restaurant
$$ | **CANTONESE** | It may look like your run-of-the-mill Hong Kong eatery, but that's where the similarities end. Here, you can taste authentic specialties that include squid, steamed shrimp, and shrimp paste fried rice—no wonder since it's located in one of Hong Kong's last traditional fishing villages. **Known for:** squid cake with dumplings; laid-back setting; shrimp paste fried rice. $ *Average main: HK$200* ✉ *52 Kat Hing St., Lantau Island* ☎ *2985–7313* 💳 *No credit cards* ⏲ *Closed Wed.*

Did You Know?

At Hong Kong Disneyland, you can catch "Momentus," a nighttime show featuring fireworks, choreographed fountains, and 3D projections.

The Tian Tan Buddha looms over his seat.

★ Po Lin Monastery Restaurant

$$ | **VEGETARIAN** | In the heart of Po Lin Monastery, surrounded by some of the best views afforded to Lantau Island, lies this Buddhist vegetarian cafeteria that's popular with tourists and locals alike. If you're traveling with others, nominate one of your party to pay for the food (do this outside of the main dining hall); seats quickly fill up given the limited hours, so guard your table well. **Known for:** veggie dishes like spring rolls and braised mushrooms; crowds; picnic tables outside. *Average main: HK$150* ✉ *Po Lin Monastery, Ngong Ping, Lantau Island* ☏ *2985–5248* *No credit cards.*

Tai O Lookout

$$$ | **ECLECTIC** | If you've made your way out to Tai O, this gorgeous glass-roofed restaurant is a great place to enjoy a leisurely afternoon tea or dinner. Formerly the Tai O Police Station, the historic building has been lovingly refurbished, and the restored colonial decor includes authentic wooden furnishings. **Known for:** Tai O fried rice; pork chop bun; cheesecake. *Average main: HK$300* ✉ *Tai O Heritage Hotel, Shek Tsai Po St., Tai O, Lantau Island* ☏ *2985–8383* *www.taioheritagehotel.com.*

Coffee and Quick Bites

Taste

$$ | **INTERNATIONAL** | This Hong Kong supermarket chain is one of the better ones, particularly if you're looking for some snacks before all of that Lantau Island hiking. Deli counters in the huge branch of the local supermarket Taste have sushi, sandwiches, salads, baked goods, and fruit. **Known for:** imported snacks; Western sandwiches; juice bar. *Average main: HK$150* ✉ *Citygate Mall, 20 Tat Tung Rd., Lantau Island* ☏ *2109–4500* *www.pns.hk/en/* Ⓜ *Tung Chung.*

Hotels

The main advantage to staying on Lantau Island is its proximity to the airport and SkyPier for late-night arrivals or early-morning departures, or to AsiaWorld-Expo if you're here on business. Most visitors come to Lantau by MTR as a day trip; popular attractions include Disneyland, the Ngong Ping cable-car ride, the Tian Tan Buddha, scenic hikes and beaches, and outlet shopping at Citygate mall. For the more adventurous, the island is also home to remote fishing villages, reached by ferry and roads less traveled. Gentrified Discovery Bay beach, easily accessible by ferry from Central, or by bus and metro on Lantau Island, hosts dragon boat races every spring.

Auberge Discovery Bay

$$ | **HOTEL** | **FAMILY** | If you need an escape from the city, Auberge Discovery Bay offers up sea views, spacious rooms, and a decadent spa. **Pros:** family-friendly; comprehensive facilities; sea and mountain views. **Cons:** 25-minute ferry ride from Central; isolated location though it's near beaches; limited nearby food options. *$ Rooms from: HK$1,450 ✉ 88 Siena Ave., Discovery Bay, Lantau Island ☎ 2295–8288 ⊕ www.aubergediscoverybay.com 325 rooms No Meals M Sunny Bay.*

Disney's Hollywood Hotel

$$$ | **RESORT** | **FAMILY** | This is Disneyland, so the focus is on kids—from chef Mickey restaurants to the piano-shape pool to well-stocked playrooms—but adults might enjoy the theme of silver-screen glamour that extends to art deco styling in the cocktail lounge and the small but comfortable guest rooms. **Pros:** good value; a children's paradise; Discovery Bay restaurants are just minutes away. **Cons:** cut off from other Hong Kong attractions; corniness factor; generic theme-park ambience. *$ Rooms from: HK$2,600 ✉ Hong Kong Disneyland Resort, Lantau Island ☎ 3510–5000 ⊕ www.hongkongdisneyland.com/hotels/disneys-hollywood-hotel/ 600 rooms No Meals M Disneyland Resort.*

Hong Kong Disneyland Hotel

$$$$ | **RESORT** | **FAMILY** | Modeled in Victorian style after the Grand Floridian at Florida's Disney resort, this hugely popular resort is beautifully done, from the spacious rooms with balconies overlooking the sea to kids' activities hosted by Disney characters. **Pros:** great for kids; handy to airport; free Wi-Fi. **Cons:** cut off from the rest of Hong Kong; can seem crowded at times; lack of good food options. *$ Rooms from: HK$3,390 ✉ Hong Kong Disneyland Resort, Lantau Island ☎ 3510–6000 ⊕ www.hongkongdisneyland.com 400 rooms No Meals M Disneyland Resort.*

★ Hong Kong SkyCity Marriott Hotel

$$ | **HOTEL** | Perks at this standard-issue airport hotel are views of the new third runway at HKG and/or the South China Sea, plus a footbridge that conveniently connects to AsiaWorld-Expo and free shuttle service to the airport. **Pros:** comfortable if generic ambience; spacious rooms good for families; across from one of the city's newest malls. **Cons:** tiny spa; low-ceilinged indoor-pool area; airport construction nearby. *$ Rooms from: HK$1,470 ✉ 1 Sky City Rd. E, Hong Kong International Airport, Lantau Island ☎ 3969–1888 ⊕ www.marriott.com 658 rooms No Meals M Asia World Expo.*

Novotel Hong Kong Citygate

$$ | **HOTEL** | Situated right at the island's main transport hub, Novotel Citygate is perfectly placed for exploring Lantau's sights. **Pros:** ideal location for exploring the island; quiet; big outdoor pool. **Cons:** distant from Kowloon/HK Island; constant stream of shoppers and airport passengers due to the adjoining mall; local food is scarce. *$ Rooms from: HK$1,720 ✉ 51 Man Tung Rd., Tung Chung, Lantau Island ☎ 3602–8888 ⊕ www.novotelcitygate.com 440 rooms No Meals M Tung Chung.*

Did You Know?

The Wisdom Path near Tian Tan Buddha features wooden pillars with carvings of calligraphy by Jao Tsung-I, an internationally renowned Sinologist and calligrapher.

Regal Airport Hotel

$$ | **HOTEL** | One of the world's largest airport hotels is more than just a place to sleep before the next flight—rooms have terrific views of take-offs and landings or overlook the swimming pool, and the spa has pleasant alfresco areas for relaxation. **Pros:** direct airport access via indoor moving walkway; refreshing pool and spa facilities; 24-hour gym. **Cons:** far removed from Hong Kong sights; limited food; hasn't been renovated since 2017. *Rooms from: HK$1,450* *Hong Kong International Airport, 9 Cheong Tat Rd., Lantau Island* *2286–8888* *www.regalhotel.com/regal-airport-hotel* *1,171 rooms* *No Meals* *Airport.*

★ The Silveri Hong Kong-MGallery

$$ | **HOTEL** | For access to Lantau Island's top sites, it's hard to beat the location of this hotel atop the Citygate Outlets, close to the airport, Ngong Ping 360 cable car, and Tung Chung bus station. **Pros:** lots of dining and shopping; airport shuttle; runway views. **Cons:** entrances are through a busy mall; two elevators are needed to reach your room; pool closed during the winter. *Rooms from: HK$1,670* *16 Tat Tung Rd., Lantau Island* *3602–8989* *www.thesilveri-hongkong.com* *206 rooms* *No Meals* *Tung Chung.*

Sha Tin

11.3 km (7 miles) from Central

Whether you enter Sha Tin by road or rail, you'll be amazed to find this metropolis in the middle of the New Territories. One of the so-called new towns, Sha Tin underwent a population explosion starting in the mid-1980s that transformed it from a town of 30,000 to a city of more than a half million. It's home to Sha Tin Park and the fantastic Hong Kong Heritage Museum, which is devoted to Chinese history, art, and culture.

Sights

The Chinese University of Hong Kong Art Museum

ART MUSEUM | Located in the Institute of Chinese Studies building, the museum is home to more than 15,000 historical objects, including well-respected collections of bronze seals, classical paintings, calligraphy, Yixing earthenware, and Lingnan school paintings. Considering the breadth of history in the region, it is helpful to take a guided tour with a docent. *Institute of Chinese Studies, The Chinese University of Hong Kong, Tai Po Rd., Sha Tin, New Territories* *3943–7416* *www.artmuseum.cuhk.edu.hk* *Free* *Closed Thurs.* *University, Exit D.*

★ Hong Kong Heritage Museum

CULTURAL MUSEUM | This history-meets-culture museum is Hong Kong's largest, yet it still seems a well-kept secret: chances are you won't have much company throughout its 11 massive galleries. The galleries ring an inner courtyard, which are benefitted by exquisite natural light flowing into the entry hall. Although many of the galleries focus on ancient Chinese art and heritage, the museum recently energized its offerings with an exhibition that displays changing exhibits of Hong Kong's pop culture. The T.T. Tsui Gallery of Chinese Art, exquisite antique Chinese glass, ceramics, and bronzes, fill hushed second-floor rooms. In spite of the museum's imposing size, the curators have gone for quality over quantity. Look for the 3½-foot-tall terra-cotta *Horse and Rider,* a beautiful example of the figures enclosed in tombs in the Han Dynasty (206 BC–AD 220). The Cantonese Opera Heritage Hall is all singing and dancing, and it's utterly hands-on. The symbolic costumes, tradition-bound stories, and stylized acting of Cantonese opera can be impenetrable; fortunately, there are well-done descriptions for even the most esoteric works. *1 Man Lam Rd., Sha Tin, New Territories*

The road is lined with golden Buddhas on the path to the Ten Thousand Buddhas Monastery.

☎ 2180–8188 🌐 www.heritagemuseum.gov.hk 🎟 Permanent exhibitions, free; special exhibitions, admission varies ⏲ Closed Tues. Ⓜ Sha Tin or Che Kung Temple.

Ten Thousand Buddhas Monastery

TEMPLE | You climb some 400 steps to reach this temple, but look on the bright side: for each step you get about 32 Buddhas. The uphill path through dense vegetation is lined with 500 life-size golden Buddhas in all kinds of positions. Be sure to bring along water and insect repellent. And once you get to the top, prepare to be dazzled: the walls of the main temple are stacked with gilded ceramic statuettes. There are nearly 13,000 here, made by Shanghai artisans and donated by worshippers over the decades. Kwun Yam, goddess of mercy, is one of several deities honored in the crimson-walled courtyard.

Look southwest on a clear day and you can see nearby **Amah Rock,** which resembles a woman with a child on her back. Legend has it that this formation was once a faithful fisherman's wife who climbed the mountain every day to wait for her husband's return, not knowing he'd drowned. Tin Hau, goddess of the sea, took pity on her and turned her to stone.

The temple is in the foothills of Sha Tin, in the central New Territories. Take Exit B out of Sha Tin station, walk down the pedestrian ramp, and take the first left onto Pai Tau Street. Keep to the right-hand side of the road and follow it around to the gate where the signposted path starts.

■ TIP→ Don't be confused by the big white buildings on the left of Pai Tau Road. They are ancestral halls, not the temple. *✉ 221 Pai Tau Village, Sha Tin, New Territories ☎ 2691–1067 🎟 Free Ⓜ Sha Tin.*

Restaurants

Sha Tin 18

$$$ | **CHINESE** | **FAMILY** | If you're exploring Sha Tin and aren't opposed to dining at a hotel, consider visiting Sha Tin 18 for a pan-Chinese feast. The restaurant is equipped with several open kitchens,

New Territories
SHENZHEN
GUANGDONG PROVINCE
HONG KONG PROVINCE
Deep Bay
Ma Chau Wetland Reserve
Mai Po Nature Reserve
San Tin
Hong Kong Wetland Park
Tin Shui Wai
Yuen Long
Ching Chung Koon Taoist Temple
Castle Peak SSSI
Tuen Mun
Tai Lam Chung Reservoir
MA WAN
Tsing Yi
TSING YI
THE BROTHERS
CHEK LAP KOK
Hong Kong International Airport (HKG)
Discovery Bay
Discovery Bay
Tung Chung
Mui Wo
0
2 mi
0
2 km

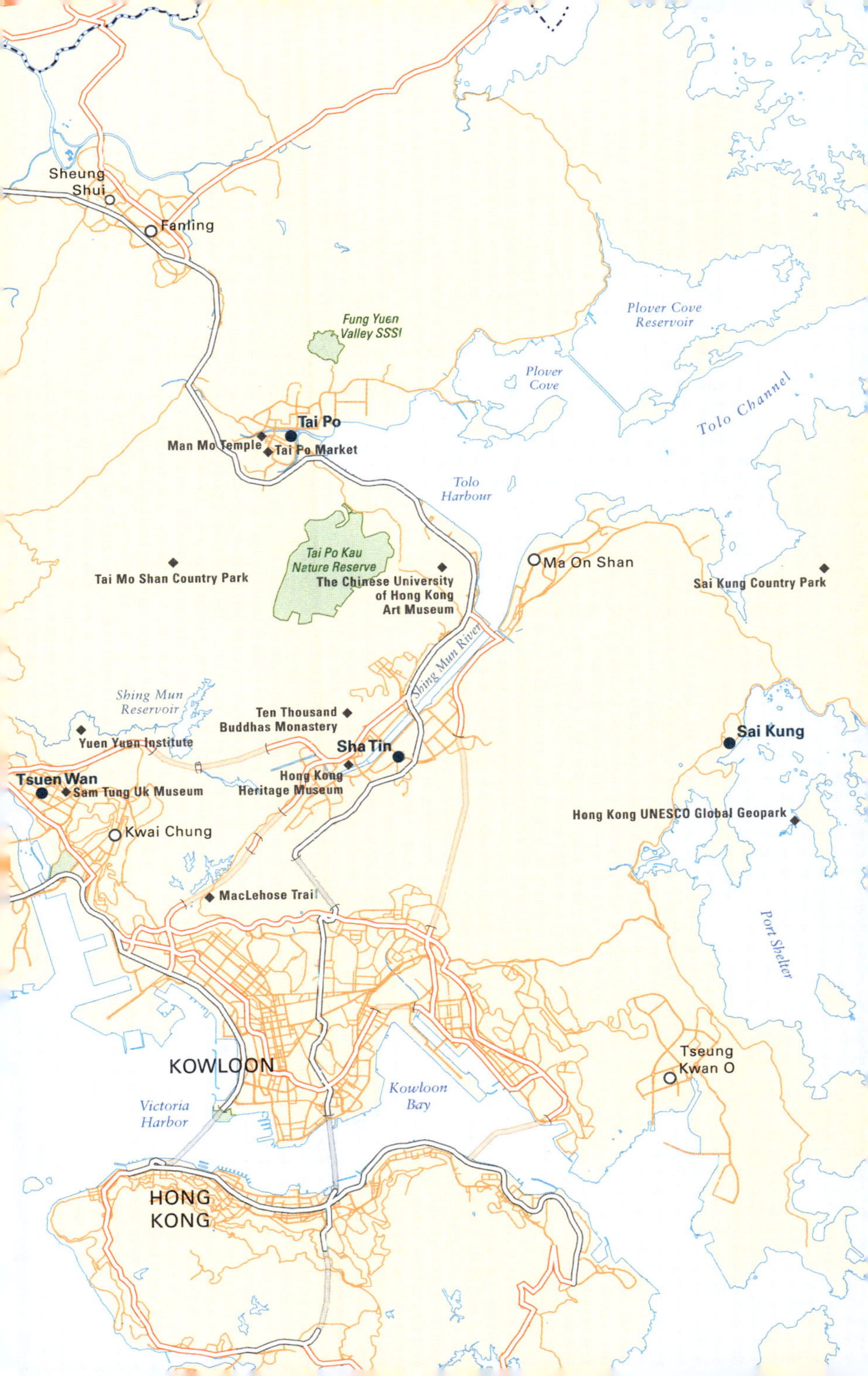

Sheung Shui
Fanling
Fung Yuen Valley SSSI
Plover Cove Reservoir
Plover Cove
Tolo Channel
Tai Po
Man Mo Temple
Tai Po Market
Tolo Harbour
Tai Po Kau Nature Reserve
Tai Mo Shan Country Park
The Chinese University of Hong Kong Art Museum
Ma On Shan
Sai Kung Country Park
Shing Mun River
Shing Mun Reservoir
Ten Thousand Buddhas Monastery
Yuen Yuen Institute
Sha Tin
Sai Kung
Tsuen Wan
Sam Tung Uk Museum
Hong Kong Heritage Museum
Kwai Chung
Hong Kong UNESCO Global Geopark
MacLehose Trail
Port Shelter
KOWLOON
Tseung Kwan O
Victoria Harbor
Kowloon Bay
HONG KONG

each with its own culinary specialty. **Known for:** dim sum; Chinese preserved tofu cheesecake; Hua Diao wine plum sherbet. $ *Average main: HK$300* ✉ *Hyatt Regency Hong Kong, 18 Chak Cheung St., Sha Tin, New Territories* ☎ *3723–7932* 🌐 *www.hyatt.com* 👔 *Smart Casual* Ⓜ *University.*

Shopping

The best shopping to be had beyond Boundary Street—the official start of the New Territories—is in malls. With big, bright windows and a stable of more than 350 stores, New Town Plaza in Sha Tin, with multiplex theaters, a Marks & Spencer department store, and even a Snoopy World theme park, is one of the top choices in the region.

MALLS AND CENTERS

New Town Plaza

MALL | If you're looking to come down to fashion earth after the designer heaven that is Central, Sha Tin's New Town Plaza is a great bet. Unless you're on the way to Shenzhen, it's somewhat detached from the usual tourist circuit. However, the New Territories' best mall has more than 350 mid-range shops and restaurants anchored by the U.K.'s Marks & Spencer. The usual local suspects abound, but lesser known local brands like Pedder Red have stores here, too. A huge multiplex cinema draws crowds on weekends. New Town Plaza is also home to one of Hong Kong's kitschier attractions: Snoopy's World, celebrating Schultz's famous cartoon dog. ✉ *18 Sha Tin Centre St., Sha Tin, New Territories* ☎ *2608–9329* 🌐 *www.newtownplaza.com.hk* Ⓜ *Sha Tin.*

Sai Kung

16 km (10 miles) from Central

Known as the "back garden of Hong Kong," Sai Kung in the New Territories is most famous for its eponymous country park. Trails run throughout this region, Hong Kong's second largest in terms of landmass. Hiking trails include the 100-km (60-miles) MacLehose Trail, Sharp Peak, and High Island Reservoir. The town of Sai Kung is well-known for its seafood restaurants and relaxed waterside vibes.

Sights

★ Hong Kong UNESCO Global Geopark

STATE/PROVINCIAL PARK | Spanning across 150 square km of the New Territories, the Geopark consists of two geological regions: the Sai Kung Volcanic Rock Region and the Northeast New Territories Sedimentary Rock Region. The sites comprise islets, sea caves, and villages, but the star may be on the honeycomb-shape columns formed by volcanic eruptions 140 million years ago, the most dramatic of which can be witnessed on the coast of High Island. The Volcanic Discovery Centre located in downtown Sai Kung provides helpful information about the area and serves as the gateway to the Geopark. Tours by Recommended Geopark Guides (R2G)—a number of which are available through the Volcanic Discovery Centre—is the best way to experience the park. ✉ *New Territories* 🌐 *www.geopark.gov.hk.*

★ MacLehose Trail

TRAIL | Named after a former Hong Kong governor, the 97-km (60-mile) MacLehose Trail is the grueling course for the annual MacLehose Trailwalker charity event. Top teams finish the hike in an astonishing 15 hours. Mere mortals should allow three to four days or simply tackle one section on a day hike.

This isolated trail starts at Tsak Yue Wu, beyond Sai Kung, and circles High Island Reservoir before breaking north. A portion takes you through the Sai Kung Country Park and up a mountain called Ma On Shan. Turn south for a high-ridge view, then walk through Ma On Shan

Sai Kung Country Park offers rewarding hiking trails, including those leading to Sharp Peak, which offers panoramic views.

Country Park. From here, walk west along the ridges of the mountains known as the Eight Dragons, which gave Kowloon its name.

After crossing Tai Po Road, the path follows a ridge to the summit of Tai Mo Shan (Big Hat Mountain), which, at 3,140 feet, is Hong Kong's tallest mountain. Continuing west, the trail drops to Tai Lam Reservoir and Tuen Mun, where you can catch public transport back to the city. To reach Tsak Yue Wu, take the MTR to Diamond Hill, then Bus 92 to Sai Kung Town. From Sai Kung Town, take Bus 94 to the country park.

An easier way to access Tai Mo Shan is via an old military road. En route you'll see the old British barracks, now occupied by the People's Liberation Army. Take the MTR to Tsuen Wan and exit the station at Shiu Wo Street, then catch Minibus 82.

★ Sai Kung Country Park

NATURE SIGHT | To the east of Sha Tin, the Sai Kung Peninsula is home to one of Hong Kong's most beloved nature preserves, Sai Kung Country Park. It has several hiking trails that wind through majestic hills overlooking the water. The hikes through the hills surrounding High Island Reservoir are also spectacular. Seafood restaurants dot the waterfront in Sai Kung Town as well as the tiny fishing village of Po Toi O in Clear Water Bay. At Sai Kung Town you can rent a sampan that will take you to one of the many islands in the area for a day at the beach. ✉ *Sai Kung Peninsula, Kowloon* ☎ *2792–7365 Sai Kung Country Park Visitors Centre* 🌐 *www.discoverhongkong.com/us/explore/neighbourhoods/sai-kung.html* 🎟 *Free* Ⓜ *Hang Hau.*

Tap Mun Island

ISLAND | **FAMILY** | Fishing villages and a nearly 400-year-old temple highlight Tap Mun Island, also known as Grass Island, where strong waves periodically beat the shores. Many visitors opt to have a seafood lunch at the New Hon Kee Seafood Restaurant. Thereafter, enjoy an "is this still Hong Kong?" moment while watching cattle graze at the hilltop pavilion. A *kaito* (local ferry) from Wong Shek pier in Sai Kung Country Park will speed you to the island; however, public transit access

The energy of a metropolis and the serenity of green hills and fishing boats coexist in Tsuen Wan.

to Wong Shek pier is limited to weekends and holidays. ✉ *New Territories.*

Restaurants

Sai Kung is worth a visit, if only for a meal. The many restaurants lining the main street and the giant fish tanks with the dizzying selection of fresh fish, crabs, prawns, clams, and oysters are a sight to behold. Point to your catch of choice and have the kitchen cook it up in any way your stomach desires. Or, sample the new wave of international flavors entering downtown Sai Kung, including those from bars, a French cheese store, and quaint cafés.

Jaspas Bar & Grill

$$$ | **INTERNATIONAL** | **FAMILY** | The food at Jaspas Bar & Grill is delicious and filling, a fitting end to a day of hiking in the hills or enjoying the beach. The international menu is wide-ranging enough to satisfy all tastes. **Known for:** chicken Parmesan; barbecue meat platter; convivial outdoor seating. *$ Average main: HK$230* ✉ *Ground fl., 13 Sha Tsui Path, Sai Kung, New Territories* ☎ *2792–6388* 🌐 *www.instagram.com/jaspasbarandgrill* Ⓜ *Hang Hau.*

Loaf On

$$ | **SEAFOOD** | Off Sai Kung's main drag, this hidden gem stands out as one of the finer seafood joints for those in the know. Unlike its big and boisterous competitors, this tiny store has no flashy fish tanks outside and the number of seats is extremely limited, so it's best to book in advance. **Known for:** deep-fried abalone; stir-fried razor clams in black bean sauce; Michelin star. *$ Average main: HK$200* ✉ *49 See Cheung St., Sai Kung, New Territories* ☎ *2792–9966* 🌐 *loafon.com/hk* Ⓜ *Hang Hau.*

Sun Tung Kee Seafood Restaurant

$$$ | **SEAFOOD** | Lobsters, clams, abalone, crabs, prawns, fish, and everything else from the deep blue sea is here for the tasting on Sai Kung's picturesque harbor. Crustaceans and fish are quickly cooked by steaming and wok frying, but are first presented whole, leaving no doubt as to the freshness of your food. **Known for:** salt and pepper squid; steamed grouper;

cheese lobster spaghetti. $ *Average main: HK$300* ✉ *96–102 Man Nin St., Sai Kung, New Territories* ☎ *2792–7453* Ⓜ *Hang Hau.*

Coffee and Quick Bites

★ Honeymoon Dessert

$ | **CHINESE** | Open since 1995, this Sai Kung store sells homemade traditional Chinese desserts, such as black-sesame sweet soup and the refreshing mango-pomelo sweet soup. It also does newfangled items, including durian pancakes and glutinous rice dumplings dusted with desiccated coconut and filled with fresh mango. **Known for:** sweet soups; durian pancakes; rice dumplings. $ *Average main: HK$35* ✉ *9–10 ABC Po Tung Rd., Sai Kung, New Territories* ☎ *2792–4991* 🌐 *www.honeymoon-dessert.com* Ⓜ *Hang Hau.*

Hotels

WM Hotel Hong Kong, Vignette Collection

$$ | **HOTEL** | Opened in 2021, this IHG property offers something for nearly everyone: terrace views of the inlet from some rooms and tents for glamping in others, and even wedding and convention space. **Pros:** the only sizable hotel in the area; big rooftop infinity pool; some rooms have patios with waterfront views. **Cons:** not the cleanest waterside location; busy when its wedding chapel and convention rooms are used; must use a keycard for all floors in the elevator. $ *Rooms from: HK$1,560* ✉ *28 Wai Man Rd., Sai Kung, New Territories* ☎ *2196–6805* 🌐 *www.wmhotel.hk/en/home* 🛏 *260 rooms* Ⓜ *Hang Hau.*

Tsuen Wan

11 km (7 miles) from Central

Until the 1940s, present-day Tsuen Wan represented a smattering of fishing villages. But once the Chinese Civil War broke out, Shanghai business people flocked to the region, constructing textile factories.

Favorite Places

Jonathan DeLise: The first attraction I ever visited in Hong Kong, way back in 2003, was the Sam Tung Uk Museum in Tsuen Wan. Even back then, I marveled at its anomalous existence, surrounded by apartment towers in an unabashedly urban setting. The stories told both by the historic museum itself, and the captions inside—relating to local and Hakka history from centuries ago—fascinate me to this day.

While there are remnants of Tsuen Wan's recent industrial past, the Hong Kong government has turned it into a "new town," meaning apartment buildings and shopping choices have proliferated. And while the imposing Nina Tower, Hong Kong's sixth tallest building at 1,050 feet (320 meters), graces the skyline, the town still has gems like Sam Tung Uk, a quaint cultural museum dedicated to the erstwhile residents of the area, the Hakka.

Sights

★ Sam Tung Uk Museum

MUSEUM VILLAGE | A walled Hakka village dating from 1786 was saved from demolition to create this museum. It's just east of Tsuen Wan MTR, adjoining giant apartment complexes and a small park. Indeed, the quiet courtyards and small interlocking chambers contrast with the nearby residential towers. The structure looks more like a large home than a village—not surprisingly, the name translates as "Three Beam House." Rigid symmetry dictated the construction: the ancestral hall and two common chambers form a central axis flanked by private areas. Traditional furniture and farm tools are on display, as well as temporary exhibits. ✉ *2*

Tai Po Market brims with vendors selling everything from fresh produce to fish balls.

Kwu Uk La., Tsuen Wan, New Territories ☎ *2411–2001* 🌐 *www.icho.hk/en/web/icho/sam_tung_uk_museum.html* 🎫 *Free* 🕓 *Closed Tues.* Ⓜ *Tsuen Wan.*

Tai Mo Shan Country Park

VIEWPOINT | The name means Big Hat Mountain, and at 3,140 feet this volcanic outcropping is Hong Kong's highest point. Due to particularly mercurial weather, the peak, often called "Foggy Mountain," is covered in clouds almost daily. But when the mist—and pollution—clears, the view stretches all the way to Hong Kong Island. Trails to the peak pass by caves created by Japanese soldiers during World War II and countless wild tea bushes. ✉ *Tai Mo Shan Rd., Tsuen Wan, New Territories* ☎ *2498–9326 visitor center* Ⓜ *Tsuen Wan.*

Yuen Yuen Institute

RELIGIOUS BUILDING | These pavilions and prayer halls, founded in 1950, bring together the three streams of Chinese thought: Buddhism (which emphasizes nirvana and physical purity), Taoism (nature and inner peace), and Confucianism (following the practical and philosophical beliefs of Confucius). The main three-tier red pagoda is a copy of the centuries-old Temple of Heaven in Beijing, and houses 60 statues representing the full cycle of the Chinese calendar—you can look for the one that corresponds to your birth year and make an incense offering. To reach the institute from Tsuen Wan MTR, head to Shiu Wo Street and take the #81 minibus. ✉ *Lo Wai Rd., Sam Dip Tam, Tsuen Wan, New Territories* ☎ *2492–2220* 🌐 *www.yuenyuen.org.hk* 🎫 *Free* Ⓜ *Tsuen Wan.*

Coffee and Quick Bites

Brilliant Thai

$ | **THAI** | This blink-and-you'll-miss-it Hong Kong chain entirely focused on Thai desserts has locations throughout the city, primarily in the New Territories. Try the coconut milk pandan cake (it's neon green), the osmanthus cake, or the butterfly pea flower coconut cake. **Known for:** sweet treats; solid chain; coconut milk pandan cake. 💲 *Average main: HK$40* ✉ *Carson Mansion, Level C1, Lo*

Tak Court, Tsuen Wan, New Territories ☎ 2952–3339 🌐 www.instagram.com/brilliant_thai_desserts 💳 No credit cards.

Tuen Mun

24 km (15 miles) from Central

For most of its history, Tuen Mun was a fishing village inhabited by the southern Chinese ethnic group Shuishangren, "people on the water." However, in the 1960s, the Hong Kong government developed it to accommodate the region's quickly expanding population.

To reach the area, the most convenient are buses 960 and 961; it is just over an hour's drive. By metro, take the Tung Chung line to Nam Cheong station, then switch to the Tuen Ma line for Tuen Mun.

Sights

Ching Chung Koon Taoist Temple
TEMPLE | This temple has room after room of altars filled with the heady scent of incense. On one side of the main entrance is a cast-iron bell with a circumference of about 5 feet—all large monasteries in ancient China rang such bells at daybreak to wake the monks and nuns for a day of work in the rice fields. On the other side of the entrance is a huge drum that was used to call the workers back in the evening. Inside, some rooms are papered with small pictures; the faithful pay to have these photos displayed so they can see their dearly departed while praying. Dwarf shrubs, ornamental fishponds, and pagodas bedeck the grounds. The temple sits adjacent to the Ching Chung MTR Light Rail station near the town of Tuen Mun. The entrance isn't obvious, but it's located on Tsing Lun Rd. *✉ Tsing Chung Koon Rd., Tuen Mun, New Territories ☎ 2462–1507 🌐 www.daoist.org Ⓜ Siu Hong, Exit B.*

Coffee and Quick Bites

Ching Chung Canteen
$$ | VEGAN | This restaurant is atop a nondescript office building with a security guard seated inside. Just take the elevator to the first floor, and follow the yellow tape from ticket purchase to dining room. Don't expect to see any English translations, however; just go for the Buddha's delight, a mix of vegetables, mushrooms, and soy sauce, and spring rolls with plant-based protein. **Known for:** Buddha's delight veggie mix; spring rolls with vegan duck; temple setting. *💲 Average main: HK$200 ✉ 28 Tsing Chung Koon Rd. ☎ 2461–7117 💳 No credit cards Ⓜ Tuen Mun.*

Hotels

Pentahotel Hong Kong, Tuen Mun
$ | HOTEL | Inspired by the neighborhood's warehouse past, this property proudly shows off its industrial-influenced design. **Pros:** close to Tuen Mun MTR station; clean, light, and modern; pool table and 24-hour gym. **Cons:** no restaurant; stark design; industrial vibes aren't to everyone's taste. *💲 Rooms from: HK$850 ✉ 6 Tsun Wen Rd., Tuen Mun, New Territories ☎ 3112–1770 🌐 www.pentahotels.com/hotels/asia/hong-kong-tuen-mun 🛏 298 rooms 🍽 No Meals Ⓜ Tuen Mun.*

Tai Po

8 km (11 miles) from Central

For centuries, Tai Po was a center of clamming, pearl-harvesting, and fishing. When the British gained control of the region from the Qing Dynasty in 1898, Tai Po was their first headquarters. Modern apartment buildings and shopping arrived in the 1970s.

To get here, take the 307 bus, which takes slightly under 1 hour 20 minutes. Or from Admiralty station on the metro, hop aboard the East Rail line to Tai Po Market station.

Man Mo Temple

TEMPLE | Close to Tai Po Market, this temple was built in 1892 to commemorate the establishment of the town of Tai Po. As you draw near, you'll feel the incense offered by worshipers. The name comes from the Cantonese words for the Taoist gods of literature, *Man Cheong*, and martial arts, *Mo Tai*. ✉ *Fu Shin St., Tai Po, New Territories* ☎ 🎫 *Free* Ⓜ *Tai Wo.*

Tai Po Market

MARKET | The name means "big market," which it more than lives up to. In the heart of the region's breadbasket, this utilitarian town's main open-air market is a feast for the eyes, with baskets of lush green vegetables, freshly cut meat hanging from racks overhead, fish swimming in tanks awaiting selection, and all types of baked and steamed treats. The ground floor is a wet market, the first floor has dried goods, and the second floor is all about hawker stands. ✉ *Fu Shin St., Tai Po, New Territories* ☎ *3183–9180* Ⓜ *Tai Po Market.*

Eat Well Canteen

$ | **VEGETARIAN** | In the New Territories, it's uncommon to find a vegetarian restaurant not attached to a temple, but this canteen, in the same cafeteria as the Old Tai Po Police Station, is strictly a no-meat, no-eggs affair. Locally sourced, organic produce is used whenever possible; their jams and preserves, dressings, and pesto are all made fresh. **Known for:** red rice with green pesto; gluten-free brownies; co-op shop that's also on the farm. $ *Average main: HK$75* ✉ *11 Wan Tau Kok La., Tai Po, New Territories* ☎ *2996–2800* 🌐 *www.greenhub.hk/en* 💳 *No credit cards* 🕒 *Closed Tues.* Ⓜ *Tai Po Market.*

Tin Shui Wai

25 km (16 miles) from Central

Present-day Tin Shui Wai was underwater in the early 1900s. That is to say, it was best known for its *gei wai* (fish ponds) to develop local aquaculture. Save for the area's most famous attraction, Hong Kong Wetlands Park, a massive land reclamation created today's Tin Shui Wai in 1990.

To arrive by bus take 969, which is just under an hour's drive. By metro, take the Tung Chung line to Nam Cheong station, then switch to the Tuen Ma line for Tin Shui Wai.

Hong Kong Wetland Park

NATURE PRESERVE | **FAMILY** | This vast wetland reserve is home to numerous species of native wildlife, including Hong Kong's own star crocodile, Pui Pui. The reserve has several walks, many suitable for families with children, including a boardwalk through a mangrove habitat and a butterfly garden. The park has a visitor center, which includes an auditorium and several indoor galleries, as well as a café, play area, and souvenir shop. ✉ *Wetland Park Rd., Tin Shui Wai, New Territories* ☎ *2617–5218 ticketing, 3152–2666 general inquiries* 🌐 *www.wetlandpark.gov.hk/en* 🎫 *HK$30* 🕒 *Closed Tues.* Ⓜ *Tin Shui Wai.*

Chapter 7

SIDE TRIP TO MACAU

Updated by
Craig Sauers

WELCOME TO SIDE TRIP TO MACAU

TOP REASONS TO GO

★ **Discover the ruins of São Paulo.** The church facade, all that remains of a former center of life and learning, is a symbol of Macau.

★ **Take a seat in Senado Square.** A bench here is the perfect perch from which to watch Macau's comings and goings while admiring the colonial surroundings.

★ **Explore the A-Ma Temple.** It's steeped in Macau's culture and history. Search for the coin-filled pool in one of the temples. Locals believe it can bring good fortune if you can create a unique sound or make the water ripple.

★ **Feast on local flavors.** Whether you prefer almond cookies or egg tarts, wonton noodles or pork chop buns, Macau's street food is a must. Be sure to try at least one Macanese restaurant, too.

★ **Place your bets.** Even if you don't gamble, it's worth a look into the buildings that butter Macau's bread. Peek inside the Hotel Lisboa, the unmissable Macau landmark, or the newer and splashier Cotai casinos, where gambling is just one part of the equation.

Macau, a Special Administrative Region (SAR) of the People's Republic of China, is on the western bank of the Pearl River Delta, about an hour from Hong Kong by hydrofoil. It consists of the Macau Peninsula, and Taipa, Cotai, and Coloane on a nearby island. The Cotai area, a glitzy, Vegas-like strip of hotels and casinos that began development in 2006, lies between Taipa and Coloane and merges the two.

Most people visit Macau to gamble, eat, and shop. But don't overlook its timeless charms and unique culture, born from centuries of Portuguese and Chinese influence.

1 The Macau Peninsula. You'll experience authentic Macau in vintage Portuguese squares and European-style sidewalk cafés, as well as in Buddhist temples, with their red lanterns and fragrant joss sticks. In this distinct place where two worlds collide, don't be surprised to find a pink colonial building housing a Chinese herbal-medicine shop.

2 Taipa. The Portuguese presence on Macau dates from the mid-1500s, but the island of Taipa wasn't occupied until the mid-1800s. It remained a garrison and a pastoral retreat until the 1970s, when it was linked to Macau by bridge. Today, some parts retain a village feel, while others are crowded with residential high-rises.

3 Cotai Strip. The 3-km (2-mile) causeway that once separated Coloane from Taipa has been bridged by a massive land reclamation and development project that includes casinos, hotels, and sporting venues.

4 Coloane. Although it's now attached to its smaller sister island, Coloane is still less populated and more intimate than Taipa. Few tourists venture this far south; however, those who do will discover parks, beaches, and golf links, as well as unchanged Portuguese architecture and cobblestone streets.

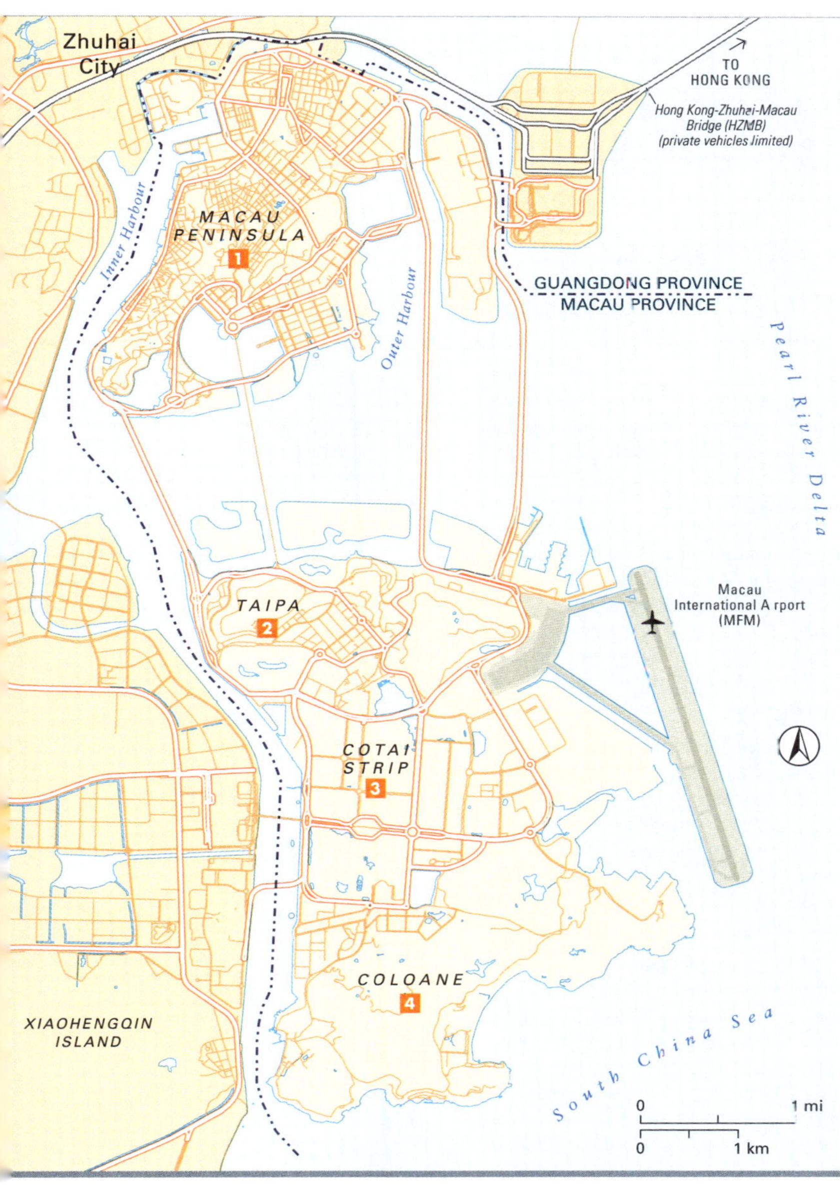
Zhuhai City
TO HONG KONG
Hong Kong-Zhuhai-Macau Bridge (HZMB) (private vehicles limited)
Inner Harbour
MACAU PENINSULA
1
Outer Harbour
GUANGDONG PROVINCE
MACAU PROVINCE
Pearl River Delta
TAIPA
2
Macau International Airport (MFM)
COTAI STRIP
3
COLOANE
4
XIAOHENGQIN ISLAND
South China Sea
0
1 mi
0
1 km

Macau is a city that refuses to be just one thing. It's the world's casino capital, where high rollers bet more in a night than most Vegas visitors do in a week. It's also a place where Buddhist temples sit beside baroque churches, where you can sip espresso on a cobblestoned square before stepping into a neon-lit megacasino dripping in gold.

Once a trading post under Portuguese rule, Macau has become a high-gloss spectacle of luxury, wealth, and reinvention. Staggering land reclamation projects have expanded its boundaries and enabled a robust gambling industry to boom, transforming a formerly barren fishing village into something far mightier than anyone could have dreamed. (Anyone except Dr. Stanley Ho, of course.) Today, it has one of the world's highest GDPs. But beneath the surface, the city is at a crossroads.

The average length of stay for travelers is a hair over one night. Tourists come in, visit the historic center, gamble, and go. As global competitors like Thailand, Japan, and the UAE push into the gambling market, Macau is waking up to the need to be more than a one-note destination.

In 2023, the local government unveiled a tourism strategy to diversify the economy through food, entertainment, conferences, events, technology, and health care. Whether they believe in the efficacy of this scheme or not, the casino operators have begun to move pieces on the chessboard to support it. Lavish resorts, exclusive cocktail bars, and high-profile concerts are drawing in new crowds. Major events are in the works, joining the annual Grand Prix. Guest chefs keep flying in for pop-ups at top-tier restaurants.

Macau once had a reputation for sheer vice—for sucking desperate punters dry and enabling crime to thrive. Those days aren't exactly gone, but times are changing. Whether it's the luxurious spas, elite fine dining, or ever-expanding line-up of events, these things all speak the same truth: Macau isn't the sin city it once was.

Planning

Getting Here and Around

Most international travelers generally arrive one of two ways: by ferry from Hong Kong, at either the Outer Harbour Ferry Terminal or Taipa Ferry Terminal, or by air.

For a city the size of Macau, getting around is harder than it should be. The best way to get around is by foot.

Although the downtown and Taipa are separated by water, and Coloane is distant from both, it is easy to walk from site to site—and with planning, it is often the most rewarding method.

AIR

Macau International Airport (🌐 *www.macau-airport.com*) operates 24 hours a day, with popular routes flying to capital cities like Bangkok, Beijing, Seoul, Singapore, Taipei, and Tokyo. It's a small and convenient airport, just 10 minutes by taxi from most hotels in Cotai.

BUS

Now, you can also travel between Hong Kong and Macau by bus. Buses travel the 55-km (34-mile) Hong Kong-Zhuhai-Macau bridge—the world's longest sea crossing—24 hours a day, depart from HKZM Frontier Post in Macau (near the Gongbei Border Gate) and travel to the HKZM Hong Kong Port on Lantau Island in Hong Kong. They cost just MOP$65 between 6 am and midnight, and MOP$70 from midnight to 6 am. Getting to the Frontier Post is perhaps the hardest part of the journey, with limited bus routes and infrequent taxis.

In Macau, buses are relatively convenient, although not for nonresidents. Fares cost MOP$6 if you pay by cash, and you don't receive change.

The casino-resorts offer free shuttle buses from the ferry terminals to their properties, as well as routes between their properties in Cotai and the peninsula. They are free for anyone to use, even nonguests. The queues, however, can be enormous at peak hours.

If you are staying a week or more and intend to use public transport, consider getting a Macau Pass. This card is similar to Hong Kong's Octopus card and is sold at Circle K and 7-Eleven minimarts—as well as the Macau Pass office in the NAPE district. It requires a nonrefundable MOP$30 deposit, but it reduces bus fares to MOP$3 and allows you to tap to pay at many mom-and-pop shops and minimarts as well as on the bus.

FERRY

Ferries travel to and from Hong Kong 24 hours a day. During peak daytime hours, they run every 30 minutes; between midnight and 6 am, they slow to once every hour.

The journey takes about one hour and is straightforward. You can purchase tickets online in advance from the two operators, Turbojet (🌐 *www.turbojet.com.hk*) and Cotai Water Jet (🌐 *www.cotaiwaterjet.com*), or buy them at the ferry terminals. Typically, you can buy a ticket on-site and depart immediately, although note that ferries fill up on holidays and for major events.

Prices for economy tickets range from MOP$175 to MOP$220 depending on departure time. Weekday tickets are cheapest while nighttime ferries cost the most.

TAXI

Macau is infamous for its taxi shortages, and it doesn't allow ride-sharing apps like Uber or DiDi to operate. Flagging down a taxi is not easy, and few drivers speak or read English. If time is of the essence, it's best to ask your hotel for help arranging transport.

TRAIN

Macau's Light Rapid Transit (LRT) operates limited routes between Barra on the peninsula, Taipa, and Cotai. It's a good option for those exploring by foot, but they will be of little use otherwise.

Casinos

In February 2006, Macau surpassed Las Vegas in gambling revenue. By June 2008, Macau's casinos were turning over 2.6 times the revenue of their Vegas Strip counterparts. Small wonder that international casino groups have swarmed the region, and they continue to transform the once sleepy city into a high-dollar tourism hub.

From the late 1960s until 2001, Dr. Stanley Ho—Macau's biggest *taipan* ("big boss")—owned all the casinos, making him one of the world's wealthiest people. One of the first steps the Chinese government took after the 1999 handover was to break up his monopoly and award casino licenses to several consortiums from Las Vegas. The grand plan to transform Macau from a quiet town that offered gambling into one of the world's top casino destinations took shape.

Since 2004, when an ambitious land reclamation project linked the islands of Coloane and Taipa, forming the Cotai Strip, American-style casino-resorts have exploded. Unlike the dark, dingy parlors of Macau's past, these palatial projects please both casual tourists and serious players for their variety of games and attractions, relatively clean and well-lit atmospheres, free 24/7 accessibility, and overall glamour-resort experience.

But the industry is undergoing changes. In 2023, the local government awarded its six casino operators new 10-year concessions, with a caveat: they must collectively invest around MOP$130 billlion over that period to help Macau diversify its economy. While the casinos continue to bring billions to the city, they are now accompanied by plans for state-of-the-art conference facilities and event venues, advanced clinics that support medical tourism, and new shows, sporting events, and amusement parks.

For those who want to play at the tables, there are a few things to remember. No one under 18 is allowed into casinos. Most use Hong Kong dollars, not Macau patacas, but you can easily exchange currencies at cashiers. High- and no-limit VIP rooms, where minimum bets range from HK$50,000 to HK$100,000 per hand, are available on request. You can get cash from credit cards and ATMs 24 hours a day, and every casino has a program to extend additional credit—and typically offer comped accommodation—to frequent visitors. Although most casinos don't have strict dress codes outside of VIP rooms, men are better off not wearing shorts or sleeveless shirts.

Unlike Las Vegas, where a lively atmosphere invites otherwise disinterested passersby to get in on the action, Macau is much more serious. Many people gamble until they're exhausted or broke, usually the latter. Finding a blackjack table can be an Orphean expedition, and poker is nearly nonexistent—the game of choice here is baccarat.

Dining

There are few better places to eat than Macau. The city has one of the highest densities of Michelin-starred restaurants on Earth, representing nearly every cuisine you can imagine—French, Italian, Japanese, Portuguese, regional Chinese specialties, and more.

Now, Macanese cuisine—a fusion of flavors uniting ingredients and techniques from Portugal's former colonies—is enjoying a revival. Once confined to family kitchens, these dishes appear on menus with refined execution and deep personal significance, as local chefs increasingly celebrate Macau's unique culinary heritage.

But Macau's great food isn't all highbrow. Some of the city's best bites are found in back-alley noodle shops, rustic Taipa eateries, and downtown diners. Don't leave without trying *zhu pa bao* (a crispy pork chop in a toasted bun) or the quintessential *p'ou tát*, Macau's take on Portuguese *pastel de nata*, better known as egg tarts.

If an espresso and egg tart aren't your style, hotel breakfast buffets offer a mix of Chinese and Western dishes, often from very early in the morning.

Dining costs vary—expect MOP$150–MOP$300 per meal without wine, though a simple noodle shop meal can cost as little as MOP$50. For an unforgettable dinner, budget at least MOP$800 per person. Most mid-range and high-end restaurants add a 10% service charge, and rounding up the total is common. While major credit cards are widely accepted, smaller establishments often prefer cash.

Meals in Macau are meant to be savored—especially at traditional Portuguese and Macanese restaurants, where slow dining is part of the experience.

⇨ *Restaurant reviews throughout this guide have been shortened. For full information, visit Fodors.com. Restaurant prices are the average cost of a main course at dinner or, if dinner is not served, at lunch.*

What It Costs in MOP$

$	$$	$$$	$$$$
AT DINNER			
under MOP$100	MOP$100–MOP$300	MOP$300–MOP$500	over MOP$500

Hotels

Over the past two decades, luxury hotels have poured into the city, transforming the old Portuguese trading post into a posh getaway. Aging three-star properties still linger in the downtown area, but the five-stars are generally worth the splurge citywide.

When choosing a hotel, consider the surroundings. In downtown Macau (or the Outer Harbour, connected to downtown via frequent casino shuttles), the city's most important historic and cultural sites are all steps away. So are excellent Macanese restaurants, wine bars, and cafés. Hotels across the harbor in residential Taipa may require a taxi or bus ride to reach the UNESCO-listed historic center, but they often have sweeping sea or city views, plus the convenience of being minutes from Taipa Village. Cotai is a completely different animal. Asia's answer to the Las Vegas Strip offers one-stop sleeping, shopping, dining, drinks, and entertainment (and, of course, casinos). Then, for otherworldly quiet, there's Coloane, where you can hit the beach or hike with almost no crowds outside of weekends.

Macau hotels are busiest during the Grand Prix (mid- to late November) and all official Chinese holidays—especially Lunar New Year in January or February. Book at least a couple of weeks in advance at these times. Year-round, weekends fill up fast and walk-ins can be prohibitively expensive. Visit on a weekday to avoid crowds and inflated prices.

Hotel reviews have been shortened. For full information, visit Fodors.com. Prices in the lodging reviews are the lowest cost of a standard double room in high season. ⇨

What It Costs in MOP$

$	$$	$$$	$$$$
LODGING FOR TWO			
	MOP$700–MOP$1,000	MOP$1,001–MOP$3,000	over MOP$3,000

Nightlife

Macau's nightlife has come a long way from its wilder past. Old movies, novels, and gossip through the years have portrayed it as a combustible mix of vices—gambling, drugs, crime, and ladies of the night. Nothing could be further from reality today. Now you can enjoy live jazz in luxurious hotel lounges, Portuguese wine in the shadows of the city's heritage sites, and exclusive whiskies and craft cocktails at independently owned bars downtown.

Shopping

Like Hong Kong, Macau is a free port for most goods, so prices for electronics, jewelry, and clothing are lower here than they are in other international cities. Yet the shopping experience is completely different, with a low-key atmosphere, small crowds, and compact areas. It is also a hub for traditional Chinese arts, crafts, and even some antiques (but be aware that there are many high-quality reproductions in the mix, too).

Macau's major shopping district runs along its main street in the downtown area, Avenida Almeida Ribeiro, more commonly known by its Chinese name, **San Ma Lo** ("New Road"). There are also shops downtown on **Rua Dos Mercadores** and its side streets; on **Rua de Cinco de Outubro;** and on the **Rua do Campo,** colloquially known as "Shoe Street" for its lifestyle and sporting goods stores. There are also bustling street markets downtown that sell clothes on **Rua de São Domingos** (near Senado Square) and **Rua da Palha.**

Increasingly, though, the casino-hotels offer more modern shopping experiences. **The Shoppes at The Venetian** and **The Shoppes at The Londoner** house everything from Lululemon and Japanese lifestyle brand Muji to Louis Vuitton, Christian Louboutin, and Bottega Veneta boutiques, and all in air-conditioned comfort. For luxury goods, peruse the **Galaxy Cotai** and **City of Dreams.** In the downtown area, **One Central,** next to the Mandarin Oriental, is a convenient destination for high-end fashion, jewelry, tea, and more.

In the downtown core, you'll also find local shops keeping Macau heritage crafts alive. Joss stick makers ply their trade in small, fragrant shops on **Rua dos Ervanários;** tailors like Choi Sang Long on **Rua dos Mercadores** still make Chinese wedding dresses by hand; and herbal tea and traditional Chinese medicine vendors operate everywhere from the historic center to the **Three Lamps District,** near Avenida Horta e Costa.

Jewelry shops near the casinos in the downtown area sell luxury watches, pendants, and rings, some of which have been pawned by desperate gamblers. Prices are generally more reasonable than in Hong Kong. For gold purchases, head to trusted Hong Kong stalwarts **Chow Tai Fook** and **Chow Sang Sang,** which have locations throughout Macau and are known for transparent pricing and knowledgeable staff with good English.

Most Macau shops operate year-round with a short break for Lunar New Year and are open from 10 am to 8 pm (later on weekends). While most accept all major credit cards, specialty discount shops usually ask for cash, and street vendors typically accept only cash.

Downtown Macau

There was a time when Macau's downtown was synonymous with crime and casinos. Today, it's whatever you want it to be. Yes, mainland gamblers still crowd around baccarat tables and gamble away savings—the house, you'll recall, always wins. And yes, you'll still see pawn shops and a seedy sauna or two somewhere in the shadows of towering casino complexes. But Macau isn't the sin city it once was. Young locals have opened fun-loving cocktail bars and boutique coffee roasters next to mom-and-pop shops and old-school noodle joints. Restaurateurs have revived forgotten quarters like the St. Lazarus district. And even the gambling groups have begun to seek new channels for profits. Each year, they bring in international artists for exhibitions, one-up each other with flashier fine dining restaurants, and open ever-fancier five-star hotels, all to the benefit of global travelers.

The Guia Lighthouse was the first western-style lighthouse built on China's coastline.

Sights

Shaped by colonial Portuguese architecture, squares, and cobblestone plazas, Macau's old town carries distinct East-meets-West influences. The best way to experience this area is on foot, wandering slowly between the major landmarks, sampling everything you can, and uncovering hidden corners.

Camões Garden

GARDEN | From dawn to dusk, Macau's most popular park comes alive with tai chi practitioners, palm readers, couples, students, and men locked in Chinese chess battles under banyan trees. Developed in the 18th century, the gardens were built on the estate once occupied by the chairman of the British East India Company. When the British moved out in 1835, the land's new Portuguese owners built a grotto around the country's greatest poet, Luís de Camões, who spent years in exile in Macau. Now the park's most iconic spot, Camões Grotto shelters a bronze bust of the poet within a rocky niche, while a bronze sculpture at the entrance symbolizes Portugal and China's historic ties Nearby, **Casa Garden,** a smaller park that now houses the Orient Foundation, features landscaped grounds, a brick pathway, and a lily-filled pond. ✉ *13 Praça Luis de Camões, Downtown* 🎫 *Free.*

★ Casa do Mandarim

(*The Mandarin's House*)

NOTABLE BUILDING | Macau's largest representation of Guangdong residential architecture spans 43,055 square feet and has more than 60 lovingly restored rooms. Built in 1869 and refurbished in 2010, the compound blends Chinese and Western architectural elements. It was the home of Zheng Guanying, a late Qing Dynasty literary figure, who completed his influential *Words of Warning in Times of Prosperity* here. Just steps away, **Lilau Square,** a banyan-shaded plaza near one of Macau's first Portuguese residential quarters, reflects the city's deep cultural ties. ✉ *10 Travessa de António da Silva,*

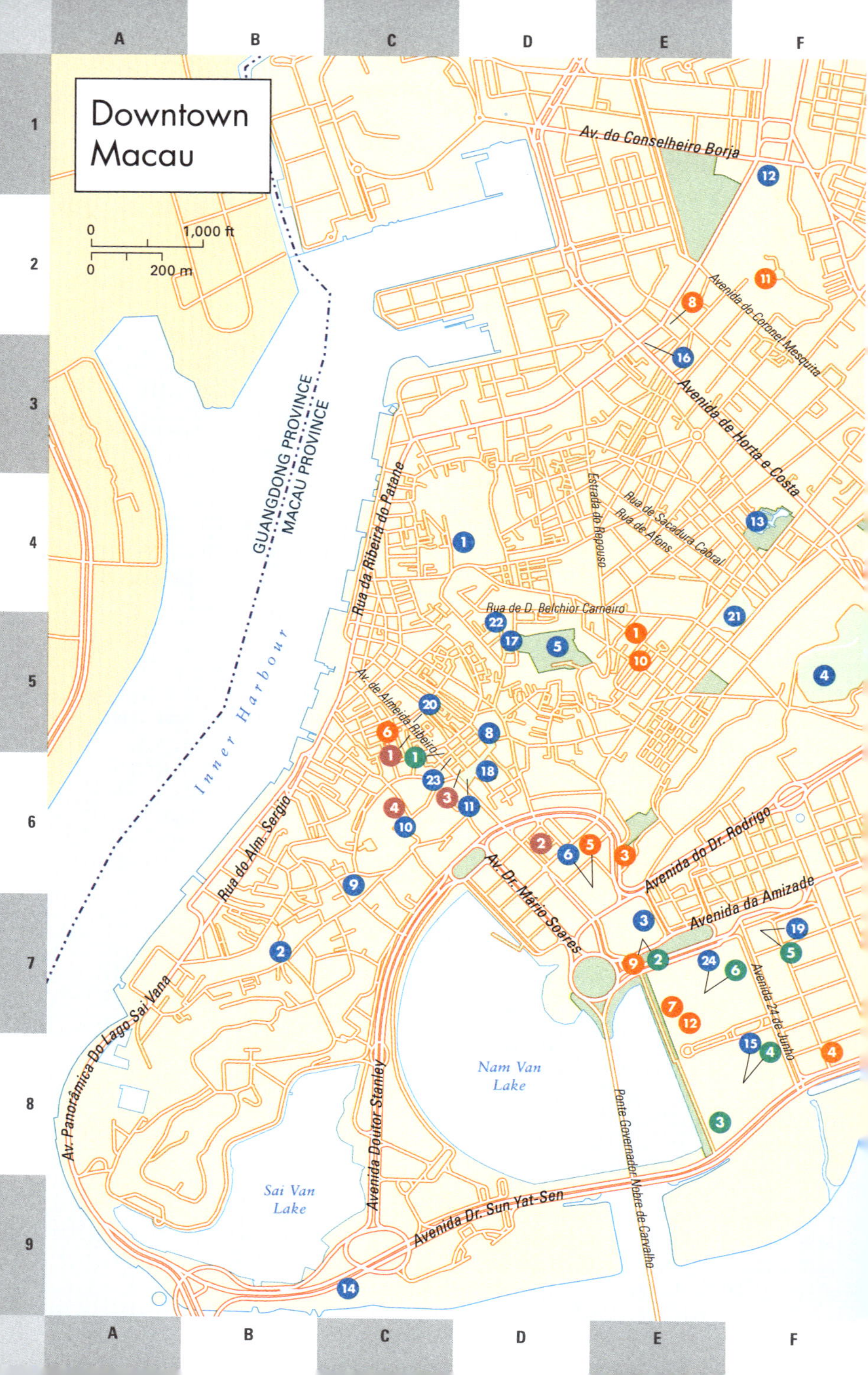

Downtown Macau
0
1,000 ft
0
200 m
A
B
C
D
E
F
1
2
3
4
5
6
7
8
9
Av. do Conselheiro Borja
Avenida do Coronel Mesquita
Avenida de Horta e Costa
GUANGDONG PROVINCE
MACAU PROVINCE
Rua da Ribeira do Patane
Estrada do Repouso
Rua de Sacadura Cabral
Rua de Afons
Rua de D. Belchior Carneiro
Inner Harbour
Av. de Almeida Ribeiro
Rua do Alm. Sergio
Avenida do Dr. Rodrigo
Avenida da Amizade
Av. Dr. Mário Soares
Avenida 24 de Junho
Av. Panorâmica Do Lago Sai Vana
Nam Van Lake
Avenida Doutor Stanley
Ponte Governador Nobre de Carvalho
Sai Van Lake
Avenida Dr. Sun Yat-Sen

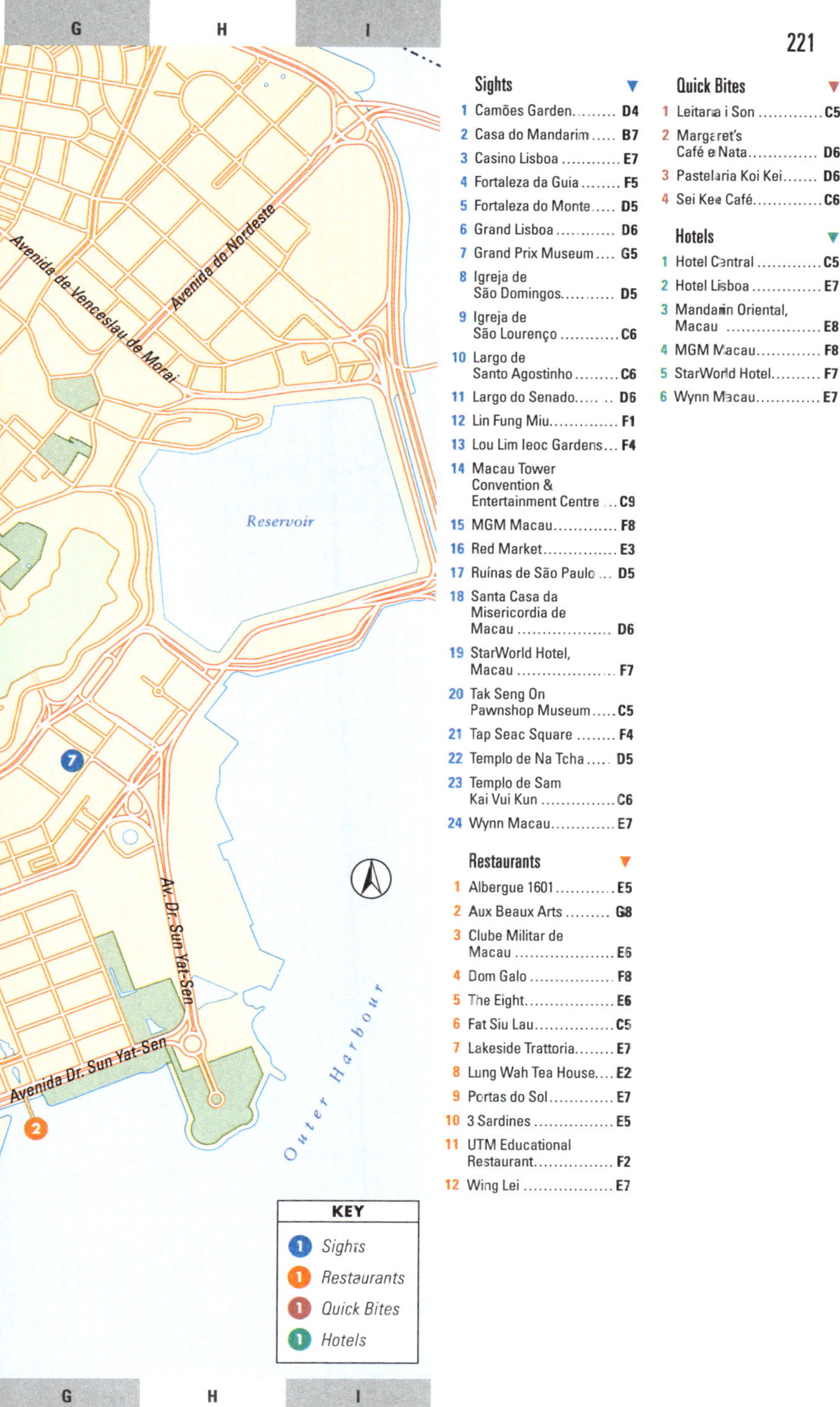

Sights

1 Camões Garden D4
2 Casa do Mandarim B7
3 Casino Lisboa E7
4 Fortaleza da Guia F5
5 Fortaleza do Monte D5
6 Grand Lisboa D6
7 Grand Prix Museum G5
8 Igreja de São Domingos............ D5
9 Igreja de São Lourenço C6
10 Largo de Santo Agostinho C6
11 Largo do Senado....... D6
12 Lin Fung Miu.............. F1
13 Lou Lim Ieoc Gardens... F4
14 Macau Tower Convention & Entertainment Centre ... C9
15 MGM Macau............. F8
16 Red Market............... E3
17 Ruínas de São Paulo ... D5
18 Santa Casa da Misericordia de Macau D6
19 StarWorld Hotel, Macau F7
20 Tak Seng On Pawnshop Museum C5
21 Tap Seac Square F4
22 Templo de Na Tcha D5
23 Templo de Sam Kai Vui Kun C6
24 Wynn Macau............. E7

Restaurants

1 Albergue 1601 .... E5
2 Aux Beaux Arts G8
3 Clube Militar de Macau E6
4 Dom Galo F8
5 The Eight.................. E6
6 Fat Siu Lau................ C5
7 Lakeside Trattoria........ E7
8 Lung Wah Tea House.... E2
9 Portas do Sol............. E7
10 3 Sardines E5
11 UTM Educational Restaurant................ F2
12 Wing Lei E7

Quick Bites

1 Leitaria i Son C5
2 Margaret's Café e Nata.............. D6
3 Pastelaria Koi Kei....... D6
4 Sei Kee Café.............. C6

Hotels

1 Hotel Central C5
2 Hotel Lisboa E7
3 Mandarin Oriental, Macau E8
4 MGM Macau............. F8
5 StarWorld Hotel.......... F7
6 Wynn Macau............. E7

The feather-shaped Grand Lisboa is an instantly identifiable landmark in the Macau skyline.

Downtown ☎ *853/2896–8820* 🌐 *www.wh.mo/mandarinhouse/en* 🎫 *Free.*

Casino Lisboa

CASINO | Opened in 1970 by Dr. Stanley Ho, this iconic Macau gaming den, unmissable with its flashing neon marquee, is replete with ancient jade ships in the halls, gilded staircases, and more baccarat tables than you can shake a craps stick at. Most of the gamblers are from neighboring Guangdong province, and Cantonese is the lingua franca. Other popular pastimes at this storied casino revolve around international fine-dining venues and colorful coffee shops, if you care to wander around the maze of marbled floors and low ceilings. ✉ *Av. de Lisboa, Downtown* ☎ *853/2888–3888* 🌐 *www.hotelisboa.com.*

★ **Fortaleza da Guia** (*Guia Fortress*)

MILITARY SIGHT | This fort, built between 1622 and 1638 on Macau's highest hill, was key to protecting the Portuguese from invaders. You can take a short cable-car ride from the entrance of Flora Garden on Avenida Sidónio Pais or walk the winding road up to it—a journey made easier thanks to elevators inside a pedestrian tunnel linking the Flora Garden and Avenida Dr. Rodrigo Rodrigues. On the hill, follow the signs for the **Guia Lighthouse**—you can't go in, but you can get a good look at the gleaming white exterior that's lit every night. Next to it is the **Guia Chapel,** built by Clarist nuns to provide soldiers with religious services. Restoration work in 1996 uncovered elaborate frescoes mixing Western and Chinese themes. They're best seen when the morning or afternoon sun floods the chapel, which is no longer used for services. The views from here are among the best, sweeping across all of Macau. Beneath the lighthouse, you'll find exercise paths popular with runners, walkers, and tai chi practitioners in the morning and evening. ✉ *Guia Hill, Downtown* ☎ *853/8399–6699* 🎫 *Free.*

Fortaleza do Monte (*Mount Fortress*)

MILITARY SIGHT | Perched on a hill overlooking the Ruins of St. Paul's, this 17th-century Jesuit fort played a pivotal role in Macau's history. In 1622, during Macau's most legendary battle, a priest's lucky cannon shot struck a Dutch ship's powder supply, thwarting an invasion. Though fire destroyed the interior buildings in 1835, the outer walls, cannons, and artillery pieces still stand. Next door, the **Macau Museum** traces the territory's history, from its origins to modern-day development. ✉ *Monte Hill, Downtown* ☎ *853/2835–7911* 🌐 *www.macaumuseum.gov.mo* 🎫 *Free.*

Grand Lisboa

CASINO | This blooming lotus-shape landmark towers over the Macau skyline. Inside, the main gaming floor features hundreds of tables—including some offering Texas hold 'em poker rings and craps, plus low minimums—and about 1,000 slot machines centered around a giant glowing orb. While the casino's famed Paris cabaret show is no more, there are plenty of ways to stay entertained. The Grand Lisboa has fantastic dining choices, for example, from the baroque Casa Don Alfonso to the elegant Lotus Lounge. If the slots have been kind, celebrate by having a divine dinner on-site at Michelin-starred stalwarts Robuchon au Dôme or The Eight. ✉ *2–4 Av. de Lisboa, Downtown* ☎ *853/2838–2828* 🌐 *www.grandlisboahotels.com.*

Grand Prix Museum

HISTORY MUSEUM | **FAMILY** | Inaugurated in 1993 to celebrate the 40th anniversary of the Macau Grand Prix, this museum tells the stories of the best drivers from every year—including German legend Michael Schumacher—but the highlights are the actual race cars on display. More than 20 Formula vehicles are exhibited in the hall, the centerpiece being the red-and-white Formula Three car driven by the late Brazilian champion Aryton Senna. Though Macau has lost its premier Formula Three race, replaced by a Formula Regional championship, its sporting legacy lives on here as well as the tough, twisting Guia Circuit. ✉ *431 Rua Luis Gonzaga Gomes, Downtown* ☎ *853/8593–0515* 🎫 *MOP$80* ⏲ *Closed Tues.*

Igreja de São Domingos (*St. Dominic's Church*)

CHURCH | The cream-and-white interior of Macau's oldest church takes on a heavenly golden glow when illuminated for service. Originally a convent founded by Spanish Dominican friars in 1587, St. Dominic's is steeped in history. In 1822, China's first Portuguese newspaper, *The China Bee,* was published here, and the church became a repository for sacred art in 1834 when convents were banned in Portugal.

TIP→ Admission to all churches and temples is free, though donations are suggested. ✉ *Largo de São Domingos, Downtown* ☎ *853/2836–7706.*

Igreja de São Lourenço (*Church of St. Lawrence*)

CHURCH | Founded by Jesuits in 1560, the Church of St. Lawrence is one of Macau's three oldest churches and has been carefully rebuilt over the centuries, with its current form dating to 1846. Set amid palm-shaded gardens overlooking the sea, it once drew families of Portuguese sailors, who gathered on its steps to pray for their loved ones' safe return, hence its Chinese name, Feng Shun Tang (Hall of the Soothing Winds). Inside, elegant wood carvings, striking stained glass, a baroque altar, and crystal chandeliers create a breathtaking display of craftsmanship and devotion. ✉ *2–4 Rua de S. Lourenco, Macau, Downtown* ☎ *8399–6699* ☞ *Access from Rua da Imprensa Nacional.*

Largo de Santo Agostinho

PLAZA/SQUARE | Like a snapshot of a Portuguese *praça*, St. Augustine Square is paved with black-and-white tiles laid out in mosaic wave patterns and lined with leafy overhanging trees and lots of wooden benches. It's easy to feel as if you're in a European village, far from South China. One of the square's main structures is the **Teatro Dom Pedro V,** a European-style performance hall with an inviting green-and-white facade, built in 1859. It's an important cultural landmark for Macau and was regularly used until World War II, when it fell into disrepair. The 300-seat venue once again hosts concerts and recitals—especially during the annual Macau International Music Festival—as well as important public events. **Igreja de Santo Agostinho (Church of St. Augustine),** to one side of the square, was built by Spanish Augustinians in 1591. The Catholic landmark has a grand, weathered exterior, a drafty interior with a high, turquoise-color wood-beam ceiling, and a magnificent stone altar with a statue of Christ on his knees, bearing the cross, with small crucifixes in silhouette on the hill behind him. On the first day of Lent each year, devotees carry this statue, called Our Lord of Passos, in a procession through the downtown streets. ✉ *Off R. Central, Downtown.*

★ **Largo do Senado** (*Senado Square*)
PLAZA/SQUARE | Paved with swirling *calçada portuguesa* (black-and-white mosaic tiles), this pedestrian-only plaza has been Macau's beating heart for centuries. Lined with pastel-hued neoclassical buildings, Largo do Senado offers a picture-perfect backdrop. Across Avenida Almeida Ribeiro, the **Edifício do Leal Senado** ("Loyal Senate" building)—erected in 1784 as Macau's original city hall—still serves as the Municipal Affairs Bureau today. Open to the public, it features a Portuguese-style garden adorned with striking *azulejos* (blue-and-white glazed tiles), a foyer hosting art and history exhibits, and an elegant meeting room that leads to a magnificent library inspired by Portugal's Convent of Mafra. Nearby alleys brim with restaurants and shops, although they are increasingly branches of Koi Kei Bakery and health and beauty chain Mannings. **TIP→ Visit early on weekdays to avoid crowds, and try to come back at night, when the square is beautifully lit.** ✉ *Largo do Senado, Downtown.*

Lin Fung Miu (*Temple of the Lotus*)
TEMPLE | Built in 1592, the Temple of the Lotus honors several Buddhist and Taoist deities, including Tin Hau (goddess of the sea), Kun Iam (goddess of mercy), and Kwan Tai (god of war and wealth). The front of the temple is embellished with magnificent clay bas-reliefs of renowned figures from Chinese history and mythology, while inside there are several halls, shrines, and courtyards. But the temple is best known as the place where, for centuries, Chinese Mandarins traveling from Guangdong would stay. The most famous of these was Commissioner Lin Zexu, whose confiscation and destruction of British opium in 1839 helped kick off the First Opium War. There's even a six-foot statue of him in the courtyard. ✉ *Av. do Almirante Lacerda, Downtown* ☎ 🎫 *Free.*

Lou Lim Ieoc Gardens
GARDEN | These beautiful gardens were built in the 19th century by a Chinese merchant named Lou Kau, who considered every last detail, from the rock formations and angle of the sunlight to the placement of the ponds and pavilions. The balanced landscapes bear the hallmark of Suzhou's gardening style. The government took possession and restored the grounds in the mid-1970s, opening up this space for tranquil walks among delicate flowering bushes framed by bamboo groves. A large auditorium frequently hosts concerts and other events, most notably recitals during the annual Macau International Music Festival. Adjacent to the gardens, a yellow, European-style building houses the **Macau Tea Culture House,** a small museum with exhibits on Chinese tea culture. ✉ *10 Estrada de Adolfo Loureiro, at Av. do Conselheiro Ferreira de Almeida, Downtown* ☎ *853/2831–5566* 🌐 *www.icm.gov.mo* 🎫 *Free.*

Senado Square is an important gathering place in downtown Macau for festivals, markets, and performances.

Macau Tower Convention & Entertainment Centre

SPORTS VENUE | Rising above Sai Van Lake, this 338-meter (1,109-foot) freestanding tower recalls Sky Tower, a similar structure in New Zealand—and it should, as both were designed by New Zealand architect Gordon Moller. The Macau Tower offers a variety of thrills, including the Tower Climb, which challenges the strong of heart and body with a two-hour ascent on steel rungs 100 meters (328 feet) up the tower's mast for incomparable views of Macau and the mainland. Other thrills include the Skywalk, an open-air stroll around the tower's exterior—without handrails; SkyJump, an assisted, decelerated 233-meter (765-foot) descent; and what was until recently the world's highest bungee jump. More subdued attractions inside the tower include a revolving restaurant (the 360° Café) serving lunch, high tea, and a dinner buffet. ✉ *Largo da Torre de Macau, Macau, Downtown* ☎ *853/2893–3339* 🌐 *www.macautower.com.mo* 🎫 *MOP$788 Skywalk; MOP$2,688 Tower Climb; MOP$2,188 bungee jump; photos extra.*

MGM Macau

CASINO | This stylish part of Macau's gambling scene offers lavish lounges, Dale Chihuly glass sculptures, Portuguese-inspired architecture, and fine dining. The gambling floor itself is popular with high rollers from Hong Kong, including business tycoons who are just in for a few days. One of the owners, Pansy Ho, is the daughter of Macau's "gambling godfather," Dr. Stanley Ho. She is a high-octane business professional in her own right, and her discerning touch shows up in the property's glitz-and-glam energy and high-society appeal. ✉ *Av. Dr. Sun Yat Sen, Downtown* ☎ *853/8802–8888* 🌐 *www.mgm.mo.*

Red Market

MARKET | A cornerstone of local life since 1936, Macau's oldest operating wet market reopened in 2024 with a fresh new look. A two-year renovation fortified the three-story art deco building, replacing walls and tiles, improving lighting, and

Ready, Set, Go!

Since 1954, Grand Prix racing has been Macau's premier sporting event in the annual calendar. Held in mid- to late November, the 6.2-km (3.8-mile) Guia Circuit tests supercharged engines along city roads that trace the Outer Harbour to Guia Hill and around the reservoir. Racers say the route rivals Monaco's challenge, featuring rapid gear changes at sharp corners, like the right-angle Statue Corner, the Doña Maria bend, and the 22-foot-wide Melco hairpin. Cars reach speeds of 275 kph (171 mph); the lap record, set by Estonian Jüri Vips, is a blistering two minutes and six seconds. Until 2024, the main event was the Formula 3 Macau Grand Prix. It has been replaced by a Formula Regional championship, but the event remains as action-packed as ever, with races for motorcycles and production cars also on the docket. The city fills up during this period, however. Expect travel disruptions, including rerouted roads and scarce hotel vacancies.

adding more floor space (not to mention air-conditioning). Now more than 130 vendors venture to the revitalized red brick building each day, offering fresh seafood, vegetables, fruit, flowers, and more. A long-awaited clock now adorns the tower, too, completing architect Júlio Alberto Fernandes Basto's original vision, back when the building still bordered the sea. ✉ *Av. do Almirante Lacerda, Downtown* 🎫 *Free.*

★ Ruínas de São Paulo

(Ruins of St. Paul's Cathedral)

HISTORIC SIGHT | Only the towering facade, with its intricate carvings and bronze statues, remains from the original Church of Mater Dei, built between 1602 and 1640 and destroyed by fire in 1835. The sanctuary, an adjacent college, and Mount Fortress—all Jesuit constructions—once formed East Asia's first Western-style university. Now a tourist attraction, the ruins are the widely adopted symbol of Macau. Tucked behind the facade of São Paulo is the small **Museum of Sacred Art and Crypt,** which contains statues, crucifixes, and the bones of Japanese and Vietnamese martyrs. There are also some intriguing Asian interpretations of Christian images, including samurai angels and a Chinese Virgin and Child. Note that admission to the site isn't allowed after 5:30 pm. ✉ *Top end of Rua de São Paulo, Downtown* ☎ *853/2836–6866* 🌐 *www.icm.gov.mo/en/StPaul* 🎫 *Free.*

Santa Casa da Misericordia de Macau

(The Holy House of Mercy)

NOTABLE BUILDING | Founded in 1569 by Dom Belchior Carneiro, Macau's first bishop, the Macau Holy House of Mercy is coastal China's oldest Christian charity. It continues to take care of the underprivileged with regular donations and a range of social services, operating a nursery, a house for the elderly, and a center for the blind. The exterior of the heritage-listed building is neoclassical, but the interior is done in an opulent, modern style. The second floor houses a museum of Roman Catholic relics, displaying portraits of its earliest benefactors, including pioneering patroness Marta da Silva Merop. ✉ *2 Travessa da Misericordia, Downtown* ☎ *853/2833–7503* 🌐 *www.scmm.mo* 🎫 *MOP$5.*

StarWorld Hotel, Macau

CASINO | Galaxy's former flagship venue has always been known for its over-the-top service and entertainment. As you enter the towering StarWorld empire you're greeted by hosts in high heels, while a band serenades you from across the lobby. The gaming floors are small and dominated by baccarat tables, but the drink service is excellent. If you seek respite from the trenches, visit the Whisky Bar on the 16th floor of the adjacent hotel—an atmospheric place to begin or end your evening with a single malt or cocktail. The neon-blue building is just across from the Wynn Macau and down the block from the MGM Macau. Live lobby entertainment and local holiday attractions add a kitschy, friendly feel. ✉ *Av. da Amizade, Downtown* ☎ *853/2838–3838* 🌐 *www.starworldmacau.com.*

Tak Seng On Pawnshop Museum

HISTORY MUSEUM | Tak Seng On, "the virtue and success" store, offers a unique look at early-20th-century pawnshops and the important role they played in China for centuries. The architecture, interior design, and furniture date back to 1917, when this shop was established. It includes old abacuses, metal safes, accounting books, signboards in Chinese and Portuguese, and other items from that era. Public guided tours run Saturday from 3 to 5 pm. ✉ *396 Av. Almeida Ribeiro, Downtown* ☎ *2892–1811* 🌐 *www.icm.gov.mo/en/Pawnshop* 🎟 *Free.*

Tap Seac Square

PLAZA/SQUARE | Tap Seac Square is Macau's largest and perhaps most dynamic public space. Designed by Macanese architect Carlos Marreiros, it's home to institutions like the Macau Central Library and Tap Seac Gallery, which hosts excellent exhibitions of Macau-made modern art. Framed by ketchup- and mustard-color heritage buildings, the square buzzes during major events like Lunar New Year, the Mid-Autumn Festival, and the Macau Grand Prix, when pop-up markets and performances take over the space. Nearby cafés, vintage shops, and *cha chaan teng* (old-school café-restaurants) add to its charm, while locals gather daily for tai chi, badminton, and chats in the shade. ✉ *Av. do Conselheiro Ferreira de Almeida, Downtown.*

Templo de Na Tcha (*Na Tcha Temple*)

TEMPLE | This small Chinese temple was built in 1888 as a plague ravaged the peninsula, the devotees hoping it would appeal to a Chinese protector deity. The **Troço das Antigas Muralhas de Defesa** (Section of the Old City Walls), all that remains of Macau's original defensive barrier, borders the left side of the temple. These crumbling yellow walls were built in 1569 and illustrate the durability of *chunambo,* a local material made from compacted layers of clay, soil, sand, straw, crushed rocks, and oyster shells. ✉ *Top end of Rua de São Paulo, Downtown* 🎟 *Free.*

Templo de Sam Kai Vui Kun

TEMPLE | Built in 1750, this temple is dedicated to Kuan Tai, the bearded, fierce-looking god of war and wealth in Chinese mythology. Statues of him and his two sons sit on an altar. A steady stream of people comes to pray and ask for support before they go wage battle in the casinos. May and June see festivals honoring Kuan Tai throughout Macau. ✉ *10 Rua Sui do Mercado de São Domingos, Downtown.*

★ **Wynn Macau**

CASINO | Every 30 minutes, from noon until 10 pm, punters and passersby flock to the Wynn to witness flames and fountain jets flicker to tracks like "Diamonds Are Forever" at Performance Lake outside Macau's first Vegas-style casino-hotel. Inside, they crowd around the rotunda to watch the "Tree of Prosperity" unfold with feng shui glitz, every hour on the dot from noon until 10 pm. Elaborate shows aside, the Wynn's expansive, brightly lit gaming floor, exquisite fine dining options, luxury boutiques, deluxe spa, and trendy suites make this one of the finer resorts in Macau. Its 1,000 rooms span the glamorous suites in the Encore Tower, all offering views of Nam Van Lake and no less than 1,100 square feet, and the Wynn Tower's luxurious suites and guestrooms,

The Games

Macau's casinos are geared to Asian gamblers, so most tables are dedicated to baccarat and popular Asian dice games. In the past there were few poker or roulette tables, though casinos such as the Galaxy, Venetian Macao, MGM Macau, and Wynn Macau have introduced more of these Western games to the market. Similarly, slot machines, though abundant, remain less popular than baccarat, which makes up nearly 84% of the total revenue the city makes from all casino games.

Baccarat is by far the most popular game in Asia, so casinos devote most of their floors to it. Many Chinese gamblers believe it's the fairest game, even if the house still wins more than 50% of the time. You can bet on four items: the player's hand, the banker's hand, a tie, or a pair. Macau rules stipulate that you can't take the house, and there are maximum payouts, but that doesn't dissuade the masses from betting on baccarat round the clock.

Big and Small (*Sic bo*) is based on guessing the values of three dice covered under a glass canister. You can bet on values, number combinations, and, most commonly, the "big" or "small" value. Hear the collective groan when three-of-a-kind turns up and the house takes all.

Fan-tan is an ancient Chinese game largely unknown in the West. The croupier (counter) plunges an inverted silver cup into a pile of porcelain buttons on the table. They then move the cup containing several buttons to one side. The goal is to guess correctly how many buttons will be left once they are counted off in groups of four. Cash bets are placed on the table on numerals one, two, three, or four; odds or evens; or divisions between numbers (called "corners"). Only a few casinos, including the original Sands and the dingier Jai Alai and Oceanus, still offer this game.

Pacapio is a Qing-era game that amounts to a Chinese version of keno. Tickets are printed with 80 Chinese characters. You select 10 of them to bet on from a computerized draw of 20 characters. The most popular location for Pacapio betting is the Lisboa Betting Centre.

Pai gow has been a popular Chinese game since the 19th century. It's played with dominoes and a revolving banker system, where one player assumes the role of the house, while the casino gets a percentage of all bets. The rules are relatively complicated, and the game is only offered at the Hotel Lisboa and a few other casinos.

Roulette is played using the European wheel with a single 0, giving you a slightly better chance of winning over the American wheel, which has both a 0 and a 00 slot. Some casinos even offer a simplified picture version, with relatively better odds. Roulette isn't as popular as the dice and card games, but you can still find a few live tables plus a handful of electronic tables in the larger casinos.

clad with marble-floored bathrooms, subdued cream-and-gold palettes, and Chinese artwork. ✉ *Rua Cidade de Sintra, Downtown* ☎ *853/2888–9966* 🌐 *www.wynnmacau.com.*

Restaurants

Lively and busy in its center, local and real on its edges, the downtown is the best place to sample Chinese dishes and Macau-only specialties like *zhu pa bao* (porkchop buns) and *minchi* (fried pork and potato hash topped with a fried egg). In the casino-resorts, you'll find some of the finest restaurants the city has to offer.

★ Albergue 1601

$$$ | **PORTUGUESE** | Tucked into a charming cobblestone courtyard in Macau's historic St. Lazarus district, Albergue 1601 serves up classic Portuguese flavors in a setting steeped in Luso culture. Chaves-born chef Pedro Almeida's specialties—seafood rice stew, braised Ibérico pork cheek, piri piri chicken, grilled octopus bathed in garlic and olive oil—pair beautifully with a deep Portuguese wine list. **Known for:** alfresco dining; quaint setting in a canary-yellow heritage house; extensive Portuguese wine list. $ *Average main: MOP$500* ✉ *8 Calçada da Igreja de São Lázaro, Downtown* ☎ *9383–1601* 🌐 *www.albergue1601.com.*

Aux Beaux Arts

$$$$ | **FRENCH** | This Parisian-style brasserie in the MGM Macau delivers refined renditions of classic dishes, from beef bourguignon to lobster bisque, in a setting that recalls old-world France. Imagine mahogany walls, rattan chairs, and cast-iron coat racks. **Known for:** art deco–esque decor with copper-toned interiors; steak Parisien with French fries; impressive wine list and top-notch sommeliers. $ *Average main: MOP$550* ✉ *MGM Macau, Av. Dr. Sun Yat Sen, NAPE, Outer Harbour* ☎ *853/8802–2319* 🌐 *www.mgm.mo* ⏲ *Closed Mon.*

Clube Militar de Macau

(*Macau Military Club*)

$$ | **PORTUGUESE** | Founded in 1870 as a private military club, the stately pink-and-white structure was restored in 1995 and reopened as a restaurant. Although the club itself is members-only, the dining room is open to the public for lunch and dinner. **Known for:** stately setting; refined Portuguese cuisine, including rice pudding with mango and other tasty desserts; enormous lunch buffet. $ *Average main: MOP$250* ✉ *975 Av. da Praia Grande, Downtown* ☎ *853/2871–4004.*

Dom Galo

$$ | **PORTUGUESE** | **FAMILY** | Quirky and one-of-a-kind, long-standing Dom Galo is as famous for flamboyant decor—rooster paraphernalia, bright yellow chairs, spray-painted disco balls strung from the ceiling—as for its generously portioned Portuguese dishes. The clientele ranges from couples on dates to gambling-compliance lawyers and Cantonese families celebrating birthdays and special occasions. **Known for:** insalada de polvo (octopus salad), bachalau a bras (salt cod with potatoes and eggs), grilled steak with French fries; giant pitchers of sangria; reservations are recommended. $ *Average main: MOP$200* ✉ *Av. Sir Andars Ljung Stedt, Downtown* ☎ *853/2875–1383.*

The Eight

$$$$ | **CANTONESE** | Designed by Hong Kong's Alan Chan, The Eight dazzles with its food as well as its decor, both of which have kept it in the Michelin guide for more than a decade. The red and gold interiors feature swimming goldfish motifs and the number eight—considered lucky in Chinese culture. **Known for:** Michelin-caliber Cantonese cuisine; eye-popping 17,800-label wine list; tea-smoked pigeon, suckling pig, and dim sum. $ *Average main: MOP$1,000* ✉ *Grand Lisboa Hotel, 2nd fl., Av. de Lisboa, Downtown* ☎ *853/8803–7788* 🌐 *www.grandlisboa.com/en/restaurants-n-bars/the-eight.*

Fat Siu Lau

$$$ | CANTONESE | A Macau institution since 1903, Fat Siu Lau keeps locals and visitors coming back for its legendary roasted pigeon, *shek ki*—a family recipe perfected over generations. Still run by its founding family, the restaurant blends classic Macanese flavors with modern creations, making it a popular stop for those craving a taste of history. **Known for:** the famous roasted pigeon dressed in a secret marinade; nostalgic setting and lengthy history; baked seafood rice and fusion fare. *Average main: MOP$350* ✉ *64 Rua da Felicidade, Downtown* ☎ *853/2857–3585* 🌐 *www.fatsiulau.com.mo.*

Lakeside Trattoria

$$$ | ITALIAN | FAMILY | Lakeside Trattoria delivers classic Italian flavors in a scenic setting overlooking Nam Van Lake. Roman-style pizzas, handmade pastas, and seafood dishes shine, but don't miss the chef's lasagna with hearty meat ragù. **Known for:** simple but well-executed Italian cuisine; peaceful lakeside setting; rich, can't-miss desserts. *Average main: MOP$600* ✉ *Rua Cidade de Sintra, Downtown* ☎ *8986–3663* 🌐 *www.wynnresortsmacau.com.*

Lung Wah Tea House

$$ | CANTONESE | This timeless dim sum restaurant near the Red Market is a living museum: hard-backed booths, slow-whirring fans, pastel green frames, and wooden bird cages by windows that are almost always open—there's no air-conditioning—keep the look and feel of Macau's traditional teahouses alive. Order *yum cha* (dim sum) classics like *siu mai* (dumplings), steamed meatballs, barbecued pork buns, and pork ribs; pair it with a pot of pu'er tea; and recall the fading glory of mid-20th-century Macau. **Known for:** throwback teahouse look and feel; classic dim sum breakfasts; aged Chinese teas. *Average main: MOP$150* ✉ *3 Rua Norte do Mercado Almirante Lacerda, Downtown* ☎ *2857–4456.*

Portas do Sol

$$$ | CHINESE | Despite its Portuguese name, Portas do Sol is one of Macau's top destinations for exquisite dim sum. Traditional favorites—barbecue pork buns, pan-fried turnip cakes, and delicate soup dumplings—share the menu with Chinese seasonal delicacies and haute cuisine creations. **Known for:** exquisite but popular weekend dim sum; fish-shape mango and coconut pudding; extravagant interiors, including a dance floor. *Average main: MOP$500* ✉ *Hotel Lisboa, 2nd fl., Av. de Lisboa, East Wing, Downtown* ☎ *853/8803–3100* 🌐 *www.hotelisboa.com.*

★ 3 Sardines

$$ | PORTUGUESE | Full-flavored *petiscos*—Portugal's answer to tapas—take center stage at this stylish bar-restaurant in São Lázaro, alongside Portuguese craft beer, wine, and cocktails. Sip a bottle of *vinho verde* or a port-and-lychee cocktail while splitting plates of *pica-pau* (beef cubes with pickles), tender fried octopus, baby snails, and *bacalhau com broa* (baked cod with a cornbread crumble and black olives). **Known for:** Portuguese petiscos and hearty bacalhau (codfish) dishes; cocktails made with port, ginjinha, and other Portuguese spirits; time capsule-like interior design. *Average main: MOP$200* ✉ *34 Rua de São Roque, Downtown* ☎ *6363–3328.*

★ UTM Educational Restaurant

$$$ | MACANESE | Part of the Macao University of Tourism (UTM), this restaurant is a training ground for students pursuing future careers in hospitality. They work in the kitchen, the bakery, and the front of the house on a variety of Macanese, Portuguese, and Western dishes, and they do it all at a high level. **Known for:** student-run service and kitchen teams; Macanese tasting menus; sustainability initiatives that have earned it a Michelin green star. *Average main: MOP$500* ✉ *Educational Restaurant, Macao University of Tourism, Colina de Mong-Há,*

Downtown ☎ *8598–3077* 🌐 *www2.utm.edu.mo/RESTAURANT* 🕒 *Closed Sun.*

Wing Lei
$$$$ | **CANTONESE** | As you walk into Wing Lei, you're greeted by a dragon sculpted from a single piece of glass and 90,000 Swarovski crystals, dangling delicately above a yellow-and-coral room inspired by Van Gogh. The Michelin-starred restaurant lives up to this lavish look with signature dishes like steamed grouper with aged tangerine peel and succulent barbecued Ibérico pork. **Known for:** extravagant interiors; affordable dim sum at lunch; Michelin-caliber Chinese cuisine. 💲 *Average main: MOP$2,000* ✉ *Rua Cidade de Sintra, Downtown* ☎ *8986–3663* 🌐 *www.wynnresortsmacau.com.*

Coffee and Quick Bites

Leitaria i Son
$ | **CANTONESE** | **FAMILY** | Look for the cow logo marking Leitaria I Son, the original shop of Yee Shun Milk Company on Avenida Almeida Ribeiro. This nostalgic milk bar is known for its silky steamed milk and ginger pudding desserts, served hot or cold, plain or with toppings like red beans. **Known for:** cold and hot puddings; nostalgic Old Macau look and feel; fruit milk shakes in flavors like papaya and banana. 💲 *Average main: MOP$35* ✉ *381 Av. de Almeida Ribeiro, Downtown* ☎ *853/2858–3384.*

Margaret's Café e Nata
$ | **INTERNATIONAL** | **FAMILY** | Founded by the ex-wife of the late Andrew Stow (of Lord Stow's fame), Margaret's Café e Nata has been dishing out piping-hot egg tarts since 1992. Nestled in an alleyway between the Grand Lisboa and Senado Square, the café provides a cool, shaded environment to enjoy its buttery, caramelized tarts and a signature milk tea or iced coffee. **Known for:** buttery, creamy egg tarts; milk tea and fresh juices; huge sandwiches and bread products. 💲 *Average main: MOP$45* ✉ *Rua Comandante Mata e Oliveira, Downtown* ☎ *853/2871–0032* 💳 *No credit cards* 🕒 *Closed Wed.*

Pastelaria Koi Kei
$ | **CHINESE** | A staple of Macau's souvenir scene, Pastelaria Koi Kei is best known for its almond biscuits, peanut brittle, and beef jerky. It also sells egg tarts, if you find yourself craving one but far from superior options like Lord Stow's, Margaret's, or Portuguese import Manteigaria. **Known for:** Portuguese custards; almond cakes, ginger candy, beef jerky, and egg rolls; ubiquitous shops lining the historic center. 💲 *Average main: MOP$20* ✉ *70–72 Rua Felicidade, Downtown* ☎ *853/2893–8102* 🌐 *www.koikei.com* ☞ *Cash is preferred.*

★ **Sei Kee Café**
$ | **MACANESE** | This grab-and-go spot hidden in an alley in the historic center isn't much to look at, but it really nails its specialty: Macau's signature pork chop bun. Since 1965, the shop has served juicy, bone-in pork chops wedged between crusty bread and fluffy scrambled eggs. **Known for:** juicy, sinful pork chop buns; secret-recipe milk tea and charcoal-boiled coffee; tucked-away location in the historic center. 💲 *Average main: MOP$50* ✉ *15 Patio da Palha, Downtown.*

Hotels

Most travelers stay in the five-star hotels and casino-resorts near Nam Van Lake, where rooms maintain high standards, though the quality of their dining, nightlife, and public spaces vary. For more character, consider Hotel Central in the historic center or the peaceful properties near the Outer Harbour.

★ **Hotel Central**
$$ | **HOTEL** | After a seven-year renovation, this 11-story icon built in 1928 (when it became Macau's first skyscraper) reopened in 2024 with exquisitely designed rooms blending vintage charm—claw-foot tubs, jade tiles, vintage rotary phones—and modern comforts,

including a free minibar and packaged coffee beans. **Pros:** one-of-a-kind design; affordable and full of character; unbeatable downtown location. **Cons:** lots of foot traffic nearby; smaller rooms; limited in-house dining options. *Rooms from: MOP$800 270 Av. de Almeida Ribeiro, Downtown 2828–6668 www.hotelcentral.com.mo 114 rooms No Meals.*

Hotel Lisboa

$$ | **HOTEL** | In Macau's lotus-shape landmark, redolent with history and intrigue, labyrinthine hallways and salons display jade and artworks, and a gilded staircase leads to 1,000 guest rooms and suites with handcrafted furniture, lush drapes, gold and red accents, and whirlpool baths. **Pros:** unique interiors; short walk from historic sites; superior restaurants. **Cons:** older building; low ceilings; intense and crowded public facilities. *Rooms from: MOP$950 2–4 Av. de Lisboa, Downtown 853/2888–3888 www.hotelisboa.com 1,000 rooms No Meals.*

★ **Mandarin Oriental, Macau**

$$$ | **HOTEL** | **FAMILY** | Offering a serene, casino-free escape, Mandarin Oriental's 213 spacious rooms and suites each boast walk-in closets, in-room work desks, and bathrooms with tubs perched next to floor-to-ceiling windows, offering panoramic views of Macau and Zhuhai while you soak. **Pros:** good option for families; lake views; excellent spa, outdoor pool, and bar. **Cons:** connected to busy One Central mall; limited food and drink options; can be hard to get a taxi. *Rooms from: MOP$1,600 945 Av. Dr. Sun Yat Sen, Downtown 8805–8888 www.mandarinoriental.com/en/macau 213 rooms Free Breakfast.*

MGM Macau

$$$$ | **HOTEL** | These chic accommodations—with their muted bronze and gold palette, picture windows, standalone tubs, and spacious seating areas—have all the comforts you'd expect from a

World Heritage

"The Historic Centre of Macau" is listed as a UNESCO World Heritage Site. The term "center" is misleading, though, as the site is really a collection of churches, buildings, and neighborhoods that colorfully illustrate Macau's 400-year history. Included in it are China's oldest examples of Western architecture and the region's most extensive concentration of missionaries and churches.

luxury brand while Portuguese accents further distinguish this hotel from the other casino-resorts. **Pros:** tasteful architecture; fine art collections; high-quality restaurants. **Cons:** inseparable from the casino; high-traffic location; pricy compared to nearby competitors. *Rooms from: MOP$4,500 Av. Dr. Sun Yat Sen, NAPE, Outer Harbour 853/8802–8888 www.mgm.mo 582 rooms No Meals.*

StarWorld Hotel

$$$ | **HOTEL** | Luminous open-plan suites have high ceilings, Jacuzzi tubs, and panoramic bay windows, and even the deluxe rooms, with their high-quality bedding and dark wood furniture, make you feel like you're somewhere special. **Pros:** celestially designed suites; live entertainment in the lobby and lounge bar; attentive service. **Cons:** high energy at all hours; in a heavy traffic area; often booked out in advance. *Rooms from: MOP$2,500 Av. da Amizade, Downtown 853/2838–3838 www.starworldmacau.com 500 rooms No Meals.*

Wynn Macau

$$$ | **HOTEL** | In this two-tower property with 1,000 rooms and suites, every glamorous room in the suite-only Encore Tower offers views of Performance Lake

and the serene Nam Van Lake while the Wynn Tower features more understated, yet equally luxurious, rooms with marble bathrooms, cream and gold color schemes, and subtle Chinese motifs, like cloud designs woven into the bedsheets. **Pros:** excellent food and drink options; Nam Van and Performance Lake views; convenient location in the heart of downtown. **Cons:** light pollution from neighboring casinos; lowest rooms on fifth floor; crowded and chaotic public spaces. *Rooms from: MOP$2,500* *Rua Cidade de Sintra, Downtown* *853/2888–9966* *www.wynnmacau.com* *1,000 rooms* *No Meals.*

Nightlife

While Macau's bar scene is more restrained than neighboring Hong Kong's, it continues to evolve and refine itself each year. Now, you can sip Portuguese wine in a heritage building, meet young entrepreneurs at a cocktail bar in the cobblestoned city center, or enjoy an exclusive nightcap at a hotel bar overlooking the still waters of Nam Van Lake.

BARS

★ MacauSoul

WINE BAR | Housed in a bright pink building with pine-green shutters, this lively wine bar is just steps away from the Ruins of St. Paul's Cathedral. The retired British couple who manage the place have assembled a wine list that includes more than 430 Portuguese varieties—many you will only find here—plus a fine selection of whiskey. Pair your port or *vinho verde* with British cheese plates, charcuterie boards, and homemade desserts. Live after-dinner music plays on select dates, particularly Friday, depending on the season. Be warned: it's cash-only and closes periodically at the owners' whims. *31A Rua de Sao Paulo, Travessa da Paixao, Downtown* *853/2836–5182* *www.macausoul.com.*

Two Moons

BARS | Coffee shop by day, whiskey bar by night, this stylish spot across from the Portuguese consulate is a haven for whiskey lovers. The selection leans heavily on small, independent producers, primarily from Scotland and Ireland. There are loads of rare bottles to discover here, including hand-filled expressions from Highlands makers Clynelish and Glendronach and Isle of Skye's Talisker. Two Moons also hosts periodic takeovers from top bartenders across Asia, promising variety whenever you visit. *32A Rua de Pedro Nolasco da Silva, Downtown* *6666–3543* *www.instagram.com/project_twomoons.*

Vida Rica

COCKTAIL BARS | This Mandarin Oriental bar-restaurant serves Cantonese during the day and Italian at night, and it merits a visit whatever the occasion, be it a business lunch, pizza dinner, or glass of champagne. It shines brightest at "The Counter," a semi-private, 10-seat bar overlooking Nam Van Lake that can be closed off to the rest of the venue. Here, bartenders serve Mandarin Oriental signatures using interesting local ingredients, like salted plum-infused gin. They are also more than happy to tailor drinks to customers, who sit in tufted leather chairs propped up against a sturdy dark wood bar. *Av. Dr Sun Yat Sen, Downtown* *8805–8918* *www.mandarinoriental.com.*

Wood House

COCKTAIL BARS | Tucked away on Rua Central near St. Augustine's Square, Wood House epitomizes the independent cocktail bar scene slowly growing outside the confines of Macau's casinos. Founded by a local who cut his teeth in Taiwan, this cozy bar fills up fast, especially on weekends, when guests often have to find space on the second floor. The menu features around 20 original cocktails, many made with homemade infusions. Not sure what to order? The bartenders

Did You Know?

At the Performance Lake in front of Wynn Macau, you can catch choreographed water shows accompanied by music. The evening shows are particularly popular.

Macau's Buzzing Coffee Culture

The third-wave coffee movement is alive and well in Macau. Open for more than a decade, **Blooom** was one of the first local roasters to elevate the city's morning pick-me-up. Today, this boutique roaster has more than 10 branches, including one at the intersection of Avenida de Praia Grande and Avenida de Almeida Ribeiro and another in the airport departures space. Near Rua dos Ervanários, you'll find **Pace** and **Tryangle** almost side by side. **Rethink** sells beans, drip and pour-over coffee, and milk-based drinks in both the NAPE district and Broadway in Cotai. In Taipa, look for **Lamgo** in the peaceful Maia de Magalhães plaza and **Pier Coffee**, about one block east of Rua do Cunha.

will gladly craft something to suit your taste. ✉ *Rua Central, 30 Edificio Cheong Seng, Downtown* ☎ *6291–2043.*

Shopping

BOOKS AND STATIONERY

Livraria Portuguesa

BOOKS | This two-story shop in the historic center carries both English and Portuguese titles, including Macanese cookbooks, but it's more than just a bookstore. Shop for Portuguese-made souvenirs, including imported soaps and perfumes, stationery, mugs, bags, and ornaments, as well as kids' books and goodies on the second floor. The shop also hosts meet-and-greets with authors, concerts, and panel discussions. ✉ *16 Rua de São Domingos, Downtown* ☎ *2835–6235* 🌐 *www.facebook.com/portuguesebookshop.*

DEPARTMENT STORES

New Yaohan

DEPARTMENT STORE | A popular shopping destination for locals, this department store offers a good mix of shops selling household goods, clothing, jewelry, sports equipment, gadgets, and beauty products. It also has an extensive food court, a well-stocked supermarket, and a large bakery. ✉ *90 Av. Doutor Mário Soares, Downtown* ☎ *853/2872–5338* 🌐 *www.newyaohan.com.*

Inner Harbour

Macau's sleepy Inner Harbour is a fragment of its free-wheeling past. The gaming action has moved elsewhere, and development has slowed everywhere except Fai Chi Kei, a growing local neighborhood on reclaimed land close to the mainland border. But this roughly 2-mile stretch facing rapidly growing Zhuhai still has it charms—in particular, the humble noodle shops and independent Chinese, dim sum, and Portuguese restaurants.

Sights

Maritime Museum

HISTORY MUSEUM | Looking like a ship, with jutting white slats and porthole windows, and set on the site where the first Portuguese explorers landed on Macau in 1553, this handsome building across from the A-Ma Temple is a great place to spend an hour brushing up on seafaring history. Multimedia exhibits cover fishermen, merchants, and explorers from Portugal, China, and Japan, displaying compasses, telescopes, and sections of ships. There's even a small aquarium gallery with local sea life and a replica dragon boat outside. Try your hand at astronomic navigation, which sailors have used for thousands of years, by looking up at the top floor's celestial dome

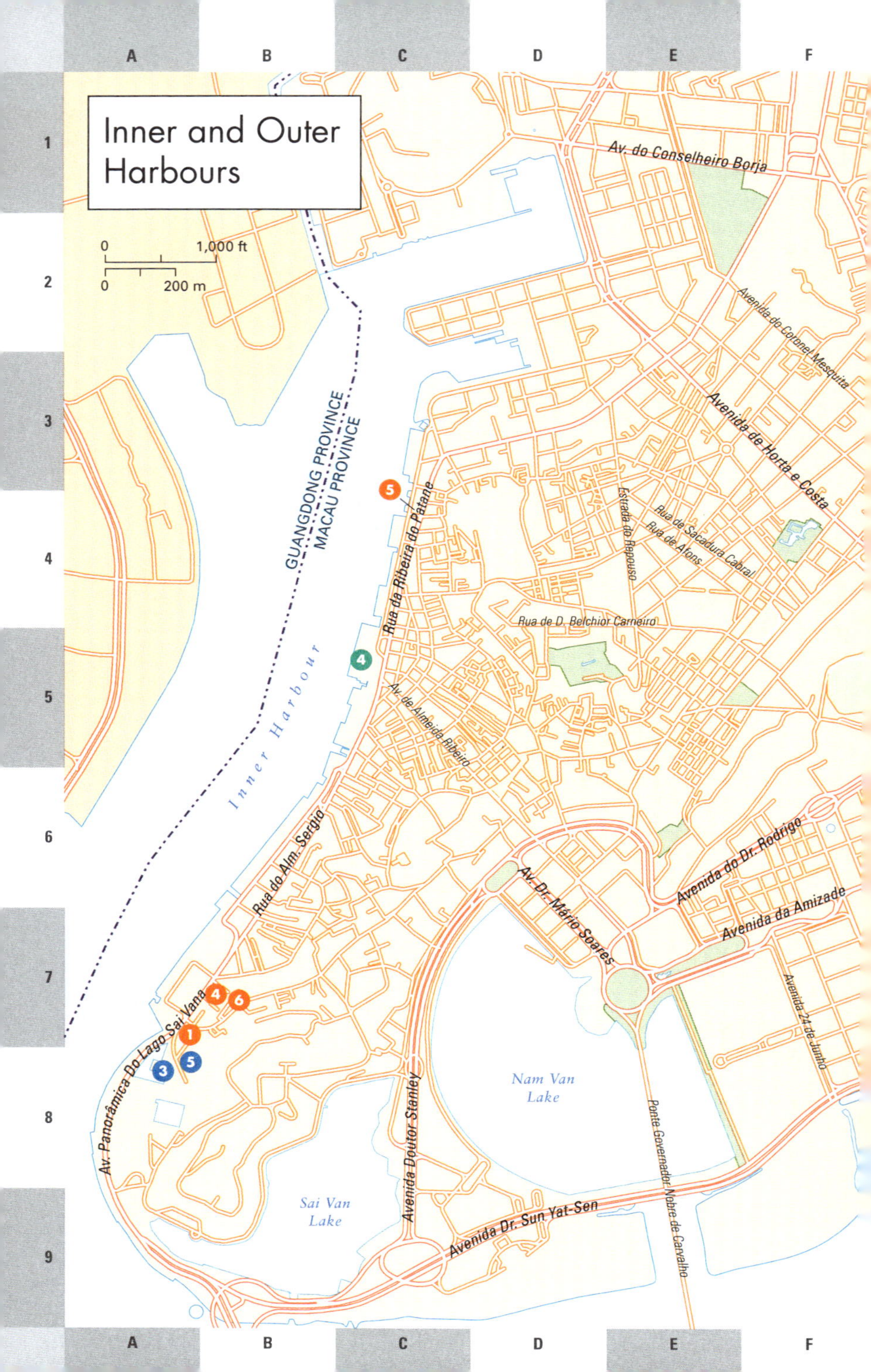

A
B
C
D
E
F
1
2
3
4
5
6
7
8
9
Inner and Outer Harbours
0
1,000 ft
0
200 m
Av. do Conselheiro Borja
Avenida do Coronel Mesquita
Avenida de Horta e Costa
GUANGDONG PROVINCE
MACAU PROVINCE
Rua da Ribeira do Patane
Estrada do Repouso
Rua de Sacadura Cabral
Rua de Afons
Rua de D. Belchior Carneiro
Inner Harbour
Av. de Almeida Ribeiro
Rua do Alm. Sergio
Avenida do Dr. Rodrigo
Av. Dr. Mário Soares
Avenida da Amizade
Avenida 24 de Junho
Av. Panorâmica Do Lago Sai Vana
Nam Van
Lake
Avenida Doutor Stanley
Ponte Governador Nobre de Carvalho
Sai Van
Lake
Avenida Dr. Sun Yat-Sen

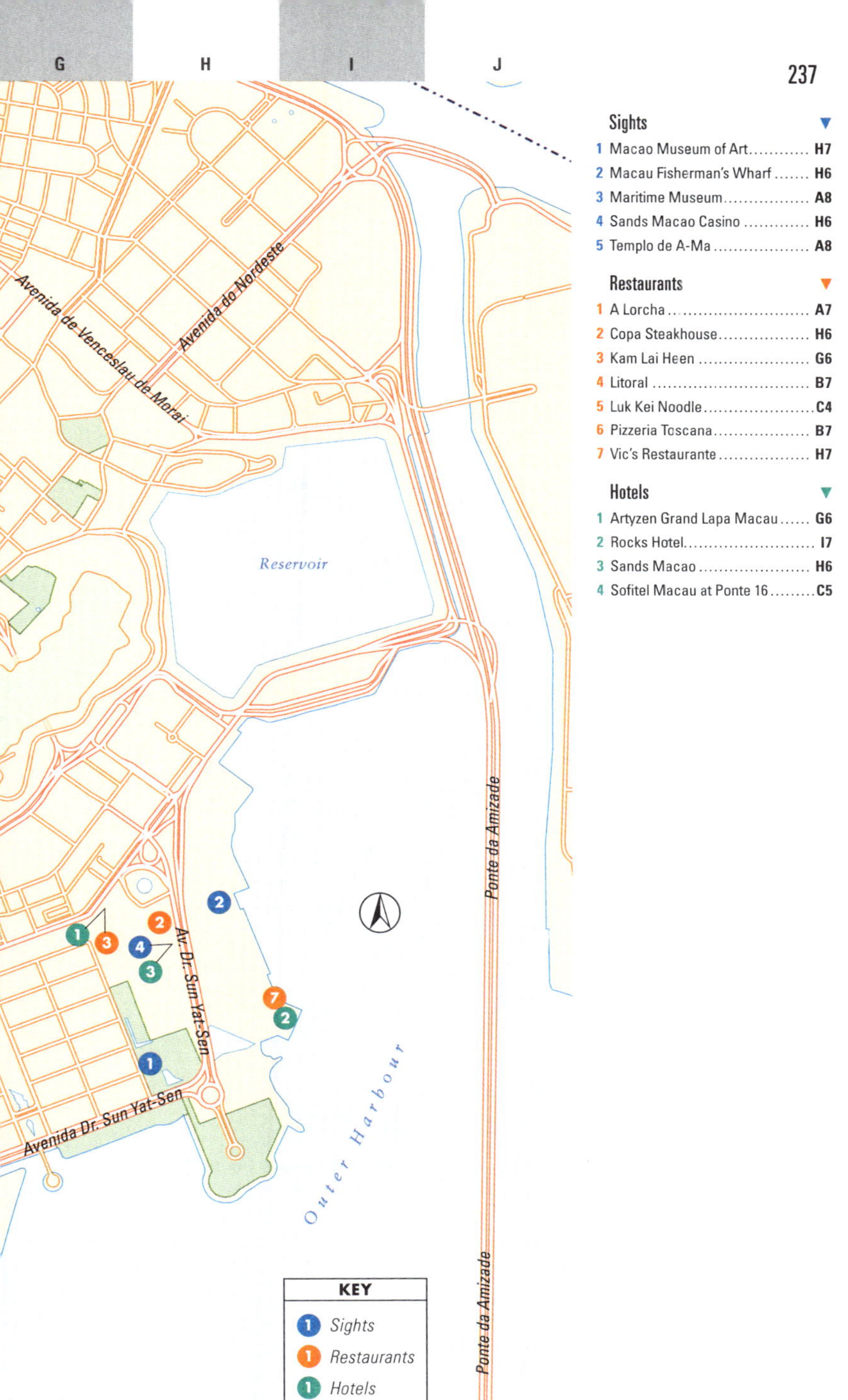

Sights

1 Macao Museum of Art H7
2 Macau Fisherman's Wharf H6
3 Maritime Museum A8
4 Sands Macao Casino H6
5 Templo de A-Ma A8

Restaurants

1 A Lorcha A7
2 Copa Steakhouse H6
3 Kam Lai Heen G6
4 Litoral B7
5 Luk Kei Noodle C4
6 Pizzeria Toscana B7
7 Vic's Restaurante H7

Hotels

1 Artyzen Grand Lapa Macau G6
2 Rocks Hotel I7
3 Sands Macao H6
4 Sofitel Macau at Ponte 16 .... C5

ceiling. ✉ *1 Largo do Pagode da Barra, Inner Harbour* ☎ *853/2859–5481* 🌐 *www.museumaritimo.gov.mo* 🎫 *Free.*

★ **Templo de A-Ma** (*A-Ma Temple*)
TEMPLE | The tiered A-Ma Temple (Ma Kok Miu) is one of Macau's oldest and most striking landmarks, as well as its likely namesake. Built during the Ming Dynasty (1368–1644) into the slopes on the Barra hill, it blends Confucian, Taoist, Buddhist, and folk influences. Vivid red calligraphy on massive boulders recounts the legend of the sea goddess A-Ma (Tin Hau). A small gate leads to prayer halls, pavilions, and caves carved directly into the hillside. ✉ *A-Ma Temple, Macau, Downtown* 🎫 *Free.*

Restaurants

★ **A Lorcha**
$$ | PORTUGUESE | Time stands still inside A Lorcha ("wooden ship"), a cozy Portuguese restaurant that has delighted local diners and travelers since 1989. The menu has barely changed since it opened; nor have the portions. **Known for:** Macanese-style chicken; airy, sinful serradura (a Macau specialty with layers of biscuits and pudding); old-school Portuguese decorations. $ *Average main: MOP$200* ✉ *289 Rua do Almirante Sérgio, Inner Harbour* ☎ *853/2831–3193* ⏲ *Closed Tues.*

Litoral
$$ | MACANESE | Just up the road from A-Ma Temple, this popular family-run restaurant has served Macanese and Portuguese favorites since 1995. The menu runs the gamut from hard-to-find specialties like *bafassá* (pork braised with saffron or turmeric) to Macau's unofficial national dish, *minchi* (wok-fried pork and potato hash topped with a fried egg). **Known for:** must-tries such as tamarind pork with shrimp paste or Portuguese vegetable cream soup; bebinca de leite (coconut-milk custard) for dessert; a line out the door on weekends, when reservations are highly recommended. $ *Average main: MOP$250* ✉ *261 Rua do Almirante Sergio, Inner Harbour* ☎ *853/2896–7878.*

Luk Kei Noodle
$ | CHINESE | Hungry diners keep coming back for its traditional noodles kneaded the old-fashioned way: by bouncing on a bamboo pool. Once ready, they're tossed into a fish-based broth, sprinkled with dried shrimp roe or served with braised beef, and paired with fried wontons and fish balls. **Known for:** traditional "bamboo" noodles; late-night eats in a quiet part of Macau; no-frills dining that's big on flavor. $ *Average main: MOP$50* ✉ *1-D, Travessa da Saudade, Inner Harbour* ☎ *2855–9627.*

Pizzeria Toscana
$$ | ITALIAN | Located across the street from the Moorish Barracks, this decades-old Italian restaurant keeps it simple with pizzas, pastas, grilled dishes, and timeless desserts like tiramisu and gelato served inside a warm, rustic space. What it lacks in "wow" factor it makes up for with affordable prices, satisfying flavors, and a family-friendly atmosphere. **Known for:** hearty pizzas and pastas; quaint dining room penned in by wooden wine racks; tender beef carpaccio and big steaks with fries. $ *Average main: MOP$140* ✉ *Calçada da Barra, 2–A Cheong Seng Bldg., Inner Harbour* ☎ *853/2872–6637.*

Hotels

Sofitel Macau at Ponte 16
$$ | HOTEL | Blending French elegance with Macau's rich heritage, the only five-star hotel in the area is a bit dated these days, but it is steps from UNESCO landmarks like the Ruins of St. Paul's. **Pros:** outdoor pool with bar; some rooms have unique views of the Inner Harbour; great high tea in the Rendez

The Zhengjiao Chanlin, or Buddhist Pavilion, in the A-Ma Temple has a circular gate designed as a symbolic entrance for spirits.

Vous lobby bar. **Cons:** some rooms can be smoky; tough to get a taxi; property is in need of a renovation. *Rooms from: MOP$1,000* *Rua do Visconde Paço de Arcos, Inner Harbour* *853/8861–0016* *www.ponte16.com.mo* *408 rooms* *No Meals.*

Outer Harbour

The first point of entry for many in Macau, the Outer Harbour offers few attractions. The hulking Sands casino and kitschy Fisherman's Wharf greet arriving ferry passengers, but most hop on shuttle buses and zip right past the district en route to glitzier casino-resorts. If you know where to look, though, you'll find some wonderful restaurants, and come Grand Prix time in November, the whole city's attention turns to the Outer Harbour.

Sights

Macao Museum of Art

ART MUSEUM | The Macao Museum of Art (MAM), the city's only dedicated art museum, spans five floors and houses over 16,000 artifacts. Opened in 1999, it showcases Chinese calligraphy, paintings, ceramics, photography, and Western works, with highlights from the Ming and Qing dynasties. Its striking, curved-roof design is as distinctive as its exhibitions, which include collaborations with Beijing's Palace Museum and the Shanghai Museum. *Macao Cultural Centre, Av. Xian Xing Hai, Outer Harbour* *853/8791–9814* *www.mam.gov.mo* *Free* *Closed Mon.*

Macau Fisherman's Wharf

OTHER ATTRACTION | **FAMILY** | This sprawling complex of rides, games, and attractions mimics foreign heritage sites with a Disney-esque flair. While the Roman Amphitheatre, Czech Baroque-inspired

Exploring Macau's Culture

Macau's historical reputation may have been eclipsed by an ever-expanding matrix of casinos, but this former Portuguese colony has much to offer in the way of heritage and beauty. From the cobblestone streets to colonial facades, museums to Moorish architecture, fortresses to street food, Macau remains a city of color, character, and top-notch cuisine.

Itinerary

1. **Leitaria I Son.** Fortify yourself by ordering a Macau-style smoothie made with frothy milk and fresh juice at one of Senado Square's favorite cafés.

2. **Largo do Senado.** See everything or just the standouts, which include the House of Holy Mercy, St. Dominic's Church, and, of course, the Ruins of St. Paul's Cathedral and neighboring Na Tcha temple.

3. **Fortaleza do Monte.** Admire the 17th-century hilltop fort; then peruse the exhibits at the adjoining museum to see how Macau has evolved.

4. **Margaret's Café e Nata.** Heading northeast along Avenida da Amizade, pop in for a quick lunch. Choose from flaky egg tarts, pastries, and made-to-order sandwiches.

5. **Guia Hill.** Take the short cable-car ride up Guia Hill, or lace up your sneakers and hike past quirky shrubs manicured to resemble dragons. Once at the top, you'll be rewarded by stunning views of all Macau.

6. **Largo do Barra.** Anchoring Barra Square, the A-Ma Temple was built in 1488 for the goddess of the sea. After seeing it, visit the Maritime Museum (also on the square) and the nearby Mandarin's House.

7. **Pousada de São Tiago.** If you're feeling peckish, stop by The Terrace at this romantic former fort for a refreshing tipple or old-school high tea.

8. **Moorish Barracks.** Originally housing a regiment from Goa to bolster local police, this neoclassical and Moghul complex has stood since 1874.

9. **A Lorcha.** Just off Barra Square, the ever-popular Macanese eatery serves up hearty favorites in a friendly atmosphere. It's best to make reservations.

10. **MacauSoul.** End the day by lingering over a glass of Portuguese wine—and perhaps listening to live music—at this jazzy venue back in Senado Square.

Harborview Hotel, and kitschy themed shops and karaoke bars won't impress world travelers, some of the restaurants offer reason to visit. **Vic's Restaurante,** for one, stands out for its rich Portuguese seafood rice and harbor views, and **Jin Yue Xuan** nails Cantonese classics and dim sum, adding a touch of authenticity to an otherwise artificial setting. ✉ *Av. da Amizade, at Av. Dr. Sun Yat-Sen, Outer Harbour* ☎ *853/8299–3300* 🌐 *www.fishermanswharf.com.mo* 🎫 *Admission free; games from MOP$1.*

Sands Macao Casino

CASINO | One of the largest casinos in Macau until Cotai's megaprojects stole the spotlight, the Sands is the first casino you'll see on the peninsula, even before disembarking from the ferry. Now more than 20 years old, it's no longer the biggest or shiniest game in town, and

Walking along Avenida Dr. Sun Yat-Sen in the Outer Harbour, you will find a statue of Kun Iam, the Buddhist Goddess of Mercy.

the focus here is clearly just gambling, often the inveterate kind—but it can still be a sight to behold. There's a sparkling 50-ton chandelier over the entrance and rotating live cabaret shows in the middle of the action, where you can play a mix of Asian and Western games, including blackjack, three-card poker, and slots. ✉ *203 Largo de Monte Carlo, Outer Harbour* ☎ *853/2888–3330* 🌐 *www.sands.com.mo.*

Restaurants

★ Copa Steakhouse

$$$$ | STEAK HOUSE | The first American steak house in Macau serves premium-quality steaks and seafood in a space that evokes 1960s Las Vegas. Chefs flame-grill your favorite cuts from an open kitchen as you dine under chandeliers and celebrity photos. **Known for:** open kitchen; perfectly cooked cuts of premium meats; fully loaded seafood towers. $ *Average main: MOP$1,000* ✉ *Sands Macao Hotel, 3rd fl., 203 Largo de Monte Carlo, Outer Harbour* ☎ *853/8118–8822* 🌐 *www.sandsmacao.com* ⏲ *No lunch weekdays except public holidays.*

Kam Lai Heen

$$ | CANTONESE | A packed house is always a good sign. The Artyzen Grand Lapa's elegant Cantonese restaurant draws local diners daily with its refined setting—crisp white linens, Chinese artwork, plush carpeting—and a menu of classics like Peking duck, tea-smoked fried chicken, and crabmeat baked in the shell. **Known for:** perfect dim sum and dumplings; elegant setting and private banquet seating; plant-based renditions of Cantonese classics. $ *Average main: MOP$300* ✉ *956–1110 Av. Da Amizade, Outer Harbour* ☎ *8793–3821* ⏲ *Closed Tues.*

Vic's Restaurante

$$$ | PORTUGUESE | Vic's Restaurante stays true to Portuguese traditions but lifts them up using top-tier ingredients and tools. Succulent 40-month-aged black Ibérico pork is put to use in a few different ways, while whole lobster rice, made for two to share, is cooked in a traditional Algarve copper pot. **Known for:** deeply satisfying seafood and lobster rice; can't-beat alfresco seaside terrace; top-tier ingredients like aged pork and Atlantic crab. *Average main: MOP$500* ✉ *Rocks Hotel, Macau Fisherman's Wharf, Av. Dr. Sun Yat-Sen, Outer Harbour* ☎ *8799–6355.*

Hotels

Artyzen Grand Lapa Macau

$$ | RESORT | FAMILY | With a more understated opulence than many of its neighbors, the Artyzen Grand Lapa weaves Portuguese charm throughout the resort. **Pros:** peaceful, palm-shaded swimming pool; tennis courts and kid's club; classic luxury facilities. **Cons:** long walk from heritage sites; quiet part of town; older, though well-maintained, property. *Rooms from: MOP$950* ✉ *956–1110 Av. da Amizade, Outer Harbour* ☎ *853/2856–7888, 2881–1288 in Hong Kong* 🌐 *www.artyzen.com* *416 rooms* *No Meals.*

Rocks Hotel

$$ | HOTEL | Convenient, quiet, and quaint, the 72-room, five-story Rocks Hotel is walking distance from the Outer Harbour ferry terminal. **Pros:** distinctive English Victorian decor; low-key fine dining; big balconies with sea views. **Cons:** no pool or spa; inside an amusement park; limited amenities and technology. *Rooms from: MOP$700* ✉ *Macau Fisherman's Wharf, Outer Harbour* ☎ *853/2878–2782* 🌐 *www.fishermanswharf.com.mo/rocks-hotel* *72 rooms.*

Sands Macao

$$ | HOTEL | The Sands Macao may show its age, but it still delivers luxury: expect spacious layouts with plush carpets, oversize beds, and marble bathrooms with whirlpool tubs. **Pros:** heated outdoor pool; close to the Outer Harbour ferry; sizable rooms and suites. **Cons:** old property; casino that caters to mass market gamblers; busy, crowded lobby. *Rooms from: MOP$900* ✉ *203 Largo de Monte Carlo, Outer Harbour* ☎ *853/2888–3330* 🌐 *www.sandsmacao.com* *289 rooms* *No Meals.*

Nightlife

BARS

The Gallery

COCKTAIL BARS | This hideaway lounge inside the Legend Palace evokes the glamour of Monte Carlo. A sleek mahogany bar, checkerboard floors, and vintage photos give the bar an air of timelessness, while light green leather booths add a cozy touch. Most come for the collection of Japanese whiskey and Scotch, including the hotel's own blend, distilled at Ardmore in the Scottish Highlands and released in limited batches each year, but the cocktail program shakes things up. Using high-tech kitchen gadgetry, the bar team creates unique redistillations, infusions, and clarified drinks that showcase Chinese flavors, from Sichuan pepper to bitter melon and guava. ✉ *1315–1339 Av. da Amizade, Outer Harbour* ☎ *8801–8003* 🌐 *www.fishermanswharf.com.mo/the-gallery.*

Activities

SPAS

The Spa at the Artyzen Grand Lapa Macau

SPA | One of the best-known spas in town takes advantage of the Artyzen Grand Lapa's sumptuous East-meets-West architecture and lets in lots of natural sunlight for a bright and airy experience. Unwind in the sauna, steam room, or vitality pool before settling into a signature treatment. The 2½-hour Macanese Sangría Ritual, created just for this hotel, includes a full body scrub using grape-seed, rosemary, and rice; a sangría bath; and an 80-minute massage with grape-seed oil. There's no rush to leave when it's done. After your treatment, relax in a private Jacuzzi tub or retreat to the 25-meter outdoor pool

The Taipa Houses overlook a tree-lined street and a modest wetland park where you can take a pause.

shaded by palm trees. ✉ *Grand Lapa, 956–1110 Av. da Amizade, Outer Harbour* ☎ *853/8793–4824* 🌐 *www.artyzen.com.*

Taipa

Directly south of peninsular Macau, Taipa is linked by four bridges. Those include the city's first: the Ponte Governador Nobre de Carvalho, which is reserved for buses, taxis, and daring pedestrians navigating its narrow roadside walkways. This largely residential district is home to quaint Taipa village, as well as Macau's international airport, several university and international school campuses, scenic trails, and a long, shaded waterfront pedestrian path stretching toward Coloane. A day is enough to explore, but the longer you spend here, hiking the Taipa Grande hill, dining at family-run restaurants, and strolling the botanical gardens by the manmade wetlands, the more it reveals its charms.

Sights

Mocha at The Altira Macau

CASINO | In the mid-2000s, this homegrown brand planted itself on the map when the property, then the Crown Hotel, became the busiest casino in the world in terms of betting volume. Since those heady days, gaming action has pivoted away from VIPs to focus on the higher end of the mass market. Now, that action takes place on the ground level and first floor, leaving the rest of the property at peace. Since the whales have left for the newer casino-resorts, the Altira Macau is much more accessible and offers great value, as well as sweeping views of the peninsula. ✉ *Av. de Kwong Tung, Taipa* ☎ *853/2886–8888* 🌐 *www.altiramacau.com.*

Pou Tai Un Buddhist Monastery

TEMPLE | Macau's largest temple is part of a functioning monastery with several dozen monks. The classically designed structure has an ornate, three-story central pavilion that houses a nearly

18-foot (5.4-meter) bronze statue of the Buddha—the tallest in Macau. Throughout, you'll find beautiful wall murals, ornamented ceilings, red wood columns, and peaceful fishponds and banyan trees, as well as resident monks who tend vegetable plots that supply the popular on-site vegetarian restaurant. ✉ *5–5B Estrada Lou Lim Ieoc, Taipa* 🌐 *www.macaotourism.gov.mo/en/sightseeing/temples/pou-tai-sin-un* 🎫 *Free* ⏲ *Restaurant closed Sun.*

Taipa Houses

NOTABLE BUILDING | These five sea-green, Sino-Portuguese buildings sit conspicuously at the edge of Taipa's man-made wetlands, surrounded by cobblestones and towering banyans. Built in 1921, they once served as residences for senior civil servants, back when they faced out over the mangroves and water toward Coloane. Today, they house rotating exhibitions and **Casa Maquista,** a beautiful, heritage-oriented restaurant serving exquisite renditions of lesser-known Macanese dishes. Nearby paths lead into the beautiful adjoining **Carmel Garden,** where palm trees provide welcome shade. Within the garden stands the brilliant white-and-yellow **Nossa Senhora do Carmo** (Church of Our Lady of Carmel), built in 1885 and featuring a handsome single-belfry tower. ✉ *Av. da Praia, Estrella de Cacilhas, Taipa* ☎ *853/2882–7527* 🌐 *www.icm.gov.mo/en/housesmuseum* 🎫 *Free* ⏲ *Closed Mon.*

★ Taipa Village

TOWN | Taipa's narrow, winding streets are packed with restaurants, bakeries, souvenir stores, temples, coffee shops, and heritage buildings defined by their traditional South Chinese and Portuguese design elements. All roads lead to perpetually busy Rua do Cunha, Taipa's famed food street. This little lane is lined by shops selling everything from matcha ice cream to pork chop buns and stewed offal. Be sure to get some egg tarts from Lord Stow's here. As you wander around the neighborhood, you'll find several Macanese and Portuguese restaurants—almost all worth a visit—alongside popular Thai, Chinese, and Western options. Come hungry, come curious. Taipa village is best explored street by street, and you'll have no shortage of tasty options to refuel. ✉ *Taipa* 🌐 *www.taipavillagemacau.com.*

Restaurants

Taipa village has several standout Macanese and Portuguese restaurants, and jam-packed Rua do Cunha offers all the Macau classics—egg tarts, steamed milk pudding, porkchop buns—in a 300-foot stretch. Thanks to its large local and expat populations, you'll also find quality and affordable ramen, burgers, and Thai food, plus well-stocked supermarkets.

Aurora

$$$$ | ITALIAN | With its fresh Italian fare and sweeping views, Aurora is a local favorite for both business lunches and dinner dates. The menu focuses on seafood, spotlighting Patagonian toothfish, Hokkaido scallops, Boston lobster, and seasonal oysters, but there are also plenty of pastas and grilled meat dishes, plus excellent wood-fired pizzas made from 48-hour fermented dough. **Known for:** wood-fired pizzas with perfectly charred crusts; striking views of the peninsula; masterfully prepared seafood dishes. $ *Average main: MOP$800* ✉ *Altira Macau, 10th fl., Av. de Kwong Tung, Taipa* ☎ *853/2886–8868* 🌐 *www.altiramacau.com/en/dining/aurora.*

★ Casa Maquista

$$$$ | MACANESE | Overseen by the two Portuguese brothers/chefs behind Albergue 1601, this spot celebrates Macanese cuisine in a unique setting: one of the charming, century-old Taipa Houses. The menu revives heirloom recipes rarely shared outside family kitchens. **Known for:** beautiful heritage home setting; Macanese dishes and decor; hearty

A Bit of History

During the age of discovery, Portuguese sailors arrived in the Pearl River Delta. Having developed good relations with Ming Dynasty rulers, in part for helping to fend off pirates, the Portuguese were able to lease land and establish a settlement in Macau. Throughout the 16th and 17th centuries, this new colony became a key hub in Portugal's global trade, as ships from Europe came to buy and sell Chinese silks and tea, Japanese crafts, Indian spices, African ivory, and Brazilian gold.

At the same time, Macau became an outpost for western religions. St. Francis Xavier used the colony as a base of operations to convert large numbers of Japanese and Chinese to Christianity. In the 1500s and 1600s, churches, missionaries, and an ambitious Christian college were erected. Today, this legacy lives on in the city's many well-preserved religious sites.

The golden age ended in the 1800s, however, when the Dutch and British gained control of most trading routes to East Asia. After defeating China in the 1842 Opium War, the British established the huge, deep-water port of Hong Kong, and Macau was relegated to a sleepy port town. It did, however, remain important to Chinese refugees during both World Wars and the Cultural Revolution.

When local officials legalized gambling in the 1960s, Macau became a freewheeling place, where espionage and Triad-related crime reigned. But the city sought to clean up its act at the turn of the 21st century. Just before the 1999 handover to the Chinese government, the Portuguese administration launched a staggering number of public works. Bridges and ports were built, and Macau International Airport opened on reclaimed land. More changes occurred following the handover to China in 1999. The gambling monopoly ended, social housing went up, and glitzy casino-resorts boomed in reclaimed Cotai, attracting tidal waves of mainland Chinese tourists.

Today, the Special Administrative Region seeks to ease gambling's stranglehold on its economy. The Macau government's "1+4" diversification strategy aims to develop four new industries to complement its strengths: healthcare, modern financial services, technology, and convention and exhibition industries, alongside culture and sports. Make no mistake: gambling still rules. Macau recorded $28.3 billion in gross gaming revenue in 2024, after all. But luxury resorts bearing the names of David Beckham and Karl Lagerfeld, NBA exhibition games, concerts, and plans for new yacht marinas signal a sea change for the city's future.

mains like turmeric-laced porco bafassá. *Average main: MOP$700* *Av. da Praia, Taipa* *6217–6332* *www.taipavillagemacau.com/directory/casa-maquista.*

★ **La Famiglia**

$$$ | **MACANESE** | Founded by local culinary legend Florita Maria Natália de Jesus Morais Alves, La Famiglia is one of the city's best places to try Macanese food. Homestyle dishes like *minchi* (wok-fried pork and potato hash topped with a fried egg), *capela* (Macanese-style meatloaf), and stuffed shrimp sautéed with butter and garlic represent the fusion of flavors that define the cuisine. **Known**

Dishing on Macanese Cuisine

Macanese cuisine is often called the world's first fusion food, but it's more than just a mix of Chinese and Portuguese flavors. It weaves together ingredients, ideas, and techniques from Southeast Asia, Africa, India, Brazil, and anywhere else the Portuguese had a footprint. Turmeric, shrimp paste, coconut milk, soy sauce, and bold spices all feature prominently from dish to dish. Deeply personal and passed down through generations, Macanese recipes are rarely standardized, with families fiercely guarding their own versions. After the 1999 handover to China, the cuisine nearly faded as families emigrated, but today, efforts to preserve and revive these unique dishes are bringing Macao's rich culinary heritage back to life. Today, you'll find dishes like *galinha à Africana* (curry-like African chicken), *casquinha* (deep-fried and baked stuffed crab), and *porco bafassá* (turmeric-laced Ibérico pork) on menus at Litoral, La Famiglia, Casa Maquista, and others.

for: family-style Macanese cuisine; local celebrity chef; colorful Taipa village setting and top-floor views. *$ Average main: MOP$500 ✉ No. 2830, Rua dos Clerigos, Taipa, Taipa ☎ 2857–6131 🌐 www.instagram.com/lafamigliamacau.*

O Santos

$$$ | **PORTUGUESE** | A busy little eatery in the heart of Taipa Village, O Santos serves up classic Portuguese fare without frills or fluff—but with a lot of warm and lively hospitality. Decorated with Portuguese soccer paraphernalia, the gregarious owner's navy keepsakes, and global currencies tacked to the walls, it's not a place for a romantic night out, but the food is great. **Known for:** hospitality that makes you feel at home; dishes like suckling pig and baked duck rice; easy-drinking house-made sangria. *$ Average main: MOP$500 ✉ Edificio Garnet, 20 Rua do Cunha, Taipa ☎ 853/2882–7508 ⏲ Closed Tues.*

Hotels

There aren't many hotels in Taipa. The ones that do exist tend to fit somewhere between upscale and basic but a bit rundown. The best properties here offer sweeping sea and city views, with the caveat that they require taxi or bus rides to reach other parts of Macau.

Altira Macau

$$ | **HOTEL** | Towering over Taipa, the luxe Altira provides stunning sea views of the Macau peninsula from all 216 rooms, suites, and villas; all come with a dedicated lounge, walk-in wardrobe, warm brown hues, and circular stone bath. **Pros:** excellent spa and dining options; open-air rooftop bar; infinity-edge swimming pool. **Cons:** a taxi or bus ride from the peninsula; rates vary throughout the year; public spaces and rooms can be smoky. *$ Rooms from: MOP$850 ✉ Av. de Kwong Tung, Taipa ☎ 853/2886–8888 🌐 www.altiramacau.com 216 rooms No Meals.*

Nightlife

Don't expect much glitz or glamour. When night falls and tourists depart Taipa village, the after-work crowds loosen their ties, take off their heels, and meet up at pubs like Old Taipa Tavern. For a loftier experience, there are bars and lounges in properties like the Altira.

BARS

Old Taipa Tavern (OTT)

PUB | A staple of Taipa's expat scene, this lively pub is a long-standing go-to for craft beers on tap, wines by the glass, and affordable mixed spirits paired with comfort food like Aussie-style pies and juicy burgers. Big-screen TVs display live sports while weeknight bar games up the excitement. For example, beat your bartender in a dice roll, and your next round is free. This pub is the perfect place to meet old friends and make new ones. ✉ *21 Rua das Negociantes, Taipa* ☎ *2882–5221.*

38 Lounge

LOUNGES | The Altira's 38 Lounge stands among the best alfresco rooftops bar in the city, literally and figuratively. Sip cocktails or a glass of champagne under the stars on the outdoor terrace 38 floors above Taipa. Trade high-floor breeze for entertainment inside, where a live band plays until the wee hours most evenings. There's a large selection of single malt whiskeys to choose from, as well as 45-plus labels of wine from Altira's sizable cellar—a reason why 38 Lounge is one of the city's few rated on the Star Wine list. ✉ *F/38, Altira Macau, Avenida de Kwong Tung, Macau, Taipa* ☎ *853/2886–8868* 🌐 *www.altiramacau.com.*

Favorite Places

Craig Sauers: Taipa is the best of Macau squeezed into a compact package. It offers the blend of Portuguese and Chinese culture and aesthetics that travelers expect, but with a fraction of the crowds of the historic center (Rua do Cunha notwithstanding). That manifests most obviously in the food you'll find—Taipa is the best place to eat Macanese cuisine, including Lord Stow's egg tarts.

Shopping

Loja das Conservas

SOUVENIRS | Rows of colorful canned Portuguese sardines bring a historic connection to the sea into the modern day as savory souvenirs. There are dozens of kinds of tinned fish in beautiful packaging to buy and bring home—from sardines to salmon, from herring to tuna; some with spices, others in olive oil. You can also pick up bottles of port wine, egg tart–shape ceramic cups, and other theme goodies from Macau and Portugal. Look for T-shirts, tote bags, and keepsakes from local brand Loving Macau. Its products make for great gifts. ✉ *No. 2, Rua do Cunha, Taipa* ☎ *6828–5689* 🌐 *www.facebook.com/lojadasconservasmacau.*

Activities

Whether you prefer leisurely walks or uphill climbs, Taipa has a trail for you. The rewards for heading up Taipa Grande and Taipa Pequena—the "big" and "small" hills—are great views of the city and the sea. To reach the **Taipa Grande** trail, walk up Estrada Colonel Nicolau de Mesquita, near the United Chinese Cemetery. (You can bypass this steep climb by taking the free inclined elevator on Estrada Governador Nobre de Carvalho.) This easy, 2.5-mile trail is shaded and cool, forming a rolling loop that's popular with both walkers and runners. You can add a hike up stone steps to Taipa's tallest point, although it's only 522 feet above sea level and the views are blocked by vegetation. About 1.5 miles long, the **Taipa Pequena** trail starts at Estrada Lou Lim Ieoc behind the Regency Hotel and takes in views of rapidly developing Hengqin Island across the estuary. Both routes are suitable for most fitness levels and ages.

Nirvana Spa

SPA | In a quiet area of town, Asian-inspired Nirvana has rooms decorated in Eastern themes. Therapists from Thailand and the Philippines are trained in deep-tissue, ayurvedic, herbal, shiatsu, and aromatherapy massages. If massage is not for you, you can opt for one of dozens of other treatments on the extensive menu. Try a manicure, pedicure, hydrating facial therapy, body wrap, or even an ear-candle cleaning. ✉ *3rd fl., Shop 328, 522–526 Av. dos Jardins do Oceano, Taipa* ☎ *853/2833–1521* 🌐 *www.nirvanamacau.com.*

Cotai Strip

Cotai is Macau's high-rolling entertainment district, packed with mega-resorts, designer shopping, and Michelin-starred dining. The Cotai Strip dazzles—or repels, depending on your view—with replicas of world landmarks, while casino-resorts lure visitors with elaborate stage shows and round-the-clock betting action. But Macau has big aspirations for Cotai to be known for more than just gambling. These days, the gaming operators are hosting big-ticket concerts, biennales and pop-up exhibitions, and sporting events at venues like the renovated Venetian Arena. All the while, new five-star hotels, including the ultra-luxe Capella, signal its ceaseless development. Whether for gambling, fine dining, or spectacle, Cotai delivers grand-scale entertainment with no signs of slowing down.

Sights

Most gravitate to the Cotai Strip, slicing between Sands China's casino-resorts, to gawk at replicas of Big Ben, the Eiffel Tower, and Venice. But you could spend days exploring Cotai's cavernous complexes, shopping, and dining, going to spas, and seeing elaborate stage shows.

Macao vs. Macau

Macau has had more name changes than you might expect. When the Portuguese arrived in 1557, they mistakenly christened it Amacao after the A-Ma Temple, believing it to be the local name for the land. In the 17th century, the Portuguese shortened it to Macao, which became Macau in 1911 when Portugal standardized its spelling. After the 1999 handover, it officially reverted to Macao to align with local linguistic traditions. So, which is correct? Technically, both—Macao for official use, Macau in Portuguese, and either for private ventures.

City of Dreams

OTHER ATTRACTION | Cotai's glitzy entertainment complex is the living definition of a megaproject. City of Dreams, or CoD for short, boasts three separate casinos with nearly 500 gaming tables, four hotels with around 2,270 total hotel rooms, and 30-plus bars and restaurants. Most know it for its entertainment options, though. The 17,000-square-foot Kids' City provides four floors of guided playtime and adventure, while the House of Dancing Water dazzled thousands with its aquatic-based spectacles until going on hiatus for improvements. ✉ *Estrada do Istmo, Cotai* ☎ *8868–6688* 🌐 *www.cityofdreamsmacau.com.*

Galaxy Macau

OTHER ATTRACTION | It's impossible to miss the six 24-karat gold cupolas of the Galaxy complex towering over the northwestern end of the Cotai Strip. This palatial complex is currently home to seven luxury hotels—including the Banyan Tree, JW Marriott, The Ritz-Carlton, and Raffles—and as of 2025, an all-suites-and-villas Capella. The whole complex spans more than 11 million square feet of space and includes 120 dining options, a 10-screen cinema, a white-sand beach and wave pool on the rooftop, a cavernous 16,000-seat arena, a VR entertainment center, and more. Smack in the center is a brightly lit casino floor packed with gaming tables, surrounded by high-end shops where you can actually hear yourself think. ✉ *Estrada da Baia de Nossa Senhora da Esperanca, Cotai* ☎ *853/2888–0888* 🌐 *www.galaxymacau.com.*

Grand Lisboa Palace

OTHER ATTRACTION | The Grand Lisboa Palace is certainly both grand and palatial. The castle-like facility blends baroque and neoclassical influences with Chinese and Portuguese design elements. Inside, the sprawling resort houses 1,350 ornate rooms and suites, including the exclusive Karl Lagerfeld and Palazzo Versace hotels. These sit alongside a massive casino and a luxury shopping complex led by NY8 New Yaohan, a 160,000-square-foot department store with a supermarket, kid's zone, and dining center, and Made in Macau, a space that displays products from local brands. Dining options range from high-end restaurants like Zuicho and Palace Garden to the indulgent Grand Buffet—one of the city's best all-you-can-eat experiences. If you need some serenity, visit Jardim Secreto, a European-style garden with grass mazes and European-style pavilions. ✉ *Rua do Tiro, Cotai* ☎ *8881–8838* 🌐 *www.grandlisboapalace.com.*

★ **The Londoner**

RESORT | **FAMILY** | Following a full-scale overhaul, the former Sands Cotai Central hotel, shopping, and casino complex re-emerged as The Londoner in 2021. Architects reconstructed the exterior to resemble, appropriately, London, complete with a replica of Big Ben along the Cotai Strip. Inside, British rock pumps through speakers as guests flit from venues like the Gordon Ramsay Pub & Grill to Churchill's Table, enjoy retail therapy at 150-plus shops and boutiques, and take selfies with black cabs, double-decker buses, and a replica of a royal carriage. There are five hotels, including The St. Regis, The Londoner, and The Londoner Grand, a high-end "resort within a resort," not to mention 14 invitation-only suites brought to life by David Beckham and British designer David Collins. ✉ *Estrada do Istmo, Cotai* ☎ *853/2882–2878* 🌐 *www.londonermacao.com.*

Studio City

OTHER ATTRACTION | **FAMILY** | Hollywood glamour hits Cotai at this Zaha Hadid–designed art deco complex. Outside, you can't miss the Golden Reel, a figure eight-shaped Ferris Wheel built into the tower. Inside, you'll find one of Asia's largest indoor water parks, a nine-house cinema including VIP rooms and a theater equipped with motion technology, about 20 different dining venues, great cocktail bars like Blind Tiger and A.P.D., and Legend Heroes Park, a family-friendly, tech-based entertainment zone. The casino, meanwhile, boasts 1,233 gaming machines and about 250 tables. When it comes time to call it a night, there are about 2,500 rooms spread across four hotels, including the glitzy W. ✉ *Studio City, Estrada do Istmo, Cotai* ☎ *8865–6868* 🌐 *www.studiocity-macau.com.*

The Venetian Macao

OTHER ATTRACTION | Twice the size of its namesake in Las Vegas, The Venetian offers ample opportunities for shopping, dining, gambling, entertainment, and sleeping. Expect faux-Renaissance decoration, built-in canals plied by crooning gondoliers, live carnival acts, and plenty of sheer spectacle. The 550,000 square feet of gaming areas, complete with 3,400 slot machines and 800 tables, make this the world's biggest casino. The sprawling property also includes 3,000 suites, plus venues like the 1,800-seat Venetian Theatre, which has hosted performances from the likes of Alicia Keys and The Beach Boys, and the newly

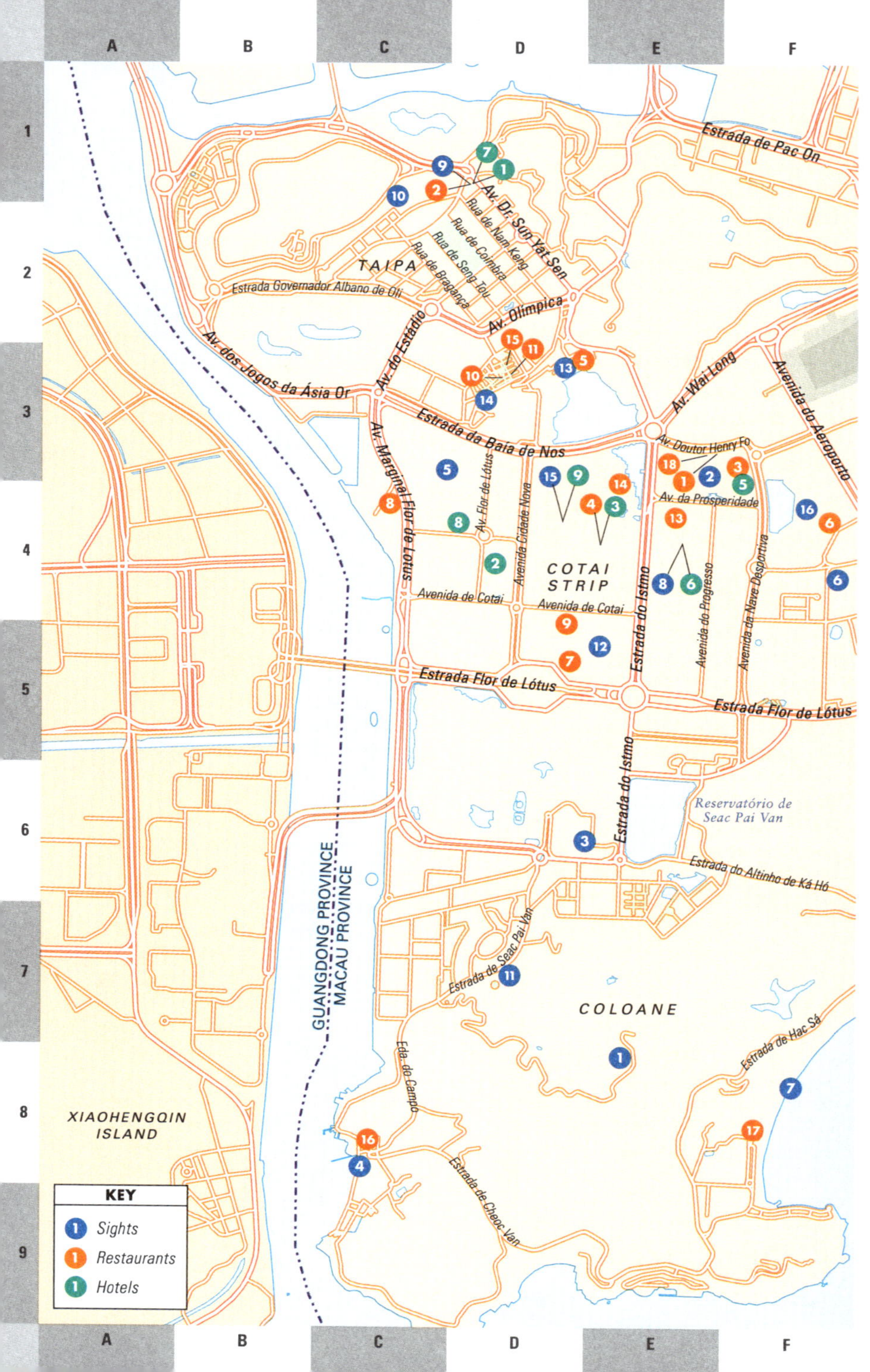
A
B
C
D
E
F
1
2
3
4
5
6
7
8
9
Estrada de Pac On
Av. Dr. Sun Yat Sen
Rua de Nam Keng
Rua de Coimbra
Rua de Seng Tou
Rua de Bragança
TAIPA
Estrada Governador Albano de Oli
Av. Olímpica
Av. do Estádio
Av. dos Jogos da Ásia Or
Av. Wai Long
Avenida do Aeroporto
Estrada da Baía de Nos
Av. Doutor Henry Fo
Av. Marginal Flor de Lótus
Av. Flor de Lótus
Avenida Cidade Nova
Av. da Prosperidade
COTAI
STRIP
Estrada do Istmo
Avenida do Progresso
Avenida da Nave Desportiva
Avenida de Cotai
Avenida de Cotai
Estrada Flor de Lótus
Estrada Flor de Lótus
Estrada do Istmo
Reservatório de
Seac Pai Van
Estrada do Altinho de Ká Hó
GUANGDONG PROVINCE
MACAU PROVINCE
Estrada de Seac Pai Van
COLOANE
Estrada de Hac Sá
Eda. do Campo
Estrada de Cheoc Van
XIAOHENGQIN
ISLAND
KEY
Sights
Restaurants
Hotels

Sights

1 A-Ma Cultural Village E8
2 City of Dreams E3
3 Coloane Karting Track............. D6
4 Coloane Village C8
5 Galaxy Macau........................ C3
6 Grand Lisboa Palace F4
7 Hác Sá F8
8 The Londoner E4
9 Mocha at The Altira Macau...... D1
10 Pou Tai Un Buddhist Monastery.............. C1
11 Seac Pai Van Park.... .... D7
12 Studio City E5
13 Taipa Houses........................ D3
14 Taipa Village......................... D3
15 The Venetian Macao D4
16 Wynn Palace F4

Restaurants

1 Alain Ducasse at Morpheus....... E3
2 Aurora.................................. D1
3 Beijing Kitchen....................... F3
4 Belcanção.............................. E4
5 Casa Maquista........................ D3
6 Chef Tam's Seasons F4
7 Din Tai Fung D5
8 Goa Nights............................. C4
9 Hawker Hawker D5
10 La Famiglia D3
11 Lord Stow's Bakery................ D3
12 Mesa by José Avillez.............. G4
13 The Mews E4
14 North E3
15 O Santos D3
16 Restaurante Espaço Lisboa....... C8
17 Restaurante Fernando F8
18 Yí.. E3

Hotels

1 Altira Macau D1
2 Andaz Macau D4
3 Four Seasons Hotel Macao E4
4 Grand Coloane Resort............. G7
5 Grand Hyatt Macau F3
6 The Londoner E4
7 Nüwa.................................... D1
8 The Ritz-Carlton, Macau.......... D4
9 The Venetian Macao D4

renovated 15,000-seat Venetian Arena. It's a must-see megaplex. ✉ *Estrada da Baía de N. Senhora da Esperança, Cotai* ☎ *853/2882–8877* 🌐 *www.venetianmacao.com.*

Wynn Palace

OTHER ATTRACTION | Wynn Palace seamlessly weaves Las Vegas–style opulence with Chinese motifs. The 28-story resort houses 1,706 lavish rooms, suites, and villas, all decorated in shades of sunrise yellow, sunset orange, peacock blue, or Wynn gold—complete with gold-hued toiletries. Guests and outsiders alike tend to congregate around Performance Lake, which stages elaborate water, music, and light shows that are best viewed from Lakeview Palace restaurant. The real standout, though, is Macau's largest spa, The Spa at Wynn Palace. There are 22 treatment rooms, including private spaces offering cryotherapy, float pods, and red-light therapy. The 424,000-square-foot casino offers round-the-clock gaming. When you tire of the tables, go for a walk around the shops to spot rare art, including Qing Dynasty Buccleuch vases; unwind by the mosaic-lined pool; or get a bite to eat one of the 13 excellent dining venues. ✉ *Av. da Nave Desportiva, Cotai* ☎ *8889–8889* 🌐 *www.wynnresortsmacau.com/en/wynn-palace.*

Restaurants

There's an abundance of great food in Cotai, but not much comes cheap. If you hit it big, you have your pick of Michelin-rated restaurants to celebrate. In the casino-resorts, you'll find familiar chains like Shake Shack, Starbucks, and Macau's Lord Stow's alongside many mid-range restaurants and grand buffets.

Alain Ducasse at Morpheus

$$$$ | **FRENCH** | The man with the most Michelin stars in the world runs this destination-dining venture in the late Zaha Hadid's ethereal Morpheus. Silver and cream hues and crystal accents set the tone for exquisite haute cuisine prepared by French chef Cedric Sabatin. **Known for:** French fine dining rooted in seasonality and precision; seafood dishes made with premium produce; huge wine list with 900-plus labels, including Ducasse's own champagne. [$] *Average main: MOP$2,988* ✉ *Morpheus, 3rd fl., City of Dreams, Estrada do Istmo, Cotai* ☎ *8868–3432* 🌐 *www.cityofdreamsmacau.com* 🕒 *Closed Mon. and Tues.*

Beijing Kitchen

$$$$ | **CHINESE** | Inspired by its sister restaurant Made In China in the Grand Hyatt Beijing, Beijing Kitchen features northern Chinese cuisine. The highlight is the Peking duck, which is cooked in a wood-fired oven, roasting away the fat and leaving the skin crispy. **Known for:** perfectly cooked Peking duck; great value set menus; juicy pan-fried pork dumplings. [$] *Average main: MOP$588* ✉ *Grand Hyatt Macau, 1st fl., City of Dreams, Estrada do Istmo, Cotai* ☎ *853/8868–1930* 🌐 *www.hyatt.com/grand-hyatt/en-US/macgh-grand-hyatt-macau/dining* 🕒 *No dinner.*

Belcanção

$$$$ | **PORTUGUESE** | Located next to the Four Seasons' Bali-inspired poolside, Belcanção offers an impressive buffet spread featuring Portuguese, Indian, Chinese, Italian, and a smaller selection of Japanese dishes. The dessert and salad bars are amply stocked, and the service is impeccable. **Known for:** extensive buffet selection; free-flow wine from the beverage cart; outdoor miniplayground for kids. [$] *Average main: MOP$608* ✉ *Four Seasons, Estrada da Baía de Nuestra Senhora da Esperança, Cotai* ☎ *853/2881–8888* 🌐 *www.fourseasons.com/macau/dining/restaurants/belcanc_ao/.*

★ Chef Tam's Seasons

$$$$ | **CANTONESE** | Cantonese chef Tam Kwok Fung creates transcendent hyper-seasonal cuisine based on the 24 solar terms of the traditional Chinese calendar. His signature tasting menu changes every two weeks, in line with subtle seasonal shifts. **Known for:** tasting menus that change every two weeks; refined Cantonese cooking from a master chef; excellent dim sum. $ *Average main: MOP$1,888* ✉ *Wynn Palace, Av. da Nave Desportiva, Cotai* ☎ *8889–3663* 🌐 *www.wynnresortsmacau.com.*

Din Tai Fung

$$ | **CHINESE** | The Taiwanese chain is famous for one thing above all: soup dumplings. Paper-thin wrappers encase fillings like truffle and pork, snow crab and scallop, and chicken. **Known for:** Taiwanese soup dumplings; wide selection of noodle dishes; affordability in an expensive part of town. $ *Average main: MOP$120* ✉ *The Countdown City of Dreams, Level 2 Estrada do Istmo, Cotai* ☎ *8868–7348* 🌐 *www.cityofdreamsmacau.com.*

Goa Nights

$$ | **INDIAN** | This popular bar-restaurant moved from Taipa to Broadway in 2024, trading a narrow, multifloor building where food and drinks were served via dumb waiter for a more spacious ground-floor setting. Now more restaurant than bar, Goa Nights still specializes in the creative Goan and Indian flavors that long made it an expat favorite. **Known for:** full-flavored Goan curries and pan-Indian dishes; cocktails inspired by Portugal's Age of Discovery; juicy kebabs featuring secret spice blends. $ *Average main: MOP$200* ✉ *Broadway Macau, Shops E-G020–G021, Av. Marginal Flor de Lotus, Cotai* ☎ *2856–7819* 🌐 *www.goanights.com.*

Hawker Hawker

$$$$ | **BUFFET** | The W Hotel's market-inspired buffet hits all the right notes with an incredible spread that features Western classics, including Portuguese dishes, alongside Chinese, Thai, and Indian cuisine. There's a walk-in seafood room filled with lobster, oysters, snow crab, and more, plus a loaded dessert station where you can try Macau diner classics, including the black ox (Coca-Cola with a scoop of chocolate ice cream). **Known for:** extensive selection; walk-in seafood room and excellent dessert bar; view of the faux Eiffel Tower outside the Parisian. $ *Average main: MOP$600* ✉ *W Macau, Level 2U, Studio City, Cotai* ☎ *8865–1366* 🌐 *www.studiocity-macau.com.*

★ **Mesa by José Avillez**

$$$$ | **PORTUGUESE** | Mesa by José Avillez is not your typical Portuguese restaurant. Its bold interior blends Chinese symbolism with Karl Lagerfeld's signature black, white, and gold aesthetic while the food also bucks norms, its plates—like succulent piri piri chicken and beef croquettes with truffle and mustard emulsion—are made to share. **Known for:** extravagant Lagerfeld design centered on a gold birdcage-like bar; piri piri chicken and beef croquettes; impressive cellar storing exclusive Douro Valley wines. $ *Average main: MOP$1,288* ✉ *The Karl Lagerfeld, 3rd fl., Grand Lisboa Palace, Rua do Tiro, Cotai* ☎ *8881–1800* 🌐 *www.grandlisboapalace.com* ⏲ *Closed Tues.*

The Mews

$$$$ | **THAI** | A British-style horse stable might not scream high-end Thai, but it works at The Mews. Designed by Ashley Sutton (known for Bangkok bars Iron Fairies and Maggie Choo's), this venue is full of surprises; enter through the "stable" (the bar), then a secret door reveals a dining room with Thai lanterns and wood carvings. **Known for:** whimsical design; classic Thai dishes like green curry made with a modern twist; world-class cocktail bar serving Thai-inspired drinks. $ *Average main: MOP$888* ✉ *The Londoner, Level 1, Estrada do Istmo, Cotai* ☎ *8118–8822* 🌐 *www.londonermacao.com.*

★ **North**

$$ | **CHINESE** | Watch in awe as chefs slice, dice, and pull noodles at staggering speed from within the show kitchen in the center of the room. Spectacle aside, the combination of Sichuan cuisine and

dishes from China's northeast are the true stars of the show at this handsome, red and black restaurant. **Known for:** action happening in the open kitchen; northeast dishes like Shanxi braised beef noodles; Sichuan influences and spicy mapo tofu. *Average main: MOP$250 The Venetian Macao, Level 1, Shop 1015, Cotai 8118–8822 www.venetianmacao.com.*

Yí

$$$$ | **CHINESE** | Perched on the 21st-floor sky bridge of the Morpheus hotel, Yí delivers sweeping views alongside an ever-evolving tasting menu inspired by the 24 solar terms of the Chinese calendar. Designed by the late Zaha Hadid, the space is stunning. **Known for:** ethereal Zaha Hadid–design dining room; hyperseasonal Chinese dishes; smoky, oven-roasted pigeon with lemongrass. *Average main: MOP$1,888 Morpheus City of Dreams, 21st fl., Estrada do Istmo, Cotai 8868–3446 www.cityofdreamsmacau.com/en/dining/yi Closed Tues.*

Hotels

In Cotai, expect to splash out on a five-star hotel—anything less tends to be worn down. The St. Regis, Four Seasons, Ritz-Carlton, Raffles, Conrad, Banyan Tree, W, and Grand Hyatt are just some of the global brands here. Then you have the gaming operator's own luxe properties, not to mention ultraposh Karl Lagerfeld- and Versace-branded resorts.

Andaz Macau

$$$ | **HOTEL** | A boutique brand under the Hyatt umbrella, the Andaz Macau hits the sweet spot between luxury and affordability. **Pros:** affordable; easy to reach Taipa; the best rooms have balconies. **Cons:** long walk to reach Cotai strip; fewer luxury amenities than competitors; business-focused atmosphere. *Rooms from: MOP$1,200 Andaz Macau, Galaxy Macau, Cotai 2888–0888 www.andazmacau.com.*

Four Seasons Hotel Macao

$$$$ | **HOTEL** | With a Sino-Portuguese aesthetic, five restaurants—including Michelin-starred Zi Yat Heen—and a sensational 20,000-square-foot spa, the Four Seasons Macao certainly upholds its brand-name reputation. **Pros:** luxury from start to finish; focus on service; extensive spa treatments. **Cons:** much larger than usual for Four Seasons; high price point; facilities beginning to age. *Rooms from: MOP$3,200 Four Seasons Hotel Macao, The Venetian Macao, Cotai 853/2881–8888 www.fourseasons.com/macau 360 rooms No Meals.*

Grand Hyatt Macau

$$$ | **HOTEL** | The Grand Hyatt Macau's two towers were inspired by waves, in keeping with the aquatic City of Dreams theme. **Pros:** stunning outdoor pool area; large spa with extensive menu; quality on-site dining options. **Cons:** surrounding neighborhood lacks character; less flashy than other hotels in Cotai; some rooms are smoky. *Rooms from: MOP$2,088 City of Dreams, Estrada do Istmo, Cotai 853/8868–1234 www.hyatt.com 791 rooms No Meals.*

★ The Londoner

$$$$ | **HOTEL** | If you really love London, you're in luck; this all-suite hotel is an over-the-top tribute to the swinging city, from the British rock soundtrack to the mahogany-lined Residence bar and lounge reserved for guests. **Pros:** loads of things to do inside the resort; handsome, thoughtful interiors; easy to find quiet nooks. **Cons:** teeming with tourists and gamblers; expensive; theme may not appeal to everyone. *Rooms from: MOP$4,500 The Londoner Macao, Cotai 8113–6167 www.londonermacao.com 614 rooms No Meals.*

Macanese vs. Portuguese Egg Tarts

If you haven't had an egg tart, then you haven't truly visited Macau. The flaky, caramelized pastry is a rite of passage, a symbol now as closely associated with Macau as it is Portugal, the country that created it. But egg tart enthusiasts can be particular about their pastries. While the SAR's tarts and their Portuguese predecessors bear many similarities, savvy tasters might notice a difference between them.

For one, there's the puff pastry shell. Portuguese bakers put butter between wafer-thin layers of puff pastry, whereas Macau makers tend to use margarine to create a crispier, crunchier exterior. Then, there's the filling and how it's prepared. Portuguese egg tarts feature a lot of egg yolks, plus whole milk, flour, cinnamon, and sugar. The flour and milk are partially cooked on the stove and the yolks are added later, creating a creamy texture. Macau egg tarts use fewer yolks but more sugar and cream, and the filling is piped into the pastry shells entirely uncooked, resulting in a wobblier, custard-like texture.

Today, visitors can taste-test both types without having to leave the city. Visit **Manteigaria** on Avenida da Praia Grande, in the heart of downtown, or **Pastéis de Chaves** on Estrada do Repouso in the St. Lazarus district to try authentic Portuguese egg tarts. For the best Macau egg tarts, visit any branch of **Lord Stow's** or **Margaret's Café e Nata** downtown.

Nüwa

$$$ | **HOTEL** | Housed within the City of Dreams, the Nüwa Macau—named after the Chinese mother goddess—offers understated luxury with a focus on design and exclusivity. **Pros:** discreet and quiet luxury; immaculate spa; high-end dining on-site. **Cons:** high price point; limited entertainment choices; subdued atmosphere. *Rooms from: MOP$2,500* ✉ *City of Dreams, 1 Estrada do Istmo, Cotai* ☎ *853/8868–6688* 🌐 *www.cityofdreamsmacau.com/en/hotels/nuwa* *290 rooms* *No Meals.*

★ **The Ritz-Carlton, Macau**

$$$$ | **HOTEL** | If cost is no concern, the Ritz-Carlton is where you want to be; the all-suite retreat set atop the Galaxy Macau makes your average luxury rooms look mundane by comparison. **Pros:** opulent interiors with abundant space; far removed from Cotai crowds; private pool and lounge. **Cons:** expensive; long walk to sites; limited, though excellent, food and drink options. *Rooms from: MOP$6,500* ✉ *The Ritz-Carlton Macau, Galaxy Macau, Cotai* ☎ *8886–6868* 🌐 *www.ritzcarlton.com* *230 suites* *No Meals.*

The Venetian Macao

$$ | **RESORT** | Love it or hate it, The Venetian Macao's strong presence in the Cotai area is both its draw and its bane. **Pros:** living rooms; comprehensive shopping and dining; plenty of options for families. **Cons:** pretentious decor; more focus on gambling and conventions than the hotel experience; lack of intimacy outside the suite. *Rooms from: MOP$1,000* ✉ *Estrada de Baía de N. Senhora da Esperança, The Venetian Macao, Cotai* ☎ *853/8118–8899* 🌐 *www.venetianmacao.com* *2,841 suites* *No Meals.*

Like its counterpart in Las Vegas, the Venetian Macao has a shopping area with a built-in canal.

Nightlife

Unlike Las Vegas, casinos don't hand out drinks to keep you at the table, and nightlife is generally subdued. There are many excellent cocktail bars and lounges in five-star hotels—dress codes often apply—but few places to roll up your sleeves and get a beer.

A.P.D. (A Perfect Dose)

COCKTAIL BARS | Hidden within the W Hotel's ground-floor Living Room lounge, A.P.D. is a speakeasy-style haven for mezcal lovers. The smoky, earthy agave spirit is the sole focus here, with a curated selection that includes more than a dozen artisanal labels, from Derrumbes, made from wild agave grown in the San Luis Potosi plateaus, to George Clooney's new premium brand Casamigos. The space is small and intimate. Go behind the open bar to examine the labels up close and chat with the friendly bartenders. ✉ *W Hotel, 1st fl., Estrada do Istmo, Cotai* ☎ *8865–1366*.

The Ritz-Carlton Bar & Lounge

LOUNGES | On the 51st floor of the Ritz-Carlton, this sophisticated lounge offers an upscale drinking experience, boasting lofty views of Cotai's skyline over a long, Italian marble bar. Gin enthusiasts will appreciate the bar's impressive selection, which includes several high-end options and rarities. For a more indulgent evening, the Ritz Hour (6 to 9 pm) offers a selection of cocktails, beers, wines, gin and tonics, and spirits for less than MOP$300. Swing by earlier for an indulgent afternoon tea from 2 pm to 5:30 pm. ✉ *Galaxy Macau, 51st fl., Estrada da Baía da Nossa Senhora da Esperança, Cotai* ☎ *8886–6868* 🌐 *www.ritzcarltonbarandloungemacau.com*.

The Roadhouse

LIVE MUSIC | It's all booze and blues at this lively brick-walled bar in Broadway's food street. The Roadhouse is one of few pubs in Cotai, if not all of Macau, serving draft beer and spirits by the glass at affordable prices. Every night from Tuesday to Sunday, rock and blues bands play on stage while sports stream on TVs in the background. If you're hungry, order a pub burger, a pizza, or appetizers like chicken wings and fried calamari rings. ✉ *Broadway Food St., E-G016–G019, Cotai* ☎ *2875–2945* 🌐 *www.galaxymacau.com.*

★ The St. Regis Bar

COCKTAIL BARS | Macau's only entry on Asia's 50 Best Bars list, the St. Regis Bar sets a high standard for cocktails and live entertainment. Inspired by the hotel's New York heritage, the signature drinks mostly nod to Big Apple history. The Cotton Club, for example, is a whiskey sour that pays tribute to Harlem's prohibition era jazz. But don't miss the Macau-inspired Maria do Leste, a bold reimagining of the Bloody Mary with cinnamon, piri piri, and a lobster tart on the side, or the Macao Egg Tart, a boozy ode to the city's favorite pastry. Both are great drinks to sip as you enjoy the live jazz. ✉ *The St. Regis Macao, 2nd fl., The Londoner Macao, Estrada do Istmo, Cotai* ☎ *2882–8898* 🌐 *www.thestregisbarmacao.com* ☞ *A smart casual dress code is enforced after 7 pm.*

Wing Lei Bar

LOUNGES | Hiding in plain sight behind jade velvet curtains inside the Wynn Palace, in the entryway to the wildly popular Lakeview Palace, Wing Lei Bar exudes an air of exclusivity. This intimate lounge, with its gilded bamboo rafters, glittering chandelier, and discreet bar seating, offers a deeply personalized drinking experience (meaning, there's no menu). The expert bartenders craft cocktails tailored to your tastes, using whichever spirits or flavor profiles you prefer. ✉ *Wynn Palace, Av. da Nave Desportiva, Cotai* ☎ *8889–3663* 🌐 *www.wynnresortsmacau.com.*

Shopping

Name a luxury brand. It's likely here. With Macau being a free port and money flowing freely, high-end shopping has become a Cotai pastime. For everyday goods and gear from brands like Hoka, Lego, Lululemon, and Uniqlo, visit The Shoppes at The Londoner and Venetian.

MALLS AND SHOPPING CENTERS

Grand Lisboa Palace Shopping Mall

MALL | FAMILY | The Grand Lisboa Palace's 800,000-square-foot, multilevel mall is a sight to behold. The flagship CDF department store houses 170 brands and is a go-to for luxury items—watches, cosmetics, jewelry, fragrances—but NY8 New Yaohan is superior if you want to shop for souvenirs. This department store is filled with Macau exclusives and has a deluxe supermarket, which is a great place to pick up artisanal goods like cured meats, fine chocolates, and wine. If you want something local to bring home, don't miss the Made in Macau shop on level one for clothes, gadgets, accessories, and food products. ✉ *Grand Lisboa Palace, Cotai* 🌐 *www.grandlisboapalace.com/en/shops.*

Shoppes at Venetian

MALL | FAMILY | The Venetian Macao's Italy-theme megamall comes complete with cobblestone walkways, arched bridges, an artificial blue sky, and working canals manned by singing gondoliers (rides are MOP$208). Its 330-plus boutiques include all the big-name lifestyle brands and luxury labels in fashion, accessories, gifts, and sporting goods. You'll also find more than 20 restaurants and a 1,000-seat international food court. Don't be surprised to see wandering stilt walkers, violinists, and juggling jesters, especially around St. Mark's Square, which hosts daily live performances. The mall also connects with the Shoppes at Four Seasons, Shoppes at Parisian, and Shoppes at The Londoner. ✉ *The Venetian Macao,*

Estrada da Baía de N. Senhora da Esperança, Cotai ☎ *853/2882–8888* 🌐 *www.venetianmacao.com/shopping.html.*

Performing Arts

Gaming operators go all out with extravagant stage shows here, including the latest permanent production, *Macau 2049*. Stay tuned for news about concerts, basketball and soccer games, and celebrity appearances—the city is dead-set on becoming a destination for major events, and all roads for those lead to Cotai.

Macau 2049

VARIETY SHOWS | From Zhang Yimou, director of the opening and closing ceremonies at the 2008 Beijing Olympics, comes MGM Cotai's spectacular eight-part show. Macau 2049 unites world-class talent to imagine ancient, regional, and largely unseen Chinese traditions in a futuristic world. Think high-flying acrobatics, cultural dances, and musical performances with high-tech visual displays. The show is breathtaking, but it can also be kitschy. Between acts, performers take a bow to prompted applause as pre-recorded scripts detail everything from the history of Miao folk singing to the payload capacity of the robotic arms used on stage. Don't expect it to have anything to do with Macau or the year its status as a special administrative region will end, either. Just sit back and enjoy. ✉ *MGM Cotai, Cotai* ☎ *8802–3833* 🌐 *www.macau2049.mgm.mo.*

★ **teamLab SuperNature Macao**

ART GALLERY | **FAMILY** | Created by the renowned Japanese art collective teamLab, this immersive art experience features large-scale digital installations that blend design, technology, and nature. Visitors can walk through expansive, ever-changing environments—many of them floral-theme, some even perfumed—where light, color, and movement respond to their presence. Unlike traditional exhibitions, this one is designed as a "body-immersive" space. That means you can physically engage with the artwork, influencing how it evolves in real time. Highlights include floating light orbs, infinite mirror rooms, and surreal digital landscapes, as well as a space for kids to create their own artwork. Best of all, it's a choose-your-own-adventure without a set route or map. ✉ *Cotai Expo, The Venetian Macao, Cotai* ☎ *2882–8818* 🌐 *www.teamlab.art/e/macao.*

Hiking Coloane 

Macau's last pocket of green, Coloane remains a serene getaway. The former island has a lush interior lined with a handful of easy hiking trails. From Estrada de Hác Sá, you can find the mostly flat, 2-mile **Trilho do Morro**, a route that overlooks Hác Sá beach, or the easy, 1-mile **Long Chao Kok Coastal Trail** below it. For a longer journey, try some or all of the five-mile **Coloane Trail**, which starts just south of Seac Pai Van on the Estrada do Alto de Coloane. The trail offers panoramic views of the sea and towering A-Ma statue.

Coloane

Quiet Coloane village is home to some of the former island's centuries-old heritage sites. Go farther afield and you'll find vacant stretches of gold sand and peaceful hiking trails.

Sights

Centuries ago, Coloane was a wild place where pirates hid in rocky caves and coves, awaiting their chance to strike at cargo ships on the Pearl River. Early in the 20th century, the local government sponsored a huge planting program to transform Coloane from barren to green. The results were spectacular—and enduring. Today this side of the island is idyllic, with lush hills and clean beaches. Once connected to Taipa by a thin isthmus, Coloane is now fused with Taipa via the huge Cotai reclaimed land project, where the "Strip" was completed in 2010. Regardless of the recent development boom elsewhere, Coloane remains the destination of choice for anyone seeking natural beauty and tranquillity, as relatively few tourists venture farther than Coloane.

A-Ma Cultural Village

TOWN | FAMILY | This huge complex built in a traditional Qing Dynasty style pays homage to Macau's namesake, A-Ma. The vibrancy and color of the details in the bell and drum towers, the tiled roofs, and the carved marble altars are awe-inspiring. It's as if you've been transported back centuries and can see temples in their true greatness. Other remarkable details include the striking rows of stairs leading to **Tin Hau Palace** at the entrance. Each row features painstakingly detailed marble and stone carvings of auspicious Chinese symbols: a roaring tiger, double lions, five cranes, the double phoenix, and a splendid imperial dragon.

Behind A-Ma Cultural Village, **Coloane Hill** rises 170 meters (560 feet) above the sea and is crowned by a 65-foot, white-marble statue of A-Ma lording over Coloane. You can make the short hike up to the top or take one of the shuttle buses that leave from the base of the hill every 30 minutes. ✉ *A-Ma Cultural Village, Estrada de Seac Pai Van, Coloane Island South* 🌐 *www.a-ma.org.mo.*

Coloane Karting Track

SPORTS VENUE | Race enthusiasts and thrill-seekers should head to the Macau Motor Sports Club, opposite the Coloane reservoir. Drivers must be at least 16 years old and have a driver's license, as 200cc engine go-karts can reach speeds up to 60 kph (37 mph). The track is 1.2 km (0.7 miles) long, 10 meters (33 feet) wide, and has 10 challenging curves. Aim for a lap time under 50 seconds on a sunny day. Take note: the track closes at even the whiff of inclement weather, and you need to wear long pants and closed-toe shoes. ✉ *Coloane Karting Track, Estrada de Seac Pai Van, Coloane Island West* ☎ *853/2888–2126* 🎟 *MOP$180 for 15 mins.*

★ Coloane Village

TOWN | Quiet, relaxed Coloane Village is home to traditional Portuguese-style houses painted in pastels, as well as the baroque-style Chapel of St. Francis Xavier and the Taoist Tam Kung Temple, dedicated to the god of seafarers. The narrow alleys reveal surprises at every turn; you may well encounter fishermen repairing their junks or a baptism at the chapel. At the village's heart is a small square adorned with a fountain with a bronze Cupid. The slow-moving pace picks up a bit on weekends, when travelers swarm the streets seeking for the perfect photo op beside wall murals and the Portuguese and Chinese restaurants fill up. ✉ *Coloane Village, Coloane Island West.*

Hác Sá

BEACH | FAMILY | Translated from Chinese, *hác sá* means "black sand." Today, though, the beaches look a shade more golden, as the once-grayish sands have been mixed with yellow sand to prevent erosion. This quiet corner of Macau is a great place to hike, enjoy a picnic, or dabble in water sports. Cool off in the Olympic-size Hác Sá Park pool (open from May 1 until October 31; MOP$15 for adults; MOP$5 for kids under 12). Hike the easy Hác Sá family trail. Play a round of 18 at the Macau Golf and Country Club. Then finish with a bite to eat on the beach. ✉ *Hác Sá, Coloane Island South.*

Did You Know?

Flanked by lush landscaped greenery, the stairs leading up to the Tin Hau Palace at the A-Ma Cultural Village are lined with auspicious Chinese symbols.

Seac Pai Van Park (*Coloane Park*)
CITY PARK | **FAMILY** | This large, family-friendly park has extensive botanical gardens, ponds, and waterfalls, as well as the popular Giant Panda Pavilion and a walk-through aviary with more than 200 bird species. There are lots of things of interest to children, including playgrounds, a minizoo with flamingos, monkeys, and other animals, and an interactive museum with exhibits on nature and agriculture. ✉ *Estrada de Seac Pai Van, Coloane Island West* 🎫 *Free.*

Restaurants

More than just the home of the original Lord Stow's, Coloane boasts some of Macau's most treasured Portuguese and Macanese restaurants. In Hác Sá, you'll also find the local legend Fernando's, plus cheap beachside eats and barbecues available for picnics.

★ Lord Stow's Bakery
$ | **PORTUGUESE** | Originally a modest, traditional bakery opened by an Englishman named Andrew Stow in 1989, Lord Stow's Bakery is now a culinary landmark in Coloane, just off the town square. Locals sit on nearby benches munching the signature hot and flaky *p'ou tát* (custard tarts) straight from the oven. **Known for:** Macau's most iconic egg tarts; cookies, muffins, and other pastries. $ *Average main: MOP$40* ✉ *Rua da Tassara, Coloane Village Square, Coloane Island West* ☎ *853/2888–2534* 🌐 *www.lordstow.com.*

★ Restaurante Espaço Lisboa
$$ | **PORTUGUESE** | Occupying a converted two-story house with a small but pleasant balcony overlooking Coloane Village, this restaurant is Portuguese-owned and has a Portuguese chef—so it's no surprise that it is a favorite of Portuguese residents. The food sticks to home-style classics, including one of the better versions of baked duck rice in town. **Known for:** codfish cakes, savory duck rice, boiled bacalhau; an extensive list of hearty Portuguese wines; house-made desserts (rice pudding or flan). $ *Average main: MOP$180* ✉ *8 Rua das Gaivotas, Coloane Island West* ☎ *853/2888–2226* 🌐 *www.facebook.com/espacolisboa.jan2003* 🕒 *Closed Wed.*

★ Restaurante Fernando
$$ | **PORTUGUESE** | Everyone in Hong Kong and Macau knows about Fernando's. The open-air dining pavilion and bar have attracted beachgoers for years, and the enterprising Fernando has built a legendary reputation for his Portuguese fare. **Known for:** suckling pig, grilled sardines, and rich caldo verde; beloved sangria and long list of Portuguese wines; informal, boisterous atmosphere. $ *Average main: MOP$200* ✉ *9 Praia de Hác-Sá Beach, Coloane Island South* ☎ *853/2888–2264* 🌐 *www.fernando-restaurant.com* 💳 *No credit cards.*

Hotels

Few travelers stay in Coloane, and those that do gravitate toward one hotel: the Grand Coloane Resort in Hác Sá. Near the southernmost point, you'll also find the older, far removed Coloane Inn overlooking Cheoc Van Beach.

Grand Coloane Resort
$$ | **RESORT** | **FAMILY** | This old resort, built into the side of a cliff with each room boasting an ocean view, is where you can truly get away from it all. **Pros:** green surroundings on Hác Sá Beach; peaceful spa and great pool area; fun for kids. **Cons:** isolated location; beach can be dirty after a storm; aging property. $ *Rooms from: MOP$700* ✉ *1918 Estrada de Hác Sá, Coloane Island South* ☎ *853/2887–1111* 🌐 *www.artyzen.com/en/hotels/grand-coloane-resort* 🛏 *208 rooms* 🍽 *No Meals.*

Index

A

B

C

Photo Credits

Front Cover: ZhengJie Wu/GettyImages [Descr.:The Temple Street night market. Late night shopping is quite typical for Hong Kong culture.] **Back cover, from left to right:** Leungchopan/Dreamstime. Photosoup/Dreamstime. Yashkru/Dreamstime. **Spine:** Dezzor/Dreamstime. **Interior, from left to right:** Vincentstthomas/Dreamstime (1). Brianngo/Shutterstock (2-3). Dax101/Shutterstock (6). Video279/Dreamstime (7). **About Our Writers:** All photos are courtesy of the writers. **Chapter 1: Experience Hong Kong:** Masterlu/Dreamstime (8-9). Courtesy of HKTB (10-11). Only Fabrizio/Shutterstock (11). AuthorLinyt/Dreamstime (11). Jack Hong/Shutterstock (12). Courtesy of HKTB (12). Sepavo/Dreamstime (12). Courtesy of HKTB (12). Pixattitude/Dreamstime (13). Nohead/Dreamstime (13). Courtesy of HKTB (14). Richard I'Anson/GettyImages (14). Noppasinw/Dreamstime (14). Courtesy of HKTB (14). Tai Kwun (15). Courtesy of HKTB (15). Be Saowaluck/Shutterstock (18). Leungchopan/Shutterstock (18). Leungchopan/Shutterstock (18). Leungchopan/Shutterstock (18) StrippedPixel.com/Shutterstock (19). Donald Yip/Shutterstock (19). Osacr_Y/Shutterstock (19). Kaykhoon/Shutterstock (19). StrippedPixel.com/Shutterstock (20). Cheryl Chan/GettyImages (20). Wendy connett /Alamy (20). Ilia Torlin/Shutterstock (20). Julien Jean Zayatz/Shutterstock (21). Courtesy of HKCTA (22). Courtesy of HKTB (22). Kobby Dagan/Shutterstock (22). Courtesy of HKTB (22). Wang Sing/Shutterstock (23). A2gxe9/Dreamstime (23). KingRobert/Shutterstock (23). Courtesy of HKTB (23). Zhongxinyashi_Photo/Shutterstock (24). Wang Sing/Shutterstock (24). Courtesy of HKTB (24). Raphin Kemthong/Shutterstock (24). Phattana Sangsawang/iStockphoto (25). **Chapter 3: Western, Central, and Southside:** Prakobkit/Dreamstime (65). Jack Hong/Shutterstock (70). Dezzor/Dreamstime (85). Gnothi Seauton/Courtesy of HKTB (94).Courtesy of HKTB (106-107). **Chapter 4: Wan Chai, Causeway Bay, and Eastern:** Gnothi Seauton_Yau Photography/Courtesy of HKTB (109). Courtesy of HKTB (114). Gnothi Seauton/Courtesy of HKTB (116). Nohead/Dreamstime (124).Gnothi Seauton/Courtesy of HKTB (133). **Chapter 5: Kowloon Peninsula:** Only_fabrizio/iStockphoto (145). Sanga Park/Shutterstock (152). Sakuragirin/Dreamstime (163). Gnothi Seauton_Night Raven/Courtesy of HKTB (176). Nikada/GettyImages (180). StrippedPixel/Dreamstime (183). Trkchon Studio/Shutterstock (184). **Chapter 6: Lantau Island and the New Territories:** Expose/Shutterstock (187). Courtesy of HKTB (193). Courtesy of Hong Kong Disneyland (195). Platongkoh/Dreamstime (196). Courtesy of HKTB (198-199). Sepavo/Dreamstime (201). Gorma Kuma/Shutterstock (205). Leungchopan/Dreamstime (206). HKTB (208). **Chapter 7: Side Trip to Macau:** CJ_Romas/iStockphoto (211). Cozyta/Shutterstock (219). F11photo/Shutterstock (222). LimLim/Shutterstock (225). Harsh - S/Shutterstock (234). Bing-Jhen Hong/iStockphoto (239). Photchara7/Shutterstock (241). Jack Hong/Shutterstock (243). Cesc_assawin/Shutterstock (256). Jui-Chi Chan/iStockphoto (260-261). **Every effort has been made to trace the copyright holders, and we apologize in advance for any accidental errors. We would be happy to apply the corrections in the following edition of this publication.*

Notes

Notes

Fodor's HONG KONG

Publisher: Stephen Horowitz, *General Manager*

Editorial: Douglas Stallings, *Editorial Director;* Jill Fergus, Alexis Kelly, Amanda Sadlowski, *Senior Editors;* Brian Eschrich, *Editor;* Angelique Kennedy-Chavannes, Yoojin Shin, *Associate Editors*

Design: Tina Malaney, *Director of Design and Production*; Jessica Gonzalez, *Senior Designer,* Jaimee Shaye, *Graphic Design Associate*

Production: Jennifer DePrima, *Editorial Production Manager,* Elyse Rozelle, *Senior Production Editor;* Carol Seigler, *Production Editor*

Maps: Rebecca Baer, *Map Director,* Mark Stroud (Moon Street Cartography), *Cartographer*

Photography: Viviane Teles, *Director of Photography;* Namrata Aggarwal, Neha Gupta, Payal Gupta, Ashok Kumar, *Photo Editors;* Zamantta Larios Salazar, Shanelle Jacobs, *Photo Production Interns*

Business and Operations: Chuck Hoover, *Chief Marketing Officer;* Robert Ames, *Group General Manager*

Public Relations and Marketing: Joe Ewaskiw, *Senior Director of Communications and Public Relations*

Fodors.com: Jeremy Tarr, *Editorial Director;* Rachael Levitt, *Managing Editor*

Writers: Piera Chen, Jonathan DeLise, Doris Lam, Thomas O'Malley, Audrey Phoon, Craig Sauers

Editor: Yoojin Shin

Production Editor: Jennifer DePrima

26th Edition

ISBN 978-1-64097-852-2

ISSN 1070-6887

SPECIAL SALES

This book is available at special discounts for bulk purchases for sales promotions or premiums. For more information, e-mail SpecialMarkets@fodors.com.

PRINTED IN CANADA

10 9 8 7 6 5 4 3 2 1